MICROSOFT CERTIFIED SYSTEMS ENGINEER

MW00814482

MCSE Planning a Windows® Server 2003 Network Infrastructure Study Guide

(Exam 70-293)

MICROSOFT CERTIFIED SYSTEMS ENGINEER

MCSE Planning a Windows® Server 2003 Network Infrastructure Study Guide

(Exam 70-293)

Diana Huggins

McGraw-Hill/Osborne
New York Chicago San Francisco Lisbon London Madrid
Mexico City Milan New Delhi San Juan Seoul Singapore Sydney Toronto

The McGraw·Hill Companies

McGraw-Hill/Osborne
2100 Powell Street, 10th Floor
Emeryville, California 94608
U.S.A.

To arrange bulk purchase discounts for sales promotions, premiums, or fund-raisers, please contact **McGraw-Hill**/Osborne at the above address. For information on translations or book distributors outside the U.S.A., please see the International Contact Information page immediately following the index of this book.

MCSE Planning a Windows® Server 2003 Network Infrastructure Study Guide (Exam 70-293)

1234567890 DOC DOC 019876543

Book p/n 0-07-222326-X and CD p/n 0-07-222327-8
parts of
ISBN 0-07-222325-1

Publisher	**Acquisitions Coordinator**	**Indexer**
Brandon A. Nordin	Jessica Wilson	Claire Splan
Vice President &	**Technical Editor**	**Composition**
Associate Publisher	Dan DiNicolo	Apollo Publishing Service
Scott Rogers		
	Copy Editor	**Series Design**
Acquisitions Editor	Robert Campbell	Roberta Steele
Timothy Green		
	Proofreader	**Cover Series Design**
Project Editor	Linda Medoff	Peter Grame
Jennifer Malnick		

This book was composed with Corel VENTURA™ Publisher.

This book is dedicated with all my love to Brandon

ABOUT THE AUTHOR

Diana Huggins is currently an independent contractor providing both technical writing and consulting services. Prior to this she worked as a senior systems consultant on projects that included a security review of Microsoft's official curriculum, content development for private companies, as well as network infrastructure design and implementation. Diana's main focus over the past few years has been on writing certification study guides. To complement her efforts, she also spends a portion of her time consulting for small- to medium-sized companies in a variety of areas and continues to work as an independent technical trainer. Diana currently has her Microsoft Certified Systems Engineer (MCSE) and Microsoft Certified Trainer (MCT), along with several other certifications from different vendors. Although her focus is on the Information Technology industry, she also holds a bachelor's degree in education. Diana runs her own company, DKB Consulting Services. The main focus of the company is on developing certification training courseware and online practice exams, as well as content delivery.

CONTENTS AT A GLANCE

CONTENTS

ACKNOWLEDGMENTS

I would like to thank all those at Osborne/McGraw-Hill—especially Tim Green, Jessica Wilson, and Jennifer Malnick—for their help in getting this book completed. Thanks to Dan DiNicolo for his knowledgeable contributions and great advice during the technical reviews of the book. Thanks once again to my son for being so patient and understanding when things get a little hectic. I hope one day he gets a chance to pick and read up one of "Mom's" books. Of course, thanks to my dad. Without him I would not be able to put in 20-hour days when they are required. Finally, thanks to all those people in my life who support me and encourage me when I'm struggling to get things done. It is a long list of people, but you all know who you are. Thanks to you all!

INTRODUCTION

This book is organized in such a way as to serve as an in-depth review for the 70-293 exam, "Planning and Maintaining a Microsoft Windows Server 2003 Network Infrastructure," for both experienced Windows 2000 and Windows Server 2003 professionals and newcomers to Microsoft networking technologies. Each chapter covers a major aspect of the exam, with an emphasis on the "why" as well as the "how to" of planning and maintaining a Windows server 2003 infrastructure as a network administrator or engineer.

Exam Readiness Checklist

At the end of the Introduction you will find an Exam Readiness Checklist. This table has been constructed to allow you to cross-reference the official exam objectives with the objectives as they are presented and covered in this book. The checklist also allows you to gauge your level of expertise on each objective at the outset of your studies. This should allow you to check your progress and make sure you spend the time you need on more difficult or unfamiliar sections. References have been provided for the objective exactly as the vendor presents it, the section of the study guide that covers that objective, and a chapter reference.

In Every Chapter

Each chapter contains several components that call your attention to important items, reinforce important points, and provide helpful exam-taking hints. Take a look at what you'll find in every chapter.

Exam Watch notes call attention to information about, and potential pitfalls in, the exam.

These helpful hints are written based on the author's exam experience.

■ Every chapter begins with the **Certification Objectives**—what you need to know in order to pass the section on the exam dealing with the chapter topic. The certification objects map to the major headings within each chapter.

■ **Practice Exercises** are interspersed throughout the chapters. These are step-by-step exercises that allow you to get the hands-on experience you need in order to pass the exams. They help you master skills that are likely to be an area of focus on the exam. Don't just read through the exercises; they are hands-on practice that you should be comfortable completing. Learning by doing is an effective way to increase your competency with a product.

■ **On The Job** notes describe the issues that come up most often in real-world settings. They provide a valuable perspective on certification- and product-related topics. They point out common mistakes and address questions that have arisen from on the job discussions and experience.

■ **Inside the Exam** further highlight important topics that are likely to appear on the exam and deserve a more in-depth discussion.

■ **Scenario and Solutions** sections lay out potential problems and solutions in a quick-to-read format:

SCENARIO & SOLUTION

James must be available to troubleshoot the computers in any office in the four buildings of the company that he works for…	Implement a roaming profile for James so that he can access his desktop no matter what computer he is using. This is especially handy since his roaming profile can include the mapping to a network drive that holds his diagnostic tools.

■ The **Certification Summary** is a succinct review of the chapter and a restatement of salient points regarding the exam.

■ The **Two-Minute Drill** at the end of every chapter is a checklist of the main points of the chapter. It can be used for last-minute review.

Q&A ■ The **Self Test** offers questions similar to those found on the certification exams. The answers to these questions, as well as explanations of the answers, can be found at the end of each chapter. By taking the Self Test after completing each chapter, you'll reinforce what you've learned from that chapter while becoming familiar with the structure of the exam questions.

■ The **Lab Question** at the end of the Self Test section offers a unique and challenging question format that requires the reader to understand multiple chapter concepts to answer correctly. These questions are more complex and comprehensive than the other questions, as they test your ability to take all the knowledge you have gained from reading the chapter and apply it to complicated, real-world situations.

Exam-Taking Pointers

Once you've finished reading this book, set aside some time to do a thorough review. You might want to return to the book several times and make use of all the methods it offers for reviewing the material:

1. *Re-read all the Two-Minute Drills*, or have someone quiz you. You also can use the drills as a way to do a quick cram before the exam. You might want to make some flash cards out of 3×5 index cards that have the Two-Minute Drill material on them.

2. *Re-read all the Exam Watch notes.* Remember that these notes are written by someone who has taken the exam and passed. She knows what you should expect—and what you should be on the lookout for.

3. *Review all the S&S sections* for quick problem solving.

4. *Re-take the Self Tests.* Taking the tests right after you've read the chapter is a good idea, because the questions help reinforce what you've just learned. However, it's an even better idea to go back later and do all the questions in the book in one sitting. Pretend that you're taking the live exam. (When you go through the questions the first time, you should mark your answers on a separate piece of paper. That way you can run through the questions as many times as you need to until you feel comfortable with the material.)

5. *Complete the Exercises.* Did you do the exercises when you read through each chapter? If not, do them! These exercises are designed to cover exam topics, and there's no better way to get to know this material than by practicing. Be sure you understand why you are performing each step in each exercise. If there is something you are not clear on, re-read that section in the chapter.

Certification Track

This book is designed to prepare you for exam 70-293 Planning and Maintaining a Windows Server 2003 Network Infrastructure. This exam is one of the requirements for both the Microsoft Certified System Engineer (MCSE) on Windows Server 2003. In order to achieve MCSE status on Windows Server 2003, you must complete a series of exams. You are required to pass six core exams and one elective exam. The core exams consist of four network system exams, one client operating exam, as well as a design exam. You can then select from a number of different exams to complete the elective. The following table summarizes the core exam requirements for obtaining an MCSE on Windows Server 2003. The exam requirements can change at any time, so it's generally a good idea to check the Web site on a regular basis for any updates or changes. You can view a complete list of elective exams from the Web site as well (www.microsoft.com/traincert/mcp/mcse/windows2003/).

Core Exams Networking Systems (4 required)
70-290—Managing and Maintaining a Microsoft Windows Server 2003 Environment
70-291—Implementing, Managing, and Maintaining a Windows Server 2003 Network Infrastructure
70-293—Planning and Maintaining a Microsoft Windows Server 2003 Network Infrastructure
70-294—Planning, Implementing, and Maintaining a Microsoft Windows Server 2003 Active Directory Infrastructure
Core Exams Client Operating Systems (1 required)
70-270—Installing, Configuring, and Administering Microsoft Windows XP Professional
70-210—Installing, Configuring, and Administering Microsoft Windows 2000 Professional
Core Exams Design (1 required)
70-297—Designing a Microsoft Windows Server 2003 Active Directory and Network Infrastructure
70-298—Designing Security for a Microsoft Windows Server 2003 Network

Test Structure

Microsoft has implemented four different testing formats:

- Case study
- Fixed length
- Adaptive
- Short form

The case study testing format is typically used only for the design exams. This test format consists of a set of case studies with each one followed by approximately 6–10 questions (the question formats will vary as discussed in the next section). Each case study will consist of a scenario that the reader must analyze. The questions following the case study will be based on the information in the scenario.

The fixed-length exams typically consist of 50–70 questions while the short-form will present the test taker with 25–30 questions. In both testing formats, you will be presented with a question for which you must supply the correct response/responses. With either format, you can move ahead to questions and return to unanswered ones until you the test is complete.

A few years ago, Microsoft introduced the Adaptive testing format where questions are ranked by difficulty (ranging from 1–5 with 1 being the easiest and 5 being the most difficult). When you begin the test you are presented with a level 3 question. If the question is answered correctly, you will be presented with a more difficult one. However, if answered incorrectly, you will be given an easy one (level 2). Once you have been presented with approximately 15–20 questions, the algorithm will be able to determine whether you would be able to answer to all the questions. In other words, once your level of performance has been determined the exam will end or the exam will end once the maximum numbers of questions have been presented (in which case the candidate will more than likely fail).

One of the main differences between an adaptive test and a fixed length or short form is that with an adaptive test questions must be answered as they are presented. In other words, once a question has been answered you can not return to it. You will not know beforehand what type of exam format you will be presented with. However, you will be able to identify an adaptive exam from the first question as there will be no box that allows you to mark questions for review. Keep in mind that Microsoft appears to be moving away from the Adaptive testing format.

Question Types

Microsoft exams consist of a variety of different question formats. You can typically expect to encounter five different question formats. Each of the flowing question types are discussed in the following sections:

- Multiple-choice, single answer
- Multiple-choice, multiple answers
- Build-list-and-reorder (list prioritization)
- Create-a-tree
- Select-and-place (drag-and-drop)

Multiple Choice

Many of the questions you will encounter will be multiple-choice format, where you are required to select a single correct answer or multiple correct answers. If more than one answer is required, the question will state how many correct answers you must choose. Example:

1. How many Schema Masters will there be in a forest that consists of a forest root domain and three child domains?

   A. 1

   B. 2

   C. 3

   D. 5

   Correct answer: A

2. Which of the following FSMO roles are domain wide? (Choose three.)

   A. Schema Master

   B. Infrastructure Master

   C. Domain Naming Master

   D. Global Catalog

   E. RID Master

   F. PDC Emulator

   Correct answers: B, E, F

Build-list-and-reorder

This question format will present the candidate with two different lists, one on the right and one on the left. In order to answer the question, objects from the list on the right must be moved to the list on the left and then placed in the correct order.

Create-a-tree

This question format will again present the candidate with a list of items. The items must be moved from the list and placed in the correct position within a tree on the left.

Select-and-place

This format is often referred to as drag-and-drop. The candidate with be presented with a list of items and a diagram with blank boxes. In order to correctly answer the question, the items must be dropped on the correct blank boxes within the diagram.

New Question Formats

Along with the question formats just outlined, Microsoft is also introducing several new question formats that you will encounter on the Windows Server 2003 exams (as well as the Windows 2000 exams). The new question formats include

- **Hot area questions**   These questions will require the candidate to select the correct elements from a given graphic.

- **Active screen questions**   These questions will present the candidate with a dialog box from which you will have to configure the settings in order to answer the question.

- **New drag-and-drop-type questions**   New drag-and-drop questions ask you to drag source elements to their appropriate corresponding targets within a work area. These types of questions test your knowledge of specific concepts and their definitions or descriptions.

- **Simulation questions**   These types of questions will ask you to indicate the correct answer by performing specific tasks, such as configuring and installing network adapters or drivers, configuring and controlling access to files, or troubleshooting hardware devices.

Preparing for the Exam

Preparing for a certification exam begins with reading through a study guide that presents you with in-depth information about the topics you will encounter on the exam. In order to increase your chance of passing the exam the first time around, you should be familiar with all the exam objectives that Microsoft posts. If this is your first exam experience, do not be discouraged if you do not pass the first time. Often times a candidate may have mastered all the topics, but the exam experience is enough to throw one off. However, on a positive note, you will definitely be more comfortable the second time around.

Good study habits get you one step closer to achieving success on the exams. I suggest that as you begin studying exam 70-293 you take a close look at the exam objectives. These objectives provide an excellent starting point for determining what you topics you need to study. You can obtain the official objectives for exam 70-293 from the Microsoft Web site.

This study guide is closely mapped to the exam objectives to ensure that all the required information is presented. Once you have read all the material for a chapter and completed the exercises, you should attempt the self test to determine if you've mastered all the topics presented. After completing the self test you should have a good idea of any areas you may still need to review, and after you thoroughly read through each chapter, you should attempt the practice test included with the book. Before taking the exam, you should aim for a score of between 75–80%. Anything lower and I would suggest taking some more time to review the areas you may be weak in.

exam

ⓦatch *When using sites that offer free practice questions, be wary of the answers. I have often encountered questions where the stated correct answer is actually incorrect.*

Practice exams are a wonderful way to test your knowledge once you've studied all the required material. A lot of study guides include practice exams designed to mimic the questions you're likely to encounter on the actual exam. There are also an abundance of Web sites that offer practice exams, some of which are free, and others that must be purchased.

For any questions you answer incorrectly, use the explanations to understand where you went wrong and why the correct answer is indeed correct. Be sure to review study material pertaining to the questions you answered incorrectly before taking the real exams.

One of the things I always like to do just before taking an exam is review a cram sheet. Several Web sites have cram sheets available free of charge and others, such as www.cramsession.com, offer them for a small price. A cram sheet does just that. It crams all the need to know exam information into a few short pages. So I recommend getting your hands on one and reviewing it shortly before taking the exam. You may even want to print one off and read it over while you are waiting to enter the exam room (at which point, however, you will have to part with it). You can also use the Two-Minute drills at the end of each chapter and the chapter summaries as a good way to review distilled facts. The glossary at the end of the book is also another resource that can be referenced for exam preparation.

Finally, and I can not stress this enough, nothing beats hands-on experience when it comes to preparing for an exam. I would recommend installing Windows Server 2003 and playing around with the various technologies discussed throughout the book.

Registering for the Exam

Once you have prepared for the exam and feel confident that you have mastered all the exam objectives, you can visit either the Pearson Vue (www.vue.com) or Prometric (www.2test.com) Web sites to schedule your exam.

On your test day, you need to arrive at the testing center where you schedule your exam at least 15 minutes prior to your schedule time. You will be required to sign in with an exam coordinator and show two pieces of identification (one of which must contain a photograph). Also, you are not permitted to take anything into the actual exam room, so you will be asked to leave your things outside the closed room.

Once in the examination room you will be provided with blank paper and a pen, or an erasable plastic board and erasable pen. You are free to make any notes prior to starting and during the exam. However, once the exam is finished and you leave the examination room, you are required to surrender the paper to the exam coordinator.

Before beginning the actual exam, you are permitted to go through a sample exam. If it is your first exam, I suggest that you take the opportunity to take the sample test so you can get a feel for what to expect. If you are an experienced exam taker, you can safely skip the sample exam and go right into the real thing.

Each exam is allotted a certain amount of time to complete. Once the exam begins, a clock will appear on the screen indicating how much time you have left. You can end the exam early if you answer all the required questions before the time expires or you can use all the available time, at which point the exam will automatically end. Once the exam is finished, your score will be tabulated and a screen will appear indicating whether it was a pass or fail.

Before you begin the exam, make sure you know how much time you have to complete all the questions. You can then average how much time you can spend on each question. Of course, some questions you may need to spend more time on than others. In my experience, Microsoft has always allocated sufficient time to complete an exam with time to spare at the end for review (if the testing format is not adaptive), so you don't need to rush through the exam. It's generally a good idea to do a quick clock check every few questions to ensure you aren't running behind.

The majority of test questions are multiple choice in format; you will be presented with a minimum of four answers to choose from. You can usually eliminate one of the answers immediately as being incorrect. From there you can then use your knowledge on the topic to begin eliminating the remaining answers. If you are unsure of the correct answer, try reading the question over.

Don't be surprised if you encounter an exam question that you can not determine the correct answer for. It often happens to those of us who have fully prepared for an exam and thoroughly studied all the necessary topics. In such cases, do not leave a question unanswered because you are unsure of the correct one. An unanswered question becomes a wrong answer. So when all else fails, a guess at least gives you a chance of answering it correctly. In some cases, you may be able to narrow the correct answer down to two choices. Carefully re-read the question. Sometimes one word can throw you off.

Some of the best advice I was ever given in such situations is to always go with your first instinct. When in doubt, go with the answer that first jumped out at you as being correct.

Exam Readiness Checklist

Official Objective	Study Guide Coverage	Ch #	Beginner	Intermediate	Expert
Planning and Implementing Server Roles and Security		9			
Configure security for servers that are assigned specific roles	Planning Security for Server Roles	9			
Plan a secure baseline installation	Planning a Secure Baseline Installation	9			
Plan security for servers that are assigned specific roles. Roles might include domain controllers, Web servers, database servers, and mail servers	Planning Security for Server Roles	9			
Evaluate and select the operating system to install on computers in an enterprise	Selecting the Appropriate Operating System	9			
Planning, Implementing, and Maintaining a Network Infrastructure		1–6, 8			
Plan a TCP/IP network infrastructure	Understanding IP Addressing and Subnetting, Planning a TCP/IP Routed Network	1, 2			
Plan and modify a network topology		1			
Plan an Internet connectivity strategy		5			
Plan network traffic monitoring. Tools might include System Monitor and Network Monitor		8			
Troubleshoot connectivity to the Internet		1, 5			
Troubleshoot TCP/IP addressing	Troubleshooting DHCP	2			
Plan a hostname resolution strategy		3			
Plan a NetBIOS name resolution strategy		4			
Troubleshoot hostname resolution	Troubleshooting DNS	3			

Exam Readiness Checklist

Official Objective	Study Guide Coverage	Ch #	Beginner	Intermediate	Expert
Planning, Implementing, and Maintaining Routing and Remote Access		1, 6			
Plan a routing strategy	Planning a Routing Strategy	6			
Plan security for remote access users	Ensuring Remote Access Security	6			
Implement secure access between private networks	Ensuring Remote Access Security	6			
Troubleshoot TCP/IP routing. Tools might include route, tracert, ping, pathping, and netsh commands and Network Monitor		1, 6			
Planning, Implementing, and Maintaining Server Availability		8			
Plan services for high availability	Planning for High Availability	8			
Identify system bottlenecks, including memory, processor, disk, and network-related bottle necks	Identifying System Bottlenecks	8			
Implement a cluster server	Planning for High Availability	8			
Manage Network Load Balancing. Tools might include the Network Load Balancing Monitor Microsoft Management Console (MMC) snap-in and the WLBS cluster control utility	Planning for High Availability	8			
Plan a backup and recovery strategy	Implementing a Backup and Recovery Strategy	8			
Planning and Maintaining Network Security		7			
Configure network protocol security	Securing Private Networks	7			
Configure security for data transmission	Securing Private Networks	7			
Plan for network protocol security	Securing Private Networks	7			
Plan secure network administration methods	Secure Network Administration	7			

Exam Readiness Checklist

Official Objective	Study Guide Coverage	Ch #	Beginner	Intermediate	Expert
Plan security for wireless networks	Wireless Network Security	7			
Plan security for data transmission	Securing Private Networks	7			
Troubleshoot security for data transmission. Tools might include the IP Security Monitor MMC snap-in and the Resultant Set of Policy (RSoP) MMC snap-in	Troubleshooting Network Security	7			
Planning, Implementing, and Maintaining Security Infrastructure		10			
Configure Active Directory services for certificate publication	Planning for Certificate Services	10			
Plan a framework for planning and implementing security	Planning a Security Framework	10			
Plan a security update infrastructure. Tools might include Microsoft Baseline Security Analyzer and Microsoft Software Update Services	Planning a Security Update Infrastructure	10			

1

Planning a TCP/IP Network

CERTIFICATION OBJECTIVES

CERTIFICATION OBJECTIVE 1.01

Understanding TCP/IP

Windows Server 2003 supports a number of different network protocols. The most common protocol used in network environments today is the Transmission Control Protocol/Internet Protocol (TCP/IP). Because it is the protocol required for accessing the Internet and because it's a routable, scalable, robust protocol, TCP/IP has quickly become the protocol of choice in many network environments. Most platforms provide support for TCP/IP, including Microsoft, which is working to make its operating systems more Internet-centric. TCP/IP is now the single default protocol for Microsoft's platforms.

TCP/IP offers the following features and benefits:

- **Security** The Windows Server 2003 implementation of TCP/IP supports IPSec for authentication and data encryption and packet filtering for filtering data.

- **Automatic private IP addressing (APIPA)** In the event that a DHCP server is not available or for single-subnet networks with no DHCP server configured, APIPA automates IP configuration. Computers assign themselves an IP address from network 169.254.0.0/16.

- **Alternate configuration** With alternate configuration, you can manually specify the IP settings to be used in the event that a DHCP server is not available. This is very useful for mobile users moving between different networks.

- **IP version 6** Windows Server 2003 supports the latest version of IP, known as IP version 6. IPv6 was designed to overcome some of the limitation now found in IPv4, such as the shortage of IPv4 addresses.

- **IGMP version 3** Windows Server 2003 supports IGMP v3. With IGMP v3, multicast group information can be obtained from all routers or only specific routers. This prevents routers from sending multicast traffic to subnets that do not have any multicast hosts.

- **ICMP router discovery** When a default gateway is not configured manually or assigned by a DHCP server, ICMP messages can be sent to automatically discover the default gateway.

- **Disabling NetBIOS over TCP/IP** NetBIOS over TCP/IP can be disabled on a network connection basis if DNS name registration is used and NetBIOS is no longer required.

TCP/IP Architecture

When we talk about TCP/IP, we are not talking about a single network protocol. Rather, TCP/IP consists of a suite of protocols and utilities that enable network communication between hosts. These hosts can be on the same local area network or span a wide area network. In any case, the protocols and utilities that make up TCP/IP enable complete network communication. The following section discusses the TCP/IP architecture and how the different protocols and utilities work to provide communication.

OSI Model

A discussion of TCP/IP would not be complete without a look at the OSI model. The Open Systems Interconnection (OSI) model, which outlines how a suite of protocols perform together, establishes an industry standard for network communication. To ensure communication between hosts, protocols must be designed according to this standard.

The OSI model consists of seven distinct layers. The protocols within a protocol suite, such as TCP/IP, operate at different layers of the model, performing different functions to enable network communication. The seven layers of the OSI model are as follows (see Figure 1-1):

- **Application** This is the top layer of the model. It defines how network applications such as databases and e-mail programs perform network-related functions.
- **Presentation** Protocols operating at this layer are responsible for converting and encrypting data. This layer defines how data is formatted, presented, and converted.
- **Session** This layer is responsible for establishing, maintaining, and ending communication sessions.
- **Transport** Protocols functioning at this layer provide flow control and error checking.
- **Network** This layer is responsible for addressing and routing to ensure information arrives at its destination.
- **Data Link** This layer controls the logical network topologies, the physical protocol assigned to the data, and sequencing.
- **Physical** This layer defines the physical characteristics of the network.

FIGURE 1-1

The seven layers
of the OSI model

As data flows through the layers, each layer adds its own header and trailer information. On the receiving end, this information is stripped off as it flows up the layers until the data arrives at the final destination.

DoD Model

The suite of protocols that make up TCP/IP also map to another conceptual model, referred to as the Department of Defense (DoD) model. This model was developed by the U.S. Department of Defense as a public standard for TCP/IP that would be independent of all software and hardware vendors. It defines communication in four layers as opposed to the seven layers of the OSI model. Each of the four layers maps to the different layers within the OSI model (see Figure 1-2), and each layer of the model also defines a specific role or function. The four layers of the DoD model include

- **Application**   This is the top layer of the model, also referred to as the Process layer, where applications such as FTP, SMTP, and HTTP gain access to the network.

- **Transport**   Protocols operating at this layer (also referred to as the Host-to host layer) are responsible for establishing sessions between two hosts. The two protocols that function at this level include the Transmission Control Protocol (TCP) and the User Datagram Protocol (UDP). The main difference between

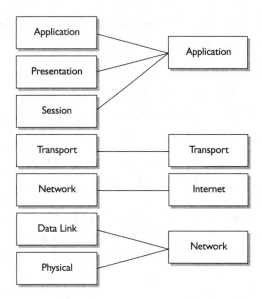

FIGURE 1-2

The four layers of
the DoD model

the two protocols is that TCP is connection orientated, which means that
it provides reliable delivery, whereas UDP is connectionless and does not.

■ **Internet**   The main responsibilities of protocols operating at this layer are
addressing and routing. The protocols working at this layer include the
Internet Protocol (IP), which is responsible for addressing and routing, the
Address Resolution Protocol (ARP), which maps IP addresses to MAC addresses,
the Internet Control Message Protocol (IMCP), and the Internet Group
Management Protocol (IGMP).

■ **Network**   Also called simply the Network Access layer, this is the bottom
layer of the model and is responsible for sending and receiving information
over the physical medium.

Now that you are familiar with the two conceptual models that define how network
protocols function, let's take a look at the specific protocols that make up Microsoft's
implementation of the TCP/IP protocol.

TCP/IP Protocols

As already mentioned, there are a number of different protocols within the TCP/IP
protocol suite. Each protocol operates at a specific layer of the conceptual models (see

Figure 1-3) and performs a specific function that enables hosts to communicate. The main protocols within the TCP/IP protocol suite include the following:

- Address Resolution Protocol (ARP)
- Internet Control Message Protocol (ICMP)
- Internet Group Management Protocol (IGMP)
- Internet Protocol (IP)
- Transmission Control Protocol (TCP)
- User Datagram Protocol (UDP)

Address Resolution Protocol (ARP) As you will see later in the chapter, each host on a TCP/IP-based network requires an IP address. To make it easier for users, hosts can be located using a friendly name such as a DNS name or a NetBIOS name. For example, instead of having to type in the IP address of a computer, you can refer to it by a host name such as WRK01. Before communication can take place, however, the friendly name must be resolved to the corresponding IP address. This is done using a method of name resolution such as DNS or WINS. Once the IP address has been determined, the resolution process does not stop there—the IP address must then be resolved to the hardware address (or MAC address). This is where the Address Resolution Protocol comes into play.

ARP is responsible for mapping IP addresses to hardware addresses. When one host needs to communicate with another host on the local network, it sends a broadcast requesting the hardware address of the destination IP address. Once the hardware address is received, it is placed in the host's ARP cache for future reference.

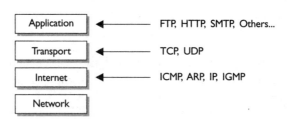

FIGURE 1-3

TCP/IP protocols mapped to the DoD model

Consider an example of what happens when an IP address needs to be resolved to a hardware address (keep in mind that the process is slightly different if the two hosts are on separate networks). If Host A wants to communicate with Host B, Host A first checks the contents of its local ARP cache to see if the mapping already exists. The purpose of this is to reduce the number of broadcasts. If there is no mapping in the cache for Host B, Host A sends out a broadcast on the local network requesting the information. Host B responds to the broadcast and returns its hardware address to Host A. A mapping is placed in the local cache. At this point, the two hosts can successfully communicate.

The process is slightly different if the two hosts are on different networks, as the broadcast must first go through at least one router. Often, to reduce network traffic, routers do not allow ARP broadcasts to flow between networks. For a host to obtain the hardware address of a host on a remote network, the following process must occur:

1. Host A attempts to connect to Host C, for example, using FTP.

2. After name resolution, the client determines that Host C is on a remote network, and Host A checks its local routing tables to determine a route to the destination host (if no entry is found, the default gateway is used).

3. Host A sends a broadcast out on the local network to determine the hardware address of the router. Once the router returns its hardware address, Host A places an entry in its local ARP cache.

4. The source will then frame the packet and forward it to the router.

5. The router strips away the framing and determines where the packet should be routed (in this case, let's assume it's attached to another network).

6. The router then ARPs for the MAC address of the destination client.

7. The router then reframes the packet and sends it to the destination host.

on the job *When an ARP broadcast is sent to determine the hardware address associated with an IP address, both the source and destination hosts will update the contents of their ARP cache. You can view the contents of the local cache using the `arp -a` command.*

Internet Control Message Protocol   ICMP is used by TCP/IP for reporting errors and status information when datagrams are sent across the network. One of the utilities that uses ICMP is the `ping` command. This command sends ICMP echo messages to a destination host to test network connectivity. The echo replies returned from the destination host will enable you to determine whether there are host or network connectivity problems. For example, if you ping a remote host and receive a destination unreachable message, this may indicate that the remote host is unavailable or there is a problem with a router (see Figure 1-4).

Internet Group Management Protocol   The Internet Group Management Protocol (IGMP) is used for multicasting purposes. With multicasting, a group of hosts share a single destination IP address. IP hosts use IGMP to report their multicast group status to routers on the network. Routers are then aware of which multicast groups are on which networks.

With multicasting, information is sent to a single IP address but processed by more than one host. All hosts listening for traffic to a specific multicast IP address are said to be *members* of the same multicast group. Therefore, all information sent to a specific multicast address is received and processed by all members of that multicast group. Membership in a multicast group is dynamic, so hosts can join and leave a group on-the-fly. IGMP is used by hosts to report their group membership status. It is also used by multicast routers to exchange multicast group information.

Internet Protocol   The Internet Protocol (IP) performs a number of functions at the Internet layer of the DoD model. Its main purpose is to address and route packets. Each host on an IP network is assigned a unique identifier known as an *IP address*, which is used to route packets between hosts. As information flows through the protocol

FIGURE 1-4	
Testing connectivity using the **ping** command	

```
C:\>ping 192.168.0.21

Pinging 192.168.0.21 with 32 bytes of data:

Destination host unreachable.
Destination host unreachable.
Destination host unreachable.
Destination host unreachable.

Ping statistics for 192.168.0.21:
    Packets: Sent = 4, Received = 0, Lost = 4 (100% loss),

C:\>_
```

stack, IP is responsible for addressing all packets, adding both the source and destination IP addresses to the packet. The IP protocol will also determine whether a destination host is on the local network or on a remote network. If the host is on a remote network, the routing table is used to determine which gateway the packet must be sent to. If the host is on the local network, the packet can be sent directly to the host once the hardware address is obtained.

Transmission Control Protocol   The Transmission Control Protocol (TCP) is a connection-based protocol, meaning that before data can be sent between two hosts, a session must first be established. TCP offers reliable delivery of data through sequencing, error checking, and flow control.

As already mentioned, before two hosts can exchange data, a session must first be established. This is done through a process known as a *three-way handshake*. Once a session is established, information can be reliably sent. Each datagram that is sent is assigned a sequence number. The sequence numbers ensure that the destination computer can reassemble the data in the proper order as it arrives. The destination computer will send acknowledgments for segments that are received. If the source computer does not receive an acknowledgment within a certain amount of time, the segment will be retransmitted, thus ensuring delivery of information.

FTP and Telnet are examples of programs that use TCP to transfer data between two TCP/IP hosts.

User Datagram Protocol   Unlike TCP, UDP is a connectionless protocol. This means that UDP does not establish a session before sending data, nor does it provide for reliable delivery. When information is sent, acknowledgments are not returned, so it is just assumed to have been received. UDP is more often used in one-to-many situations where information is sent using a broadcast or for multicasting (TCP is used for one-to-one communication). If reliable delivery and sequencing of datagrams is required, it is the responsibility of the application or a higher-level protocol to provide these services. For example, UDP is often used by videoconferencing and streaming media applications because they require fast delivery of data. The Session Information Protocol (SIP) used for streaming media relies on UDP but also uses its own retransmission mechanisms because UDP does not offer reliable delivery of data.

TCP and UDP Ports   Both TCP and UDP communicate using ports. Port numbers are application specific, ranging between 0 and 65535, that define logical endpoints for sending data between two hosts. An application will have a sending port as well as a receiving port. Some of the common TCP and UDP ports are shown next.

TCP Port Number	Application
20, 21	File Transfer Protocol (FTP)
23	Telnet
25	Simple Mail Transfer Protocol (SMTP)
110	Post Office Protocol (POP3)

UDP Port Number	Application
23	Telnet
25	Simple Mail Transfer Protocol (SMTP)
53	Domain Name System (DNS)

Application Layer Protocols   There are a number of other protocols within the protocol suite that function at the Application layer of the DoD model. Some of these protocols include

- **Simple Network Management Protocol (SNMP)**   This protocol is used to collect information about network devices and store the information in a centralized database.
- **File Transfer Protocol (FTP)**   This protocol provides a way to transfer files between two TCP/IP hosts. Using FTP, you can browse directories and files and transfer text and binary files from one host to another.
- **Hypertext Transfer Protocol (HTTP)**   This is the protocol used to enable communication between a web browser and a web server.
- **Post Office Protocol (POP)**   This protocol is used to retrieve e-mail from a POP server.

Now that you're familiar with the architecture of TCP/IP and the different protocols that make up the protocol suite, let's take a look at one of the most important concepts when discussing TCP/IP: IP addressing.

CERTIFICATION OBJECTIVE 1.02

Understanding IP Addressing and Subnetting

TCP/IP is one of the more difficult protocols to understand (and configure). For packets to be routed on an IP network, every host requires a unique IP address (hosts can include workstations, servers, routers, printers, or any other device with a network interface card). The IP address is a 32-bit number, represented in decimal format, that identifies each host. In order to achieve exam success as well as to design an efficient IP network, you must have an understanding of the concepts discussed in the following section. You should have an understanding of IP addresses and be able to perform binary calculations as well as basic subnetting.

IP Addressing

An IP address consists of two parts: the *network ID* and the *host ID*. The network ID is used to identify a specific network or subnet, whereas the host ID identifies the hosts on a given network or subnet. For example, with the IP address of 132.10.26.2 and the default subnet mask of 255.255.0.0, the network ID is 132.10 and the host ID is 26.2.

If you are familiar with IP addresses, you may have also heard them compared to streets and house addresses. This is one of the most common analogies used to explain the idea behind IP addresses. A residence is identified by its street name and house number. Each residence on a specific street requires a unique house number (so that mail can be delivered, for instance). Turning to IP addresses, the network ID is similar to the street name in that it identifies a specific network, whereas the host ID is similar to a house number in that it specifically identifies a specific computer on that network. So just as the street address and the house number are used to deliver information to a specific residence, the network ID and the host ID are used to determine what computer information should be delivered to and where that computer is located on the network.

We see IP addresses in decimal format. Computers, on the other hand, understand only binary. Therefore, every IP address can be converted from decimal format to binary and vice versa. An IP address consists of four octets. The value of each octet can range from 0 through 255. When an octet is converted to binary, it will consist of eight bits, each with a specific value. When converting from binary to decimal, you can add up the bit values to arrive at the decimal value. The eight bit values are as follows:

1 1 1 1 1 1 1 1

128 64 32 16 8 4 2 1

An IP address of 131.107.2.10 can therefore be converted to the following binary number:

10000011 01101011 00000010 00001010

You might now be asking yourself how a computer determines which part of an IP address identifies the network and which part identifies the hosts on a given network. So to clarify this, consider the subnet mask.

A quick-and-easy way to convert to binary if you have access to the Windows calculator is to switch to Scientific view, ensure the Bin button is selected, type in the bit pattern you want to convert, and click the Dec button.

Subnet Masks

In order to determine if a destination host is on the local network or a remote network, a computer must be able to identify which portion of an IP address is the host ID and which part represents the network ID. This is where the subnet mask comes into play.

A *subnet mask* is a 32-bit number that uses 1's and 0's to distinguish the network ID in an IP address from the host ID. The portion of the subnet mask that is sent to all 1's identifies the network ID, while the portion set to all 0's identifies the host ID. For example, the IP address of 192.168.0.1 would have a default subnet mask of 255.255.255.0. The first three octets of the subnet mask are set to all 1's. This means that the first three octets of the IP address identify the network ID. Since the last octet of the subnet mask is set to all 0's, only the last octet of the IP address is used to identify a specific host on the network.

on the
Job

A subnet mask can be written in a different, much faster format. For example, the subnet mask of 255.0.0.0 can also be represented as /8 because the first eight bits represent the network ID.

The subnet mask is used to determine whether a destination computer is on the local network or a remote network. So how is the subnet mask used to determine this? The answer is, through a process known as *ANDing*. Basically the 1's in the binary address of the subnet mask are masked against the IP address to determine if the address is on the local network or a remote network.

So let's take a look at the process of ANDing. The important thing to remember when comparing the 1's and 0's in the subnet mask to those of the IP address is that all combinations except 1 and 1 result in a value of 0:

192.168.0.1 in binary is 11000000 10101000 00000000 00000001

255.255.255.0 in binary is 11111111 11111111 11111111 00000000

Since the first three octets in the subnet mask are set to 1's, they are masked against the first three octets of the IP address to get the following result (keep in mind that 1 and 1 result in a value of 1, while all other combinations result in 0):

11000000 10101000 00000000 00000000

For example, consider how ANDing is used to determine that two hosts are on the same subnet. Host A has an IP address of 192.168.2.10 and a subnet mask of 255.255.255.0. Host B has an IP address of 192.168.2.25. Looking at the IP addresses, you can tell that the hosts are on the same network. However, the following process is used by the computer to determine this:

- **192.168.2.10**   11000000 10101000 00000010 00001010
- **255.255.255.0**   11111111 11111111 11111111 00000000
- **Results of ANDing**   11000000 10101000 00000010 00000000
- **192.168.2.25**   11000000 10101000 00000010 00011001
- **255.255.255.0**   11111111 11111111 11111111 00000000
- **Results of ANDing**   11000000 10101000 00000010 00000000

As you can tell from the results of ANDing, the computers are both on the same network. When the results for each IP address are converted back to decimal, the network IDs are the same (192.168.2.0). Now take a look at the results for two hosts on different networks. Host A has an IP address of 192.168.2.10 and a subnet mask of 255.255.255.0. Host C has an IP address of 192.168.6.20.

- **192.168.2.10**   11000000 10101000 00000010 00001010
- **255.255.255.0**   11111111 11111111 11111111 00000000
- **Results of ANDing**   11000000 10101000 00000010 00000000
- **192.168.6.20**   11000000 10101000 00000110 00010100
- **255.255.255.0**   11111111 11111111 11111111 00000000
- **Results of ANDing**   11000000 10101000 00000110 00000000

As you can tell from the results of ANDing, the computers are on different networks. Once the results are converted back to decimal format, you get two different network IDs, 192.168.2.0 and 192.168.6.0. This tells the computer that the destination host is not local.

Address Classes

In order to use TCP/IP, you must have an understanding of the various address classes. The class of IP used will determine the number of subnets you can create and the maximum number of hosts per subnet.

e x a m
w a t c h

Be prepared to encounter exam questions pertaining to the private reserved ranges of IP addresses. These *include 10.0.0.0/8, 172.16.0.0/12, and 192.168.0.0/16. Addresses that fall within these ranges cannot be used on the public Internet.*

Class A addresses range from $1.x.y.z$ to $126.x.y.z$ with a default subnet mask of 255.0.0.0. A network ID within this range would allow for more than 16 million host IDs. So with a class A address, you are looking at support for a small number of networks but a large number of hosts. The problem is that there are no unused class A addresses available. So if you need the flexibility of a class A address, meaning a lot of flexibility in terms of subnetting and the number of hosts, you are forced to use the private reserved range. On a private network, this does not pose a problem so long as you have no intention of attempting to use the IP addresses on the Internet. If you do want to connect machines on this network to the Internet, you will need to implement some sort of Internet gateway that is assigned a valid Internet IP address (although not a class A address) through which internal hosts would gain Internet access.

e x a m
w a t c h

With automatic private IP addressing (APIPA), computers can assign themselves an IP address within the range of 169.254.0.1 to 169.254.255.254. When a computer is configured as a DHCP client and there is no DHCP server available, it will assign itself an IP address within this *range. Keep in mind that only the IP address and corresponding subnet mask are assigned, so the computer has very limited functionality on the network. In any case, be prepared to encounter exam questions pertaining to the topic.*

Class B addresses fall in the range of 128.*x.y.z* to 191.*x.y.z* with a default subnet mask of 255.255.0.0. Class B addresses allow for more than 16,000 networks and more than 65,000 hosts per network. Remember as well that the IP address range used for automatic private IP addressing (169.254.0.0) also falls within the class B range.

Class C addresses fall within the range of 192.*x.y.z* to 223.*x.y.z* with a default subnet mask of 255.255.255.0. The class C address range allows for more than one million networks and 254 hosts per network.

Class	IP Address Range	Default Subnet Mask
Class A	1–126	255.0.0.0
Class B	128–191	255.255.0.0
Class C	192–223	255.255.255.0

As you will notice from the preceding table, 127 is not included in any of the address ranges. This value is known as the loopback address and has been reserved for diagnostic testing.

The class of address you use will depend on the size of the network and the projected growth. For example, a class B network address can give you more than 65,000 host IDs per network. If your network has only a few thousand users and you have no plans for it to grow much larger in size, all those IP addresses will go unused. At the other extreme, using a class C address would give you only 254 host IDs per network. Keep in mind as well that valid IP addresses are expensive to obtain, so if you plan on implementing a public range of IP addresses on the internal network, be prepared to pay.

The typical solution when implementing IP addresses is to use one of the private ranges on the internal network (remember these are the three ranges of IP addresses that cannot be used on the Internet), for example, by using the network ID of 192.168.0.0 and assigning all internal hosts an IP address from this range. To allow for Internet access, a limited number of public IP addresses can be obtained from an ISP and assigned to your NAT server (this would be the computer that has an interface connected to the public Internet). Hosts on the private network would then gain access to the Internet through the network address translator. Not only does this reduce the cost associated with obtaining IP addresses but it also protects the hosts on the private network, as their IP addresses are never exposed on the Internet.

Subnetting

One of the problems with using the default subnet masks is that you end up with a single network. If the infrastructure is small, then this may be a viable implementation. In a large infrastructure, however, a single network can result in a lot of broadcast traffic (although most routers are configured not to pass most broadcasts). One of the solutions to this problem is to implement subnetting to logically segment the network.

The inventors of the Internet Protocol figured the 32-bit addressing scheme would be sufficient; they never predicted that the Net would so grow in size and popularity that a shortage of IP addresses would result. Subnetting introduces a solution to the shortage of IP addresses.

Subnetting allows administrators to take a large network and logically divide it into smaller networks. Some of the benefits of this include

- **Simplified administration** A large network can be broken down into smaller logical networks that can be managed independently.
- **Reduced network traffic** Once a network has been subnetted, all broadcast traffic remains isolated within a logical network.
- **Increased security** Traffic can be isolated so that it remains localized, if necessary.

Subnetting works by taking away some of the bits used for host IDs and using them to identify the logical networks. For example, the default subnet mask for a class C address is 255.255.255.0. Changing that to 255.255.255.254 means some of the bits from the fourth octet used to identify hosts are now being used as part of the network number. The result is fewer host IDs but more networks.

The number of bits you use will determine the number of subnets you can create. So when planning your subnets, you will need to first consider the number of subnets you will require and the number of hosts per subnet. Once you have determined this, you can then establish the subnet mask to use. Table 1-1 outlines the subnet expansion. For example, if you require seven subnets, you can determine from Table 1-1 that you will need to use four bits from the host ID.

You can determine the number of subnets and hosts that a subnet mask will provide by using the formula $2 \wedge n - 2$, where n is the number of bits used for the subnet ID or the number of bits remaining for the host IDs.

For example, with a subnet mask of 255.255.255.192, two bits are used from the fourth octet for the subnet mask. Using the preceding formula, $2 \wedge 2 - 2$ will equal 2. This means that a subnet mask of 255.255.255.192 will allow for two subnets. To determine the number of host IDs available with this subnet mask, use the same formula, only this time set n equal to the number of bits left over for the host IDs. Using the same subnet mask, two bits were used for the subnet mask, which leaves six bits for

TABLE 1-1	Bit Pattern	Subnet Mask	Number of Subnets
Subnet Expansion	11000000	192	2
	11100000	224	6
	11110000	240	14
	11111000	248	30
	11111100	252	62
	11111110	254	126
	11111111	255	254

host IDs. Therefore, $2 \wedge 6 - 2$ equals 62 hosts. Thus the subnet mask of 255.255.255.192 will allow for 62 hosts per subnet.

watch *Be prepared to encounter exam questions related to subnetting. When given a range of IP addresses, you must be able to determine the corresponding subnet mask.*

The following example illustrates subnetting a class B address of 131.107.0.0 where the default subnet mask would be 255.255.0.0. If 10 subnets are required, a total of four bits must be used from the host ID. Referring back to Table 1-1, the subnet mask will then be 255.255.240.0. You can determine the number of subnets this subnet mask will allow by using the preceding formula. Since $2 \wedge 4 - 2$ equals 14, 14 subnets can be created using the subnet mask. Since $2 \wedge 12 - 2$ equals 4094, the subnet mask will provide for up to 4094 hosts/subnet.

EXERCISE 1-1

Subnetting a Class A Network Address

In this exercise, you will use the steps outlined in the preceding section to subnet a class A network address. You use the following scenario to determine the appropriate subnet mask.

You have been assigned the IP address range of 125.0.0.0 and a default subnet mask of 255.0.0.0. You want to subnet your network into ten different subnets. Determine the subnet mask to use. Calculate the number of hosts and subnets that will be available.

INSIDE THE EXAM

Subnetting

Subnetting is often one of the most difficult concepts to grasp. But it is one that is important to understand for success both in passing the exam and on the job. At first, the concept may seem mind boggling, but once you've done it a few times, it really turns out to be less complex than it first appeared to be.

When you take the exam, be prepared to encounter at least one exam question (if not several) related to subnetting. You should be able to perform basic subnetting for a given scenario. For example, if you are presented with a scenario outlining the required number of subnets and the expected number of hosts per subnet, you must be able to select the appropriate subnet mask. Also, be sure to read the scenario carefully. In order to choose the correct subnet mask, you must take into consideration any expected growth. Thus a scenario may tell you that 6 subnets are required, but if you read carefully, you may notice that there are plans to add 6 more in the near future. This means you'll need

to choose a subnet mask that will allow for at least 12 subnets.

You also need to be able to determine the number of subnets that can be created for a given subnet mask as well as the number of hosts per subnet. You can determine this using a simple formula. For example, the subnet mask of 255.255.255.224 would allow for 6 subnets. You can determine this by using the following formula: $2 \wedge n - 2$, where n is the number of host bits used for the subnet mask. Since 224 uses three bits, using the formula means $2 \wedge 3 - 2$ equals 6 subnets. You can use the same formula to determine the number of hosts, where this time n equals the number of bits remaining for the host ID. Since three bits are used for the subnet mask, this leaves five bits. $2 \wedge 5 - 2$ equals 30, which means each subnet can have a maximum of 30 hosts. If you can remember that formula, you will be able to determine the number of subnets and hosts that a specific subnet mask will allow for.

Determining the Valid Network IDs

As another aspect of subnetting that you may encounter on the exam, you may be asked to calculate the range of network IDs for a given subnet mask. To begin figuring out the range of IP addresses for a given subnet mask, you must first convert the subnet mask to binary and place the bits used to extend the subnet mask in every possible combination of 1's and 0's.

For example, a class B address of 182.20.0.0 has been extended and the subnet mask used is 255.255.192.0, or 11111111.11111111.11000000.00000000. Two bits are used from the third octet to extend the subnet mask. Begin by placing the two bits in every possible combination of 1's and 0's as follows. Remember, the extended portion of the subnet mask cannot be all 1's or all 0's as these values would not be considered valid network IDs.

- 00000000   Not a valid network ID
- 01000000   64
- 10000000   128
- 11000000   192 not a valid network ID

Therefore, the two valid subnet IDs are 182.20.64.0/14 and 182.20.128.0/14 (and if you refer back to Table 1-1, you can see that an extended subnet mask of 192 will produce two valid subnets). From this you can determine that the valid host IDs for the two subnets are

- 182.20.64.1–182.20.127.254
- 182.20.128.1–182.20.191.254

EXERCISE 1-2

Determining the Valid Network IDs

In this exercise, you will use the following information to determine the valid network IDs for a given subnet mask.

1. You have been assigned a class B address of 132.10.0.0/8. You want to create eight subnets. Which subnet mask will you use?

2. How many subnets will the subnet mask support?

3. How many host IDs will be supported per subnet?

4. What are the valid network IDs for the subnet mask?

5. What are the valid host IDs for the subnet mask?

Designing a TCP/IP Network

Once you have an understanding of some of the fundamental concepts underlying TCP/IP, you can begin to design a functional TCP/IP network. There are a number of aspects you need to consider to come up with a functional plan. These include the addressing scheme you will implement, the subnet requirements, and how IP addresses will be assigned to computers.

Choosing an Addressing Scheme

One of the decisions you will be faced with when designing an IP network is whether to use a public or private addressing scheme on the internal network. First of all, if any computers have a direct connection to the Internet, they will obviously require at least one public IP address. But for those computers with no direct Internet connection, you have the option of using public or private addresses. A list of the available private address blocks is shown here:

IP Address Class	Private Address Range
Class A	10.0.0.0–10.255.255.255
Class B	172.16.0.0–172.31.255.255
Class C	192.168.0.0–192.168.255.255

As you begin to design IP networks, you will soon see that only rarely will all computers have a direct Internet connection. This is a good thing in terms of security, as the fewer direct connections there are, the less entry points attackers have. In these situations, you have the option of implementing a private addressing scheme. Not only is this more secure, it is also inexpensive.

Internet access can still be provided through the use of a proxy or NAT server. Only a minimum number of public IP addresses need to be acquired, and the only IP address visible to the Internet is that of the proxy or NAT server.

You also have the option to implement a public IP addressing scheme. If a large number of computers require a direct Internet connection, they will need to be assigned public addresses. Also, if you've been assigned a range of IP addresses that is sufficient for all computers on the network, you may choose to use them instead of private ones. Even though the private network uses public Internet addresses, security can still be achieved by implementing some form of firewall between the Internet and the private network. One of the disadvantages of this scheme is that it may not provide flexibility in terms of growth, depending on the number of IP addresses you've been allocated by your ISP. Table 1-2 summarizes some of the advantages and disadvantages of each addressing scheme.

Subnet Requirements

Earlier in the chapter, you were introduced to the concept of subnetting. There are a number of things that you must think about when considering a subnet mask design. First of all, you need to consider the number of subnets that you will require or that currently exist, along with the number of hosts that exist on each subnet. Drawing on this information, you can determine the subnet mask to use. Keep in mind that a good subnet mask design will not limit growth, so when you are considering the number of subnets and hosts, also factor future growth into the equation. It is always better to design for excess than to face having to completely redesign your IP network because the existing subnet mask design won't support network growth.

TABLE 1-2	A Comparison of Public Versus Private IP Addressing Schemes	
Scheme	**Advantages**	**Disadvantages**
Private IP addressing	• Inexpensive • Offers increased security • Flexible in terms of growth • Allows for expansion	• At least one public address still required. • A proxy server or NAT server is required for Internet access.
Public IP addressing	• Allows computers to directly access the Internet	• It is expensive. • It offers limited flexibility in terms of growth. • It can be less secure.

In the past, subnetting has always been a popular exam topic. If you encounter questions where you are required *to choose the appropriate subnet mask, be sure to read the question carefully and factor in any projected growth.*

Allocating IP Addresses

One topic not yet touched upon is how IP addresses are allocated to computers. As already mentioned, every host (including computers, printers, and routers) requires an IP address. How these hosts will be assigned IP addresses needs to be considered when designing an IP network. IP addresses can be assigned manually, automatically using a DHCP server, or through APIPA.

Manually assigning IP addresses requires visiting every host and typing in the required IP parameters. This is not the preferred or most efficient method of assigning IP addresses. However, for hosts such as servers and routers or for those hosts that do not support DHCP, IP parameters must be configured manually. Keep in mind as well that certain services and applications may require a computer to have a static IP address. For example, when you install DNS on Windows Server 2003, a message will appear indicating that the server must be configured with a static IP address.

Using a DHCP server, you can have IP addresses assigned to hosts automatically. An administrator defines a scope or range of IP addresses on the DHCP server. DHCP clients are then dynamically allocated IP addresses from the scope. If the majority of clients support DHCP, this is the preferred method for allocating addresses.

o n t h e

ꙸo b

DHCP is the preferred method for assigning IP addresses. Especially in complex subnetted networks, using a DHCP server will centralize the administration of IP addresses.

The third option is to use automatic private IP addressing. This option would be most viable in a single-subnet network that does not require Internet access. With this method, a host will assign itself an IP address from the 169.254.0.0 address block and a subnet mask of 255.255.0.0. No optional parameters such as the default gateway and DNS servers are assigned, which means this method provides a host with very limited functionality. However, this feature does add some level of functionality for those networks that implement DHCP. If a DHCP server is temporarily unavailable and DHCP clients are unable to lease or renew an IP address, they can use an IP address within the 169.254.0.0 block. This will enable DHCP clients to communicate on their local subnet with other hosts using APIPA. For example, servers on the subnet will more than likely be assigned static IP addresses, and therefore clients using APIPA will not be able to communicate with them. Keep in mind as well that since APIPA does not include a default gateway address, communication outside of the local network will fail.

on the
()ob

APIPA can be disabled through the Windows Registry by editing the following Registry key: IPAutoConfigurationEnabled hklm\system\ currentcontrolset\services\tcpip\parameters\interfaces. By changing the value of IPAutoConfigurationEnabled to 0, you can disable APIPA for a given interface.

SCENARIO & SOLUTION

What are three methods for assigning IP addresses?	• Statically • DHCP Server • Automatic private IP addressing
When would APIPA be appropriate as a method for assigning IP addresses?	APIPA would be a viable method of IP address assignment for small single networks that are not connecting to the Internet.
What is the alternate configuration?	Alternate configuration allows an administrator to manually configure IP parameters that should be used when a DHCP server is unavailable.
What are the benefits of using DHCP?	• It centralizes the administration of IP addresses. DHCP can assign optional parameters such as default gateways, DNS servers, and WINS servers. • It eliminates the chance of hosts being given incorrect IP parameters.

Configuring TCP/IP

TCP/IP is installed by default with Windows Server 2003. In terms of configuration, TCP/IP is the most difficult of the network protocols to configure. If you are using DHCP, however, some of the configuration can be automated. The following section will briefly look at how to configure TCP/IP.

TCP/IP Properties

You can configure the TCP/IP protocol through the properties dialog box for the network connection. To do so:

1. Click Start, point to Control Panel, point to Network Connections, and click the network connection for which you want to configure TCP/IP.

2. From the status window, click Properties.

3. Select the Internet Protocol (TCP/IP) from the list of installed components and click Properties.

4. The Internet Protocol (TCP/IP) Properties dialog box will appear as shown here.

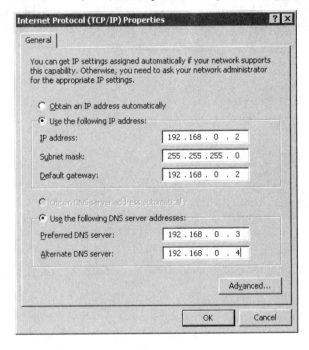

From the General tab, you can configure how the computer will obtain an IP address. The default is set to automatically, so if there is a DHCP server on the network, the computer will lease an IP address from it. You have the option of manually configuring an IP address. If so, you must specify the IP address, subnet mask, and default gateway that the computer will use. The same holds true for the IP address of the DNS servers. They can be obtained from a DHCP server or configured manually.

You can configure additional settings for the protocol by selecting the Advanced tab (see Figure 1-5). From the IP Settings tab, you can add additional IP addresses as well as additional default gateways. Many of these advanced settings will be discussed in detail in subsequent chapters.

The DNS tab, shown in Figure 1-6, enables you to configure various advanced DNS settings. The settings you can configure include the IP addresses of additional DNS servers, the order in which DNS servers are contacted when resolving hostnames, and the process that occurs when appending DNS suffixes for name resolution.

FIGURE 1-5

Configuring
advanced
protocol settings

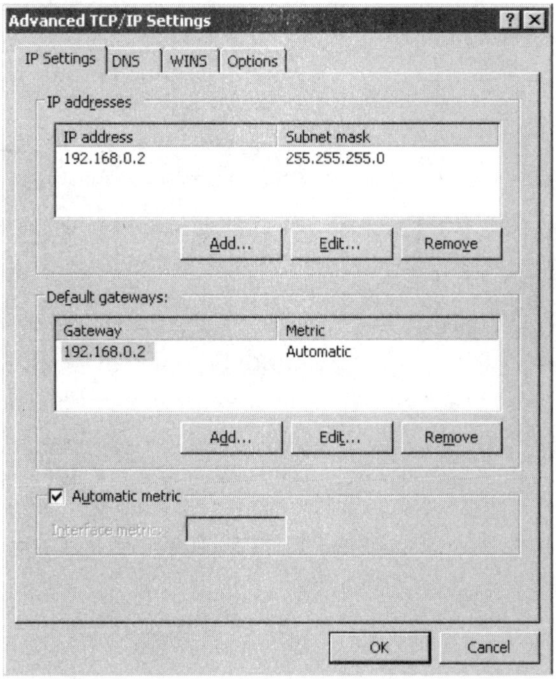

Configuring
advanced DNS
settings

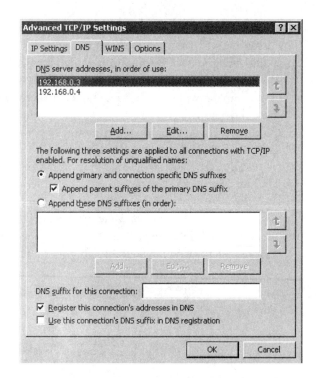

The WINS tab allows you to enable WINS for NetBIOS name resolution (see Figure 1-7). Ideally, you will want to disable NetBIOS over TCP/IP, unless the network supports legacy clients (pre–Windows 2000). From here, you can specify the IP addresses of the WINS servers on the network, enable LMHOSTS for NetBIOS name resolution, and configure various NetBIOS settings (all of which are discussed further in Chapter 4).

The final tab available from the Internet Protocol (TCP/IP) Properties dialog box is the Options tab. From here, you can configure TCP/IP filtering to control the type of traffic permitted by the host computer. Clicking Properties brings up the TCP/IP Filtering dialog box (see Figure 1-8). You can allow the local computer to permit all types of traffic, or you can permit traffic by TCP and UDP port as well as by IP protocol.

FIGURE 1-7

Configuring
WINS settings

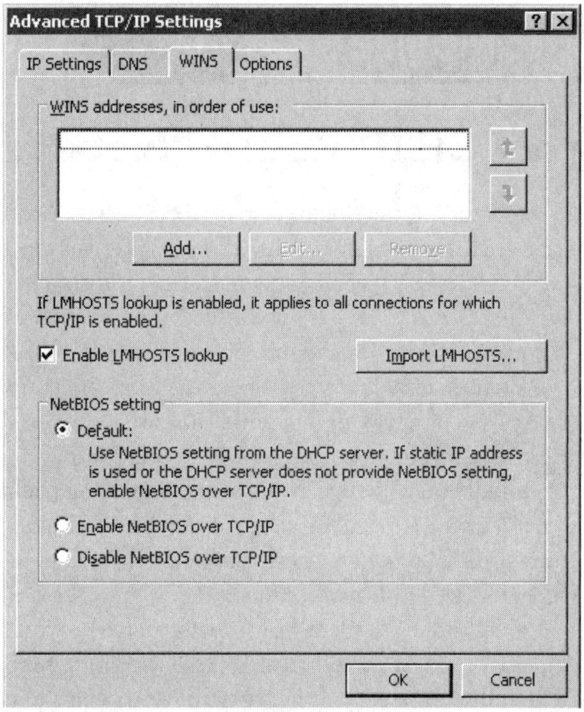

FIGURE 1-8

Configuring
TCP/IP filtering

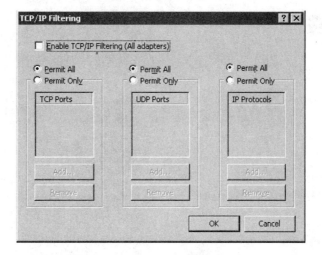

CERTIFICATION OBJECTIVE I.03

Planning a TCP/IP-Routed Network

In order for information to be routed between networks, the protocol used must provide a mechanism for determining if the packet is for a local host or a remote host. If the packet is destined for a remote host, the protocol must also provide a way of determining where to send it. As you saw earlier in the chapter, TCP/IP provides this functionality through IP addresses and subnet masks, which make it a routable protocol.

What exactly is a routed network? In very simplistic terms, a routed network is two physical network segments that are connected using a router (see Figure 1-9) for the purpose of moving data between point A and point B. The router acts as sort of "middle man" between the subnets, passing packets from one subnet to another router, and eventually to the subnet where the destination host resides. Of course, most TCP/IP-routed networks are much more complex than this, consisting of multiple segments and multiple routers.

So let's take a look at how routing actually works. Using the example shown in Figure 1-9, Host A and Host B are on separate subnets connected by a single router. The following steps outline how routing occurs between them.

FIGURE 1-9   TCP/IP subnets connected using a router

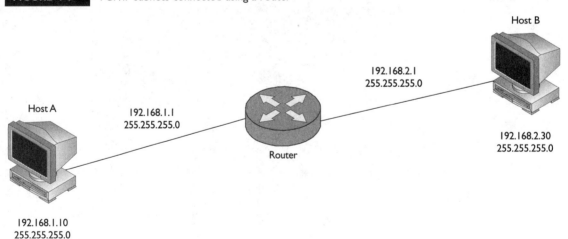

1. Host A pings the IP address of Host B (192.168.2.30).

2. Host A will use the process of ANDing (described earlier in the chapter) to determine if the destination host is local or remote.

3. In this example, the ANDing results will not match and Host A will determine that Host B is on a remote network.

4. Since Host B is remote, the packet must be sent to Host A's default gateway (which in this case is the router interface of 192.168.1.1). Before the packet can be sent to the gateway, Host A must know its MAC address. Host A checks in the ARP cache to find the MAC address.

5. If it does not find it there, Host A will send an ARP broadcast for the MAC address of 192.168.1.1. The router will send back a reply with the hardware address for the interface of 192.168.1.1.

6. The packet is placed within a frame and sent to the router interface. Once the router receives the frame, it determines that the packet is for another host, in this case 192.168.2.30.

7. The router will check the entries within the routing table and determine that the network 192.168.2.0 is a directly connected interface.

8. Next the router will need to determine the MAC address of the destination host by checking the contents of the ARP cache or by performing an ARP broadcast.

9. Host B will respond with its MAC address, and the frame will be sent to the destination host.

As you will see in the following section, routers and routing play a crucial role in an IP-routed network. When planning an IP routing infrastructure, you must have some knowledge of how IP packets are sent between subnets, how routers determine the path to a destination host, and the two different routing protocols that are supported. These topics will be discussed in the following sections.

Planning an IP Routing Infrastructure

As you already saw from the discussion on TCP/IP addressing, all IP packets are assigned source and destination IP addresses. Routing is the process of delivering an IP packet to a destination IP address. Of course, this is routing in its most simplistic terms, whereas the real process of routing is far more complex.

Routers use the information within an IP packet header to determine the destination IP address. Routers maintain information within a table about the physical network, such as the path to a destination network and the metric associated with the route, the metric being the distance between the source and destination networks.

In order for routers to know where to forward IP packets, they must be aware of other routers on the network. This information is stored within the routing table. When a router receives a packet, it checks the routing table to determine which path a packet must take to reach the destination host. The router will examine the network ID of the destination address and use the routing table to determine where the packet should be forwarded.

The information stored within a routing table can be configured statically or dynamically. Statically configuring routing tables entails manually typing in the paths to destination networks. Dynamic routing entails the use of routing protocols that enable routers to communicate with one another to share information about remote networks. Static and dynamic routing is discussed in the following section.

Static Routing

With *static routing,* an administrator must manually configure the routing table by adding entries that tell the router how to reach other networks. Using the `route` command, an administrator updates the routing table by specifying the network addresses, the subnet masks, and the metrics associated with each route (see Figure 1-10).

FIGURE 1-10 Statically updating the routing table using the `route` command	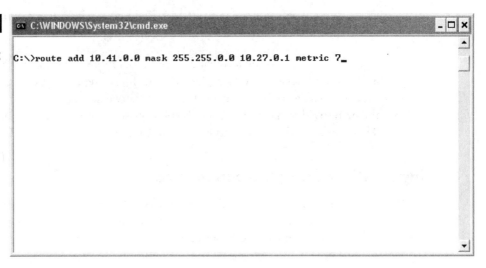

When deciding whether to use static routing, keep in mind that it works best for networks that do not change on a regular basis. If the network configuration is constantly changing, the administrative overhead associated with constantly having to update the routing tables will greatly increase because the changes must be made on each router. In such cases, it may be more beneficial and more efficient to implement dynamic routing.

Dynamic Routing

Dynamic routing eliminates the overhead associated with manually updating routing tables. Routers can dynamically build their own routing tables by communicating with other routers on the network.

With dynamic routing, the routing tables are built automatically through router communication. Using a routing communication protocol (such as RIP), routers periodically exchange messages containing location information about routes through the network. This information is used to build and update routing tables.

The major advantage of dynamic routing is that it reduces the administrative overhead associated with manually updating routing tables. For example, if a router goes down, the change is automatically propagated to all routers on the network so that they are all aware of the change in the network topology. However, this is also a disadvantage because it causes an increase in network traffic.

Routing Protocols

For routers to share information and dynamically update their routing tables, a routing protocol must be used. As already mentioned, the two routing protocols supported by Windows Server 2003 are the Routing Information Protocol (RIP) and Open Shortest Path First (OSPF). Although both routing protocols are used for dynamic routing, there are some distinct differences between the two that you should be aware of before deciding which protocol to implement.

Routing Information Protocol

The Routing Information Protocol (RIP) is designed for small to medium-sized networks. One of the main benefits for choosing RIP is that it's very simple to configure and deploy. One of the major drawbacks associated with this protocol is that it's limited to a maximum hop count of 15, which means any networks more than 15 hops away are considered unreachable. So if your network has a hop count of greater than 15, you

exam
@**atch**

As mentioned earlier, all routes to a destination network are assigned a metric, which defines the distance between the source and the destination. RIP uses

a hop count to identify the distance between two networks. A value of 1 is added to the hop count for each router between a source network and a destination network.

will not be able to use RIP for IP. Also, as a network increases in size, excessive traffic can be generated from RIP announcements.

When a router is first configured as an RIP router, the only entries in the routing table are for those networks to which it is physically connected. It then begins to send announcements of its availability to notify other routers of the networks it services. RIPv1 sends the announcements as broadcasts, whereas RIPv2 can send multicast packets to make the announcements.

When changes occur to the network topology, RIPv2 uses triggered updates to communicate the changes to other routers. With triggered updates, the change to the network topology can be propagated immediately.

If you are considering using RIPv1, keep in mind that it does not support multicasting, it does not support any type of security between routers, and it does have known issues with routing loops. Since it may take several minutes for routers to reconfigure themselves after a change in network topology, such as when an existing router becomes unavailable, routing loops can occur where routers send data in a circle. Also, RIPv1 does not support Classless Interdomain Routing (CIDR) or variable-length subnet masks, so if the network consists of more than one subnet mask, RIPv2 is required.

The Windows Server 2003 implementation of RIP supports the following features:

- The capability to select the version of RIP to implement for incoming and outgoing packets
- Support for routing filters to configure which routes should be accepted or denied
- Password authentication between routers
- Split horizons to avoid router loops
- Triggered updates to ensure changes to the network topology are propagated immediately

Open Shortest Path First

Open Shortest Path First (OSPF) is designed for large internetworks (especially those spanning more than 15 router hops). The disadvantage of OSPF is that it's generally more complex to set up and requires a certain amount of planning.

OSPF uses the Shortest Path First (SPF) algorithm to calculate routes. The shortest path (the route with the lowest cost) is always used first.

Unlike RIP, which uses only announcements to update and share routing information, OSPF maintains a map of the network, known as the *link state database*. This map is synchronized between adjacent routers, or those neighboring OSPF routers. When a change is made to the network topology, the first router to receive the change sends out a change notification. Each router then updates its copy of the link state database, and the routing table is recalculated.

One of the main differences between OSPF and RIP is that OSPF divides the network into different areas. Each of the routers maintains information in the link state database only about those areas to which it is connected. Another difference is that OSPF replicates only the changes to the routing table, not the entire table, which means less network traffic is generated from routing table updates. OSPF does not support nonpersistent demand-dial connections. Table 1-3 summarizes the criteria to follow when deciding whether to implement static routing, RIP, or OSPF.

TABLE 1-3	Option	Criteria
Criteria for Choosing Static or Dynamic Routing	Static routing	• Small routed environments • Routing information rarely changes • Requires manual update of the routing tables
	RIP	• Routing tables are updated automatically • Routing information changes frequently • Maximum router hop is 15 • Existing routers on the network use RIP • Supports nonpersistent demand-dial connections
	OSPF	• Routing information changes frequently • Existing routers use OSPF • Designed for those networks spanning more than 15 hops

An *area* is a group of neighboring networks. The areas are connected to a backbone area. Area border routers connect the different areas to the backbone area.

TCP/IP Troubleshooting Utilities

When you are planning and maintaining a TCP/IP network, you may find the utilities outlined in the following section helpful for troubleshooting different connectivity and routing problems. Table 1-4 summarizes some of the utilities that can be used to troubleshoot TCP/IP, some of which are further discussed in the following headings.

The ipconfig Utility

From a command prompt you can use the `ipconfig` utility to view the IP configuration information on a computer (see Figure 1-11).

Configuration information that is displayed includes the following:

- IP address
- Subnet mask
- Default gateway
- DNS servers

If IP parameters are being assigned from a DHCP server, you can also use the `ipconfig` command to renew lease information. The `ipconfig /release`

| **TABLE 1-4** | TCP/IP Troubleshooting Utilities |

Utility	Description
ipconfig	Used to view the IP configuration parameters on a local computer
ping	Used to test connectivity with another IP host
netstat	Used to display statistics for current TCP/IP connections
arp	Can be used to view the contents of the ARP cache
hostname	Used to verify the hostname assigned to the computer
nbtstat	Used to view NetBIOS over TCP/IP information and manipulate the NetBIOS name cache
NetDiag	Used to check various aspects of network connections
tracert	Used to trace the path taken to a remote computer
route	Used to view and manipulate the routing table

FIGURE 1-11

Viewing IP
configuration
information using
the `ipconfig`
command

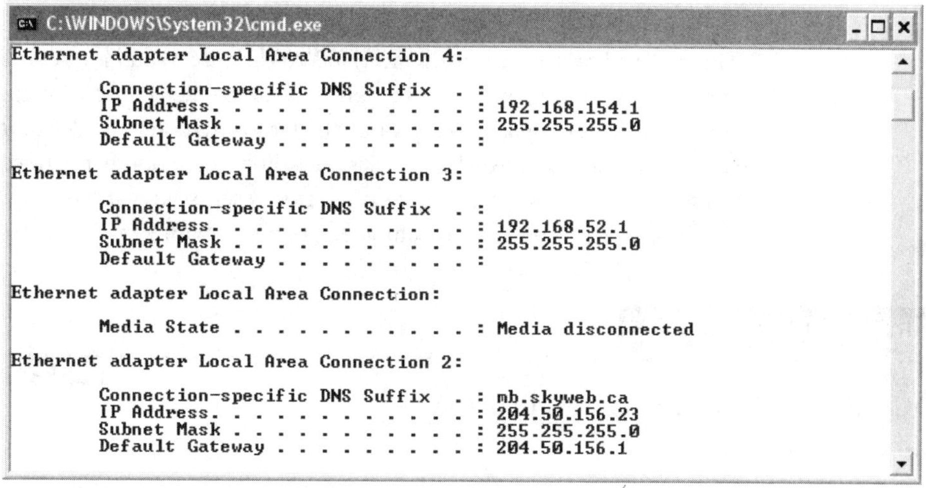

```
C:\WINDOWS\System32\cmd.exe                                        _ □ x
Ethernet adapter Local Area Connection 4:

        Connection-specific DNS Suffix  . :
        IP Address. . . . . . . . . . . : 192.168.154.1
        Subnet Mask . . . . . . . . . . : 255.255.255.0
        Default Gateway . . . . . . . . :

Ethernet adapter Local Area Connection 3:

        Connection-specific DNS Suffix  . :
        IP Address. . . . . . . . . . . : 192.168.52.1
        Subnet Mask . . . . . . . . . . : 255.255.255.0
        Default Gateway . . . . . . . . :

Ethernet adapter Local Area Connection:

        Media State . . . . . . . . . . : Media disconnected

Ethernet adapter Local Area Connection 2:

        Connection-specific DNS Suffix  . : mb.skyweb.ca
        IP Address. . . . . . . . . . . : 204.50.156.23
        Subnet Mask . . . . . . . . . . : 255.255.255.0
        Default Gateway . . . . . . . . : 204.50.156.1
```

command followed by the `ipconfig /renew` command will update the information
from a DHCP server.

The ping Utility

The command-line utility `ping` is used to verify connectivity between two hosts or
devices using TCP/IP. The `ping` command sends an ICMP request for response to the
remote host, which will typically return one of the following three answers:

- Reply from <IP address>:bytes= time=TTL=
- Request timed out
- Reply from <IP address of a router on the route>: destination host unreachable

If the remote host replies, connectivity is confirmed. If the request times out, the
remote machine may be configured not to respond to ICMP traffic, may not be able
to send a response to your address, or may not be responding on the network at all.
If a router replies with the "destination host unreachable" message, you should confirm
the path traffic is taking using the `tracert` command.

The tracert Utility

The `tracert` tool is used to track the path that traffic is taking between two hosts.
By using the output of this command, you can determine this path or the point at which
communications fail between the hosts.

The pathping Utility

The `pathping` tool was introduced in Windows 2000 and is essentially a combination of `ping`, `tracert`, and a traffic monitor. The `pathping` command generates output as it determines the path from your computer to a remote host. Next, it monitors traffic for a set amount of time, which varies according to the number of hops taken. After the traffic monitoring is complete, `pathping` presents time and packet loss statistics for each hop so that you can determine where performance losses are occurring.

EXERCISE 1-3

Viewing the TCP/IP Configuration of a Workstation

In this exercise, you will use the `ipconfig` command to analyze the TCP/IP configuration of a workstation.

1. From the command prompt, type **ipconfig /all**.

2. Identify the following information:
   - DNS suffix
   - Physical address
   - IP address
   - Subnet mask
   - Default gateway
   - DHCP server
   - DNS server
   - DHCP enabled
   - Autoconfiguration enabled
   - IP address lease expiration

3. Type **ping 127.0.0.1**. Describe the results.

4. How could you determine if your workstation is accessible to other hosts on the network? What message would appear if your workstation was not responding?

CERTIFICATION OBJECTIVE 1.04

Optimizing a TCP/IP Network

One of the goals when planning a TCP/IP network is to ensure that IP packets are transmitted on the network within a reasonable amount of time. When planning an IP network, you can take a number of steps to optimize performance.

Optimizing TCP/IP

Optimizing a TCP/IP network begins when you are planning the IP addressing and subnetting scheme. Implementing an address scheme that is too large for a network will result in IP addresses going unused. It is always good to plan for excess, but within reason. On the other hand, an address scheme that is too small can result in having to implement multiple IP address ranges, which can lead to complex routing. By implementing variable-length subnet masks, you can further subdivide an existing subnet, thereby making better use of the IP addresses. Keep in mind that in order to do so, you must be using RIPv2 or OSPF.

Networks today often span geographical locations, and IP subnets may be connected by WAN links. Although TCP/IP is generally self-tuning, some configuration changes can be made to optimize network performance (especially across WAN connections). TCP/IP uses window sizes to determine how much data can be stored within the send and receive buffers. The receive buffer size determines the number of bytes in the buffer before an acknowledgment must be sent. Plan to increase the buffer size from the 16KB default for links with high delay and latency. Of course, before you do this, you should take a close look at the type of traffic flowing across a WAN link. If a lot of the traffic is delay or latency sensitive, such as authentication negotiations, consider making this change.

Depending on the network configuration, data may end up having to travel through several routers to reach its destination. This may pose a problem for traffic that is time sensitive, such as videoconferencing, especially when routers do not prioritize traffic and handle it on a first-come, first-served basis. To overcome this, you can implement Quality of Service (QoS), which allows you to reserve bandwidth for users, services, and applications, and prioritize network traffic.

CERTIFICATION SUMMARY

TCP/IP is the most widely used protocol both on the public Internet and on private networks. Due to its increase in popularity, most operating systems introduced now support this protocol. In this chapter, we looked at some of the important concepts underlying the TCP/IP protocol suite.

The TCP/IP protocol suite maps to two conceptual models: the OSI Reference model and the DoD model. These models consist of different layers that define how network communication occurs between two hosts. The different protocols that make up the protocol suite operate at the different levels of the conceptual models. Each protocol performs a specific function, and when they work together, they enable network communication.

The chapter went on to look at IP addressing and subnet masks. An IP address is used to route information between hosts or devices on an IP network. Each device on a network requires a unique 32-bit IP address. The subnet mask is used to determine which portion of the IP address identifies the network.

IP networks can be broken up into physical segments known as subnets. These subnets can be connected via routers. Routers use information within routing tables to determine where to send a packet to reach a specific destination. The information in routing tables can be generated manually or dynamically. Windows Server 2003 supports RIP over IP and OSPF for dynamic routing.

When planning an IP network, you have a number of things to consider, including the number of subnets and hosts per subnet that is required, whether to use a public or private addressing scheme, and how IP addresses will be allocated. If the network is routed, you will also need to decide which routing protocols will be used on the network.

TWO-MINUTE DRILL

Understanding TCP/IP

❑ TCP/IP allows computers running various operating systems to communicate with each other on a network.

❑ TCP/IP is the default protocol in Windows Server 2003.

❑ TCP/IP maps to the seven-layer OSI model and the four-layer DoD model.

❑ The seven layers of the OSI model are Application, Presentation, Session, Transport, Network, Data Link, and Physical.

❑ The four layers of the DoD model are Application, Transport, Internet, and Network.

❑ TCP/IP is a suite of protocols. The core protocols include TCP, UDP, IP, ARP, ICMP, and IGMP.

❑ The Address Resolution Protocol (ARP) is responsible for mapping IP addresses to hardware addresses.

❑ The Internet Control Message Protocol (ICMP) reports errors and status information when datagrams are sent across the network. The Internet Group Management Protocol (IGMP) is used for reporting multicast group status.

❑ The Internet Protocol (IP) is responsible for addressing and routing packets.

❑ TCP and UDP operate at the Transport layer. TCP is a connection-based protocol offering reliable delivery of data. UDP is connectionless.

Understanding IP Addressing and Subnetting

❑ Every host on a TCP/IP network requires an IP address. An IP address consists of a network ID and a host ID. The host ID must be unique on a given network.

❑ Subnet masks are used to identify which part of an IP address represents the network ID. This information is used in determining if a destination host is on the local network or a remote network.

❑ Subnetting allows you to divide a large network into smaller logical networks. When planning an IP network, you must consider the number of subnets that are required and the number of hosts per subnet.

Planning a TCP/IP-Routed Network

❑ During the planning phase, you must decide whether to use public or private IP addresses. Public addresses are assigned from an ISP. Each address class also contains a block of private addresses that cannot be used on the Internet.

❑ Also during the planning phase, you must decide how hosts will be assigned IP addresses. IP addresses can be assigned statically, using a DHCP server, or through APIPA.

❑ In a routed IP network, routing tables are used to determine where packets must be sent to reach a host on another network. Routing tables can be built statically or dynamically using a routing protocol. Windows Server 2003 supports RIPv1, RIPv2, and OSPF.

Optimizing a TCP/IP Network

❑ Implementing variable-length subnet masks can make better use of IP addresses.

❑ Increase the TCP/IP buffer size for links with high delay and latency.

❑ Implement Quality of Service (QoS) to reserve bandwidth for users, services, and applications and to prioritize network traffic.

SELF TEST

Understanding TCP/IP

1. Bob is using a class A address range of 12.0.0.0/8. He wants to extend the subnet mask to create 20 subnets on the internal network. Which of the following subnet masks should he implement?
   A. 255.192.0.0
   B. 255.224.0.0
   C. 255.240.0.0
   D. 255.248.0.0

2. You have implemented a class C address on your network with the default subnet mask of 255.255.255.0. How many hosts will be supported per network?
   A. 254
   B. 500
   C. 1024
   D. 256

3. Bob is planning the IP network for his organization. The plan calls for an addressing scheme that will support 6 subnets with possible expansion of up to 12. You have been assigned a class C address. Which of the following subnet masks will meet the subnet requirements?
   A. 255.255.255.192
   B. 255.255.255.224
   C. 255.255.255.240
   D. 255.255.255.248

4. There are five subnets on your internetwork. You will be configuring Windows Server 2003 RRAS servers to route between the subnets. Your goal is to do this while minimizing the administrative overhead associated with maintaining the routing tables and minimize the amount of traffic generated between routers when updating routing tables. Which of the following should you implement to support these requirements?
   A. Static routes on all routers
   B. OSPF
   C. RIPv1
   D. TCP/IP

5. Which layer of the TCP/IP DoD model is responsible for addressing and routing?

   A. Application
   B. Transport
   C. Network
   D. Internet

Understanding IP Addressing and Subnetting

6. An IP address of 192.168.0.1 belongs to which of the following address classes?

   A Class A
   B. Class B
   C. Class C
   D. Class D

7. You are trying to verify connectivity between two TCP/IP hosts. Which utilities can you run to do this? (Choose all correct answers.)

   A. ipconfig
   B. ping
   C. tracert
   D. route

8. There are three subnets within the network infrastructure. All subnets are connected using Windows Server 2003 RRAS servers. The subnets are connected using nonpersistent demand-dial connections. Routing tables should be updated automatically. You also want any changes made to the network topology propagated immediately. Which of the following should you implement?

   A. Static routes
   B. ICMP
   C. OSPF
   D. RIPv2

Planning a TCP/IP-Routed Network

9. Sean is designing a TCP/IP solution for his organization using a private class B address. The plan calls for 25 subnets, with this number possibly growing as high as 40. Which of the following subnet masks will allow for the required number of IP subnets?

A. 255.255.240.0

B. 255.255.192.0

C. 255.255.254.0

D. 255.255.252.0

10. DKB International is planning to enable NAT on a computer running Windows Server 2003 and implement a private address range on the internal network. Which of the following ranges can be used?

A. 12.0.0.0/8

B. 192.168.0.0/24

C. 126.0.0.0/8

D. 131.107.0.0/16

11. John has taken a class B address range and extended the subnet mask. The address range being used is 172.60.0.0, with a subnet mask of 255.255.224.0. Which of the following are valid network IDs for the given subnet mask?

A. 172.60.0.0/19

B. 172.60.32.0/19

C. 172.60.64.0/19

D. 172.60.224.0/19

12. Which of the following utilities can be used to manipulate a routing table?

A. route

B. tracert

C. NetStat

D. ping

13. You have a class B network address. There are six subnets on the network. What is the default subnet mask?

A. 255.192.0.0

B. 255.255.248.0

C. 255.255.224.0

D. 255.255.255.248

14. John is assigned a class A address. He extends the subnet mask to create subnets within the existing network infrastructure. He chooses to use the subnet mask of 255.248.0.0. How many subnets does this subnet mask support?

    A. 2
    B. 30
    C. 6
    D. 60

15. What is the total number of host IDs available with a class C address?

    A. 254
    B. 1024
    C. 65,533
    D. 16 million

Optimizing a TCP/IP Network

16. David is the network administrator of a Windows Server 2003 network. There are currently four subnets and routing tables are updated statically. David wants to reduce the administration associated with updating the routing tables and to implement a routing protocol but does not want an increase in broadcast traffic. Which of the following should he implement?

    A. RIP version 1
    B. ICMP
    C. ARP
    D. RIP version 2

17. Tom is planning the IP addressing scheme for a Windows Server 2003 network. The network consists of 5 subnets, approximately 1000 hosts, as well as two DNS servers and a WINS server. What would be the best method to assign IP addresses to clients on the network?

    A. DHCP
    B. APIPA
    C. Static
    D. Alternate configuration

18. Which of the following correctly identifies the number 192 in binary format?

    A. 11100000
    B. 11000000
    C. 11000001
    D. 01100001

19. Jim is the network administrator of a Windows Server 2003 network. A user calls to report that they are unable to communicate with hosts on a remote subnet. Jim verifies that the workstation is configured with the correct IP parameters; he suspects a problem with one of the routers. Which of the following commands can Jim use to determine the path a packet takes to a remote network?

    A. `ping`
    B. `route`
    C. `tracert`
    D. `arp`

20. Mary is the network administrator of a Windows Server 2003 network. A user reports that they are having trouble communicating with other hosts on the network. Mary pings the loopback address to verify TCP/IP is initialized on the local computer and pings the IP address assigned to the workstation. Both return successful results. What should Mary try next?

    A. Ping the IP address of a local host.
    B. Ping the IP address of a remote host.
    C. Ping the IP address of a remote server.
    D. Ping the IP address of the default gateway.
    E. Ping the IP address of a remote gateway.

LAB QUESTION

You are a consultant hired to help a growing company restructure their existing network and upgrade to Windows Server 2003. The existing network consists of a single subnet. The new infrastructure will call for 5 additional subnets with future plans to increase this number to 10. You recommend the company implement a private IP addressing scheme and use a DHCP server to assign IP addresses to all workstations. Using the private IP address of 172.16.0.0, determine the subnet mask that will allow for 10 subnets. Then determine the range of IP addresses that can be used for each of the 10 subnets.

SELF TEST ANSWERS

Understanding TCP/IP

1. ☑ D. The subnet mask of 255.248.0.0 will allow you to create 20 subnets.
   ☒ A is incorrect because this subnet mask will allow for a maximum of only 2 subnets.
   B is incorrect because this subnet will allow for a maximum of only 6 subnets.
   C is incorrect because this subnet mask will allow for a maximum of only 14 subnets.

2. ☑ A. The default subnet mask for a class C address will allow for 254 hosts.
   ☒ B, C, and D are incorrect because they do not represent the correct values.

3. ☑ C. Using a subnet mask of 255.255.2255.240 will provide for a maximum of 6 subnets.
   ☒ A is incorrect because the subnet mask will provide for only 2 subnets. B is incorrect because the subnet mask will provide for only 6 subnets. Although this would meet the current requirements, it does not take into account the future expansion. D is incorrect because this subnet mask will provide for more subnets than will ever be required.

4. ☑ B. OSPF is the best choice in this situation because it does not generate as much traffic as RIPv1.
   ☒ A is incorrect because using static routing will increase the administrative overhead associated with updating the routing tables. D is incorrect because TCP/IP is not a routing protocol.

5. ☑ D. The Internet layer of the DoD model is responsible for addressing and routing.
   ☒ A is incorrect because this layer is used by applications to gain access to the network. B is incorrect because protocols functioning at this layer are responsible for establishing sessions between hosts. C is incorrect because the network layer is responsible for sending and receiving information over the physical medium.

Understanding IP Addressing and Subnetting

6. ☑ C. The IP address of 192.168.0.1 belongs to the class C address range.
   ☒ A, B, and D are incorrect because they do not represent the correct address class for the given IP address.

7. ☑ B and C. Both the `ping` utility and `tracert` can be used to test TCP/IP connectivity.
   ☒ A is incorrect because `ipconfig` is used to view the TCP/IP configuration of a computer. D is incorrect because the `route` command is used to manipulate the routing tables.

8. ☑ **D.** To meet the requirements of not having to manually update the routing tables and having changes propagated immediately, a routing protocol must be used. Since nonpersistent demand-dial connections are being used, RIPV2 must be implemented.
☒ **A** is incorrect because implementing static routes means the routing table must be manually updated. **B** is incorrect because ICMP is not a routing protocol. It is used for reporting errors and status information. **C** is incorrect because OSPF does not support nonpersistent demand-dial connections.

Planning a TCP/IP-Routed Network

9. ☑ **D.** The subnet mask of 255.255.252.0 will allow you to create the number of subnets required.
☒ **A** and **B** are incorrect because these subnets do not allow for the required number of subnets. **D** is incorrect because this subnet mask allows for more subnets than will ever be required.

10. ☑ **B.** The IP address range of 192.168.0.0/24 is reserved for use on private networks and cannot be used on the Internet.
☒ **A, C,** and **D** are incorrect because these all represent public IP address ranges.

11. ☑ **B** and **C.** 172.60.32.0/19 and 172.60.64.0/19 are both valid network IDs.
☒ **A** and **D** are incorrect because the extended subnet cannot be represented as all 1's or all 0's, which is the case for these two network IDs.

12. ☑ **A.** The `route` command can be used to view and manipulate the contents of the routing table.
☒ **B** is incorrect because `tracert` is used to trace the path to a remote computer.
C is incorrect because `NetStat` is used to display current TCP/IP connections.
D is incorrect because `ping` is used to test connectivity between two hosts.

13. ☑ **C.** The default subnet mask will be 255.255.224.0.
☒ **A** is incorrect because this subnet mask would be used for a class A network. **B** is incorrect because this subnet mask provides for more than 6 subnets. **D** is incorrect because this subnet mask is used for a class C network.

14. ☑ **B.** The subnet mask of 255.248.0.0 will allow you to create 30 subnets.
☒ **A** is incorrect because a subnet mask of 255.192.0.0 will allow you to create 2 subnets.
C is incorrect because a subnet mask of 255.224.0.0 will allow you to create 6 subnets.
D is incorrect because the subnet mask of 255.252.0.0 will allow you to create 60 subnets with a maximum of 62.

Optimizing a TCP/IP Network

15. ☑ **A.** A class C address supports 254 hosts.
☒ **B, C,** and **D** are incorrect because they do not represent the correct number of hosts.

16. ☑ **D.** RIP version 2 does not rely on broadcast packets for announcements. It can use multicast announcements. **A** is incorrect because RIP version 1 only uses broadcast announcements. **B** is incorrect because ICMP is a protocol used to status and error reporting. **C** is incorrect because ARP is the protocol used to resolve IP addresses to hardware addresses.

17. ☑ **A.** DHCP can be used to automatically assign IP addresses to clients. The DHCP server can also provide clients with the IP addresses of the DNS and WINS server.
☒ **B** is incorrect because APIPA should only be used for single subnet networks. With APIPA workstation will assign themselves an IP address and a subnet mask only. Therefore this method will not work in an environment with multiple subnets. **C** is incorrect because statically configuring all workstations with IP addresses would drastically increase the administrative overhead associated with managing and maintaining an IP network. **D** is incorrect because the alternate configuration can be used in the event that a DHCP server is unavailable. This also requires manual configuration by an administrator.

18. ☑ **B.** 11000000 represents the number 192 in binary format.
☒ **B, C,** and **D** are incorrect because they represent incorrect values when converted to decimal format.

19. ☑ **C.** The `tracert` command can be used to trace the path a packet travels to reach a destination host. The information can be used to determine if a problem exists with a router.
☒ **A** is incorrect because the `ping` command is used to test connectivity with another host. **B** is incorrect because the `route` command is used to manipulate the routing tables. **D** is incorrect because the `arp` protocol is used to resolve IP addresses to hardware addresses.

20. ☑ **D.** When troubleshooting TCP/IP connectivity, use the `ping` command to test connectivity with the default gateway once you have successfully pinged the IP address of the workstation.
☒ **A, B, C,** and **E** are incorrect because they do not represent the correct sequencing of steps when troubleshooting TCP/IP using the `ping` command.

LAB ANSWER

The subnet mask of 255.255.240.0 will allow for a maximum of 14 subnets. The valid host IDs for each subnet include these:

- 172.16.16.1–172.16.31.254
- 172.16.32.1–172.16.47.254
- 172.16.48.1–172.16.63.154
- 172.16.64.1–172.16.79.254
- 172.16.80.1–172.16.95.254
- 172.16.96.1–172.16.111.254
- 172.16.112-1–172.16.127.254
- 172.16.128.1–172.16.143.254
- 172.16.144.1–172.16.159.254
- 172.16.160.1–172.16.175.254

2

Planning a DHCP Implementation

CERTIFICATION OBJECTIVE 2.01

Understanding the Dynamic Host Configuration Protocol

As you saw in Chapter 1, every host on an IP network requires a unique IP address. One of the options for assigning IP addresses is to do so manually. In smaller network environments, this may be a viable solution. In larger environments, and in ones that are constantly growing, this can become a huge administrative burden, as each workstation needs to be assigned an IP address, a subnet mask, and most likely, a default gateway and a DNS server. Making any changes to the existing IP network can require an administrator to reconfigure several workstations. A more efficient way of assigning and managing IP addresses would be to implement DHCP.

The Dynamic Host Configuration Protocol (DHCP) eliminates most of the administrative overhead associated with configuring IP addresses. It automates the process of assigning IP addresses and other parameters to hosts as well as centralizes administration. To better understand the importance of DHCP, imagine having a network that consists of thousands of workstations, all running TCP/IP. Assigning IP addresses manually on all workstations would be a tremendous task, as would be updating them all whenever changes needed to be made to the parameters. Not only that, but there would always be a chance of making an error when typing in the required information. So DHCP greatly reduces the administration associated with assigning IP addresses.

DHCP was introduced in Windows NT 3.5. Since then, there have been many improvements and new features added to the service. Some of the new features of the DHCP service in Windows Server 2003 include

- **DHCP Client Alternate Configuration**   With this feature, DHCP clients (Windows XP and Windows Server 2003) can be configured to use specific IP parameters in the event that a DHCP server is not available. This means that computers that move between networks need not be reconfigured with each move. For example, if a mobile computer is moved from a network that uses DHCP to one that does not, the alternate configuration can be used.

- **DHCP database backup and restore**   The DHCP database can be backed up and restored through the DHCP management console.

How DHCP Works

Once the DHCP service is installed, DHCP clients can automatically obtain an IP address as well as optional parameters such as the IP address of the default gateway and name servers. When a DHCP server receives a request from a client for an IP address, it leases the client an address from a pool of IP addresses also known as a *scope*. Each DHCP server must be configured with at least one scope, which defines the range of IP addresses that can be leased to clients.

The steps that a DHCP client goes through to obtain an IP address from a DHCP server are known as the *lease process*. Each time a workstation is rebooted or when an IP address is manually released and renewed using the `ipconfig` command, the lease process will occur. In order to fully understand how DHCP works, it is important to be aware of what occurs during the lease process.

DHCP Lease Process

The DHCP lease process occurs in four distinct phases: DHCPDISCOVER, DHCPOFFER, DHCPREQUEST, and DHCPACK. These are described as follows:

- **DHCPDISCOVER** This is the first phase of the lease process. During this phase, a DHCP client broadcasts a DHCPDISCOVER message on the network in an attempt to locate a DHCP server. The broadcast message contains the computer name and the hardware address of the client.

- **DHCPOFFER** This is the second phase of the lease process. During this phase, any DHCP server that receives the discover message will respond with a broadcast known as a DHCPOFFER. The message includes an offered IP address, a subnet mask, and a lease length. Any DHCP servers that respond with an offer will temporarily reserve the offered IP address to eliminate the possibility of having the IP address offered to another client.

- **DHCPREQUEST** During the third phase, the client broadcasts a DHCPREQUEST message accepting the first offered IP address it received. If multiple DHCP servers responded with an offer, the remaining servers place the offered IP addresses back into their address pool.

- **DHCPACK** The last phase of the lease process occurs when the DHCP server sends the client a DHCPACK message permitting the client to use the IP address. This message will also contain any optional IP parameters, such as the IP addresses of the default gateway and name servers.

Keep in mind that some DHCP broadcasts are not forwarded between subnets. This poses a problem if the DHCP server is located on another subnet. In such cases, it may be necessary to enable a DHCP relay agent to forward the broadcasts on behalf of the clients. This topic is discussed in the next section.

Now that you are familiar with the different phases of the lease process, let's take a look at what actually occurs when a client attempts to lease an IP address from a DHCP server (see Figure 2-1).

1. A DHCP client sends a DHCPDISCOVER message on the network to locate a DHCP server. The client will continue to send the broadcast messages at 2-, 4-, 8-, and 16-second intervals until a DHCP server responds. If no response is received, the client will continue to send out a broadcast every five minutes.

2. Any DHCP server that receives the broadcast will respond with a DHCPOFFER that includes an IP address available for the client to lease.

3. If multiple DHCP servers respond to the request for an IP address, the client will respond to the first request it receives by broadcasting a DHCPREQUEST. All other DHCP servers will retract their offers and place the IP addresses back in their address pools.

4. The DHCP server responds with a DHCPACK message confirming the client's lease and providing the client with any optional IP parameters.

IP Address Renewal

Once a client leases an IP address from a DHCP server, it is permitted to use the IP address for a specific period of time, referred to as the *lease duration*. Once the lease duration expires, the client must contact a DHCP server to lease another IP address.

IP address lease
process

DHCP client

DHCPDISCOVER

DHCPOFFER

DHCPREQUEST

DHCPACK

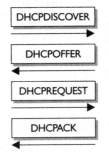

DHCP server

Remember that if a DHCP server does not respond to the DHCP discover message, the client will continue to broadcast. During this time, however, it will also use automatic private IP addressing and assign itself an IP address from the range of 169.254.0.0/16. If you are using the Alternate Configuration feature, on the other hand, clients can use the IP parameters specified.

The actual renewal process between a DHCP client and a DHCP server begins when 50 percent of the configured lease time expires. At this point, the client will attempt to contact a DHCP server to renew its lease. A DHCPREQUEST message is sent by the client requesting to renew the IP address it is currently configured with. If the DHCP server is available, it will respond to the client with a DHCPACK, renewing the client's IP address.

If the DHCP server does not respond, the client will again attempt to renew its IP address, this time when 87.5 percent of the lease time expires. If the server is available, it will respond to the client's request for a renewal. If the DHCP server does not respond, the client will continue to use the IP address until the lease duration expires, when the lease process outlined in the preceding section is started again.

An IP address can be manually renewed using the `ipconfig /release` and `ipconfig /renew` commands.

CERTIFICATION OBJECTIVE 2.02

Designing DHCP

In order to achieve success on the exam as well as on the job, you should be aware of the factors that will influence your DHCP design. In certain environments, such as a single network with no subnets, your DHCP implementation may be very straightforward, consisting of a single DHCP server. In larger subnetted environments, however, the DHCP implementation can become more complex. In either case, planning is crucial and there are a number of factors you should consider before going ahead with the installation.

DHCP Design Decisions

Certain factors are going to affect your DHCP implementation. Considering these factors prior to installation can save you a lot of time, money, and headaches down the road. When designing a DHCP strategy, you need to consider the following points:

- Planning the number of DHCP servers
- Planning the placement of DHCP servers
- Planning for a routed DHCP network

Number of DHCP Servers

There is really no limit to the number of clients a single DHCP server can service. Therefore, the main factors that will influence the number of servers you do implement will be the existing network infrastructure and the server hardware. If your network consists of a single subnet, a single DHCP server is sufficient, although you may choose to implement more than one for a high level of availability. Implementing a single DHCP server does create a single point of failure, although clients can use APIPA in the event the DHCP server is unavailable. You can also use the Alternate Configuration option and manually specify the IP address parameters a client should use if a DHCP server is not available.

If you are familiar with DHCP, you may recall a couple of popular options. First, if you want to add redundancy to your DHCP implementation, you can implement two DHCP servers, one to be the primary server and the other as a standby. If the primary server becomes unavailable, you can bring the standby online. The major disadvantage to this approach is that one server is sitting idle. The second option is to use the 80/20 rule, where the primary DHCP server is configured with 80 percent of the IP addresses for a scope and another DHCP server (which can be on another subnet if DHCP broadcasts can be forwarded through routers) is configured with the remaining 20 percent of the addresses. If the primary DHCP server goes offline, clients can still obtain an IP address from the server configured with the remaining addresses (see Figure 2-2).

In terms of the network infrastructure, if the network consists of multiple subnets, routers can be configured to forward DHCP broadcasts between subnets. Or you may choose to place a DHCP server on each of the subnets. Another option is to configure a DHCP relay agent on those subnets that do not host DHCP servers. The DHCP relay

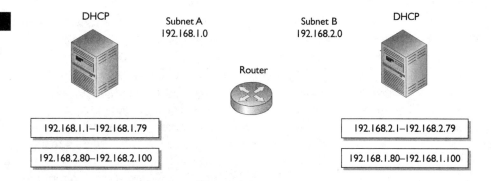

FIGURE 2-2

Using the 80/20 rule to add redundancy for DHCP servers

agent can forward IP address requests to DHCP servers on other subnets on behalf of clients.

In any case, before you implement any DHCP servers on the network, consider the following points:

- DHCP servers should be configured with fast disk subsystems and as much RAM as possible. If your DHCP server lacks the hardware and you have many clients, you may need to implement more than one DHCP server to improve response time for clients.

- Implementing a single DHCP server does create a single point of failure.

- If there are multiple subnets, you can extend the functionality of a DHCP server across subnets using the DHCP relay agent. The other solution is to place a DHCP server on each subnet.

- Consider the speed of the links connecting various networks and segments. If a DHCP server is on the far side of a slow WAN link or a dial-up connection, you may choose to place DHCP servers on either side for increased performance. Since DHCP servers do not share any information, there would be no increase in network traffic. Network traffic on the slow link would actually be reduced, because clients can obtain leases locally as opposed to using a remote DHCP server.

Placement of DHCP Servers

When it comes time to determine where on the network DHCP servers should be placed, keep in mind that your overall goals are to provide high levels of client performance and server availability. The placements of DHCP servers will depend upon the routing configuration, how the network is configured, and the hardware installed on the DHCP servers.

If you are implementing a single DHCP server, this server should be placed on the subnet that contains the highest number of clients. All other subnets will have a DHCP relay agent installed, or the routers will be configured to forward DHCP broadcasts. Keep in mind as well that with a single-server implementation, the network connections should be high speed and the server should be configured with the appropriate hardware.

You may choose to use multiple DHCP servers for a number of reasons. An obvious one is high availability and redundancy. When you are determining where to place the DHCP servers, again, they should be located on the subnets that contain the most clients. Also assess the connections between networks. If certain subnets or segments are connected with slow WAN links such as a dial-up connection, a DHCP server should be placed at these locations so that clients do not have to use the slow connection when attempting to lease or renew an IP address. Having clients obtain IP addresses across slow, unreliable links creates another point of failure should the link be unavailable.

Routed Networks

As you learned in Chapter 1, networks can be subdivided into smaller networks known as subnets. These subnets are connected together using routers. In order to reduce network traffic, most routers do not forward broadcasts from one subnet to another. This poses a problem with DHCP, as a client must initially send out a broadcast when leasing an IP address, since the client does not yet have an IP address. One solution is to use DHCP relay agents.

<table>
<tr><td>

e x a m

w a t c h   *Be prepared to encounter exam questions pertaining to the DHCP relay agent component of Windows Server 2003. Understand what this component does and when it should be implemented.*

</td></tr>
</table>

Understanding Relay Agents   A *relay agent* is responsible for relaying DHCP messages between DHCP clients and DHCP servers that are located on different subnets. If routers are RFC 1542–compliant, they can forward the DHCP-related messages between subnets. If not, a computer running Windows Server 2003 (or Windows NT 4.0 and Windows 2000 as well) can be configured as a relay agent by installing the DHCP relay agent component.

So let's take a look at what happens when a DHCP client attempts to obtain an IP address from a DHCP server located on a remote network:

1. The DHCP client sends out a DHCPDISCOVER on its local subnet. The broadcast is done using UDP and port 67.

2. The relay agent receives the message. Since the client does not have an IP address, the address in the packet is 0.0.0.0. The router or relay agent will replace this field with their own IP address. The message is forwarded to the IP address of the DHCP server configured on the relay agent.

3. The DHCP server examines the IP address of the router or relay agent to determine which scope the client should be leased an IP address from.

e x a m

ⓦatch

Remember that in order for the DHCP server to lease IP addresses to clients on a remote subnet, the DHCP server must be configured with a scope for that subnet. For example, if clients are on Subnet A and the DHCP server is on Subnet B, the DHCP server must be configured with a range of IP addresses for Subnet A. The DHCP server will use the IP address of the relay agent to determine which scope clients should be leased an IP address from.

4. The DHCP server returns the DHCPOFFER to the relay agent, which in turn forwards it back to the DHCP client.

You configure a DHCP relay agent through the Routing and Remote Access console. Exercise 2-1 walks you through the process of enabling this component on a computer running Windows Server 2003.

EXERCISE 2-1

CertCam 2-1 ON THE CD

Enabling a DHCP Relay Agent

In this exercise, you will use the Routing and Remote Access snap-in to configure the DHCP relay agent component on a computer running Windows Server 2003.

1. Click Start, point to Administrative Tools, and click Routing And Remote Access.

2. If RRAS is not enabled yet, right-click your server listed in the console and click Configure And Enable Routing And Remote Access. Click Next. If RRAS is already enabled, you can proceed to step 6.

3. From the list of configurations, click Custom. Click Next.

4. Click LAN routing. Click Next.

5. Click Finish.

6. Click your remote access server and click IP Routing. Right-click the General container and click New Routing Protocol. Select DHCP Relay Agent and click OK.

7. Right-click the DHCP Relay Agent container and click New Interface.

8. Select the appropriate interface from the list and click OK.

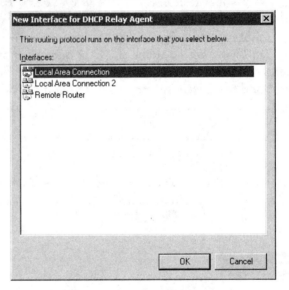

9. In the details pane, right-click the interface and click Properties. Ensure that the option to Relay DHCP Packets is selected. Click OK.

10. Right-click the DHCP Relay Agent container and click Properties.

11. From the DHCP Relay Agent Properties dialog box, type in the IP address of the DHCP server the relay agent will send messages to. Click Add. Click OK.

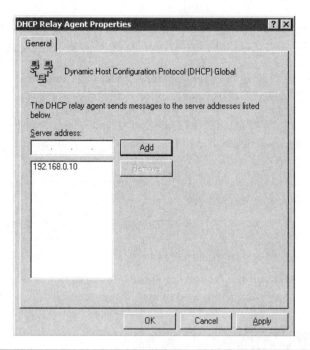

Centralized Versus Decentralized

Another point you need to consider when planning for DHCP is whether you will implement a centralized model or a decentralized one in a subnetted environment. For example, you may choose to have all the DHCP servers in a single location, servicing requests from clients on different subnets. Or you may choose to place a DHCP server on each of the different subnets instead. Before you make your decision, you should be aware of the advantages and disadvantages associated with each choice.

A decentralized approach would result in DHCP servers being placed in each of the different subnets. Doing so would offer the following advantages and disadvantages:

- Local administrators can administer their own DHCP servers and configure them in a way that meets their own needs.
- Clients do not have to rely on WAN links to obtain an IP address.

■ Obviously, placing a DHCP server at each location will result in an increase in cost due to the fact that multiple servers are required.

A centralized approach would result in all DHCP servers being located in a specific location. Using this approach will offer the following advantages and disadvantages:

■ Administration of DHCP may be simpler because there will be fewer servers and having them in a single location where technical support is on hand makes problems easier to troubleshoot.

■ Obviously, if fewer DHCP servers are required, the cost associated with implementing DHCP will be reduced.

■ Clients in remote sites may have to rely on WAN links to obtain an IP address. This means if the WAN link is down, clients will not be able to contact a DHCP server. Again, this creates a single point of failure.

■ It can, on the other hand, make administration more difficult because it is hard for an administrator to know the configuration requirements of a remote site.

CERTIFICATION OBJECTIVE 2.03

Implementing DHCP

Now that you are familiar with how DHCP works on a network, you can decide whether it is a beneficial solution for your network environment. If you opt to implement DHCP, it is important that you have a general idea of what is involved in implementing the service. The following section will give you a brief overview of the steps that must be completed to successfully implement DHCP on a network.

DHCP Requirements

As with the installation of most services and applications, there are requirements that must be met and specific steps to follow to successfully implement the product. Before a DHCP server can be fully functional on a network, the following steps must be completed:

■ The computer that will function as a DHCP server on the network must be configured with a static IP address.

■ The DHCP service must be installed.

■ After the DHCP service is installed, the DHCP server must be configured with at least one scope. The scope must be activated after it is created.

■ The DHCP server must be authorized within Active Directory. This step is required only if your network is running Active Directory.

Installing DHCP

The first step in configuring a DHCP server (of course, after you have taken the time to plan the implementation) is to install the service on a computer running Windows Server 2003. The DHCP service can be installed in a few different ways. It can be installed during the installation of the operating system, or it can be added afterward using the Add or Remove Programs applet within the Control Panel or by using the Configure Your Server Wizard (see Figure 2-3). In any case, the installation is a relatively straightforward process. To install the DHCP service using the Configure Your Server Wizard:

1. Click Start and click Manage Your Server.

2. Click Add Or Remove A Role.

3. Review the list of preliminary steps and verify they have been completed. Click Next.

FIGURE 2-3

Using the Configure Your Server Wizard to install DHCP

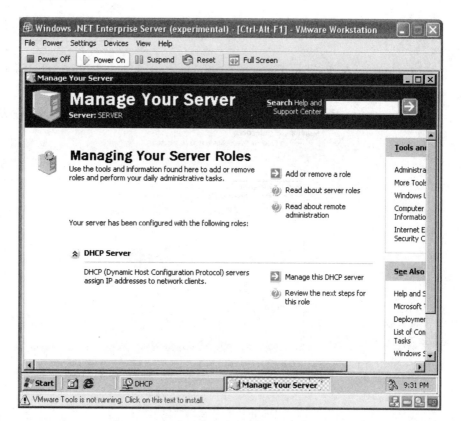

4. From the list of server roles, select DHCP server. Click Next.

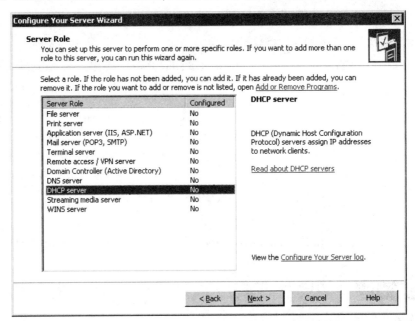

5. Review the summary of selections and click Next. The DHCP service is installed, and the New Scope Wizard appears.

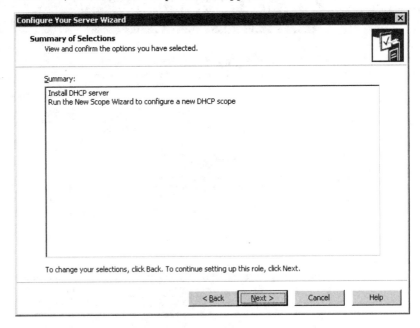

6. Click Next. The wizard walks you through the process of creating the initial scope. This process will be outlined later in the chapter.

7. Once you've created the scope, click Finish.

The steps involved in installing the DHCP service using the Add or Remove Programs applet are outlined in Exercise 2-2.

EXERCISE 2-2

CertCam 2-2 ON THE CD

Installing DHCP

In this exercise, you will install the DHCP service on a computer running Windows Server 2003 using the Add or Remove Programs applet within the Control Panel.

1. Click Start, point to Control Panel, and click Add Or Remove Programs.

2. Within the Add or Remove Programs applet, click Add/Remove Windows Components.

3. From the list of components, select Network Services and click Details.

4. Select Dynamic Host Configuration Protocol and click OK.

5. Click Next. Click Finish.

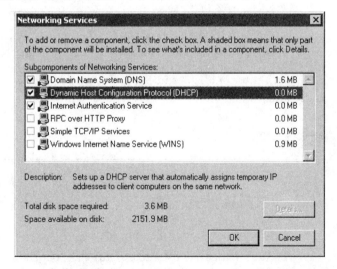

---

on the
❶ o b

It is sometimes easier to use the Configure Your Server Wizard when installing services because the wizard not only installs the component but also walks you through the process of configuring it. For example, when you install DHCP using this method, the wizard will also walk you through the process of creating the initial scope.

Creating Scopes

Scopes determine the range of IP addresses that a DHCP server can lease to clients. Before a DHCP server is fully functional on a network, it must be configured with at least one scope. Since a scope is a range or pool of IP addresses that can be leased to DHCP clients on a given subnet, you may have to create multiple scopes if your network consists of multiple subnets.

Before jumping in and creating your scopes, you should be aware of the following guidelines:

- As already mentioned, in order for a DHCP server to lease IP addresses, it must be configured with at least one scope.

- Any IP addresses that should not be leased to clients should be excluded from the scope. This eliminates the chances of duplicate IP addresses on the network.

- In the event that your network is divided into subnets, a single DHCP server can be configured with multiple scopes. This means a single DHCP server can assign IP addresses to clients from multiple subnets.

- Scope information is not shared between DHCP servers. Therefore, you must ensure that scopes do not overlap to avoid duplicate IP addresses on the network.

With those guidelines in mind, Exercise 2-3 walks you through the process of creating a new scope.

EXERCISE 2-3

CertCam 2-3 ON THE CD

Creating a Scope

In this exercise, you will create a new scope through the DHCP console.

1. Click Start, point to Administrative Tools, and click DHCP.

2. Within the DHCP console, right-click your DHCP server and click New Scope. This launches the New Scope Wizard. Click Next.

3. Type in a name and description for the scope. This name will be displayed within the DHCP console, making it easy to distinguish one scope from another. Click Next.

4. Enter the range of IP addresses for the scope. Verify the correct length and subnet mask.

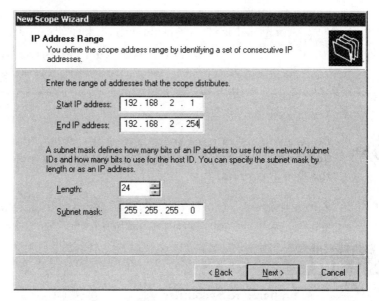

5. From the Add Exclusions dialog box, type in the IP address range for those addresses you do not want included within the scope. Click Add to have the range added to the list of exclusions. Click Next.

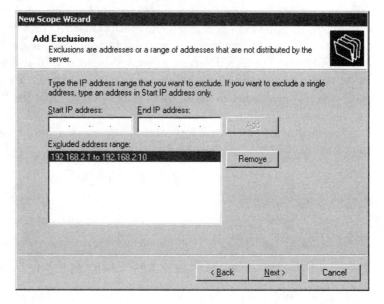

6. Specify a lease duration (this topic will be discussed in more detail later in the chapter). The default value is 8 days. Click Next.

7. At this point, you can configure the optional parameters or they can be configured at a later time through the DHCP console. Click Next. Click Finish.

8. The scope will now appear under your DHCP server. You will now need to activate the scope. To do so, right-click the scope and click the Activate option.

on the Job

Be sure you activate the scope once it is created; this step is often overlooked. Scopes that are not activated will appear with a red arrow beside them within the DHCP console.

Superscopes   Along with regular scopes described in the preceding section, you can also create a second type of scope, known as a *superscope*. In an environment that consists of multiple subnets (also referred to as multinetted environments), superscopes are created to enable a DHCP server to assign leases to clients on multiple subnets. Multinets are created when there are two or more logical subnets on a single subnet or router interface.

Be prepared to encounter exam questions related to superscopes. Make sure you understand why they are necessary.

Let's look at an example of how superscopes are used. A network is divided into two subnets, Subnet 1 and Subnet 2. The subnets are connected via a router. Subnet 2 is further divided into two multinets. The network contains a single DHCP server located on Subnet 1. The DHCP server contains a single scope with a range of IP addresses to lease to clients on the local subnet. To have the DHCP assign IP addresses to clients on Subnet 2, you can create a superscope and add to it the IP address ranges for the multinets on Subnet 2 (assuming of course that the relay agent component is configured). The DHCP server may be configured with the following scopes:

- Subnet 1
  - Scope 1: 192.168.0.2–192.168.0.254
- Subnet 2
  - Superscope for Subnet 2
    - Scope 2: 192.168.1.2–192.168.1.254
    - Scope 3: 192.168.2.2–192.168.2.254

Probably the biggest advantage to creating superscopes is that it eases the administration in a multinetted environment. With multiple scopes configured, it can be difficult to determine which scopes go with which subnets. Creating superscopes and grouping scopes in some logical manner can make them easier to administer. Think of an office building that has multiple floors. You can create superscopes within the DHCP console and group all scopes from a single floor into a superscope, making them easier to manage. Exercise 2-4 takes you through the steps involved in creating a new superscope within the DHCP management console.

on the **Job**

Before you can add a scope to a superscope, the scope must already be created. As you will see when you walk through the New Superscope Wizard, you will be prompted to select those scope you want to include.

EXERCISE 2-4

Creating a Superscope

In this exercise, you will practice creating a new superscope within the DHCP console.

1. Right-click the DHCP server and select the New Superscope option. This launches the New Superscope Wizard. Click Next.

2. Type in a descriptive name for the superscope (make sure this is something that makes it easy to identify). This is the name that will appear within the DHCP management console. Click Next.

3. From the list of available scopes, select the scopes you want to include in the superscope. Keep in mind you can add only active scopes. Click Next.

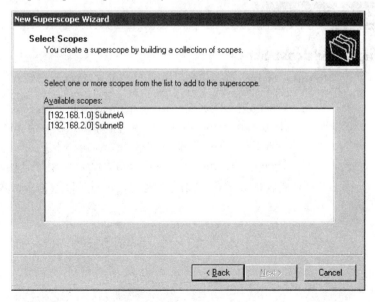

4. Click Finish.

Your scopes must be created and activated first before they can be grouped into a superscope.

Multicast Scopes A third type of scope that can be configured is a *multicast scope*. As discussed in Chapter 1, multicasting is the process of sending a message to a group of recipients, for example, to a group of users participating in a group discussion using NetMeeting.

Normally DHCP is used to assign each DHCP client a single unique IP address from a range of IP addresses configured in a scope. Windows .NET Server 2003 extends the functionality to allow you to create multicast scopes so that messages destined to a multicast IP address can be sent to all clients in a multicast group.

Multicast scopes are supported through a protocol known as the Multicast Address Dynamic Client Allocation Protocol (MADCAP). MADCAP controls how the DHCP servers dynamically assign IP addresses on a TCP/IP network.

The multicast server (in this case the DHCP server) is configured with a group of class D IP addresses (in the range 224.0.0.0–239.255.255.255) that can be assigned to multicast clients. The server is also responsible for maintaining the group membership list and updating the list as members join and leave a group. Exercise 2-5 walks you through the process of creating a multicast scope.

EXERCISES 2-5

Creating a Multicast Scope

In this exercise, you will practice creating a new multicast scope.

1. Within the DHCP management console, right-click the DHCP server and choose the New Multicast Scope option. This launches the New Multicast Scope Wizard. Click Next.

2. Type in a name and description for the scope. Click Next.

3. Specify a range of IP addresses and a TTL. Click Next.

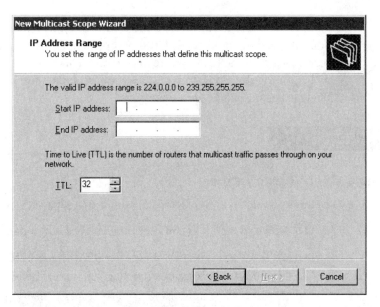

4. Type in any IP addresses you want to exclude from the range. Click Next.

5. Specify a lease duration, which defines how long a client can lease a multicast address from the scope. The default is 30 days. Click Next.

6. Click Yes to activate the scope. Click Next.

7. Click Finish.

Client Reservations   Client reservations enable you to configure a workstation as a DHCP client while at the same time still assigning the workstation the same IP address. This means every time the client leases an IP address, that client will receive the same IP address. In terms of administration, IP addressing still remains centralized and the clients can be assigned optional parameters through the DHCP server.

One thing you need to keep in mind when using client reservations is that if multiple DHCP servers are configured with a range of IP addresses that cover the reserved address, the client reservation must be duplicated on all DHCP servers. If not, there is a chance that the client may end up receiving an incorrect IP address (one other than the address that has been reserved for the client). For example, if you have configured the 80/20 rule between two DHCP servers, you must configure any client reservations on both servers.

A client reservation can be created within the DHCP console. Before you do so, you will need the hardware address of the client. This address is used by the DHCP server to determine the client reservation. You can obtain the hardware address of a client using the `ipconfig /all` command. Exercise 2-6 outlines the process of creating a new client reservation.

EXERCISE 2-6

Creating a Client Reservation

In this exercise, you will practice creating a new client reservation.

1. Within the DHCP console, click your DHCP server and click the scope.

2. Right-click the Reservation container and click New Reservation.

3. From the New Reservation dialog box, enter the required information.

Configuring Lease Durations

Lease durations were briefly mentioned when you were creating a scope. The lease duration for a scope determines how long a client can use an IP address before it must be renewed. The default lease time is eight days; this value can be changed to meet your specific requirements. Now if your range of IP addresses is relative to the number of DHCP clients, you may want to shorten the lease time to ensure that there are always available IP addresses. On the other hand, if the range of IP addresses exceeds the number

SCENARIO & SOLUTION

What is the IP address lease duration for?	The lease duration determines how long a client can use an IP address before it must be renewed. The default value is eight days.
When should I decrease the value of the lease duration?	A general rule of thumb is if the number of IP addresses available within a scope is close to the number of DHCP clients on the network, decrease the lease duration.
When should I increase the value of the lease duration?	If the number of IP addresses within a scope exceeds the number of DHCP clients, the lease duration can be increased.
Will the fact that I have a number of mobile users on the network impact the value of the lease duration?	Yes. If there are a lot of mobile users, shorter lease durations should be configured so that addresses are released more quickly. However, an alternative to configuring shorter lease times is to configure the 002 Microsoft Release DHCP Lease On Shutdown option. This way, all mobile users will release their IP addresses when they are properly shut down.

of DHCP clients, you may choose to increase the lease duration. Doing so will decrease the number of DHCP broadcasts on the network.

As you saw in the preceding section, the lease duration can be configured during the creation of the scope. You can change the value any time afterward by right-clicking the scope within the DHCP console and clicking Properties (see Figure 2-4). From the properties dialog box, you can increase or decrease the value of the lease duration.

Scope Options

One of the major benefits of using DHCP is that it can also be used to dynamically assign optional parameters to DHCP clients. As you saw when you walked through the process of creating a scope, optional parameters can be configured at this time or they can be created later through the DHCP management console. The scope options can be configured at four different levels. The level at which you configure an option will determine its scope or which DHCP clients will receive the parameter. In any case, the four levels at which you can configure these options are

■ **Server** Options configured at this level will apply to all DHCP clients regardless of the subnet they are on. For example, if all network clients use the same DNS server, you can configure this option at the server level.

■ **Scope** Options configured at the scope level will apply to DHCP clients on a specific subnet. For example, in a subnetted environment, clients on different subnets will be using different default gateways. Therefore, this option should be configured at the scope level.

■ **Class** Configuring options at this level allows you to apply DHCP options to a group of clients or workstations with similar needs. For example, options can be applied to mobile users or to a group of users based on vendor information such as Windows 98 or Windows 2000.

■ **Client** Optional parameters can be applied to specific clients for whom there are client reservations created.

on the

J o b

Keep in mind, when you are configuring scope options, that any options configured at the scope or client level will override those configured at the server level. When options are applied at the various levels, they are applied in the following order: server, scope, class, and client. This means options applied at the client level will override all others.

Now that you are familiar with the different levels at which scope options are configured, let's take a look at some of the common options that can be configured.

<table>
<tr><td>**FIGURE 2-4**</td></tr>
</table>

Configuring the
lease duration
of a scope

Scope [192.168.1.0] SubnetA Properties   ? ✕

General | DNS | Advanced |

📁 Scope

S̲cope name: SubnetA

S̲tart IP address: 192 . 168 . 1 . 1

E̲nd IP address: 192 . 168 . 1 . 254

Subnet mask: 255 . 255 . 255 . 0   Length: 24

┌─ Lease duration for DHCP clients ──────────────
│ ⦿ L̲imited to:
│   D̲ays: Ho̲urs: Minutes:
│   [8 ⬍]   [0 ⬍]   [0 ⬍]
│
│ ○ U̲nlimited

Descri̲ption: [   ]

                    [OK]   [Cancel]   [Apply]

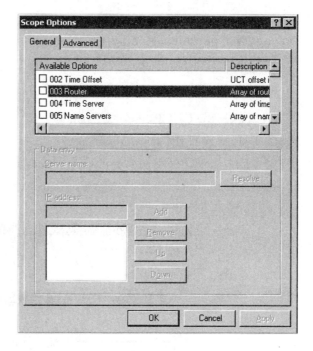

FIGURE 2-5

Options that can
be configured for
DHCP clients

DHCP Options

As already mentioned, not only can a DHCP server be used to lease IP addresses and
subnet masks, but it can also be used to assign optional parameters. Many different options
can be configured, some of which are shown in Figure 2-5. Table 2-1 outlines some of
the more common options used.

TABLE 2-1   Common DHCP Options

Option	Description
006 DNS Servers	Specifies the IP address of the DNS servers available to clients on the network.
015 DNS Domain Name	Specifies the DNS domain name used for client resolutions.
003 Router	Specifies the IP address of the router or default gateway.
044 WINS/NBNS Servers	Specifies the IP addresses of the WINS servers on the network available to clients.
046 WINS/NBT Node Type	Specifies the name resolution type. The available options include 1= B-node (broadcast), 2 = P-node (peer), 4 = M-node (mixed), 8 = H-node (hybrid).

Remember that once your DHCP server is configured with an active scope and any optional parameters, it must still be authorized within Active Directory. This topic is discussed further later in the chapter in "Optimizing DHCP."

To configure an option at the scope level:

1. Within the DHCP console, expand your DHCP server.

2. Double-click the appropriate scope.

3. Right-click the Scope Options container and click Configure Options.

4. Select the option you want to assign to clients and type in the necessary parameters. Click OK.

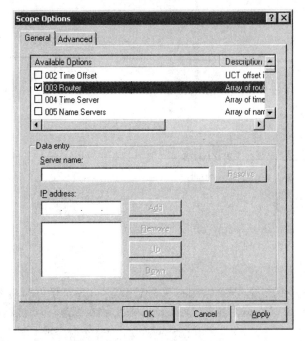

DHCP Clients

Configuring DHCP clients is a very straightforward process, although the steps may vary slightly depending on the platform you are working with. If you are using Windows 2000, Windows XP, or Windows Server 2003, the default configuration for computers using TCP/IP is to obtain an IP address from a DHCP server. If a workstation is using a static IP address, you can use the steps in the following exercise to change the configuration so that the workstation obtains an IP address from a DHCP server instead.

EXERCISE 2-7

Configuring DHCP on a Windows XP Client

1. Click Start and click the Control Panel.

2. Open the Network Connections applet.

3. Right-click your local area connection and click Properties.

4. From the properties dialog box, select Internet Protocol (TCP/IP) and click Properties.

5. From the Internet Protocol (TCP/IP Properties dialog box), select the option to Obtain An IP Address Automatically. Click OK.

Once you've configured a client to automatically obtain an IP address, you can use the `ipconfig` command to verify the client is indeed obtaining an IP address. To do so, open the command prompt and type in **ipconfig /all** (see Figure 2-6).

Integrating DHCP and DNS

Prior to Windows 2000, DHCP did not integrate with DNS: DNS is used to resolve hostnames to IP addresses. But what happens if the IP address changes because the workstation is a DHCP client? Without the integration of the two services, the IP address

FIGURE 2-6

Using the ipconfig command to verify an IP address lease

```
C:\WINDOWS\System32\cmd.exe                                                    _ □ X
Ethernet adapter Local Area Connection:

        Media State . . . . . . . . . . : Media disconnected
        Description . . . . . . . . . . : 3Com 3C920 Integrated Fast Ethernet
Controller (3C905C-TX Compatible)
        Physical Address. . . . . . . . : 00-08-74-03-8D-77

Ethernet adapter Local Area Connection 2:

        Connection-specific DNS Suffix  . : mb.skyweb.ca
        Description . . . . . . . . . . : SMC 10/100 PC Card
        Physical Address. . . . . . . . : 00-04-E2-3B-DE-1B
        Dhcp Enabled. . . . . . . . . . : Yes
        Autoconfiguration Enabled . . . . : Yes
        IP Address. . . . . . . . . . . : 206.186.217.31
        Subnet Mask . . . . . . . . . . : 255.255.255.0
        Default Gateway . . . . . . . . : 206.186.217.1
        DHCP Server . . . . . . . . . . : 10.10.10.11
        DNS Servers . . . . . . . . . . : 209.5.243.59
                                          204.50.251.17
                                          209.5.243.54
        Lease Obtained. . . . . . . . . : Wednesday, June 04, 2003 10:03:46 PM

        Lease Expires . . . . . . . . . : Thursday, June 05, 2003 4:03:46 AM
```

within the DNS database that is associated with a host could be incorrect. For example, if a host acquires a new IP address from a DHCP server, the update may not be reflected within the DNS database and name resolution for the host may fail.

Dynamic DNS was introduced in Windows 2000 and is included in Windows Server 2003. With dynamic updates, the DNS server allows DHCP servers and DHCP clients to dynamically register A records and PTR records. Windows 2000, Windows XP, and Windows Server 2003 clients are capable of updating their own records. For those clients that cannot perform this function, a DHCP server can perform the updates on their behalf. For example, when a Windows 95 client leases an IP address, the DHCP server can update the client's records with the DNS server on its behalf.

By default, Windows 2000 clients and later are configured to update their own A records with the DNS server; the DHCP server updates the PTR records. Alternatively, you can configure the DHCP server to also update A records on their behalf. For pre–Windows 2000 clients, the DHCP server will perform the update of both A and PTR records.

So how do updates actually occur? The process is slightly different depending on the platform the client is running. Records are updated during the IP address lease process outlined earlier in the chapter. Once the client receives a DHCPACK from the server, it will update its own A record and the DHCP server will update the PTR record. The client will know whether or not to update its A record using the information returned in the DHCPACK.

Now if the client that is requesting an IP address is a legacy client that does not support dynamic updates, the client will simply lease an IP address using the process outlined earlier in the chapter. Once the DHCPACK is sent to the client, the DHCP server will send the updates to the DNS server.

on the
job *For Windows 2000 clients and later, the DHCPACK will contain "Option 81."*
This instructs the client as to how the updates should be performed. In other
words, should the client update the A record, or is the DHCP server configured
to update both A and PTR records?

Configuring DHCP for DNS Integration

You can configure a DHCP server for dynamic updates through the DHCP console. To do so, right-click your DHCP server and click Properties. From the properties dialog box, select the DNS tab (see Figure 2-7).

As you can see, the DHCP server is by default enabled to perform updates if requested to do so by the DHCP client. The available options are summarized here:

■ Dynamically update DNS A and PTR records only if requested by DHCP clients. This option specifies that the DHCP server update records only if requested to do so by the client.

■ Always dynamically update A and PTR records. This option specifies that the DHCP server always update records regardless of the client request.

■ Discard A and PTR records when lease is deleted. This option specifies that the records be deleted when a lease expires.

■ Dynamically update DNS A and PTR records for DHCP clients that do not request updates. By selecting this option, you enable the DHCP server to perform updates on behalf of those clients that do not support this feature.

On the client side, you can also configure whether or not dynamic updates are performed. On a Windows XP client, click the Advanced tab on the properties dialog box for the TCP/IP protocol. From the DNS tab, select or deselect the option to Register This Connection's Addresses In DNS (see Figure 2-8).

FIGURE 2-7

Configuring
DHCP for DNS
integration

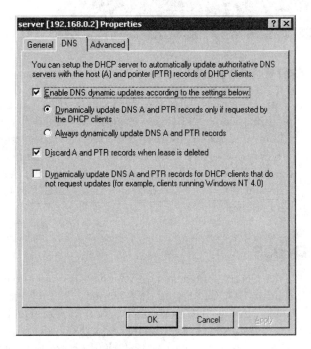

server [192.168.0.2] Properties

General DNS Advanced

You can setup the DHCP server to automatically update authoritative DNS servers with the host (A) and pointer (PTR) records of DHCP clients.

☑ Enable DNS dynamic updates according to the settings below:

   ⦿ Dynamically update DNS A and PTR records only if requested by the DHCP clients

   ○ Always dynamically update DNS A and PTR records

☑ Discard A and PTR records when lease is deleted

☐ Dynamically update DNS A and PTR records for DHCP clients that do not request updates (for example, clients running Windows NT 4.0)

OK   Cancel   Apply

FIGURE 2-8

Enabling or
disabling dynamic
updates on a
Windows XP
client

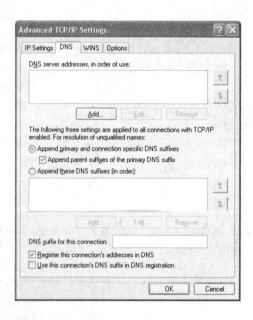

CERTIFICATION OBJECTIVE 2.04

Optimizing DHCP

Optimization of a DHCP server includes three categories: security, availability, and performance. A DHCP server plays an extremely important role. Your goal as an administrator is to ensure that the service is available to clients and that the DHCP server responds to client requests in a timely manner. To achieve these goals, you need to be aware of the different options you have to optimize DHCP. The following section will look at how you can optimize DHCP in terms of security, availability, and performance.

Securing DHCP

Since DHCP is integrated with Active Directory, you can take certain steps to ensure that your DHCP servers are more secure. You have two ways to do this: first, by implementing DHCP on domain controllers or member servers to ensure all servers are authorized to lease IP addresses, and second, by using Windows groups to control which users have access to the DHCP servers. Both of these topics are discussed in more detail in the sections that follow.

Authorizing DHCP

The authorization of DHCP servers is a feature introduced in Windows 2000 and included with Windows Server 2003. Before a DHCP server can lease IP addresses to clients on a network, it must first be authorized within Active Directory to do so. This prevents a DHCP server with incorrect information from being introduced to the network. For example, a DHCP server with incorrect scope information cannot be introduced onto the network and so provide DHCP clients with incorrect IP parameters.

How a server is authorized depends on whether it is a member of a domain or a stand-alone server. In order for a server to be authorized within Active Directory, it must be a domain controller or a stand-alone server. In either case, when the server is brought online, it will query Active Directory for the list of IP addresses of authorized DHCP servers. If the server's IP address is not in the list, the DHCP service will not start and the server will be unable to respond to client requests. If you are installing DHCP on a stand-alone server, bear this important point in mind: The stand-alone server must be placed on a subnet that contains no other DHCP servers. If an authorized server is on the same subnet, the stand-alone server will not be able to lease IP addresses to clients.

DHCP servers are authorized through the DHCP management console and must be performed by a user that is a member of the Enterprise Admins group. Exercise 2-8 walks you through the process of authorizing a DHCP server that is also configured as a domain controller.

EXERCISE 2-8

Authorizing a DHCP Server

In this exercise, you will authorize a DHCP server within Active Directory to lease IP addresses to clients on the network.

1. Click Start, point to Administrative Tools, and click DHCP.

2. Within the DHCP console, right-click your DHCP server.

3. Click the Authorize option.

4. The DHCP server will now appear with a green arrow beside it, indicating that it has been authorized to lease IP addresses to clients on the network.

e x a m

ⓦ a t c h

In order for a DHCP server to be authorized, it must be a domain controller or a member server. Stand-alone servers are not authorized. If a Windows 2000 or Windows Server 2003 stand-alone server is placed on a subnet *with an authorized DHCP server, the service will fail to start. However, this does not hold true for any other DHCP servers, such as Windows NT 4.0. All other DHCP servers will still function correctly, potentially interfering with the network.*

Using Windows Groups to Secure DHCP

Once the DHCP service is installed, two groups are added that can be used to define the type of access users have to your DHCP servers. The two groups are the DHCP Administrators and the DHCP Users (see Figure 2-9). Any users who are members of the DHCP Administrators group will have administrative access to the DHCP servers. Members of the DHCP Users group have read-only access to the DHCP servers. They can view information and server properties but are unable to make any configuration changes.

FIGURE 2-9

The DHCP Administrators and DHCP Users groups

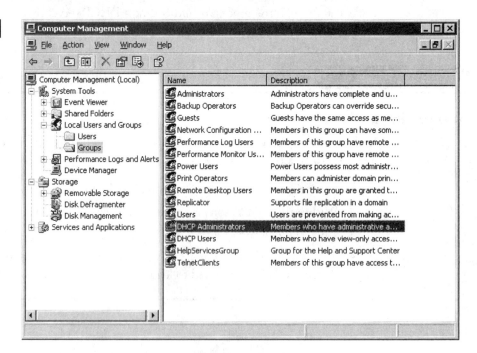

INSIDE THE EXAM

Authorizing a DHCP Server

With earlier versions of Windows (prior to Windows 2000), you could easily install the DHCP service on a computer and add it to the network without the need for authorization. Now this may not seem like an overly huge deal, unless of course the DHCP server is misconfigured. Imagine a DHCP server being introduced into a network with incorrect scope information or incorrect scope options. Havoc, both for the clients and the administrator.

With Windows Server 2003, and Windows 2000, DHCP servers must be authorized within Active Directory before they can begin leasing IP addresses to clients. This is a welcome security change. First of all, it gives administrators the opportunity to verify the configuration of a DHCP server before it is introduced onto the network. Second, it eliminates the chance of someone maliciously adding a DHCP server to the network with the sole intention of leasing clients incorrect IP addresses. So, good luck to the individual who takes the time to install and configure a DHCP server with the intent

to provide incorrect information to clients, only to discover that an Enterprise Administrator must authorize the DHCP server. One thing to keep in mind, though, is that authorization does nothing to stop rogue or unauthorized servers that are not running Windows 2000 or Windows Server 2003. So a Windows NT 4.0 DHCP server could be placed on the network and cause potential network problems.

You may be wondering exactly how a DHCP server determines if it is authorized to lease IP addresses. Well, when the DHCP service is started, the server will query Active Directory for a list of authorized DHCP servers. If the server's IP address is not on the list, it is not authorized, and the DHCP service will be shut down.

The authorization of DHCP servers was introduced in Windows 2000 and is included with Windows Server 2003. Since it is still a relatively new feature and since it is a feature that greatly improves network security, be prepared to answer exam questions pertaining to the topic.

When you add a user to either of these two groups, the permissions do not apply to all DHCP servers. The user is granted permission to configure (or view, depending on the group) the DHCP service only on the local computer. So if you have multiple DHCP servers within the domain, you will have to add the user account to the group on each one. Alternatively, if you have multiple DHCP servers, you can add the user to the Domain Admins group, which will grant them permission on all DHCP servers within the domain. Now this is not the recommended solution, as Domain Admins have permissions to far more than just DHCP. The more secure approach is to create a universal group and add the users that will be responsible for administering DHCP. You can then add the new universal group to the appropriate group on each DHCP server within the domain.

Enhancing DHCP Availability

A DHCP server plays a very important role within a network environment. A DHCP server that is not available can cause some havoc throughout your network. As with most network services, one of your goals is to ensure that services have a high level of availability, that is, that a service is available to users when they need it. The following section will look at ways in which you can increase the availability of DHCP.

Distributed Scopes

One of the easiest ways to increase the availability of DHCP is to use distributed scopes (if you recall, this goes back to the 80/20 rule). With distributed scopes, you take the IP addresses available for a scope and split them between two DHCP servers. If there are two DHCP servers on a single subnet, you can pretty much split the IP addresses 50/50; that is, each server will be configured with 50 percent of the IP addresses in the scope range.

You can also use distributed scopes if there are DHCP servers on other subnets (and DHCP relay agents have been enabled). In this case, in order to ensure client performance, you should configure the local DHCP server with the majority of the IP addresses within the scope. A DHCP server on another subnet can be configured with the remaining IP addresses. This ensures clients will use the local DHCP server unless it is unavailable, at which point clients can lease an IP address from the remote DHCP server.

Clustering DHCP

Another option available for increasing the availability of DHCP is to use Windows Clustering. The DHCP service included with Windows Server 2003 is cluster-aware. A cluster requires at least two DHCP servers bound to a single virtual IP address. If one DHCP server fails, the other is ready to take its place. With this configuration, downtime can be reduced to seconds or the amount of time it takes for automatic failover to occur.

When DHCP is installed in a cluster configuration, one server is active while the other is passive. All DHCP information is stored on a shared disk that both servers are connected to. If the active DHCP server should fail, the passive DHCP server will take over almost immediately.

Enhancing DHCP Performance

Optimizing DHCP also includes optimizing the performance of a DHCP server. The overall goal is to ensure quick response times for DHCP clients. Here are some of the steps you can take to optimize the performance of your DHCP:

- Performance can be increased by configuring the DHCP server with the appropriate hardware. A DHCP server should be configured with a fast disk subsystem, ample memory, and a high-bandwidth network card.
- If you have multiple DHCP servers, consider distributing the scope between servers to load-balance client requests and increase availability.
- To increase response time for users, place the DHCP servers on the subnets that have the most clients.
- If segments are connected using WAN links, consider placing a DHCP server on either side to improve performance for DHCP clients.
- Adjusting the lease time will affect performance. If the number of available IP addresses within a scope is relative to the number of clients, shorten the lease time, making IP addresses available for other hosts, although this approach will increase network traffic. If the number of available IP addresses exceeds the number of clients, consider increasing the lease time.

Monitoring DHCP Performance

Part of any good maintenance plan will include regularly monitoring servers to ensure they continue to perform at an acceptable level. Over time as networks change, as additional components are installed on a server, and as configuration changes are made, the performance of a server can begin to deteriorate and bottlenecks can begin to appear. Regularly monitoring DHCP servers will assist you in determining what is "normal" performance for a DHCP server under given circumstances and so help you detect bottlenecks before they become a serious problem.

System Monitor

Windows Server 2003 comes with a performance monitoring tool built in. Using System Monitor, you can monitor the real-time performance of a computer. It allows you to monitor the various components, including hardware, services, and applications. Once the DHCP service is installed, you can use System Monitor to monitor the performance of the service. Several counters are added to System Monitor as well once the service has been added (see Figure 2-10). The available counters are summarized in Table 2-2.

Network Monitor

Network Monitor is a "sniffer" that can be used to capture network traffic coming to and from a computer. In terms of DHCP, you can use it to view and analyze traffic, such as the IP address lease process, between a DHCP server and DHCP clients. Both System Monitor and Network Monitor will be discussed in more detail in Chapter 8.

FIGURE 2-10

DHCP
performance
counters

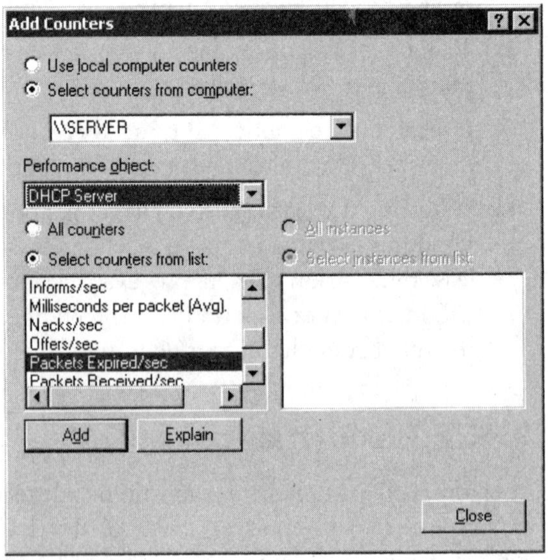

TABLE 2-2   DHCP Performance Counters

Performance Counter	Description
Acks/Sec	The number of DHCPACKS sent by the DHCP server to clients per second.
Active Queue Length	The current length of the internal DHCP message queue. This is the number of messages waiting to be processed. A high number may indicate heavy traffic to the server.
Conflict Check	The current length of the conflict check queue.
Queue Length	This is the number of messages waiting for a response while the server performs conflict detection.
Declines/Sec	The number of DHCP decline messages received by the DHCP server by DHCP clients.
Discovers/Sec	The number of DHCPDISCOVER messages received by the server per second.
Duplicates Dropped/Sec	The number of duplicate packets per second that are dropped by the server.
Informs/sec	The number of DHCPINFORM messages received by the server per second.
Nacks/sec	The number of DHCP negative acknowledgment messages sent by the server to clients. A high value can indicate a deactivated scope.
Offers/sec	The number of DHCP offers per second sent by the server to clients.
Packets Expired/sec	The number of packets per second that expire and are dropped by the DHCP server. A high value can indicate that there is too much traffic for the server to handle.
Packets Received/sec	The number of message packets received by the DHCP server per second. If this number is high, it indicates a heavy amount of DHCP-related traffic.
Releases/sec	The number of DHCPRELEASE messages received per second from DHCP clients.
Requests/sec	The number of DHCP REQUEST messages received from DHCP clients per second.

CERTIFICATION OBJECTIVE 2.05

Troubleshooting DHCP

Troubleshooting is something that network administrators spend a large amount of time doing. If you have an understanding of how DHCP operates, it will make it easier for you to troubleshoot the problems as they arise. In any case, the following section will look at some of the more common DHCP-related problems you may encounter and how you can remedy them.

Common Problems Related to DHCP Clients and DHCP Servers

A number of problems can arise when troubleshooting DHCP clients. Problems can range from clients being unable to lease an IP address to clients leasing an IP address but receiving incorrect parameters. On the server side, problems can occur when the DHCP service will not start or the DHCP server is unable to respond to client requests. If you are responsible for administering DHCP, you should be aware of some of the common problems you can encounter with DHCP clients and servers.

- If the DHCP client has no IP address or its IP address is 0.0.0.0, it is unable to contact the DHCP server. In this case, verify that the network card on the client workstation is functioning. Also verify that the DHCP server is online and the service is started.

- If the DHCP client has assigned itself an IP address in the range of 169.254.0.0, verify network connectivity using the ping command. Verify that the DHCP server is online and the service is started. Use the ipconfig command to attempt to manually renew an IP address with the DHCP server.

- If a client is missing optional parameters or has been assigned incorrect parameters, verify that the optional parameters have been configured and that they are configured at the correct level: server, scope, class, or client.

- If the DHCP service on the server is stopped, verify that the server has been authorized within Active Directory. If it's a Windows 2000 or Windows Server 2003 stand-alone server, make sure there are no authorized DHCP servers on the same subnet. Also be sure to check the System log in the Event Viewer for any DHCP-related messages. This may give you an indication of what is causing the problem.

- If the DHCP server has been authorized but is unable to lease IP addresses, verify that the scope has been activated.

- If a DHCP server is unable to provide service to some of the DHCP clients, verify that the relay agent is enabled if necessary. Check to ensure that any superscopes have been properly configured.

Troubleshooting Automatic Private IP Addressing

Recall from Chapter 1 that automatic private IP addressing was introduced in Windows 98. APIPA is supported by the following platforms:

- Windows 98
- Windows ME
- Windows 2000 (all platforms)
- Windows XP
- Windows .NET Server 2003

With the feature enabled, clients can assign themselves an IP address

- If a DHCP client is unable to contact a DHCP server
- If a DHCP client's attempt to renew its IP address fails

In both cases, the client will assign itself an IP address in the range 169.254.0.1–169.254.255.254. Using the `ipconfig` command at the command prompt, you can verify if APIPA is being used. Remember as well that this feature is enabled by default and can be disabled through the Registry.

One of the limitations of APIPA is that clients assign themselves only an IP address and a subnet mask. If your network consists of multiple subnets, clients using APIPA will be able to communicate only with hosts on their local subnet because they do not assign themselves a value for the default gateway. In other words, APIPA does not include optional parameters.

Troubleshooting DHCP Server Authorization

As already mentioned previously in this chapter, before a DHCP server can assign IP addresses to clients, it must be authorized within Active Directory. This was a security feature introduced in Windows 2000 to eliminate the possibility of rogue servers on the network.

The steps involved in authorizing a DHCP server were outlined earlier in the chapter. If you are unable to authorize a DHCP server, keep in mind that you must be logged on with a user account that is a member of the Enterprise Admins group.

Another problem you may encounter in regards to authorizing DHCP servers can arise if you have configured a Windows 2000 or Windows Server 2003 stand-alone server as a DHCP server. Although this configuration is acceptable, the stand-alone server cannot be placed on a subnet that already hosts a DHCP server that has been authorized.

When the DHCP service starts on a stand-alone server, it sends out a DHCP information message (DHCPINFORM). The DHCPINFORM message is sent to determine if there are any DHCP servers on the network. If the DHCP server does not receive a DHCPACK, it will initialize and begin leasing IP addresses to clients. If the stand-alone server receives a reply from a DHCP server that has been authorized within Active Directory, the DHCP service on the stand-alone server will be shut down and will not be able to lease IP addresses to clients.

Troubleshooting Scope Options

As pointed out earlier in the chapter, scope options can be configured at different levels. The level at which an option is configured will determine which DHCP clients are assigned the parameter. For example, an option configured at the server level will apply to all DHCP clients regardless of the scope from which they are leased an IP address.

One of the most common problems that can occur with DHCP options is that clients end up being assigned incorrect parameters. In such cases, you will need to verify at which level the option has been configured. For example, configuring the router option at the server level when the network consists of multiple subnets will result in some DHCP clients being configured with an incorrect gateway. In this case, the option needs to be configured at the scope level, as opposed to the server level.

Using Log Files to Troubleshoot DHCP

One of the first things an administrator should do when troubleshooting events is to examine the contents of log files, which are a rich source of valuable information. You can use the System log within the Event Viewer to monitor and troubleshoot DHCP-related events. When an event does occur, such as the DHCP Server service being restarted, it is written to the log file, providing useful information, including a description of the event and when it occurred (see Figure 2-11).

Windows Server 2003 also supports audit logging of the DHCP service. The audit logs are by default stored in the %systemroot%\system32\DHCP directory (see Figure 2-12). Audit logging for a DHCP server can be enabled by right-clicking the appropriate DHCP server within the management console and selecting Properties. Using the General tab, audit logging can be enabled or disabled (see Figure 2-13). You can also use the Advanced tab from the DHCP server's properties dialog box to change the default location of the log files.

As events occur, they will be written to a log file. Entries in the log will contain an event ID and the date and time at which the event occurred, as well as the IP address, hostname, and MAC address of the workstation that generated the event. Some of the common event IDs are listed in Table 2-3.

FIGURE 2-11

Using the system
log to monitor
DHCP

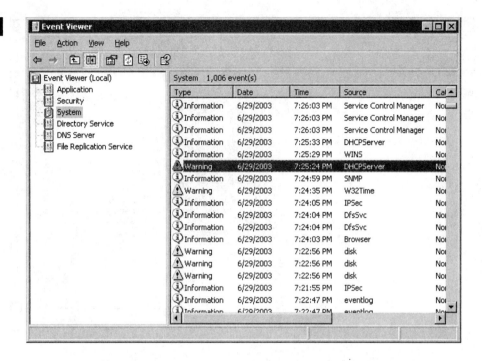

FIGURE 2-12

DHCP audit log

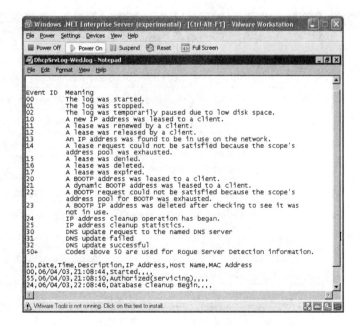

FIGURE 2-13

Enabling logging
for the DHCP
service

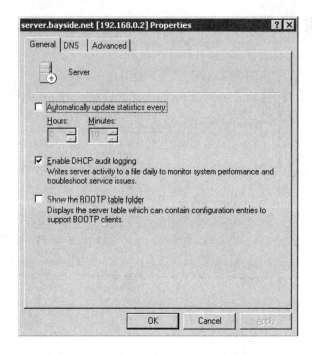

TABLE 2-3	Code	Description
Common DHCP Audit Codes	00	The log was started.
	01	The log was stopped.
	02	The log was temporarily paused due to low disk space.
	10	A new IP address was leased to a client.
	11	A client renewed an existing lease.
	12	A client released an IP address.
	13	An IP address was found in use on the network.
	14	A client is unable to lease an IP address because the address pool is exhausted.
	15	A lease request was denied.
	30	DNS dynamic update request.
	31	DNS dynamic update failed.
	32	DNS dynamic update successful.

TABLE 2-3	Code	Description
Common DHCP Audit Codes (continued)	55	DHCP server was authorized to start on the network.
	56	DHCP server was not authorized to start on the network.

CERTIFICATION SUMMARY

Every TCP/IP host requires a unique IP address. IP addresses can be assigned dynamically using the Dynamic Host Configuration Protocol (DHCP). DHCP is built into the Windows Server 2003 operating system.

During the IP address lease process, four distinct phases occur: DHCPDISCOVER, DHCPOFFER, DHCPREQUEST, and DHCPACK. The lease duration determines how long a client can lease an IP address. Once a client leases an IP address, it must begin the renewal process when 50 percent of the lease duration expires.

A DHCP implementation requires some level of preplanning. You need to consider the number of DHCP servers, where on the network DHCP servers should be placed, and if your network is routed. If the network is routed, you may have to enable the relay agent component.

Installing a DHCP server is a fairly straightforward process. Once the service itself is installed, you must configure the DHCP server with at least one active scope. If your network is multinetted and the DHCP server is assigning IP addresses to clients on different subnets, you must configure superscopes. For security purposes, before a DHCP server can lease IP addresses, it must be authorized to do so within Active Directory (unless it is a stand-alone server).

DHCP and DNS can be integrated so that A records and PTR records are dynamically updated. Windows 2000, Windows XP, and Windows Server 2003 clients can update their own A records. For legacy clients (pre–Windows 2000), the DHCP server can be configured to perform the updates on their behalf.

Optimization of DHCP falls into three categories: security, availability, and performance. A more secure DHCP implementation can be achieved by using member servers and domain controllers to act as DHCP servers. This allows you to take advantage of Active Directory and ensure that all DHCP servers are authorized before leasing IP addresses. You can also use Windows groups to configure the level of access users have to DHCP servers. In terms of availability, using distributed scopes and clustering can ensure that the service is always available to clients. Performance of a DHCP server can be tuned, for example, by ensuring that the computer has the appropriate hardware installed, including a high-end disk subsystem and sufficient RAM. You can monitor the performance of the DHCP service using the various DHCP-related counters within System Monitor.

TWO-MINUTE DRILL

Understanding the Dynamic Host Configuration Protocol

❑ Dynamic Host Configuration Protocol (DHCP) is used to dynamically assign IP addresses and optional parameters to DHCP clients.

❑ DHCP client Alternate Configuration enables an administrator to configure the IP address and other parameters that a client should use when a DHCP server is not available.

❑ The DHCP lease process occurs in four distinct phases: DHCPDISCOVER, DHCPINFORM, DHCPREQUEST, and DHCPACK.

❑ DHCP clients will attempt to renew their IP addresses when 50 percent of the lease time expires.

Designing DHCP

❑ To add redundancy to DHCP, you can implement the 80/20 rule. Here, the primary DHCP server is configured with 80 percent of the IP addresses, and another server is configured with the remaining 20 percent.

❑ DHCP servers should be placed on the subnet that contains the highest number of clients.

❑ A DHCP relay agent forwards DHCP messages from clients on one subnet to a DHCP server on another subnet.

❑ DHCP broadcast messages are not forwarded between subnets unless the router is configured to do so (is RFC 1542 compliant). A broadcast forwarder such as the DHCP relay agent included with Windows Server 2003 must be used.

Implementing DHCP

❑ The DHCP service can be installed using the Add or Remove Programs applet, using the Configure Your Server Wizard, or during the installation of Windows Server 2003.

❑ Scopes define the range of IP addresses that a DHCP server can lease to clients. Once a scope is created, it must be activated.

❑ DHCP servers must be authorized in Active Directory.

❑ The lease duration determines how long a client can use an IP address until it must be renewed.

❑ The default lease duration is eight days. The main factor when determining the value to set for the lease duration is the number of IP addresses available compared to the number of DHCP clients.

❑ Scope options can be configured at four different levels: server, scope, class, and client. The level at which you configure an option will determine which IP clients receive the configuration information.

❑ DHCP and DNS can be integrated so that A records and PTR records are dynamically updated as IP address information changes.

Troubleshooting DHCP

❑ If the DHCP service fails to start, verify that the server has been authorized within Active Directory.

❑ If an authorized DHCP server is unable to lease IP addresses, verify that a scope has been configured and activated.

❑ The System log can be used to monitor and troubleshoot DHCP related events.

Optimizing DHCP

❑ The performance of the DHCP service can be monitored using System Monitor. Network Monitor can be used to monitor DHCP traffic on the network.

❑ The availability of DHCP can be increased by implementing distributed scope and Windows clustering.

SELF TEST

Understanding the Dynamic Host Configuration Protocol

1. Joe is responsible for maintaining the network infrastructure. He recently purchased another server for the network. He installs the DHCP service on the new computer that is a member of the domain and configures the scope. When he places the server on the network, he notices that the service will not start. What is causing the problem?

   A. The scope has not been activated.

   B. The new server is not a domain controller.

   C. The new server has not been authorized in Active Directory.

   D. The server has not been activated.

2. The Bayside network consists of multiple subnets connected using routers. You install DHCP on a member server running Windows Server 2003. The server is placed on subnet 1. You configure the 003 router option at the server level. All clients are able to lease an IP address. However, users soon report that they are unable to communicate outside their local subnets. When you investigate the problem, you determine that only clients on subnet 1 are able to do so. What could be causing the problem to occur?

   A. The scopes have not yet been activated.

   B. The server has not been authorized within Active Directory.

   C. Users on the remaining subnets do not have permission to lease an IP address.

   D. The 003 router option should be configured at the scope level.

3. Bob is the junior network administrator who is in charge of implementing a DHCP solution. He installs and configures DHCP on a member server and places it on Subnet A. When he tests his configuration, he discovers that clients in subnet A can lease an IP address. However, the clients on the remaining subnets are using IP addresses in the range of 169.254.0.0. What is causing the problem?

   A. The DHCP service is not started.

   B. The DHCP relay agent must be enabled.

   C. The DHCP server has not been authorized.

   D. Clients are not configured to automatically obtain an IP address.

Designing DHCP

4. The DHCP service has recently been installed on a computer running Windows Server 2003. When you place the server on the network, you notice that the service is constantly being shut down. How can you fix the problem?

A. Configure the DHCP server with at least one active scope.

B. Install the service on a domain controller.

C. Activate the DHCP service.

D. Authorize the DHCP server within Active Directory.

5. Over the past year, the Bayside network has grown drastically. John, the network administrator, is now concerned that the number of IP addresses within the scope is relative to the number of DHCP clients that are now on the network. What can he do to ensure IP addresses are available?

A. Add a standby DHCP server.

B. Increase the lease duration.

C. Decrease the lease duration.

D. Configure static IP addresses on clients.

6. The Bayside Corporation is in the process of upgrading from Windows NT 4.0 to Windows Server 2003. It has been suggested that static IP addresses should be used to eliminate the havoc that occurred when a junior administrator brought a DHCP server online with incorrect scope information. You assure your managers that features of Windows Server 2003 will prevent this from occurring again. When you are installing DHCP, on which computers should the service be installed? (Choose all correct answers.)

A. Windows XP Professional workstations

B. Windows Server 2003 domain controllers

C. Windows Server 2003 member servers

D. Windows Server 2003 stand-alone servers

7. Riverside Corporation consists of two subnets. A DHCP server was recently placed on each subnet. Marge, the network administrator, has been asked to implement some sort of redundancy for the DHCP servers without additional costs. Which of the following options should be implemented?

A. Windows clustering

B. Distributed scopes

C. DHCP relay agent

D. Multicast scopes

Implementing DHCP

8. Bob is planning a DHCP implementation for his organization, so administration of IP addresses becomes be centralized. There are three print servers on the network. You want to enable these servers as DHCP clients while at the same time ensuring they are always leased the same IP address. How should Bob proceed?

    A. Bob should plan to create client reservations.

    B. Bob should plan to create separate scopes for each of the print servers.

    C. Bob should plan to continue to use static IP addressing for these servers.

    D. Bob should plan to enable APIPA on the print servers.

9. A user calls the help desk and reports that they are unable to access any other computers on the network. Upon examining the IP configuration, you determine that the computer has assigned itself an APIPA address. You want to attempt to manually obtain an IP address with the DHCP server. Which of the following commands should be used?

    A. `ipconfig /all`

    B. `ipconfig /renew`

    C. `ipconfig /update`

    D. `ipconfig /release`

10. Westside is deploying a DHCP server. The DHCP server will be responsible for assigning IP addresses to clients on different subnets. The IP address ranges are as follows:

    192.168.0.1–192.168.0.254

    192.168.1.1–192.168.1.254

    192.168.2.1–192.168.2.254

    192.168.3.1–192.168.3.254

When configuring the DHCP server, what should be done first?

    A. Configure a single scope containing all IP address ranges.

    B. Configure a scope for each IP address range.

    C. Configure a superscope containing all the IP address ranges.

    D. Configure a superscope for each range of IP addresses.

11. One of the DHCP clients on the network has reported errors in communicating with other hosts on the network. You determine that the client is using an IP address of 169.254.1.10. How can you manually renew the IP address and attempt to lease one from a DHCP server?

    A. `ipconfig`

    B. `ipconfig /lease`

    C. `ipconfig /renew`

    D. `ipconfig /restore`

12. Which of the following clients support dynamic update of their own A records with the DNS server?

    A. Windows 95

    B. Windows ME

    C. Windows 2000

    D. Windows XP

Troubleshooting DHCP

13. John is the network administrator of a Windows Server 2003 network. He is installing the DHCP service on a Windows Server 2003 member server, and configures the scope and the required scope options. When he attempts to authorize the DHCP server, the operation fails. Which group must John be a member of in order the authorize a DHCP server within Active Directory?

    A. Administrators

    B. Domain Admins

    C. DHCP Administrators

    D. DHCP Users

    E. Enterprise Admins

14. David is planning the implementation of DHCP on his company network. There are 5 subnets. A single DHCP server will be used and the DHCP relay agent will be enabled on those subnets that do not have a DHCP server. Some of the workstations will be required to lease the same IP address so client reservations will be configured. When planning for optional parameters, David is trying to recall the order in which they are applied. Which of the following is correct?

    A. Client, class, scope, server

    B. Class, client, server, scope

    C. Scope, server, class, client

    D. Server, scope, class, client

15. Mary is the network administrator of a Windows Server 2003 network. There is a single DHCP server used by all workstations on the network. Mary enables audit logging to monitor and troubleshoot DHCP. What is the default location where the audit logs are stored?

    A. %systemroot%\System32\DHCP

    B. %systemroot%\DHCP

    C. %systemroot%\DHCP\Logging

    D. %systemroot%\System32\DHCP\Logging

Optimizing DHCP

16. Joe has installed a DHCP server on the network. The network consists of both Windows 95 and Windows XP clients. The DHCP server is configured with default settings. Joe soon discovers that the Windows XP clients are updating their own A records with the DNS server while the records for the Windows 95 clients are not being updated. What is causing the problem and how can it be resolved?

    A. The Windows 95 clients do not support dynamic updates and must be upgraded to Windows XP.

    B. The DHCP relay agent is not configured and must be added.

    C. The Windows 95 clients are not configured to perform updates and must be configured to do so through the properties of TCP/IP.

    D. The DHCP server is not configured to perform updates for legacy clients and must be configured to do so through the DHCP server's properties dialog box.

17. Which of the following tools can be used to monitor the real-time performance of the DHCP service?

    A. Network Monitor

    B. System Monitor

    C. Performance Monitor

    D. DHCP Monitor

18. Which of the following IP address lease phases signifies the end of the lease process and that the client has successfully obtained an IP address?

    A. DHCPACK

    B. DHCPREQUEST

    C. DHCPOFFER

    D. DHCPEND

19. Don is the network administrator for a Windows Server 2003 network. A new subnet is being added to the existing infrastructure. Don has been asked to recommend the most cost-effective way of implementing automatic IP addressing on the new subnet. There is an existing DHCP server located on another subnet. However, the existing routers do not forward DHCP/BOOTP broadcasts. Which solution should you recommend?

    A. Add an additional DHCP server to the new subnet.

    B. Purchase routers capable of forwarding DHCP/BOOTP broadcasts.

    C. Enable the DHCP relay agent on the new subnet.

    D. Use Automatic Private IP Addressing.

20. Diane is the network administrator of a Windows Server 2003 network. She is planning the implementation of DHCP. Currently there are 6 subnets on the network. A DHCP server will be placed on one subnet and the DHCP relay agent will be enabled on the remaining subnets. Diane will have to configure the 003 Router option so all workstations are assigned the IP address of a default gateway. At which level should this option be configured?

   A. Server

   B. Scope

   C. Class

   D. Client

LAB QUESTION

FKB International has hired you to assist in planning the implementation of DHCP in one of the new branch offices. You have gathered the following information to assist you in planning a DHCP implementation:

- The head office already hosts a DHCP server.

- The new subnet will use the IP address range of 172.16.32.0/20.

- The branch office will host approximately 100 workstations.

- There will be 3 servers, two print servers, and a DNS server. All of which will be configured with static IP addresses.

- Fault tolerance is crucial. All clients should be able to obtain an IP address in the event that a DHCP server fails or if the WAN connection to the head office fails.

Based on this information, document a DHCP implementation plan for the new branch office, taking into consideration such things as DHCP server placement, fault tolerance, and scope options.

SELF TEST ANSWERS

Understanding the Dynamic Host Configuration Protocol

1. ☑ **C.** In order for a DHCP server to lease IP addresses to DHCP clients, the server must first be authorized to do so within Active Directory. DHCP servers that are configured as member servers or domain controllers must be authorized.

   ☒ **A, B** and **D. A** is incorrect because failure to activate a scope would not cause the DHCP service to fail to start. **B** is incorrect because DHCP can be installed on a domain controller, a member server, or a stand-alone server. **D** is incorrect because DHCP servers are not activated but rather authorized.

2. ☑ **D.** Each of the subnets will have different default gateways. Therefore, this 003 router option should be configured at the scope level instead of the server level.

   ☒ **A, B,** and **C. A** and **B** are incorrect, since the server is already leasing IP addresses to clients. Therefore, the server must already be authorized and the scope must be activated. **C** is incorrect because any client that is configured for DHCP can lease an IP address. They do not require any special permissions.

3. ☑ **B.** In order for clients on the remote subnets to successfully lease an IP address, the DHCP relay agent must be enabled. The relay agent will then forward the DHCP messages on behalf of the clients to the DHCP server on the remote subnet.

   ☒ **A, C,** and **D. A** and **C** are incorrect, since clients are already leasing an IP address, which means the DHCP server has been authorized and the service is started. **D** is incorrect because APIPA is used when DHCP clients cannot contact a DHCP server.

Designing DHCP

4. ☑ **D.** The server must be authorized within Active Directory, whether it is a domain controller or a member server. If the DHCP server is not authorized, the service will fail to start.

   ☒ **A, B,** and **C. A** is incorrect because although a DHCP server not configured with a scope would be unable to lease IP addresses to clients, this would not cause the DHCP service to fail. **B** is incorrect because the DHCP service can run successfully on a domain controller, member server, or stand-alone server. **C** is incorrect because DHCP servers are not activated; rather, they are authorized.

5. ☑ **C.** The lease duration determines when a client must renew its IP address lease. Configuring a shorter lease time forces clients to release their IP addresses more often, thereby ensuring that IP addresses not being used are available for other clients.

☒ **A, B**, and **D. A** is incorrect because adding a standby server will not increase the availability of IP addresses. Rather, it will increase the availability of the DHCP service itself. **B** is incorrect because increasing the lease duration should be done only when the number of IP addresses within a scope exceeds the number of DHCP clients. **D** is incorrect because configuring static IP addresses will also not increase the number of available IP addresses.

6. ☑ **B** and **C.** In order to eliminate rogue servers on the network, Windows Server 2003 uses DHCP authorization. To take advantage of this feature, DHCP must be installed on a domain controller or a member server.
   ☒ **A** and **D. A** is incorrect because DHCP cannot be installed on Windows XP. **D** is incorrect because stand-alone servers are not authorized within Active Directory.

7. ☑ **B.** By implementing distributed scopes, fault tolerance for DHCP servers can be achieved without incurring additional costs. The primary DHCP server for a subnet is configured with the majority of IP addresses for a scope. A second server, which can be on another subnet, is configured with the remaining IP addresses.
   ☒ **A, C**, and **D. A** is incorrect because although Windows clustering does offer a solution, it will require that additional hardware be purchased. **C** and **D** are incorrect because the DHCP relay agent component or multicast scopes will not increase the availability of a DHCP server.

Implementing DHCP

8. ☑ **A.** Client reservations ensure that a computer is always leased the same IP address. This allows all computers to be DHCP clients, even those that require a specific IP address.
   ☒ **B, C**, and **D. B** is incorrect because scopes define the range of IP addresses a server can lease. **C** is incorrect because static IP addressing is not necessary and does centralize the administration of IP addresses. **D** is incorrect because automatic private IP addressing is suitable only for small single-subnet networks. If the print servers are assigned a private address, they will not be accessible to other hosts. There is also a good chance the IP address of the print servers would change.

9. ☑ **B.** Using the `ipconfig` command with the `renew` parameter allows you to attempt to manually contact a DHCP server to obtain an IP address.
   ☒ **A, C**, and **D. A** is incorrect because `ipconfig /all` is used to view detailed IP configuration information of a host. **C** is incorrect because no update parameter is used with the `ipconfig` command. **D** is incorrect because `ipconfig /release` is used to relinquish the IP address currently being used.

10. ☑ **B.** A scope must be defined for each range of IP addresses.
   ☒ **A, C**, and **D. A** is incorrect because each range of IP addresses requires its own scope be configured. **C** and **D** are incorrect because superscopes are required only when a single broadcast domain hosts multiple logical subnets.

11. ☑   **C.** Using the `ipconfig` command with the `renew` parameter allows you to manually attempt to lease an IP address from a DHCP server.
      ☒   **A, B**, and **D. A** is incorrect because although this is the command used, it must be used with the correct parameter. Using the `ipconfig` command on its own will display only basic TCP/IP configuration information on the host. **B** and **D** are incorrect because the `ipconfig` command does not support these parameters.

12. ☑   **C** and **D.** Windows 2000, Windows XP, and Windows Server 2003 clients are all capable of updating their own A records with a DNS server as their IP address information changes.
      ☒   **A** and **B. A** and **B** are incorrect because these clients do not support this feature. The DHCP server must be configured to perform updates on behalf of legacy clients.

Troubleshooting DHCP

13. ☑   **E.** In order to authorize a DHCP server, you must be a member of the Enterprise Admins group.
      ☒   **A, B, C** and **D** are incorrect because members of these groups do not have sufficient privileges to authorize a DHCP server.

14. ☑   **D.** Optional DHCP parameters are applied in the following order: server, scope, class, client. This means options configured at the client level will override the same values configured at the other three levels.
      ☒   **A, B**, and **C.** These answers are incorrect because they do not represent the correct order in which optional parameters are applied.

15. ☑   **A.** The DHCP audit logs are by default stored in the %systemroot%\system32\DHCP directory.
      ☒   **B, C**, and **D.** These answers are incorrect because they do not represent the default location where the audit logs are stored.

Optimizing DHCP

16. ☑   **D.** By default, a DHCP server is not configured to perform updates on behalf of legacy clients. To change this, you must use the DNS tab found within the properties dialog box of the DHCP server.
      ☒   **A, B**, and **C. A** is incorrect because although the clients do not support this feature, the DHCP server can perform the updates for them, making it unnecessary to upgrade them. **B** is incorrect because the DHCP relay agent is used to update records. Also, that the Windows XP clients can successfully perform updates eliminates this as the problem. **C** is incorrect because you cannot configure legacy clients to perform their own updates.

17. ☑ **B.** System Monitor can be used to monitor the real-time performance of a DHCP server.
☒ **A, C,** and **D.** A is incorrect because Network Monitor is used to capture and analyze network traffic. **C** is incorrect because Performance Monitor was a tool included with Windows NT 4.0. It is now known as System Monitor in Windows 2000 and Windows Server 2003. **D** is incorrect because there is no such monitoring utility.

18. ☑ **A.** Once the client receives a DHCPACK from the DHCP server, the lease process is complete and the client has successfully leased an IP address.
☒ **B, C,** and **D.** B and C are incorrect because these phases occur earlier in the lease process, when the client is attempting to acquire an IP address. **D** is incorrect because it does not represent a phase of the IP address lease process.

19. ☑ **C.** Enabling the DHCP relay agent will allow workstations on the new subnet to obtain an IP address from a DHCP server on another subnet.
☒ **A, B,** and **D.** A and B are incorrect because both of these solution would not be the most cost effective to choose. **D** is incorrect because using APIPA would only allow workstations to communicate on their local subnet.

20. ☑ **B.** Configuring the 003 Router option at the scope level will ensure that computers on each of the subnets are configured with the IP address of the correct default gateway.
☒ **A, C,** and **D.** A is incorrect because configuring the 003 Router option at the server level would result in clients on the various subnets being given the incorrect IP address of their default gateway. **C** and **D** are incorrect because options configured at the class level allow you to apply DHCP options to a group of clients or workstations with similar needs and at the client level, options can be applied to client reservations.

LAB ANSWER

A DHCP server should be placed in the new branch office. This will ensure that clients can lease an IP address should the WAN connection to the head office go down. The local DHCP server should be configured with 80 percent of the available IP addresses. The DHCP server in the head office should be configured with the remaining 20 percent. This will ensure that clients can still lease IP addresses should the local DHCP server go down. The DHCP relay agent must also be enabled for clients to obtain an IP address from the remote DHCP server if necessary.

Optional parameters on the local DHCP server can be configured at the server or scope level. Optional parameters on the remote DHCP server must be configured at the scope level. Optional parameters should include the IP addresses of the default gateway and DNS server.

When configuring the scopes on each server, the IP addresses for the servers must be excluded to avoid IP address conflicts.

MICROSOFT CERTIFIED SYSTEMS ENGINEER

3

Planning and Maintaining Windows Server 2003 DNS

CERTIFICATION OBJECTIVE 3.01

Planning a DNS Strategy

Every computer on a TCP/IP network must be assigned an address that uniquely identifies the computer on the network. These addresses, referred to IP addresses, are decimal numbers that can be used to determine a computer's location on the network. Since IP addresses are represented in dotted-decimal notation (a set of four three-digit decimal numbers), they can be difficult for users to remember, especially when there are a large number of computers on the network. Instead, we can use friendly names, what are called hostnames, to locate other computers on the network. In order for this system to work, special services such as the Domain Name Service (DNS) are required to translate these hostnames for us into the corresponding network addresses.

DNS is not a new concept but has been around on the Internet for many years. Prior to DNS, Hosts files were used to map hostnames to IP addresses. The problem with this is that Hosts files needed to be manually updated. Considering how fast the Internet has grown in size, I am sure you see where the problem lies: hosts files became pretty much impossible to keep up to date. As a result, the more efficient DNS system was introduced.

If you have worked with older versions of Windows such as Windows NT 4.0, you will be familiar with the Network Basic Input/Output System (NetBIOS). NetBIOS names were used to identify computers on the network and the services they were running. Name resolution for NetBIOS names was done using LMHOSTS files or NetBIOS name servers. The LMHOSTS file is a static text file that mapped the NetBIOS names to IP addresses. Of course, the limitation of using this method for name resolution is that the file needed to be statically updated. Microsoft introduced its own version of a NetBIOS name service, known as the Windows Internet Name Service (WINS). Since NetBIOS is no longer required with a pure Windows 2000 or Windows Server 2003 environment, WINS is used only for backward compatibility; in this capacity, it remains an important service. However, DNS is the required service in a Windows Server 2003 domain. Many services, including Active Directory, are dependent on DNS.

The following chapter will introduce you to the DNS Service included with Windows Server 2003. You will learn the fundamental concepts behind DNS, what needs to be considered before implementing the service, and how to implement it. The chapter begins by discussing the important concepts behind DNS, some of the issues that need to be considered when implementing it, and how to maintain and troubleshoot the service.

Understanding DNS

Traditionally, DNS is used to provide name resolution services to clients. One of the major changes since Windows NT 4.0 is that Windows Server 2003 now relies on DNS as a locator service, as opposed to just resolving hostnames to IP addresses. Operating system services such as Kerberos now use DNS as well.

In Windows NT 4.0, the NetBIOS name service is used. A NetBIOS name consisted of 16 characters, where the first 15 characters identified a specific computer on the network and the sixteenth character (a hexadecimal character) identifies a network service running on that computer. Each computer on the network will dynamically register one or more NetBIOS names (depending on the services it was running) with a NetBIOS name server. The NetBIOS name server could then answer queries to resolve the NetBIOS names to IP addresses.

Due to the limitations of using NetBIOS, Microsoft has moved away from this system beginning with the release of Windows 2000 and continuing with Windows Server 2003. Now, in order to successfully implement Active Directory, DNS is required. Keep in mind, however, that NetBIOS is still supported by Windows Server 2003 to remain backward compatible with legacy clients such as Windows 98 and Windows NT 4.0.

Windows NT 4.0 was the first Windows operating system that included an official "DNS" component. The version of DNS included with Windows Server 2003 is greatly enhanced and includes a number of new features:

- **SRV records**   These records are used to locate services running on computers, much like the sixteenth character used in a NetBIOS name environment.

- **Dynamic updates**   Using this feature, resource records no longer need to be manually added to the DNS database. Windows 2000, Windows XP, and Windows Server 2003 clients can dynamically update their own resource records with a DNS server. For legacy clients (pre–Windows 2000), a DHCP server running Windows 2000 or Windows Server 2003 can be configured to perform updates on their behalf. Pre–Windows 2000 clients do not support dynamic updates.

- **Secure updates**   This feature is an extension to the dynamic updates. With secure updates, only those computers that are authorized can make modifications to the DNS database.

- **Incremental zone transfers**   Zone information can be replicated between DNS servers for fault tolerance and increased availability. With incremental zone transfers, only new and updated information is replicated between DNS servers, as opposed to having to replicate an entire zone file regardless of what has been changed.

■ **Active Directory**   One of the most important new features is the ability to use DNS with Active Directory. Traditionally, updates to a zone file must occur on the primary DNS server and then be replicated to the secondary servers. That DNS is integrated with Active Directory means that changes to the zone file can be made on any DNS server and then replicated.

Name Resolution

Now that you have a general idea behind the history of the DNS service and what it is used for, let's take a look at how name resolution occurs. A fully qualified domain name (FQDN) identifies a particular host within a DNS hierarchy. The FQDN can be broken down into different levels indicating the host, the domain, and the type of organization, which are written from right to left. For example, with the FQDN of srv01.klnsweep.net, the .net is the top-level domain, which indicates the type of organization, such as a commercial organization (.com) or an educational organization (.edu). The second-level domain (klnsweep in the preceding example) identifies a specific domain. The third level may identify a subdomain or a specific host in that domain such as srv01. In any case, a DNS server is required to resolve these FQDNs to IP addresses.

Odds are you have often typed in an Internet address, or Universal Resource Locator (URL), to open a web site. Before you can access the web site, the name must be resolved to an IP address behind the scenes. This is done by querying one or more DNS servers. There are three different types of queries that can be performed: recursive, iterative, and inverse.

Recursive Queries   With a *recursive* query, when the client sends a name resolution request to a DNS server, it must respond with the information or return an error message that the requested information does not exist. If the DNS server is unable to resolve the request, it cannot refer the client to another DNS server.

Iterative Queries   When an *iterative* query is performed, the DNS server will return an answer to the client. This may be the requested information or a referral to another DNS server. For example, when a user enters **www.klnsweep.net** into a browser, the following process occurs:

1. The client sends the request to a DNS server for the IP address of www.klnsweep.net. The request may be sent to a DNS server on the local network or a DNS server hosted by an ISP.

2. The DNS server uses its local cache and zones to determine if it can resolve the request.

3. If no entry exists in the cache for the hostname and if there is no zone information matching the DNS client's request, the request is sent to a root name server.

4. The root name server will respond with the IP address of a name server responsible for the top-level domain within the FQDN.

5. The local DNS server queries the top-level DNS server to map the request to an IP address. This net name server will refer the DNS server to another name server authoritative for the klnsweep.net domain.

6. The local DNS server sends the query for www.knlsweep.net to the klnsweep.net name server.

7. The klnsweep.net name server responds with the IP address. The local DNS server returns the information to the DNS client that made the initial request.

on the Job   *You can use the Monitoring tab from the DNS server's properties dialog box to verify the configuration of DNS by manually sending queries against the server. You can perform a simple query that uses the DNS client on the local server to query the DNS service to return the best possible answer. You can also perform a recursive query where the local DNS server can query other DNS servers to resolve a query.*

Inverse Queries   With an *inverse* query, a DNS client sends a request to a DNS server to return the hostname that is associated with a specific IP address. For example, a client may query for the hostname associated with the IP address of 192.168.0.1. A DNS server can use the information stored within a reverse lookup zone to return the information to the client. Inverse queries are also used in conjunction with mail servers. A mail server can be configured to do a reverse lookup on a server to ensure that a server it is receiving mail from is valid.

Reverse lookup is used to map a known IP address to a computer name. It is the opposite of performing a forward lookup. The reverse lookup zone stores the PTR records that are used to resolve IP addresses to computer names.

PTR records are contained within the reverse lookup zone and provide the IP address–to–hostname mappings. A PTR record is created by reversing the numbers within the IP address. The string "in-addr.arpa" is added to the end to create the PTR record. For example, the PTR record for WRK01 with an IP address of 192.168.0.28 may look as follows:

28.0.168.192.in-addr.arpa. IN PTR wrk01.bayside.net

DNS Servers

Before you install DNS, you should have an understanding of the different roles in which a DNS server can be configured. The three roles a DNS server can be configured in are

- Primary
- Secondary
- Caching-only

A DNS server can function in more than one role. For example, a single DNS server can be a primary DNS server for one zone and act as a secondary for a zone hosted on another DNS server.

Primary DNS Servers   A *primary* DNS server hosts the main, working copy of a specific zone file locally. A *zone file* consists of the various resource records for a specific domain. The information within a zone file is used to resolve hostnames to IP addresses. If a change needs to be made to the zone file, such as the addition of a resource record, it must be done on the primary DNS server (the changes are then replicated to secondary DNS servers as described in the next section).

Secondary DNS Servers   A *secondary* DNS server obtains the zone file from another DNS server. It hosts only a read-only copy of the zone file, which is kept up to date through zone transfers. The DNS server that the secondary server receives zone information from is referred to as a *master* name server. This can be a primary DNS server or another secondary DNS server.

As already mentioned earlier in the chapter, Windows Server 2003 DNS supports incremental zone transfers where only the changes made to a zone file are replicated. The version of DNS included with Windows NT 4.0 supported only full zone transfers, where the entire zone file had to be replicated regardless of the changes made. The benefit of performing incremental zone transfers is that it reduces the network traffic associated with keeping zone files on secondary servers up to date.

Let's take a look at an example to help clarify the difference between the two roles. If Server1 is the primary DNS server for klnsweep.net, it would maintain the working copy of the zone file and any changes would be made on this server. Server2 could be configured as a secondary server for klnsweep.net. When a change to the zone file is made on Server1, these changes would be replicated to Server2.

Implementing secondary DNS servers provides a number of benefits, including

- **Fault tolerance**   Should the primary DNS server go offline, the secondary DNS server can still provide name resolution services for the zone, although no changes can be made to the zone file until the primary DNS server is back online.

- **Less network traffic**   If branch offices are connected to a main office using WAN links, name resolution traffic across the connection can be reduced by placing a secondary DNS server in each location. Clients can then resolve queries locally.

- **Load balancing**   The secondary server can respond to name resolution requests as well, in turn reducing the load placed on the primary DNS server.

Caching-Only Server   DNS servers have a local cache file known as cache.dns. Whenever a DNS server resolves a query, it places the information within the cache. The next time a request for the same hostname is received, the information can be retrieved from the local cache instead of having to resolve the name using other DNS servers.

The difference between caching-only servers and primary or secondary servers is that caching-only servers do not store any zone information. Just as its name indicates, this type of DNS server only caches results. It resolves hostnames using either the cache or other DNS servers, places the results in the local cache, and returns the results to the requesting client.

Caching-only servers are useful when you want to implement a DNS server but do not want an increase in traffic from zone transfers. In the beginning, you will see a slight increase in traffic as the cache file is built up. But there will be no traffic generated from zone transfers, because the server does not host any zone files.

e x a m

watch

Be sure you understand when to choose a caching-only server. This type of DNS configuration is useful in remote locations where **you want to provide local DNS name resolution but do not want an increase in network traffic resulting from zone transfers.**

EXERCISE 3-1

MasterSim 3-1 ON THE CD

Planning DNS Server Roles

In this exercise, you will use the information within the scenario to determine the type of NDS server role to implement.

AbleCom is a large consulting company. Rapid growth has forced the company to open a new branch office in a remote location. The branch office will be connected to the head office using a slow WAN link. As the network administrator, you have been asked to make a recommendation as to how DNS should be implemented within the branch office. DNS is the only name resolution service implemented on the network. The head office currently has three domain controllers configured as DNS servers. Your managers are concerned about network traffic on the slow link as well as being able to provide an acceptable response time for branch office users when resolving hostnames. Given these concerns and the existing configuration, how would you implement DNS in the new branch office?

1. Should a DNS server be placed in the branch office? Explain your answer.

2. If yes, what type of DNS server will be placed in the branch office and what impact will it have? If no DNS server will be placed in the branch office, how will branch office users resolve hostnames?

Now that you are familiar with the different DNS server roles, Exercise 3-2 will walk you through the process of installing the service. DNS can be installed in three different ways: it can be added during the installation of the operating system, using the Configure Your Server Wizard, or by using the Add or Remove Programs applet within the Control Panel.

EXERCISE 3-2

Installing DNS

In this exercise, you will install the DNS service on a computer running Windows Server 2003, assuming that the service was not installed during the installation of the operating system.

1. Click Start, point to Control Panel, and click Add or Remove Programs.
2. Click Add/Remove Windows Components.
3. From the list of Windows Components, select Networking Services and click the Details button.
4. Select Domain Name System (DNS) and click OK.

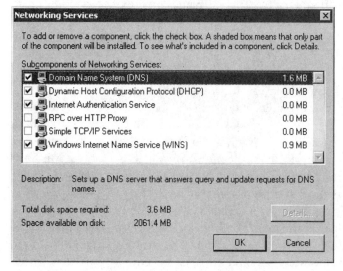

5. Click Next. If prompted, insert the Windows Server 2003 installation CD.
6. Click Finish.

If you install DNS using the Configure Your Server Wizard, once the service is installed, the wizard will walk you through creating the initial forward lookup zone. This approach is sometimes simpler for novice administrators.

INSIDE THE EXAM

Caching-Only DNS Servers

Caching-only DNS servers can sometimes be difficult to understand. Students often ask why you would want to use them and when it would be appropriate to configure this type of DNS server (as well as the "how" of configuring it).

Since you are likely to encounter exam questions surrounding this topic, it deserves a little more attention and a more detailed explanation. First of all, as the name certainly implies, the sole purpose of this type of DNS server is to resolve queries and cache the results.

Remember, every DNS server has a local cache. When queries are resolved, the results are stored for future use. It is kind of like adding a web site to your list of favorites. When you find a web site you are looking for, it is much more efficient to add it to your favorites instead of having to search for the site when you need to access it again. So when a DNS server resolves a query the first time, it stores the results for future use. When another DNS client requests the same information, it is far more efficient to get the information locally than having to query other servers to find it—both reducing network traffic and decreasing the amount of time it takes to resolve queries for clients.

So the next question is, when would you want to use a caching-only server? Well, take for instance an organization that consists of multiple sites connected together by WAN links. Installing a primary or secondary DNS server at each site will increase traffic over the WAN link because zone transfers can be intense.

Not placing a DNS server at each site reduces availability. If the WAN link is unavailable, clients are unable to resolve hostnames. The work-around is to implement caching-only servers. Now keep in mind that these servers have no zone information, and when they are initially configured, the cache is empty; it must be built up over time. So in the beginning, you may not see a decrease in traffic until the DNS server has time to build up the contents of the cache. But once it does, many requests will be resolved locally.

Any responses a caching-only server receives from other DNS servers will contain more than just the IP address of the hostname being resolved. Additional information is included in the response that is used to tell the caching-only server how long the record can remain in the cache. So once a record is cached, the Time to Live (TTL) associated with the record determines when the record must be purged from the cache. When a record is cached, the countdown to the TTL begins, and once the value reaches zero, the record is removed from the cache. This ensures that the information within the cache is correct.

The last question is, how exactly does one configure a caching-only server? Well, simply install the DNS service and verify that the root hints are properly configured (the root hints enable a DNS server to locate other DNS servers to assist in resolving queries). No zone information is required.

DNS Server Placement   Now that you are familiar with the different types of DNS servers that can be configured, you also need to consider where on the network your DNS servers should be located. The main goal here is to provide clients with optimal response time when resolving hostnames (of course, you also want to consider network traffic as well).

In a network that is routed, you have two options. Ideally, you want to be able to place a DNS server on each subnet. Or if the subnets are connected via high-speed links, you can place all the DNS servers in a central location (which may be more ideal for administrators). However, in choosing the second option, the loss of a connection can mean clients are temporarily without name resolution services.

If zones are not integrated within Active Directory, secondary servers should be used for fault tolerance and increased availability. Ideally, the primary DNS servers should be located near those who are responsible for administering them. Consider placing the secondary servers on subnets that contain the most hosts or on those that generate the most name resolution traffic. For those subnets that generate a large amount of traffic, you may want to place both primary and secondary servers for load-balancing purposes.

You also need to consider if there are any remote sites connected to the main sites via slow WAN connections. In these situations, caching-only servers are ideal. Once the cache is built up, there will not be as much need to resolve queries over the WAN connection. The WAN link will also not be used for zone transfers (which can generate a large amount of network traffic), because the server does not store any zone information.

If you are looking to reduce the amount of traffic on a WAN link generated by DNS queries, caching-only servers can offer a viable solution. Initially, you may not see a reduction in network traffic, because the cache is empty at first and must be built up as the DNS server resolves client queries.

DNS Zones

Once the DNS service is added, you can begin configuring zones (except in the case of a caching-only server, which does not host any zone information). The DNS server role will determine where the zone information is retrieved. For example, a secondary DNS server will be retrieving the zone file from a master name server, which means the zone file will already be created.

A DNS *zone* is a section of the DNS database that is administered as a single unit. It maintains the configuration information for the zone as well as the various types of resource records. A zone can consist of records from a single domain or multiple domains. Any DNS server that hosts a zone file can resolve queries for the corresponding domain/domains. Keep in mind, however, that domains in the same zone must be contiguous. For example, sales.bayside.net and bayside.net can be in the same zone, but riverside.net and bayside.net cannot.

Resource records are stored within a forward lookup zone and, optionally, a reverse lookup zone. The forward lookup zone is used to resolve queries for the IP address associated with a specific hostname. Conversely, the reverse lookup zone does just the opposite of this. It allows for queries to be sent to a DNS server to map an IP address to the associated hostname. This is also referred to as a reverse query. Reverse queries are often used to troubleshoot DNS using the NSLookup command.

There are various types of zones that can be created. Before you begin configuring zones, you should know the differences among them and when each should be implemented. Windows Server 2003 supports four different types of zones (see Figure 3-1):

- **Primary zone**   A primary zone stores the master copy of the zone file locally in a text file. Any updates must be performed on the primary zone.

- **Secondary zone**   Secondary zones are configured for fault tolerance and load balancing. The zone data is obtained from a master name server, which can be a primary or secondary server. When you configure a secondary zone, you must supply the IP address of at least one server from which the zone information will be retrieved (see Figure 3-2).

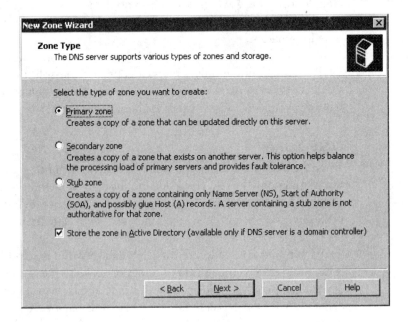

FIGURE 3-1

Zone types supported by Windows Server 2003

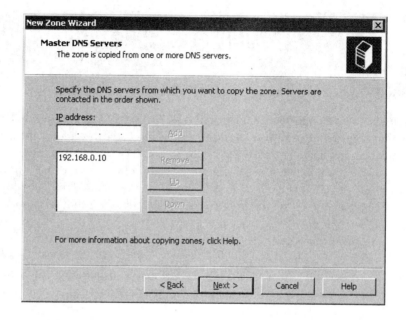

FIGURE 3-2

Specifying the master name server for a secondary zone

■ **Active Directory integrated zone** This zone type stores its information within Active Directory. Doing so allows zone information to be replicated using Active Directory. You can also take advantage of secure updates. Keep in mind that Active Directory integrated zones can only be domain controllers running DNS.

■ **Stub zone** This type of zone is new in Windows Server 2003. A stub zone maintains a list of authoritative name servers only for a particular zone. The purpose of a stub zone is to ensure that a DNS server hosting a parent zone is aware of authoritative DNS servers for its child zones.

ⓦatch   *A new feature of Windows   to encounter an exam question pertaining*
Server 2003 is the stub zone. Be prepared   to this topic.

INSIDE THE EXAM

Stub Zones

If you like to challenge new certification exams as they are released, you know that new features and upgrades are often popular topics on the exam. Since stub zones are a new feature introduced in Windows Server 2003, be prepared to encounter at least one exam question on them. And since it is a new feature, one that was not included with Windows 2000, it deserves some added attention.

Stub zones are used to keep track of which DNS servers are authoritative for a domain. The root DNS server for an organization can be used to determine which DNS servers are authoritative over which domains.

So how exactly are stub zones beneficial? Well, when you use zone delegation, stub zones can be used to determine which servers are authoritative for zones in the DNS namespace, as opposed to having to contact the primary DNS server that is authoritative for the parent zone. In other words, the stub zones are used only to determine what servers are authoritative for a particular zone. For example, if the subdomain sales.klnsweep.net is delegated to a different DNS server from its parent, a stub zone can be used to determine which DNS server is authoritative for that zone instead of having to contact the DNS server that is authoritative for the klnsweep.net zone.

watch *Stub zones and primary zones can be stored within Active Directory. Secondary zones must be stored on the local machine only.*

Active Directory Integration

As previously mentioned, DNS zones can be integrated within Active Directory, meaning the zone information is stored within the Active Directory database rather than stored locally in a text file. When deciding what type of zone to configure, it is important that you are aware of the benefits associated with Active Directory integrated zones.

■ **Multimaster replication** Normally, DNS updates are performed using a single master update model. This means that updates occur on a single DNS server that is authoritative for the domain and are then replicated to secondary DNS servers. When zone information is stored within Active Directory, a multimaster update model is used and any DNS server acting as a domain controller becomes authoritative for the zone. Updates can then be performed on any domain controller running the DNS service. This also eliminates the primary DNS server as a single point of failure, as it is in the single master update model.

- **Simplified administration** By storing zone information in Active Directory, you can take advantage of the Active Directory replication topology. This eliminates the need to plan and administer two separate replication topologies. Zone information and directory information can be replicated using a single topology.

- **More efficient replication** Information stored within Active Directory is replicated on a per-property basis, which means that only the updates and changes are replicated.

EXERCISE 3-3

Creating a Forward Lookup Zone

In this exercise, you will create a new Active Directory integrated zone on a computer running Windows Server 2003. This exercise assumes that the computer is configured as a domain controller.

1. Click Start, point to Administrative Tools, and click DNS.

2. Under your DNS server, right-click Forward Lookup Zones and click New Zone.

3. Click Next at the Welcome To The New Zone Wizard screen.

4. Select Primary Zone and ensure the option to Store The Zone In Active Directory is selected. Click Next.

5. From the Active Directory Zone Replication Scope screen, leave the default option selected to replicate zone data to all DNS servers in the Active Directory domain. Click Next.

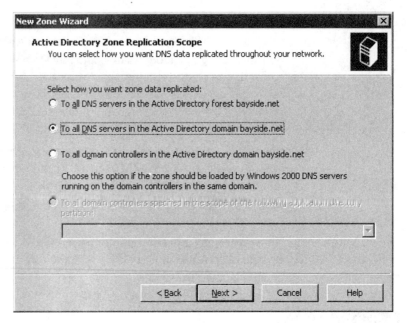

6. Type in a name for the zone, such as **klnsweep.net**. Click Next.

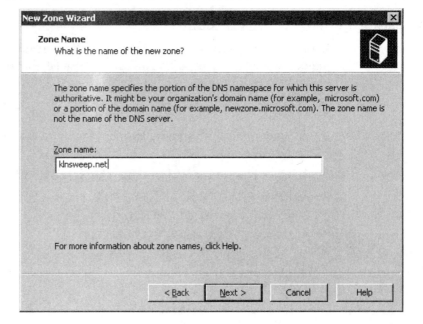

7. From the Dynamic Updates screen, select Allow Both Nonsecure And Secure Dynamic Updates. Click Next.

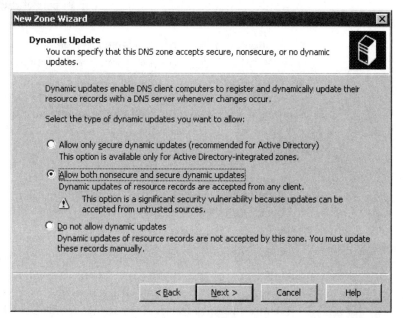

8. Click Finish. The new zone should now appear within the Forward Lookup Zones container.

Zone Delegation

Delegation is the process of designating a portion of the DNS namespace to another zone. It gives administrators a way of dividing a namespace among multiple zones. For example, an administrator may place the klnsweep.net domain in one zone and place the sales.klnsweep.net subdomain in another, delegated, zone. Normally, the klnsweep.net zone would contain all the records for the sales subdomain if it were not delegated. With delegation, the klnsweep.net zone contains information for only klnsweep.net, as well as records to the name servers authoritative for the sales.klnsweep.net subdomain, but the host entries for any machines in sales.klnsweep.net are contained only on the delegated server.

Zone delegation can provide the following advantages:

- It allows you to delegate management of part of the DNS namespace to other departments or locations.
- It allows you to distribute a large DNS database across multiple servers for load balancing, faster name resolution, and increased performance.
- It allows you to extend the namespace for business expansion.

Before you delegate a zone, all the subdomains must first be listed in the current zone. Once they've been added, you can use the following procedure to create a zone delegation:

1. From within the DNS management console, right-click the subdomain you want to delegate and select New Delegation. The New Delegation Wizard opens. Click Next.

2. Type a name for the delegated domain in the Delegated Domain text box. Click Next.

3. Click Add to specify the name servers that will host the delegated domain. The New Resource Record dialog box appears, allowing you to specify the names and IP addresses of the name servers. Click OK. Click Next.

4. Click Finish.

SCENARIO & SOLUTION

Are secondary DNS servers required?	No, although it is highly recommended that you have at least one secondary server for fault tolerance. Implementing a single DNS server creates a single point of failure.
Should zones be converted to Active Directory integrated?	Yes. When at all possible, zones should be converted to Active Directory integrated to take advantage of features such as the multimaster replication model and secure updates.
What types of zones can be converted to Active Directory integrated?	Both primary and stub zones can be converted to Active Directory integrated. Secondary zones must be stored locally.
What are the requirements for using Active Directory integrated zones?	The only requirement is that the DNS service must be running on a domain controller.

EXERCISE 3-4

Planning for DNS Zones

In this exercise, you will use the information within the scenario to plan the implementation of DNS zones.

Klnsweep is an organization that provides various cleaning services to large corporations. Due to its rapid growth in popularity, a new branch office is being added in the suburb of a major city center. The branch office will be connected to the head office via a T1 link.

The head office currently has three Windows Server 2003 domain controllers. A fourth domain controller will be added to the new branch office. The organization currently uses klnsweep.net for both its Internet and forest root domain name. Your job is to plan the DNS zones.

1. Identify the DNS needs of users in the new branch office.

2. Identify the type of DNS zone you would create and explain why.

3. Explain how you can secure the DNS zone.

4. What impact will your implementation have on network traffic on the T1 connection?

Resource Records

Once a zone has been created, it can be populated with *resource records*. Remember, if your clients are all running Windows Server 2003, Windows XP, or Windows 2000 and the zone is configured for dynamic updates, the clients can add and update their own resource records. You can also manually add resource records to a zone file through the DNS management console. Resource records appear as entries within the DNS server database files. Each resource record contains information about a specific machine such as the IP address or specific network services running. The type of information within a resource record will depend on the type of resource record that is created. For example, an A (address) record contains the IP address associated with a specific computer. It is used to map a hostname to an IP address.

There are a number of resource records that can be created. Table 3-1 summarizes some of the more common resource records you may come across. To view all of the resource records supported by Windows Server 2003 DNS, right-click a zone and select Other New Records (see Figure 3-3).

FIGURE 3-3

Resource records
supported by
Windows Server
2003

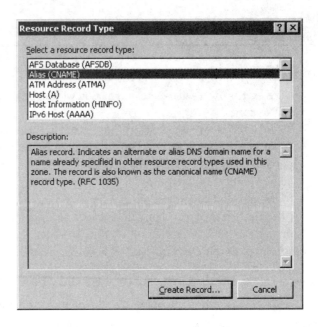

As already mentioned, resource records can be created using the DNS management
console. To create a new host record, simply right-click the zone in which you want
to create the record and select the New Host (A) option. In the New Host dialog
box, type the name and IP address for the host (see Figure 3-4). To automatically
create a pointer record, select the Create Associated Pointer (PTR) Record check
box. PTR records can be created automatically only if the reverse lookup zone exists.
Keep in mind that if you want to use the NSLookup command, which is useful for
troubleshooting hostnames, the necessary PTR records must exist.

TABLE 3-1 Common DNS Resource Records

Resource Record	Description
Host Address (A) Record	Maps a DNS name to an IP address.
Mail Exchanger (MX) Record	Routes messages to a specified mail exchanger for a specified DNS domain name.
Pointer (PTR) Records	Points to a location in the DNS namespace. PTR records are normally used for reverse lookups.
Alias (CNAME) Record	Specifies another DNS domain name for a name that is already referenced in another resource record.

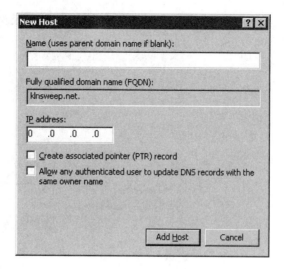

FIGURE 3-4

Creating a new
host record

Dynamic DNS

Windows 2003 Server, Windows XP, and Windows 2000 clients can interact directly with a DNS server. With dynamic updates, clients can automatically register their own resource records with a DNS server and update them as changes occur.

Dynamic updates greatly reduce the administration associated with maintaining resource records by eliminating the need for administrators to manually update these records. In terms of DHCP, with a short lease duration configured, the IP addresses assigned to DNS clients can change frequently. If dynamic updates are not enabled, an administrator can end up spending a large amount of time updating zone information. Additionally, there is always the chance for human error when updates are carried out manually. Dynamic updates can be enabled on a per-zone basis (see Figure 3-5).

Dynamic updates basically provide the following advantages:

- DHCP servers can dynamically register records for clients. This is particularly important because DHCP servers can perform updates on behalf of clients that do not support dynamic updates, such as Windows 95, 98, or NT 4 clients.

- The administrative overhead is reduced because A records and PTR records can be dynamically updated by Windows DNS clients that support this option. An A (address) record lists the IP address associated with a specific machine, while a PTR record lists the specific machine associated with an IP address.

- Domain controllers can be dynamically registered through SRV records.

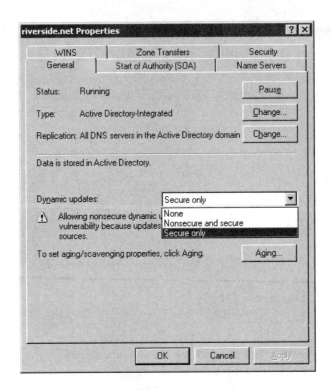

FIGURE 3-5

Enabling or
disabling dynamic
updates

If you are experiencing problems with dynamic updates, verify that the zone is properly configured, that the clients on the network support the dynamic update feature, and that dynamic updates have not been disabled on the client side (for Windows 2000 clients and later).

Planning a Namespace Strategy

Another aspect you need to consider before deploying DNS is the namespace strategy. At this point, there are a few things you need to consider, such as

- Do you already have a DNS name that is registered on the Internet?
- Will the DNS servers be used on the private network or on the Internet?
- Are you implementing DNS to support Active Directory?
- Are there any particular requirements that need to be adhered to when assigning hostnames to computers on the network?

Determining the answers to these questions will certainly assist in implementing an appropriate naming strategy. In any case, when planning the namespace strategy, you basically have three different options. Of course, the option that you select will be dependent on the answers to these questions.

Using the Same Public and Private DNS Domain Name

Most organizations these days have an Internet presence, meaning they have a name registered on the Internet—for example, klnsweep.net. You can choose to use the same name for your Active Directory namespace, which means you will be sharing your private namespace on the Internet. There will thus be no difference between the internal and external DNS names; the split between the two ultimately occurs at the firewall. External resources are resolved using the public DNS servers, and internal resources are resolved using the private DNS servers. Any external resources that must be accessible to users on the private network must have resource records manually added to the internal DNS servers. Likewise, any internal resources that must be accessible from the Internet must be defined on the external DNS servers.

For example, suppose you decide to use bayside.net on the internal network, which is also the name being used on the Internet. Your local ISP hosts your web server and your mail server. The external DNS servers will resolve names such as mail.bayside.net and www.bayside.net. However, unless additional records are created on the internal DNS servers, queries for www.bayside.net made by a user on the private network will fail (if the user is configured to query the internal DNS server). The user's name resolution request will never be forwarded to the Internet-based DNS server, because as far as the internal servers know, they are authoritative for bayside.net. Additional records must be created on the internal DNS servers, mapping www and mail to external IP addresses.

If you are using this namespace strategy, you must also take care with dynamic updates. Since you do not want your domain controllers to register themselves with the external DNS servers, be sure to turn off dynamic updates outside the firewall (if these DNS servers support dynamic updates).

Using Subdomains

Again, if an organization has an Internet name registered, you can use a subdomain for the internal Active Directory namespace. For example, if an organization has registered klnsweep.net, you can begin your Active Directory namespace with ad.klnsweep.net. This creates a distinction between the internal and external namespaces. ad.klnsweep.net will be your Active Directory root domain. Any child domains will inherit this namespace.

Using Different Internal and External DNS Domain Names

The third option is to implement an internal namespace that is completely different from the external namespace. Doing so creates a very clear distinction between internal and external resources. This strategy requires registering a second domain name and may get confusing for users, as their logon IDs may be different from their corporate e-mail addresses.

DNS Integration

When planning a DNS strategy, be sure to confirm that the version of DNS included with Windows Server 2003 will integrate with the other DNS servers. In some cases, a network will already have a DNS implementation and you may be required to add a Windows Server 2003 DNS server to the infrastructure. Before you do, it's critical that you know how DNS will integrate with these existing versions. For example, if you were installing a Windows Server 2003 domain, how would an existing BIND DNS server function within the domain?

You also need to consider the existing name service used for resolution. Many networks today still implement WINS servers to support legacy clients such as Windows NT 4.0 or clients that still use NetBIOS names. Since Active Directory requires the use of DNS, you will need to be aware how Windows Server 2003 DNS can integrate with WINS servers.

Windows Server 2003 DNS with Other Versions

Many networks already have a DNS infrastructure in place. And as the old saying goes, if it ain't broke, then don't fix it. Many administrators may be reluctant to switch over to another DNS server when the infrastructure currently in place is fine. However, if you plan to implement Windows Server 2003 Active Directory, you will require at least one additional DNS server. In such cases, you should be aware of how Windows Server 2003 DNS will interoperate with other versions of DNS.

BIND   One of the most prevalent DNS services is known as the Berkeley Internet Name Daemon (BIND), which is Unix based. Even those organizations that are predominantly Windows based implement BIND and are often hesitant to migrate over. Fortunately, Windows Server 2003 can integrate with BIND servers and has been tested with the following versions of BIND:

- BIND 4.9.7
- BIND 8.1.2

- BIND 8.2
- BIND 9.1.0

Watch

Be prepared to encounter questions about Windows Server 2003 coexisting with BIND servers. Make sure you are familiar with which versions of BIND support which features. For example, BIND 4.9.7 will support SRV records but not dynamic updates.

There are various versions of BIND, and the version in use will determine how it can interoperate with Windows Server 2003 DNS. As mentioned earlier, Windows Server 2003 uses SRV records to locate domain controllers. SRV records are mandatory, and in order for another version of DNS to coexist with Windows Server 2003, it must support this feature. BIND versions 4.9.7 and later support SRV records.

Although not mandatory, it is recommended that DNS servers support dynamic updates. This eliminates the need to manually update the zone files. BIND version 8.2.2 provides support for dynamic updates.

Other DNS Servers   Microsoft Windows NT 4.0 DNS will support SRV records if service pack 4 has been installed. Also, Windows NT 4.0 DNS will not perform dynamic updates. This means that the Active Directory SRV records must be manually updated every time a domain controller, global catalog server, or site is added or deleted. Windows 2000 DNS servers support both SRV records and dynamic updates and so are capable of functioning within a Windows Server 2003 environment.

Windows Server 2003 domain controllers must use a DNS server with SRV record support. Dynamic update is strongly recommended, because changes in the domain controllers or Active Directory may require updates to SRV record information. Therefore the primary DNS server must support dynamic updates.

DNS and WINS

Windows Server 2003 DNS provides the ability to use WINS servers to resolve hostnames if they cannot be resolved using information within zone files. WINS lookup is useful in a mixed environment. For example, if you have some Unix-based clients that only use DNS and other clients the require the use of NetBIOS, you can enable WINS lookup so that the DNS clients can resolve the names of WINS clients.

So how exactly do WINS and DNS integrate? If a client sends a query to its local DNS server for HostA.sales.klnsweep.net, the process outlined earlier in the chapter occurs. When the DNS server that is authoritative for the sales.klnsweep.net domain receives the request from the original DNS server, it attempts to resolve the name using cache and zone information. If it cannot find the information, the host part of the name (in this case HostA) is separated from the fully qualified domain name. The request for HostA is then sent to the WINS server. If the WINS server can resolve the name, the information is sent back to the DNS server. The IP address of HostA is returned to the original DNS server and then to the requesting client.

Keep in mind that by default, WINS lookup is not enabled. This feature can be enabled on a per-zone basis from the zone's properties dialog box (see Figure 3-6).

on the **Job** *In a pure Windows 2000 and Windows Server 2003 environment, WINS is not required and therefore you would not need to use WINS lookup. This feature would be used only in an environment that needs to support legacy clients that use NetBIOS.*

Planning Zone Replication

Zone transfers are performed to make zone information available on more than one DNS server to provide high availability and fault tolerance. If a single server is used, name resolutions for the zone can fail if the server is unavailable. How zone information is replicated will depend on whether the zone is Active Directory integrated or not.

FIGURE 3-6

Enabling WINS
lookup

riverside.net Properties

General | Start of Authority (SOA) | Name Servers
WINS | Zone Transfers | Security

You can use WINS to resolve names not found by querying the DNS namespace.

☑ U̲se WINS forward lookup

☐ Do n̲ot replicate this record

IP address:

[. . .]   Add

192.168.0.10   Remove

Up

Down

Advanced...

OK   Cancel   Apply

Understanding Zone Transfers

As mentioned earlier in the chapter, secondary servers get their zone information from a master name server. The master name server is the source of the zone file. This can be a primary server or another secondary server. Keep in mind that if the master name server is another secondary server, this secondary server must first get the updated zone file from a primary server. The process of replicating zone information to a secondary server is referred to as a *zone transfer*. Zone transfers occur between a secondary server and a master name server in the following situations:

- When the master name server notifies the secondary server that changes have been made to the zone file When changes occur, the secondary server will receive notification and request a zone transfer. To ensure the master name server is not overburdened with requests, the secondary servers are notified at random.
- When the refresh interval expires and the secondary server contacts the primary name server to check for changes to the zone file.
- When the DNS service is started on a secondary server.
- When a zone transfer is manually initiated through the DNS management console on a secondary server.

Windows Server 2003 DNS (as well as Windows 2000 DNS) supports two types of zone transfers. Pre–Windows 2000 implementations of DNS supported a full zone transfer (AXFR) only. With this type of zone transfer, the entire zone file is replicated to the secondary server. Most implementations of DNS support this type of zone transfer. If changes are made to the zone file, the entire file must be replicated. This type of zone transfer always occurs when a secondary DNS server is initially configured. Subsequently, after the zone file is replicated, incremental zone transfers are used.

The second type of zone transfer is known as an incremental zone transfer (IXFR). With this type of zone transfer, only the changes are replicated to the secondary server. The advantage of this is a reduction in network traffic.. You can control how often zone transfers occur from the Start Of Authority (SOA) tab within the zone's properties dialog box (see Figure 3-7). Table 3-2 summarizes the configurable options.

How Zone Transfers Occur

Zone transfers are always initiated on the secondary server by contacting one of the master name servers. The master name server then responds to the request with either a full or incremental zone transfer, depending on whether the zone file already exists on the secondary server (remember, the first time a secondary server is configured,

FIGURE 3-7

Using the Start
Of Authority tab
to control zone
transfers

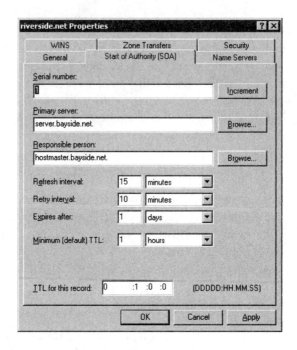

a full zone transfer is performed). So let's take a look at the process that occurs when a secondary server contacts the master name server.

1. When a secondary server is first configured, it sends a request to the master name server for an AXFR (full zone transfer).

2. The master name server responds by sending the zone information back to the requesting DNS server. A serial number is associated with the zone to determine when the zone file has been updated.

3. When the refresh interval expires (refer to Table 3-2), the secondary server sends a source of authority (SOA) query to the master name server requesting the serial number.

4. The master name server responds with the serial number. The secondary DNS server compares the response with the existing serial number. If the serial number from the master name server is higher, the secondary DNS server concludes that the zone file has changed.

5. The secondary DNS server sends an IXFR request (incremental zone transfer request) to the master name server.

6. The master name server will respond with either a full or incremental zone transfer, depending on whether or not it supports incremental zone transfers (remember, some versions of DNS do not support this feature).

DNS Notify

Normally, the secondary DNS server checks for updates to the zone file when the refresh interval expires. However, using a feature known as DNS notify, you can configure a master name server to notify a secondary DNS server when changes to the zone file occur. Once the secondary servers are notified, they can pull the changes from the master name server and update the information within the zone file.

In order to use this feature, you must configure the properties of the zone file and configure the list of secondary servers that will be notified of any changes (see Figure 3-8). One of the main reasons for using this option is to increase security. Only those secondary servers listed on the Notify tab will be permitted to request zone updates from the master name server.

TABLE 3-2   Options Used to Control Zone Transfers

Option	Description
Serial Number	Displays the number used to determine whether the zone file has changed. Each time a change is made, this number is incremented by 1. You can manually force a zone transfer by manually increasing this number.
Primary Server	Displays the hostname of the primary DNS server for the zone.
Responsible Person	Displays the e-mail address of the person responsible for administering the zone.
Refresh Interval	Specifies how often the secondary server will poll the primary server for updates. This value should be increased if zone transfers are occurring over slow network connections.
Retry Interval	Specifies how often the secondary server will attempt to contact the primary server if the server does not respond.
Expires After	Specifies when zone file information should expire if the secondary server fails to refresh the information. If a zone expires, zone data is considered to be potentially out of date and is discarded. Secondary master servers will not use zone data from an expired zone.
Minimum (Default) TTL	Specifies how long records from the zone should be cached on other servers.
TTL For This Record	Specifies how long DNS servers are allowed to store a record from the zone in their cache before it expires.

FIGURE 3-8

Configuring the
secondary
servers that will
be notified of
changes to the
zone file

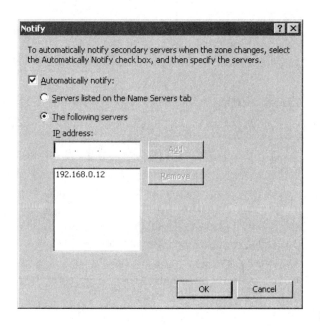

Active Directory Zone Replication

The process just described outlines how zone data is replicated between primary and secondary servers. If the zones are Active Directory integrated, the replication process is different. Replication of zone information is now based on a multimaster update model. This means that any domain controller running DNS is authoritative for the zone and can receive updates. Since the master copy of the zone is now stored within Active Directory, any domain controller running DNS can update the zone file and the changes are then replicated to all domain controllers within the domain.

on the
job

One of the benefits of using Active Directory integrated zones is that you no longer have to administer two different replication topologies. Since the zone information is stored in Active Directory, it can take advantage of the Active Directory replication topology. Only one replication topology is need to replicate directory and zone information.

If you are using Active Directory integrated zones, you can configure the scope of replication. This means you have some control over what domain controllers the zone information is replicated to (see Figure 3-9). The available options are summarized in Table 3-3.

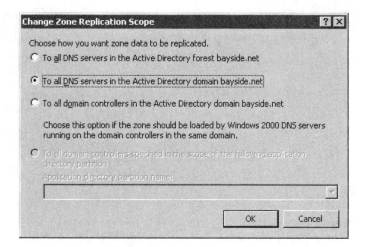

FIGURE 3-9

Configuring the
replication scope
for an Active
Directory
integrated zone

When you are determining which of the options to select, consider the fact that
the broader the replication scope, the more network traffic will be generated. For
example, replicating zone information throughout a forest will result in more traffic
than replicating zone information within a domain.

TABLE 3-3   Replication Scope Options

Replication Scope Options	Replication Scope Options
To All DNS Servers In The Active Directory Forest	Selecting this option means that the zone information will be replicated to all domain controllers within the forest running DNS.
To All DNS Servers In The Active Directory Domain	This is the default option. Zone information will be replicated to all domain controllers within the domain running DNS.
To All Domain Controllers In The Active Directory Domain	Select this option to have zone information replicated to Windows 2000 domain controllers within the domain running DNS.
To All Domain Controllers In (a specified application directory partition)	Zone data is replicated according to the replication scope of the specified application directory partition.

INSIDE THE EXAM

Application Directory Partition

Active Directory is made up of various *directory partitions* or naming contexts. A directory partition essentially forms a unit of replication. In Windows 2000, Active Directory contained at least three directory partitions: schema, configuration, and one or more domain partitions. Active Directory in Windows Server 2003 now supports application directory partitions.

Application directory partitions can contain any type of object other than security principals that can be configured to replicate to specific domain controllers within a forest. A domain directory partition, on the other hand, is replicated to all domain controllers within a single domain. Application directory partitions are normally used to store data that is dynamic and changes more frequently, since the replication frequency and scope can be configured for each application directory

partition. Thus an administrator has the ability to customize replication to reflect the type of data stored within the partition.

In terms of DNS, zone information can be stored within the domain directory partition or within an application directory partition. You can create an application directory partition within the DNS console by right-clicking your DNS server and selecting the Create Default Application Directory Partitions option. Before a zone can be stored within a specific application directory partition, the DNS server hosting the zone must be enlisted in that partition. A DNS server can be enlisted within an application directory partition using the dnscmd command-line utility. Once this step is complete, the zone replication scope can be changed so that data is replicated to only those domain controllers enlisted in the application directory partition.

CERTIFICATION OBJECTIVE 3.02

Securing DNS

Knowing that Active Directory relies heavily on DNS along with many other server services, you should take certain steps to secure your DNS infrastructure, as there are many exploits that can take advantage of security holes. Instead of waiting for an attack to occur, you should take proactive measures to secure your DNS servers. There are a number of ways in which you can secure your DNS servers, from implementing policies and procedures to changing various configuration settings.

Secure Policies and Procedures

Policies and procedures help to ensure that the required level of security within an organization is maintained. Many administrators have a set of guidelines and procedures that must be strictly adhered to. Such guidelines and procedures can also be applied to a DNS implementation to ensure that a secure DNS implementation is achieved and maintained. Consider including some of the following policies and procedures when implementing DNS:

- Once a DNS server is installed, document the configuration for future reference.
- Implement change control, where any changes to the configuration must be approved and later documented.
- Develop a sound backup strategy for your DNS servers.
- Determine which users will be responsible for administering the DNS servers.
- Review the contents of the DNS log on a regular basis.
- Determine how zone transfer will occur and, if necessary, configure which servers will receive zone transfers.
- Make sure all DNS servers have the latest service packs installed, because they often address security issues.
- Have a failover strategy in place. Since DNS is required by a number of services, having a failover plan can increase redundancy.

Namespace

There are a number of different ways in which you can secure your DNS servers. However, having a secure DNS implementation begins by securing the DNS namespace. When you are planning your DNS namespace, keep the following security recommendations in mind:

- If clients on the private network do not need to resolve names on the Internet, eliminate DNS communication on the Internet (although most organizations require that clients have Internet access, and this is therefore not a viable option).
- When planning the DNS namespace, try to create a distinction between the internal namespace and the external namespace. This can be achieved by using

an internal namespace that is a subdomain of the external namespace. If, for example, the external namespace is klnsweep.net, the internal namespace can be a subdomain such as ad.klnsweep.net.

■ Plan to host the internal namespace on internal DNS servers so that it is not exposed on the Internet. The external namespace should be hosted on external DNS servers. Any queries for external resources should be forwarded to the external DNS servers.

■ The internal and external DNS servers should be separated by a firewall. On the firewall, you can configure packet filtering to permit UCP and TCP port 53 communication between the internal and external DNS servers.

Secure Updates

Windows Server 2003 supports secure dynamic updates for those zones that store information within Active Directory. This means that only those clients authorized within the domain are permitted to update resource records. the DNS server will only accept updates from those clients that are permitted to do so. This eliminates the chance of unknown computers registering records with the DNS server. Secure updates for a zone can be configured by selecting the Secure Only option. Once this option is enabled, you can use the Security tab from the DNS zone's properties window to control who can update the zone file.

Enabling this option will increase the security of your DNS implementation. The resource records and zone files can only be changed by users who have been permitted to do so. Administrators can edit the access control list (ACL) for the zone and specify which specific users and groups can perform dynamic updates. You edit the ACL for a zone by right-clicking the zone, selecting Properties, and choosing the Security tab.

EXERCISE 3-5

Configuring Secure Updates

In this exercise, you will configure a zone to accept secure updates only. The exercise assumes that you changed the default setting from secure only in Exercise 3-3.

1. Click Start, point to Administrative Tools, and click DNS.

2. From within the DNS console, expand your DNS server and click the Forward Lookup Zones container.

3. Right-click the zone you created in Exercise 3-2 and click Properties.

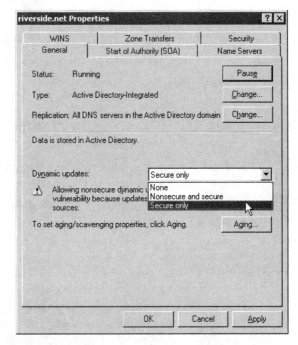

4. From the General tab, use the drop-down list beside Dynamic Updates and select Secure Only.

5. Click OK.

DNS Forwarding

DNS servers may be required to communicate with DNS servers outside of the local network. A *forwarder* is a DNS server that receives DNS queries that cannot be resolved locally and are therefore forwarded to another DNS servers.

Forwarding allows you to specify where one DNS server should forward queries. It also allows you to specify which DNS server on the network is responsible for handling external traffic, as opposed to having all DNS servers forward queries to external DNS servers. By configuring forwarding, another level of security can be added to your DNS implementation as only specified DNS servers will be capable of forwarding queries outside of the local network.

You can also use forwarding as a means of reducing network traffic. This can become an important issue if the existing Internet connection is slow, costly, or already heavily utilized. If a designated DNS server is responsible for receiving all queries from local DNS servers, it should in turn build up a large amount of cached queries. The forwarder may be able to resolve queries from the cache instead of forwarding them to an external DNS server.

DNS forwarding occurs in the following manner:

1. When a DNS server receives a DNS query, it attempts to first resolve the request using its local zone information and information within its local cache.

2. The DNS server sends a recursive query to the DNS server designated as the forwarder if it is unable to resolve the request.

3. The forwarder will attempt to resolve the query. If the forwarder does not respond, the DNS server will attempt to resolve the request by contacting the appropriate DNS server as specified in the root hints.

Using forwarding, you can configure a DNS server to send all queries it cannot resolve locally to another DNS server , and you can also configure conditional forwarders. Conditional forwarding is slightly different in that the DNS servers are configured to forward requests to different servers according to the DNS name within the query. When configuring conditional forwarding, you must specify the following information:

■ The domain name for which queries will be forwarded

■ The IP address of the DNS server for which the queries should be sent.

INSIDE THE EXAM

Conditional Forwarders

Conditional forwarding is a new feature introduced in Windows Server 2003 and therefore a topic you are more than likely to encounter on the exam. Conditional forwarders are configured to tell one DNS server to forward a query to another specific DNS server according to the domain name contained within the query.

Conditional forwarders allow queries to be sent between two networks, as opposed to having to send the queries on the Internet. For example, if two companies merge, each will more than likely have its own DNS namespace and DNS servers. You can configure conditional forwarders so that the DNS servers on one network will forward name resolution queries for clients on the other network to the specified DNS servers. This eliminates the need for recursion and having to resolve hostnames via Internet-based DNS servers, making resolution more efficient.

To configure DNS forwarders:

1. Within the DNS management console, right-click the DNS server and click Properties.

2. From the properties dialog box for the DNS server, click the Forwarders tab.

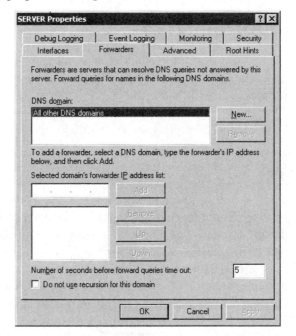

3. Under DNS Name, select a domain name. To add a new domain name, click Add.

4. In the selected domain's forwarder IP address list, type the IP address of the forwarder. Click Add.

e x a m

w a t c h

Another method of optimizing a DNS server is to delete the root hints file (cache.dns). A DNS server uses the information within this file to locate DNS servers that are authoritative for the root of a DNS namespace. Deleting this file removes the ability of a DNS server to *contact any authoritative root DNS servers. This in turn allows you to prevent internal DNS servers from accessing the Internet. To allow name resolution of Internet resources, configure these DNS servers to forward requests to a DNS server that does contain a root hints file.*

CERTIFICATION OBJECTIVE 3.03

Troubleshooting DNS

An important part of an administrator's job is to troubleshoot problems as they arise. Since the DNS service is required by Active Directory as well as by other server services such as Exchange and ISA, it is important that you know how to troubleshoot. Thankfully, a number of tools are available that can assist an administrator in tracking down the source of a problem and rectifying it as quickly and efficiently as possible.

Event Viewer

DNS-related events can be written to the DNS Server log. DNS logging can be enabled using the Event Logging tab from the DNS server's properties dialog box (see Figure 3-10). The default configuration is to log all DNS-related events.. You can optionally change this and choose to log errors only or both errors and warnings. By selecting the No Events option, you can disable event logging.

You can use the DNS log located within the Event Viewer to view events (see Chapter 8 for more information about the Windows Server 2003 Event Viewer). Once the Event Viewer is open (click Start, point to Administrative Tools, and select Event Viewer), click the DNS log. Any DNS-related events are displayed within the right pane. To view detailed information about an event, double-click the event within the right pane. The properties dialog box for the event displays information such as the date and time the event occurred, the type of event, the user and computer under which the event occurred, and an event ID. A basic description of the event is also provided.

FIGURE 3-10

Enabling logging
for the DNS
service

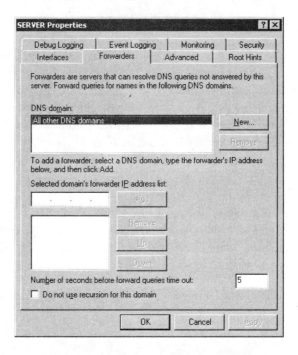

FIGURE 3-11

Using the Event
Viewer to view
the DNS log

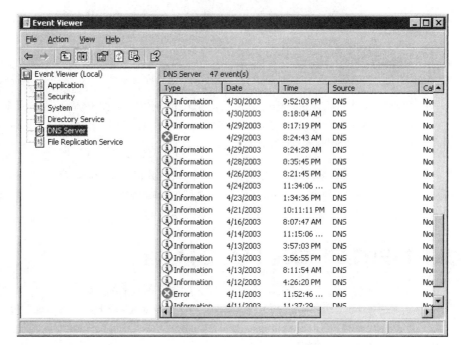

NSLookup

The NSLookup command-line utility can be used to send forward and reverse queries to a DNS server. Normally, you would use the command to perform a forward query to resolve a hostname to ensure it is able to find a specific client. It can also be used to determine the host associated with a given IP address by performing a reverse query. You can learn the syntax used for the command as well as its many other uses by typing **nslookup ?** at the command prompt.

IPCONFIG

You may already be familiar with the ipconfig command. You can use the command to perform a number of functions using the various parameters that are supported. For example, using ipconfig /all will display the TCP/IP configuration of a host. In terms of DNS, you can use the following parameters:

- **RegisterDNS**   This parameter refreshes all DHCP lease and re-registers DNS names.
- **Displaydns**   This parameter will display the contents of the DNS resolver cache.
- **Flushdns**   This parameter purges the DNS resolver cache.

Replication Monitor

Using a tool called Replication Monitor, you can monitor the status of Active Directory replication between domain controllers. If the zone information is configured as Active Directory integrated, you can use this tool to monitor replication between DNS servers.

Replication Monitor is not a tool that is installed by default. You can install the tool by browsing to the i386\Support\Tools directory on the Windows Server 2003 CD and running setup. Once it has been installed, it can be launched from the command prompt using the Replmon command.

CERTIFICATION SUMMARY

DNS has been around on the Internet for many years, so it is not a new concept. It was primarily developed to overcome the limitations of HOSTS files. DNS has now become a very critical component because many services, including Active Directory, are now dependent upon it.

Prior to installing DNS, you should take some time to plan the internal DNS namespace. The strategy you choose to implement will be dependent upon a number of different factors but primarily whether the organization has an existing Internet presence. You should also plan where on the network you intend to place your DNS servers. Your goal should be to provide clients with the best possible response time.

A DNS server can be configured in three different roles: primary, secondary, or caching-only. Primary DNS servers maintain the working copy of a zone file, and secondary DNS servers maintain a replica. Secondary servers provide fault tolerance, load balancing, and increased availability. Caching-only servers only resolve queries and cache the results. They do not maintain any zone data and therefore do not participate in zone transfers.

Windows Server 2003 supports four different zone types: primary, secondary, stub, and Active Directory integrated. If the DNS service is running on a domain controller, both primary and stub zones can be converted to Active Directory integrated. Doing so enables a multimaster replication model and secure updates to zone files. When zone information is stored within Active Directory, it can be stored in the domain directory partition or within an application directory partition.

Due to the importance of the DNS service, it's crucial that you take the necessary steps to secure it. Securing DNS begins by implementing policies and procedures that must be adhered to by administrators and other personnel and also includes making configuration changes such as enabling secure updates only.

TWO-MINUTE DRILL

Planning a DNS Strategy

❑ Windows Server 2003 Active Directory requires the DNS service to be installed.

❑ Windows Server 2003 supports three different DNS server roles: primary, secondary, and caching-only.

❑ Primary servers maintain a working copy of the zone file. Secondary servers maintain a replica. Secondary servers provide fault tolerance, load balancing, and increased availability.

❑ Caching-only servers resolve queries and cache the results. They do not host any zone information. These servers are useful in remote sites connected to a main office via WAN links.

❑ Before implementing DNS, consider where the DNS servers should be placed.

❑ Windows Server 2003 supports four different zone types: primary, secondary, stub, and Active Directory integrated.

❑ Stub zones are used to determine which DNS servers are authoritative for which domains.

❑ Primary and stub zones can be converted to Active Directory integrated if the DNS server is also configured as a domain controller.

❑ With dynamic updates, clients that support this feature can dynamically register their own resource records with the DNS server.

❑ BIND version 4.9.7 support SRV records. BIND version 8.2.2 and Windows NT 4.0 with service pack 4 or later support dynamic updates.

❑ The process of replicating zone information between a primary DNS server and a secondary DNS server is referred to as a zone transfer.

❑ Windows Server 2003 supports two types of zone transfers: full zone transfers and incremental zone transfers. With full zone transfers, the entire zone file is replicated. With incremental zone transfers, only the updates are replicated.

❑ Using DNS Notify, primary DNS servers can be configured to notify specific secondary servers when changes to the zone file have occurred.

❑ Active Directory replication uses a multimaster model in which updates can occur on any domain controller and the changes are replicated throughout the domain.

❑ Active Directory integrated zones can be stored within a domain directory partition or an application directory partition.

Securing DNS

❑ It is good security practice to implement policies and procedures that DNS administrators must adhere to so that the required level of security is maintained.

❑ By enabling secure updates, you assure that only those clients that are authorized can update the zone file. Secure updates can only be enabled on zones that are Active Directory integrated.

❑ A forwarder is a DNS server that receives request from internal DNS servers that need to be forwarded to external DNS servers.

❑ Conditional forwarders use the domain name to specify where a DNS server should forward name resolution queries.

Troubleshooting DNS

❑ When you enable DNS logging, DNS-related events can be written to the DNS log. You can the use the Event Viewer to view the contents of the log file. Logging of DNS is enabled by default.

❑ NSLookup can be used to perform reverse and forward queries against a DNS server for troubleshooting.

❑ Replication Monitor can be used to monitor the status of Active Directory replication. If zone information is stored within Active Directory, you can use this tool to monitor zone replication between domain controllers.

SELF TEST

Planning a DNS Strategy

1. John is planning a DNS implementation for his organization. The network consists of a main office and several branch offices. Most of the branch offices are connected to the main office with high-speed links with plenty of available bandwidth. However, there are two remote sites that use slow, unreliable connections. You want to implement a DNS solution for both of these sites without increasing the amount of network traffic on the links. How should you proceed?

   A. Place a primary DNS server in each site

   B. Place a secondary server within each site.

   C. Place a caching-only server within each site.

   D. Do not place a DNS server within these two sites.

2. The klnsweep organization currently has a single DNS server. DNS is installed on a member server running Windows Server 2003. You plan to install DNS on another member server to eliminate DNS as a single point of failure. For what type of DNS role should the new DNS server be configured?

   A. Caching-only server

   B. Master name server

   C. Backup DNS server

   D. Secondary DNS server

3. Which of the following DNS servers support dynamic updates? (Choose all correct answers.)

   A. Windows 2000

   B. Windows NT 4.0

   C. BIND 4.9.7

   D. BIND 8.2.2

4. You are configuring DNS servers on your network. Four new DNS servers are being added to the network infrastructure. You are planning the DNS zones and want to provide the highest level of fault tolerance and plan to configure the zones as Active Directory integrated. On which of the following can DNS be installed? (Choose all correct answers.)

   A. Windows 2000 member server

   B. Windows NT 4.0 domain controller

   C. Windows Server 2003 domain controller

   D. Windows Server 2003 member server

5. John has been informed by his senior network administrator that he needs to be able to control which users and groups can perform dynamic updates to the DNS database. What should John do to meet this new requirement?

   A. Add the appropriate users to the Dynamic Updates group.

   B. Configure the zone to accept only secure updates.

   C. Disable dynamic updates.

   D. Enable DNS notify.

6. Which of the following clients are able to dynamically update their own resource records?

   A. Windows 95

   B. Windows 98

   C. Windows 2000

   D. Windows XP

7. The klnsweep network consists of Windows XP, Unix, and some legacy clients. The Unix hosts use DNS for name resolution. They are unable, though, to resolve the NetBIOS names of the legacy clients. You want to implement a simple and efficient solution to the problem. What should be done in order to assist non-WINS clients in resolving NetBIOS names?

   A. Configure the DNS server for WINS lookup.

   B. Upgrade the legacy clients to Windows XP.

   C. Install the WINS service on the DNS server.

   D. Configure an LMHOSTS file on every Unix client.

Securing DNS

8. In order for a DNS server to support Active Directory, what type of resource record must the DNS server support?

   A. A record

   B. SRV record

   C. MX record

   D. CNAME record

9. Which of the following DNS servers support SRV records? (Choose all correct answers.)

   A. Windows NT 4.0 DNS with service pack 4

   B. Windows 2000 DNS

   C. BIND 4.9.7

   D. BIND 8.2

10. Bob is a network administrator for the klnsweep domain. He is in charge of administering DNS. Currently, the organization uses klnsweep.net as its internal namespace. There are also several subdomains that have been delegated to other DNS servers on the network. Which type of DNS zone facilitates the locating of DNS servers that are authoritative for subdomains?

    A. Secondary

    B. Primary

    C. Stub

    D. Active Directory integrated

11. Bill is planning the Active Directory zones for his organization. He wants to take advantage of the Active Directory replication topology but also be able to control which DNS servers the zone information is replicated to. Where should the zone information be stored?

    A. On the local DNS server within the DNS folder

    B. In the domain directory partition

    C. In an application directory partition

    D. In the Cache.dns file on the local DNS server

12. John wants to store a zone within an application directory partition. The partition already exists, but he needs to enlist the DNS server hosting the zone. Which of the following commands can he use to do so?

    A. NSlookup

    B. dnscmd

    C. ipconfig

    D. dnsenlist

13. How does a caching-only server determine how long to cache resource records?

    A. All records are cached for a default of 24 hours.

    B. It uses the TTL assigned to the resource record.

    C. It uses the refresh interval configured on the server.

    D. It uses the serial number.

14. An organization has recently completed a merger with another company. The new company currently has an existing DNS implementation. Robert has been asked to configure the local DNS servers so that any name resolution queries for clients within the other company are sent to that company's local DNS servers. What can he do?

    A. Configure conditional forwarding.

    B. Configure a stub zone.

    C. Configure replication between the DNS servers within each organization.

    D. Configure forwarding.

15. Since DNS is crucial in a Windows Server 2003 environment, the director of internal IT has asked you to devise a plan to increase the availability of DNS in all locations of DKB Consulting. The company has one head office and three regional offices in Europe, North America, and Asia. Which of the following would be options for increasing DNS availability within the organization? (Choose all correct answers.)

    A. Configure Active Directory integrated zones on all DNS servers.
    B. Configure caching-only servers within each of the regional offices.
    C. Enable dynamic updates for all zones.
    D. Place at least two DNS servers within each of the different regions.

Troubleshooting DNS

16. Your network currently has a single DNS server. You are concerned about fault tolerance and the impact it will have on the network if the DNS server crashed. You decide to install another DNS server on the network. Which type of server should you configure?

    A. Secondary server
    B. Caching-only server
    C. Forwarder
    D. WINS server

17. Mary is the network administrator of a Windows Server 2003 network. There is a single DNS server on the network. The zone is standard primary. Mary has created all the required resource records. Two new servers are added to the network that host network services. Users soon report that they cannot access the new servers. What can Mary do to resolve this problem? Select two possible answers.

    A. Change the zone to Active Directory integrated.
    B. Manually add the resource records to the zone file.
    C. Enable dynamic updates for the zone.
    D. Clear the contents of the DNS cache

18. FKB International has a head office and two branch offices. The primary DNS server, SRV01, is located within the head office. Each branch office has a caching-only server (SRV02 and SRV03) that forwards requests to the primary DNS server. You want to reduce the amount of DNS traffic on the WAN links. How can this be accomplished?

    A. Decrease the TTL on SRV02 and SRV03.
    B. Increase the TTL on SRV02 and SRV03.
    C. Decrease the TTL on SRV01.
    D. Increase the TTL on SRV01.

19. Felicia is the administrator of a Windows Server 2003 network. The network consists of a head office and two branch offices connected by WAN links. Users in the branch office resolve hostnames using the single primary DNS server in the head office. However, users report that name resolution within the company is slow. You discover that a lot of traffic is being generated on the WAN links from name resolution queries. What should you do? Select two answers.

   A. Increase the TTL on the primary DNS server.

   B. Place secondary DNS servers in each branch office. Configure the primary DNS server as the master name server.

   C. Configure a caching-only DNS server in each site. Configure the servers to forward all requests to the primary DNS server.

   D. Configure clients in the branch offices with the IP address of the local DNS server.

20. Dan is restructuring his company's DNS infrastructure. There are currently three DNS servers. The primary DNS server is installed on one of three domain controllers. Two member servers are configured as secondary DNS servers. Dan wants to simplify replication and zone transfers as well as increase fault tolerance. What should he do? Select two answers.

   A. Increase the Time to Live on the primary DNS server.

   B. Remove DNS from the member servers. Install DNS on the remaining domain controllers.

   C. Enable dynamic updates for the zone.

   D. Change the zone to Active Directory integrated.

LAB QUESTION

FKB International has asked you to assist in the deployment of DNS. FKB International consists of two companies: FKB Sales and FKB Manufacturing. In order to assist in the deployment of DNS, FKB International has provided you with the following information:

- Each company has its own IT department.
- Each company maintains its own DNS domain name.
- All workstations are running Windows XP Professional.
- There is a single head office for both companies. Branch offices are connected to the head office using T1 connections.
- DNS will be installed on computers running Windows Server 2003.

FKB International has some distinct requirements for their DNS implementation. All users must be able to resolve hostnames from both companies. Fault tolerance is required for the branch offices, and administration of zone files should be minimal. The head office is not a computing center, but users in this location must also be able to resolve company hostnames. Using this information, develop a DNS implementation plan.

SELF TEST ANSWERS

Planning a DNS Strategy

1. ☑ **C.** By placing a caching-only server within each of the two sites, you can implement a DNS solution without experiencing an increase in traffic. Since the caching-only server does not hold any zone information, no traffic will be generated by zone transfers.
   ☒ **A** and **B** are incorrect. Placing either a primary or secondary server within each of the sites would result in zone transfers occurring over the already-slow WAN links. **D** is incorrect because making the remote sites rely on a DNS server in the main site creates a point of failure, especially since the WAN links are unreliable.

2. ☑ **D.** The new server should be configured as a secondary server. Secondary servers are designed to provide primary DNS servers with fault tolerance, availability, and load balancing.
   ☒ **A** is incorrect because caching-only servers do not maintain any zone data. They only resolve queries and cache the results. Such a server would provide fault tolerance in terms of name resolution services for clients. However, it would not provide fault tolerance for the zone data stored on the primary DNS server. **B** is incorrect because a master name server is simply the name of the server from which a secondary server pulls the updates to the zone file. **C** is incorrect because there is no such role as a backup DNS server.

3. ☑ **A** and **D.** Windows 2000 DNS and BIND versions 8.2.2 and later both support dynamic updates where clients can dynamically register their own resource records with the DNS server.
   ☒ **B** is incorrect. In order for Windows NT 4.0 to support dynamic updates, service pack 4 or later must be installed. **C** is incorrect because BIND version 4.9.7 does not provide support for this feature.

4. ☑ **C.** In order to support Active Directory integrated zones, the DNS servers must also be running as domain controllers.
   ☒ **A** and **B** are incorrect because only those DNS servers that are also acting as domain controllers can support Active Directory integrated zones.

5. ☑ **B.** When you configure a zone to accept only secure updates, only those who are authorized to do so can update the zone information. **A** is incorrect because there is no group known as the Dynamic Updates group. **C** is incorrect because disabling dynamic updates means that the zone information will have to be updated manually. **D** is incorrect because this feature enables a primary DNS server to notify secondary DNS servers of changes to the zone file.

6. ☑ **C** and **D.** Both Windows 2000 and Windows XP clients are able to dynamically update their own resource records with a DNS server that also supports this feature.
   ☒ **A** and **B** are incorrect because these clients do not support dynamic updates on their own.

In order for their records to be updated in the DNS database, a DHCP server on the network would be required to perform the updates on their behalf.

7. ☑ **A**. If you configure a DNS server for WINS lookup, the DNS server can forward queries that it cannot resolve to the WINS server on the network.
☒ **A, B**, and **D** are all incorrect. Although these options might be viable solutions, they do not represent the most efficient and simple solution.

Securing DNS

8. ☑ **B**. In order for DNS to support Active Directory, it must provide support for SRV records.
☒ **A** is incorrect because A records are used to map hostnames to IP addresses. **C** is incorrect because MX records are used to route messages to a specified mail exchanger for a specified DNS domain name. **D** is incorrect because CNAME records specify another DNS domain name for a name that is already referenced in another resource record.

9. ☑ **A, B, C**, and **D**. All answers are correct. All version of DNS listed provide support for SRV records. Windows NT 4.0 will support SRV records if service pack 4 is installed.

10. ☑ **C**. Stub zones are used to determine which DNS servers are authoritative for which portions of a DNS namespace.
☒ **A** is incorrect because secondary zones are replicas of primary zones. They contain zone information and the various resource records for hosts on the network. **B** is incorrect because the primary zone is the working copy of a zone file. It contains zone information as well as the various resource records required to resolve hostnames within a particular namespace. **D** is incorrect because with Active Directory integrated zones, zone data is stored within Active Directory. Stub zones can also be configured as Active Directory integrated zones.

11. ☑ **C**. Storing zone data within an application directory partition enables you to configure the scope and frequency of replication. Since the zone data is being stored within Active Directory, it uses the Active Directory replication topology to replicate changes.
☒ **A** is incorrect because storing the zone data locally means the zone is not Active Directory integrated and therefore does not use the Active Directory replication topology. **B** is incorrect because storing the zone information within the domain directory partition does not allow you to control which domain controllers the zone data is replicated to. **D** is incorrect because the purpose of the cache.dns file is to temporarily store hostname–to–IP address mappings.

12. ☑ **B**. You can use the dnscmd command to enlist a DNS server within a specific application directory partition.
☒ **A** is incorrect because NSLookup is used for troubleshooting. **C** is incorrect because

`ipconfig` is used to view the IP settings configured on a computer. **D** is incorrect because no such command is supported by Windows Server 2003.

13. ☑ **B**. Every resource record has an associated TTL value. DNS servers use this value to determine how long a record can remain in the cache. Once the TTL expires, the record is purged.
    ☒ **A** is incorrect because all resource records have a TTL based on the configuration of the DNS server that stores the record. This value is returned along with the hostname–to–IP address mapping to other DNS servers. **C** is incorrect because the refresh interval determines how often a secondary DNS server polls a primary DNS server for updates. **D** is incorrect because the serial number is used to determine when information within a zone has been changed.

14. ☑ **A**. Conditional forwarders enable an administrator to configure where a DNS server should send name resolution requests according to the domain name within the query.
    ☒ **B** is incorrect because stub zones are used to determine which DNS servers are authoritative for a domain. **C** is incorrect.

15. ☑ **A** and **D**. Using Active Directory integrated zones, zone information is stored within Active Directory and updates can occur on any domain controller running DNS. If one DNS server is unavailable, updates can still be performed. With two DNS servers placed within each region, clients can still resolve hostnames if one DNS server is unavailable.
    ☒ **B** is incorrect because a caching-only server is mainly used for performance, not fault tolerance. **C** is incorrect because enabling dynamic updates allows clients to update their own resource records but does not add fault tolerance to DNS.

Troubleshooting DNS

16. ☑ **A**. A secondary server provides fault tolerance by maintaining a copy of the zone database, which is replicated from a master name server (which in this case will be the primary DNS server). If the primary DNS server crashes, hosts can still resolve name by querying the secondary server.
    ☒ **B** is incorrect because caching-only servers do not hold any zone information. They only cache results as they resolve them. **C** is incorrect because a forwarder is configured to tell a DNS server where to send name resolution requests if they cannot be resolved. **D** is incorrect because a WINS server is used to resolve NetBIOS names.

17. ☑ **A** and **B**. Since Mary has been manually updating the zone file, it is not using dynamic updates. In order to allow clients to access the new servers, the appropriate records must be added to the zone file. Another solution is to enable dynamic updates so that the servers can add their own resource records to the zone file.
    ☒ **C** is incorrect because this will only change where the zone data is being stored. **D** is incorrect

because there are no resource records for the servers, and therefore there would be no entries for the new servers in the DNS cache.

18. ☑ **D.** Increasing the TTL means that the secondary DNS servers do not have to refresh resource records as often, thereby reducing traffic across the WAN link.
☒ Answers **A** and **B** are incorrect because the TTL must be configured on the DNS server that maintains the working copy of the database. **C** is incorrect because this would result in an increase in traffic.

19. ☑ **B** and **D.** With a secondary DNS server in the branch office, users can resolve hostnames using a local zone file. Each client's primary DNS server should point to the local branch office DNS server.
☒ **A** is incorrect because this will only result in a decrease in network traffic. **C** is incorrect because a caching-only server does not maintain a copy of the zone file. It simply resolves queries and caches the results.

20. ☑ **B** and **D.** Installing DNS on the domain controllers instead of the member servers allows zone information to be stored within Active Directory, thereby simplifying zone transfers and replication. It also increases fault tolerance, as each domain controller hosts a working copy of the zone file.
☒ **A** is incorrect because increasing the TTL means records do not need to be refreshed as often. **C** is incorrect because dynamic updates will allow clients to update their own resource records.

LAB ANSWERS

Answers may vary.

To provide each company with the ability to maintain its own DNS name, two primary DNS servers should be configured for each company. Secondary DNS servers should be configured for fault tolerance. If the DNS service is placed on domain controllers, zones should be Active Directory integrated. To minimize administration of zone files, zones should be enabled for dynamic updates.

In order for clients to resolve hostnames of both DNS domains, each primary DNS server can also be made a secondary DNS server for the other DNS zone. Another option is to configure conditional forwarding, where each DNS server forwards queries for the other DNS domain to the appropriate DNS server.

Users in the head office must be able to resolve hostnames from each company. A DNS server that is secondary to both zones can be configured on the head office. Another option is to configure a caching-only server within the head office.

4

Planning a WINS Strategy

CERTIFICATION OBJECTIVES

CERTIFICATION OBJECTIVE 4.01

Understanding WINS

The Windows Internet Name Service (WINS) is Microsoft's implementation of a NetBIOS name server. WINS, which was developed to overcome the problems associated with NetBIOS in a routed environment, provides a centralized method for dynamically registering and resolving NetBIOS names. WINS servers provide name resolution services by mapping NetBIOS names to IP addresses for clients on the network. Along with these features, there are a number of other advantages to implementing WINS:

■ WINS provides a dynamic database of NetBIOS name–to–IP address mappings. In other words, WINS clients can register their own computer names instead of requiring an administrator to do so manually. This also means that the database is up to date.

■ WINS eliminates the need to maintain LMHOSTS files.

■ WINS reduces the number of NetBIOS broadcasts on the network. Instead of clients having to perform broadcasts to register and resolve NetBIOS names, they can communicate directly with a WINS server. However, broadcasts can still be used in the event that a WINS server is not available.

■ WINS provides backward compatility for legacy clients on a Windows Server 2003 network. This allows these clients to interoperate within a Windows Server 2003 environment.

WINS is not a new service introduced in Windows Server 2003 but has long been used with previous versions of the operating system. The WINS service included with Windows Server 2003 does include some enhancements and new features over the WINS service included with Windows 2000:

■ **Advanced WINS database and filtering**   Using filtering and new search capabilities, you can search for records in the WINS database using the criteria specified.

■ **Accepting replication partners**   Administrators can define from which WINS servers name records can or cannot be accepted from during replication.

NetBIOS Names

Before you can fully understand WINS, it is important to have a general understanding of NetBIOS names. NetBIOS names are used to uniquely identify computers and resources on a network. All workstations running pre–Windows 2000 platforms must be assigned a unique NetBIOS name, which is also the computer name. The NetBIOS name is a 16-character string, where the first 15 characters are used to identify a specific workstation on the network and the sixteenth character is a hexadecimal value used to identify a specific network service running on that workstation, for example, the file and print service running on a specific workstation. Thus a workstation may register multiple NetBIOS names, using the sixteenth character to identify the various services it is running. Table 4-1 outlines some of the common hexadecimal values used to identify services running on a workstation.

How WINS Works

WINS consists of two main components: the WINS server and the WINS client. The WINS server maintains the centralized database of NetBIOS name–to–IP address mappings and is responsible for processing the name resolution requests from WINS clients to register their NetBIOS names and IP addresses. It also receives the queries sent by WINS clients and attempts to resolve them using the information within its database. The following section will look more closely at what happens between a WINS client and a WINS server.

WINS Resolution

WINS *resolution* consists of varied processes that occur between a WINS client and a WINS server. It refers to both the process that occurs when a client registers its NetBIOS name and the process that occurs when a client queries the WINS server to resolve a

TABLE 4-1   Common NetBIOS Hexadecimal Values

Hexadecimal Value	Description
<00H>	Registered by the Workstation service
<1CH>	Indicates a domain name that can be used to locate domain controllers
<06H>	Registered by a computer running Routing and Remote Access Server
<1BH>	Registered by each domain controller functioning as the domain master browser
<20H>	Registered by a WINS client running the Server service
<21H>	Registered by the RAS client running on a WINS client

name to an IP address. There are four different events that can occur between a WINS server and a WINS client, each of which are described in the following sections:

- Name registration
- Name renewal
- Name release
- Name resolution

WINS Name Registration   When a client is configured to use WINS, it will dynamically register its NetBIOS name with the primary WINS server. When the workstation is started or when a network service is started on the workstation, a name registration request is sent directly to the WINS server. If the name has not already been registered by another client on the network, the WINS server will respond with a successful registration message. The message also contains the Time to Live (TTL), which defines how long the client can continue to use the name registered until it must be renewed. The default TTL is six days.

When the WINS server receives a name registration request, it will parse the database to see if the name has already been registered by another client. This is done to avoid name conflicts on the network. If the name is already registered by another client, the WINS server will send a challenge message to the host that has registered the name. If the host responds to the challenge, a negative response is returned to the client requesting to register the name. However, if the host does not respond to the challenge, the requesting WINS client is permitted to register the name.

Now, when a client needs to register a NetBIOS name, the request is initially sent to the primary WINS server. If the primary WINS server is unavailable, the request is sent to a secondary WINS server that the client has been configured to use. If no WINS servers respond to the request, the client registers its NetBIOS name using a local broadcast.

Name Renewal   As already mentioned, every WINS client is required to renew its NetBIOS name that has been registered with a WINS server. The frequency at which the renewal process occurs is defined by the TTL. Clients renew their NetBIOS names by sending a refresh request to the primary WINS server. The renewal process occurs as outlined here:

1. A refresh request is sent to the primary WINS server when one-half of the TTL expires.

2. If the primary WINS server does not respond to the request, the client will continue to attempt to renew its name at ten-minute intervals for a total of one hour.

3. If the primary WINS server does not respond during this time, the client will try to renew its NetBIOS name with a secondary WINS server.

4. The WINS client will continue to renew its NetBIOS name with the primary and secondary servers.

5. If no response is received from a WINS server before the TTL expires, the client is forced to release its NetBIOS name.

Name Release   As you can see from the process outlined in the preceding section, there are times when a WINS client must release its NetBIOS name. Releasing a NetBIOS name makes it available for use by another client on the network. When a workstation is properly shut down, a name release request is sent to the WINS server. The request contains the client's IP address and NetBIOS name, which are then removed from the WINS database.

Name Resolution   Name resolution is the process of mapping a NetBIOS name to an IP address. When a client is configured for WINS, it will send any name resolution requests to the WINS server. The WINS server will attempt to resolve the request using the information within the WINS database. When a WINS client needs to resolve a NetBIOS name, the following process occurs (see Figure 4-1):

1. The client checks to see if the name it needs to resolve is its own NetBIOS name.

2. The client checks to see if it can resolve the name using its local NetBIOS name cache. Each time a client resolves a name, that name is placed within the local cache for future reference.

3. If the name cannot be resolved using this method, the client will send the name resolution request to the primary WINS server.

4. If the primary WINS server does not respond, the client will send the request to one of the other WINS servers it is configured to use.

5. If no WINS server responds, the client will attempt to resolve the name using a local broadcast.

6. The client will parse the LMHOSTS file if it is configured to do so.

7. Finally, the client will attempt to use DNS name resolution methods by parsing the HOSTS file and send the name resolution request to a DNS server.

The NetBIOS
name resolution
process

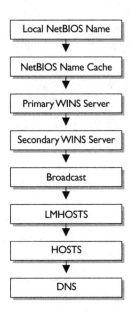

The process outlined here is the default behavior for H-node resolution. If WINS
is used, this is the default node type used by Windows 2000, Windows XP, and Windows
Server 2003 clients. Node types will be discussed in more detail later in the chapter.

WINS and Windows Server 2003

Prior to Windows 2000, Windows platforms required the use of NetBIOS for various
networking processes to occur. However, when Windows 2000 was introduced, NetBIOS
names were no longer required (Windows Server 2003, for instance, does not require
them). In a Windows Server 2003 network that does not need to support legacy clients,
NetBIOS can be disabled through the properties of TCP/IP, since hostnames and DNS
are used. WINS is still included as a network service, and NetBIOS is still supported
to support legacy Windows platforms on a Windows Server 2003 network.

NetBIOS Name Resolution

In order for workstations on a network to successfully communicate, their IP addresses
must be identified. So like the domain names discussed in Chapter 3, NetBIOS or
computer names must also be resolved to an IP address. The following section will look
at the various methods available for resolving computer names.

The three standard ways that computer names can be resolved to IP addresses are

- Local broadcast
- NetBIOS name cache
- NetBIOS name server

Name Resolution Methods

With a local broadcast, a workstation will broadcast a name resolution request on the network. The computer with the corresponding NetBIOS name will respond with its IP address. The disadvantages to this approach are the increase in broadcast traffic and the fact that broadcasts are not normally forwarded between subnets by a router. Thus, resolving the NetBIOS name of a workstation on a subnet would not be possible.

Each workstation maintains a local NetBIOS name cache. Whenever a computer name is resolved to an IP address, the mapping is added to the cache for future reference. Each entry added to the cache is maintained for ten minutes, at which point it is removed. This is the first method a client will use to resolve a computer name. The local NetBIOS name cache is always checked before using any other resolution method. Another method of name resolution is to use a NetBIOS name server, such as WINS, where name resolution requests can be sent.

These are the three standard methods for resolution. However, Microsoft also includes other methods for resolving computer names. These include

- DNS servers
- HOSTS files
- LMHOSTS files

NetBIOS Node Types

The method or methods that a client uses to resolves computer names are determined by the NetBIOS node type it is configured to use. As an example, if a client is configured for B-node, it will first attempt to resolve a NetBIOS name using a broadcast and, if this fails, try the LMHOSTS file. By using the `ipconfig /all` command, you can verify the node type that a client is configured to use (see Figure 4-2). Microsoft supports four different node types, as outlined in Table 4-2.

Keep in mind that a client configured with the IP address of a WINS server will default to

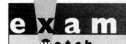

FIGURE 4-2

Verifying the
node type

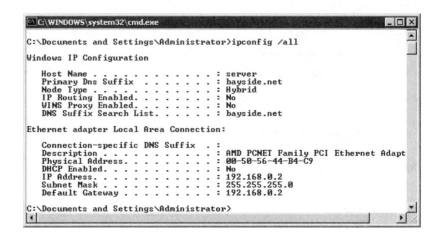

H-node. If the client is not configured with the IP address of a WINS server, it defaults to B-node.

Since Microsoft includes other methods for name resolution, the entire name resolution process can include HOSTS files and DNS servers as well. For a WINS client using H-node, the entire resolution process is performed in the following order:

- NetBIOS name cache
- WINS
- Broadcast
- LMHOSTS
- HOSTS
- DNS

TABLE 4-2   Node Types Supported by Microsoft

Node Type	Description
B-node	This method uses a broadcast. If the broadcast fails, an LMHOSTS file is used.
P-node	This method uses a WINS name server.
M-node	This method uses a broadcast. If the broadcast fails, a WINS server is used.
H-node	This method uses a WINS server. If the WINS server cannot resolve the request, a broadcast is used.

LMHOSTS

In an environment that does not implement WINS, LMHOSTS files can be used for name resolution. An LMHOSTS file is a text file that contains NetBIOS name–to–IP address mappings. Although this is not normally the most efficient means for resolving NetBIOS names, it does offer a solution in a non-WINS environment. One of the advantages of an LMHOSTS file is that the entries it contains can be loaded into the NetBIOS name cache (and as you may recall, this method is always used first for name resolution). The biggest disadvantage of using LMHOSTS files is that the contents must be updated every time there is a configuration change, such as renaming a workstation on the network. Also, if DHCP is used and IP addresses assigned to clients are constantly changing, keeping the file up to date involves high administrative overhead.

To ease the administration associated with LMHOSTS files and keeping them up to date on the workstations, you can use a central LMHOSTS and have the changes made to this file propagated to the workstations.

You can find the LMHOSTS file in the %SYSTEMROOT%\system32\drivers\etc directory. In order for the file to be used, the default name of LMHOSTS.SAM must be changed to LMHOSTS. A sample LMHOSTS file is shown in Figure 4-3. As you can see, there are a number of different directives within the file indicating the various types of entries. Table 4-3 outlines the directives appearing in an LMHOSTS file.

on the *J*ob

LMHOSTS is a solution for reducing broadcast traffic in a small environment where workstations are configured with static IP addresses.

e x a m

w a t c h *Entries within the LMHOSTS file can be preloaded into the NetBIOS name cache when the computer is booted. Any entries containing the #PRE directive will be preloaded into the cache and not removed until the computer is shut* *down. Since the LMHOSTS file is parsed from beginning to end when attempting to resolve NetBIOS names, it is generally a good idea to place those entries that will be preloaded at the end of the text file to speed up the resolution process, especially if there are numerous entries.*

FIGURE 4-3

The default
LMHOSTS file
included with
Windows
Server 2003

TABLE 4-3 LMHOSTS File Directives

Predefined Keyword	Description
#PRE	Indicates that an entry should be preloaded into the cache when the computer is booted.
#DOM:*DOMAIN_NAME*	Indicates that the record is for a domain controller.
#BEGIN_ALTERNATE #END_ALTERNATE	Indicates a list of alternative LMHOSTS files that can be used for resolution.
#INCLUDE	Indicates that entries from another LMHOSTS file, other than the default one, should be loaded.
#MH	Indicates multiple entries for a multihomed computer.

CERTIFICATION OBJECTIVE 4.02

Planning a WINS Solution

Implementing a WINS solution does require some level of preplanning. These are some of the things you need to consider before installing WINS:

- Does the network require a WINS implementation?
- How many WINS servers will be required?
- Where on the network will the WINS servers be placed?

These topics will be discussed in the following section.

Determining the Need for WINS

In network environment that supports only Windows 2000, Windows XP, and Windows Server 2003 clients, WINS is not required, as the primary namespace used is DNS. When NetBIOS over TCP/IP is enabled, traditional name resolution techniques may still be used, depending upon the manner is which a request is made. For example, when mapping a network drive using a convention like \\server01\share, NetBIOS name resolution is still used. The method used when NetBIOS over TCP/IP is enabled is determined by the server name provided with the command. If the drive is mapped as, for example, \\server01.bayside.net, or if the server name is longer than 15 characters, the DNS is used.

Pre–Windows 2000 clients require NetBIOS for such things as locating domain controllers. Thus if there are any legacy clients running, for instance, Windows NT 4.0, Windows 95, or Windows 98 on the network, WINS may be required for NetBIOS name resolution services. Otherwise, if all workstations can support DNS, WINS will not need to be implemented.

You also need to look at the physical network. If there is a single subnet with a small number of clients, WINS may not be necessary; you can rely on LMHOSTS files or broadcasts for name resolution. However, if there are a large number of hosts on the subnet or if there are multiple subnets, WINS should be implemented. In terms of the number of clients, a physical network can suffer in performance if broadcasts are relied upon for name resolution. Implementing WINS can reduce the number of broadcasts on a subnet. Also, since routers do not forward broadcasts between subnets, WINS should be used to facilitate network access between different subnets. WINS servers on different subnets can be configured for replication so that clients on one subnet can resolve the names of clients on other subnets.

Determining the Number of WINS Servers and Placement

A single WINS server is capable of handling a large number of requests. The number of WINS servers you implement on a network will be dependent on several things, such as the hardware installed on the WINS server, whether or not the network is routed, and the number of clients on each subnet. When deciding the number of WINS servers, also consider the following points:

- The number of NetBIOS names typically registered by a WINS client
- The frequency of name registrations and releases due to workstations being rebooted
- The speed and availability of the physical links connecting the various networks

A single WINS server is capable of handling approximately 10,000 clients; of course, this figure depends on the amount of NetBIOS traffic that is generated. It is always recommended, though, that at least two WINS servers be configured, to provide fault tolerance. Accordingly, when you are planning the number of WINS servers, a good guideline is to install two WINS servers for every 10,000 WINS clients. You can then configure the two WINS servers as replication partners.

When implementing multiple WINS servers, you also need to decide where they should be located. The network connections will have a major impact on where WINS servers are placed. For example, if a branch office is connected to a central office by a slow, unreliable link, you may choose to place a WINS server in the branch location so that clients can resolve names locally rather than across a WAN link (see Figure 4-4). Also, consider how clients are distributed throughout the network and plan to place the WINS servers on subnets that contain the most WINS clients or generate the most name resolution traffic.

FIGURE 4-4

Using multiple
WINS servers

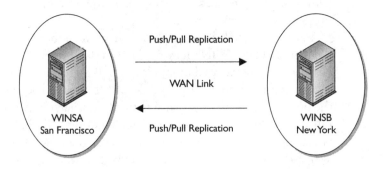

SCENARIO & SOLUTION

When planning to implement WINS, what are some of the important aspects to consider?	You should consider the need for WINS servers, how many are required (plan to install at least two for fault tolerance), and where on the network to place the servers.
Is WINS required in a Windows Server 2003 environment?	The answer depends on the types of clients you must support. If clients are running Windows 2000 and later, then no, WINS is not required. However, if you need to support pre–Windows 2000 clients, plan to implement WINS.
What would be the benefit of installing WINS as opposed to using LMHOSTS files?	The main benefit is that the WINS database is dynamic, so WINS clients can dynamically register their NetBIOS names as well as update their records when changes occur. The LMHOSTS file is static and therefore must be manually updated.
If WINS is being installed within a routed environment, does each subnet require a WINS server?	No. You can configure a WINS proxy agent on those subnets that do not host WINS servers. In an environment that is fully routed, where all clients are WINS-compatible, a WINS proxy is not required. A WINS proxy agent is necessary only if a client on a subnet does not support WINS.

WINS Replication

If there are multiple WINS servers on the network, they can be configured to replicate the contents of their databases to other servers. Doing so allows WINS information to be distributed throughout a network, such that the NetBIOS names registered with one server can be replicated to other servers on the network.

Replication is especially important in a subnetted environment—take, for example, Figure 4-5. There is a WINS server on Subnet A and a WINS server on Subnet B. Each WINS client registers its computer name with the WINS server on its own subnet. Without replication, when a client on Subnet A attempts to resolve the NetBIOS name for a host on Subnet B, resolution will fail. Replicating WINS records between servers makes it possible to resolve names in a subnetted environment.

In order for replication to occur between two WINS servers, they must be configured as replication partners. There are three different configurations for replication partners: push, pull, and push/pull.

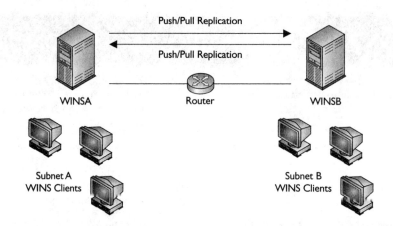

FIGURE 4-5

Distributing WINS information using replication

WINS replication is incremental, which means only the changes are replicated, not the entire database.

Replication Partners

When a WINS server is configured as a *pull* partner, it will request WINS database updates from another WINS server. Requests for updates are performed at preconfigured intervals (this is known as the replication interval; the default value is every 30 minutes). A pull partner requests any information from its push partner with a higher version ID than the last entry received. When a WINS server is configured as a pull partner, it will request updates from its push partners when it is started and when the time defined by the replication interval expires.

When a WINS server is configured as a push partner, it will send a message to its pull partners notifying them of changes to its database. The pull partners will respond to the message by requesting the updates. At this point, the push partner sends the updates to its configured pull partners. Through the WINS management console (see Figure 4-6), you can configure when the WINS server will notify its pull partners, including

- When the WINS server starts
- When there is an IP address change for a NetBIOS name mapping in the database
- When a certain number of changes have occurred

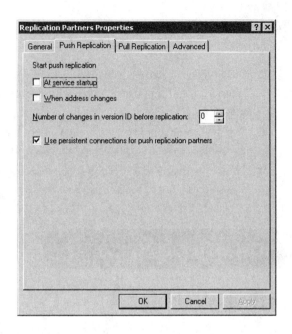

Thus in order to replicate a WINS database between two servers, you must configure at least one push partner and one pull partner. Once you do so, replication can occur in any of the following situations, depending on your configuration:

■ A pull partner will request changes each time the server is started. You can also configure a push partner to send a notification when it starts.

■ Replication can be configured to occur at specific intervals. For example, the pull partner can be configured to request updates every two hours.

■ A push partner can be configured to notify its pull partners when a certain number of changes have occurred. The pull partners will then request the updates.

■ Replication can be forced between two WINS servers.

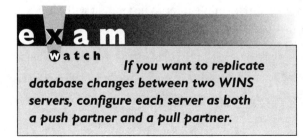

If you want to replicate database changes between two WINS servers, configure each server as both a push partner and a pull partner.

In general, it is easiest to configure push/pull partners to ensure full replication of the WINS database. This is also the default configuration in Windows Server 2003. This configuration is also required if you are implementing a secondary WINS server for fault tolerance. Push/pull partners ensure that both WINS servers replicate their database changes to each other. In any case, when you are deciding how to configure replication partners, keep the following points in mind:

- If WINS servers are connected by high-speed reliable links, configure a push partner so that replication can occur when a preset number of database changes is reached.

- A pull partner should be configured when WINS servers are connected by slow, unreliable links, as replication can be configured to occur at specific intervals.

- If changes need to be replicated between two servers, configure each to be both a push partner and a pull partner.

CERTIFICATION OBJECTIVE 4.03

Implementing WINS

Once you have determined that WINS is required on the network and considered the topics outlined in the section on planning a WINS solution, you are ready to go ahead with the installation and configuration of the service. The following section will discuss how to install and configure WINS in Windows Server 2003, how to configure a WINS client, and how to manage and maintain a WINS server once it is functioning on the network.

Installing and Configuring WINS

Installing and configuring WINS is not a very complex task. The installation is as simple as adding the service and placing the Windows Server 2003 CD into the CD-ROM drive when prompted. In some cases, once the service is installed, you will not need to make any configuration changes and can simply use all the default settings. In situations such as this, WINS is a snap to get up and running on a network. In any case, it is still important for a network administrator to be familiar with the installation process and the various settings that can be configured. These will be our next topics for discussion.

INSIDE THE EXAM

Hub and Spoke Replication Design

The topic of convergence has not yet been discussed in the chapter but may appear in an exam question. In terms of WINS replication, convergence is the amount of time it takes for a change on one WINS server to be replicated to other WINS servers on the network. You can determine the convergence time by calculating all the replication intervals. For example, if WINS01 is configured as a push/pull partner with WINS02 with a replication interval of 15 minutes and WINS02 is also configured as a push/pull partner with WINS03 with a replication interval of 15 minutes, the convergence time is 30 minutes. Obviously, when you are planning for WINS replication, you want to implement a replication model that will provide fast convergence.

Many organizations choose to implement a hub and spoke model for WINS replication. This model works well for networks that consist of a central location and various branch offices. Hence the name hub and spoke, where the central location is configured as the hub for WINS replication and the branch offices are the spokes.

In this model, there is a WINS server at the central office (hopefully at least two for fault tolerance), and WINS servers are placed within the branch offices. Each of the WINS servers in the branch offices is configured as both a push partner and a pull partner with the WINS server in the central office, which is responsible for receiving database changes from the various WINS servers and replicating them throughout the network.

Installing WINS

WINS is not a service that is installed by default. There are a number of ways in which WINS can be installed. You can do so during the installation of Windows Server 2003, using the Configure Your Server Wizard (see Figure 4-7), or using the Add or Remove Programs applet within the Control Panel. Many times, there are requirements that must be met before you can install a service or application. In terms of WINS, there are no preinstallation requirements other than that it is recommended that you configure the server with a static IP address first. Exercise 4-1 walks you through the steps of installing WINS using the Add or Remove Programs applet within the Control Panel.

FIGURE 4-7

Installing WINS
using the
Configure Your
Server Wizard

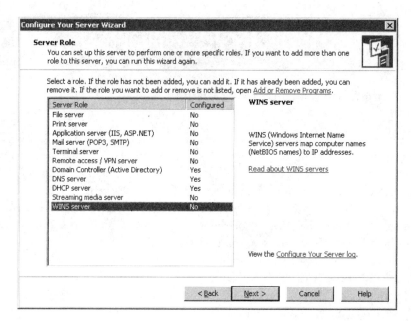

EXERCISE 4-1

Installing WINS

In this exercise, you will install the WINS service on a computer running Windows
Server 2003.

1. Click Start, point to Control Panel, and click Add or Remove Programs.

2. Click Add/Remove Windows Components.

3. From the list of components, select Network Services and click the Details
   button.

4. Click Windows Internet Name Service (WINS) and click OK.

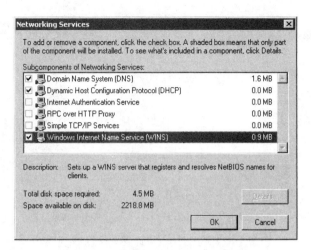

5. Click Next. Insert the Windows Server 2003 installation CD as prompted. Click Finish.

Configuring WINS

Once WINS has been installed, the WINS console is added to the Administrative Tools menu. You can use the console to configure and manage your WINS server. To configure the properties of the WINS server, click Start, point to Administrative Tools, and click WINS. Within the WINS console, right-click your WINS server and choose Properties (see Figure 4-8).

Using the options on the General tab, you can configure how often statistics are updated. By default, a WINS server refreshes its server statistics every ten minutes. You can also specify the path to which the WINS database is backed up. Using the Renewal tab shown in Figure 4-9, you can configure the various intervals at which records in the database are renewed, deleted, and verified. The renewal options are summarized in Table 4-4.

When a WINS client is properly shut down, a name release request is sent to the WINS server. At this point, the record is marked as released. The extinction interval determines how long the record remains available for the client. For example, if a workstation is simply rebooted, the NetBIOS name will be released but is still available for the client when it is restarted. The extinction timeout determines when the record is removed from the WINS database.

FIGURE 4-8

WINS server
properties
dialog box

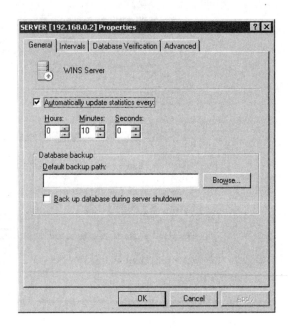

Using the Database Verification tab shown in Figure 4-10, you can control whether the WINS server will verify the integrity of the database and how often. The WINS

FIGURE 4-9

Configuring
renewal intervals

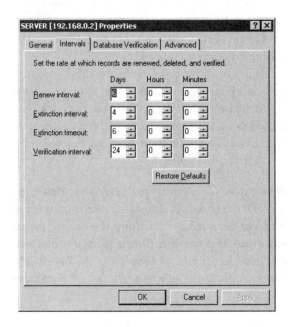

TABLE 4-4	Renewal Interval Options
Option	**Description**
Renewal Interval	This determines the number of days that a WINS client can use a registered NetBIOS name before it must be renewed.
Extinction Interval	This determines the amount of time before a record marked as released is marked as being extinct.
Extinction Timeout	This determines the amount of time before a record marked as extinct is removed from the WINS database.
Verification Interval	This determines the amount of time before a WINS server must verify that records replicated from another WINS server are still active.

server will compare its local database with other WINS servers on the network. This ensures that the database is not corrupt and that it contains correct information. This option is not enabled by default because it can affect the performance of a WINS server.

Using the Advanced tab shown in Figure 4-11, you can configure a number of various other settings. The first option allows you to enable logging of WINS-related events

FIGURE 4-10

Controlling
database
verification

FIGURE 4-11

Configuring
Advanced
properties of
a WINS server

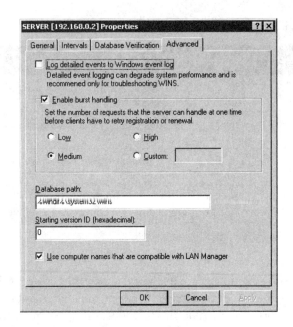

to the Windows System log. You can enable or disable Burst Handling, which determines the number of client requests the WINS server can handle at one time. The Database Path option enables you to configure where the WINS database will be stored.

Making configuration changes to any component on a server can have adverse effects. You can give a user the ability to view the contents of the WINS database by adding that user to the WINS Users group. Members of this group do not have permission to make configuration changes to the server.

Configuring WINS Clients

In order for clients to dynamically register their NetBIOS names, they must be configured with the IP address of a WINS server. Once configured, WINS clients can dynamically register their NetBIOS name with the WINS server, release and renew their registered names, and query the WINS server to resolve NetBIOS names. Windows Server 2003 supports the following WINS clients:

■ Windows Server 2003 (all platforms)

■ Windows XP (all platforms)

■ Windows 2000 (all platforms)

- Windows ME
- Windows NT Server
- Windows NT Workstation
- Windows 98/95
- Windows for Workgroups
- Microsoft LAN Manager
- OS/2 clients
- Linux and Unix clients (with Samba installed)

There are two different ways in which a WINS client can be configured. If you have implemented DHCP on the network, you can do so dynamically or else you can configure each client manually.

Using DHCP to Configure WINS clients

If you choose to use DHCP, clients must be configured to automatically obtain an IP address. The rest of the configuration is done on the DHCP server. As you should recall from Chapter 2, DHCP servers can assign option parameters to DHCP clients. Thus you can use the DHCP server to provide clients with the IP address of the WINS servers. To do so, you must configure the 044 WINS/NBNS servers (see Figure 4-12) and the 046 WINS/NBT Node Type (see Figure 4-13). The 044 WINS/NBNS option specifies the IP addresses of the WINS servers. The 046 WINS/NBT Node Type specifies the methods clients can use to resolve NetBIOS names and the order in which they are used.

Manually Configuring WINS Clients

Clients can also be configured manually, which requires visiting each workstation and configuring the properties of TCP/IP. This may be a viable solution on a smaller environment. However, where there are a large number of clients, it is normally more efficient to have WINS parameters assigned using a DHCP server. In any case, the process of manually configuring a client will vary between platforms. These steps describe the process of configuring WINS on a Windows XP client:

1. Right-click My Network Places and click Properties.
2. From the Network Connections dialog box, right-click the appropriate Local Area Connection and click Properties.
3. Select Internet Protocol (TCP/IP) and click the Properties button.

FIGURE 4-12

Configuring the
044 WINS/NBNS
option

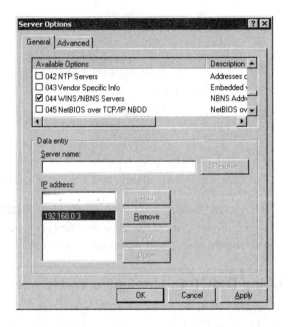

FIGURE 4-13

Configuring the
046 WINS/NBT
option

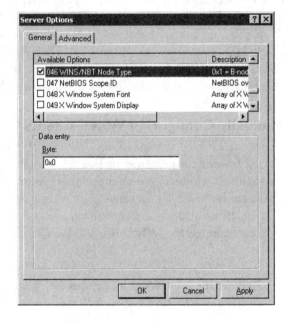

4. From the Internet Protocol (TCP/IP) Properties dialog box, click Advanced. Click the WINS tab.

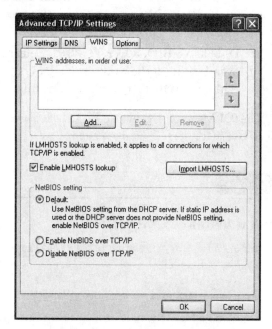

5. Click Add, type in the IP address of the WINS server, and click Add again. Repeat this process for any additional WINS servers.

There are a number of other options available on the WINS tab. Each of them is summarized here:

■ **Enable LMHOSTS Lookup**   This option is enabled by default. It enables the workstation to use an LMHOSTS file for NetBIOS name resolution. The Import LMHOSTS button enables you to import an existing file into the local LMHOSTS file.

■ **Default**   This option is selected by default. The NetBIOS setting, whether NetBIOS over TCP/IP is enabled or disabled, is determined by the DHCP server. If TCP/IP is statically configured and this option is selected, NetBIOS over TCP/IP will be enabled.

- **Enable NetBIOS Over TCP/IP** If the workstation has a static IP address, select this option to enable NetBIOS and WINS use. This option needs to be selected only if the workstation needs to communicate with other workstations running legacy platforms.

- **Disable NetBIOS Over TCP/IP** Select this option to disable NetBIOS over TCP/IP. If the workstation does not have to communicate with other workstations that require NetBIOS, this option should be selected.

The 001 Microsoft Disable NetBIOS DHCP option can be used to disable NetBIOS over TCP/IP on DHCP-enabled clients.

EXERCISE 4-2

Enabling WINS on Windows XP

In this exercise, you will configure the IP address of a WINS server on a workstation running Windows XP.

1. Click Start, and click Control Panel.

2. Double-click the Network Connections applet.

3. Right-click your local area network connection and click Properties.

4. Select Internet Protocol (TCP/IP) and click the Properties button.

5. Click the Advanced button on the General tab.

6. Click the WINS tab.

7. Click the Add button. Type in the IP address of the WINS server. Click Add.

8. Click OK.

Configuring Static Mappings

There may be instances when some clients on the network are unable to dynamically register their names with a WINS server. For example, Unix clients support only DNS and are unable to dynamically register and update their names with a WINS server. Although the WINS database is dynamic, static mappings can be created. If there are clients on the network that do not support WINS, an administrator can create a static mapping for them in the WINS database. Once the static entries are created, WINS clients can resolve the names of non-WINS clients. Any static entries do not need to be updated by the client, nor do they expire. In order to remove these entries, an administrator must manually delete them.

When a system running Unix/Linux has Samba installed, it is capable of registering with a WINS server.

To configure a new static mapping in the WINS database:

1. Click Start, point to Administrative Tools, and click WINS.

2. From within the WINS console, right-click the Active Registrations container and click New Static Mapping.

3. Type in the computer name for the host.

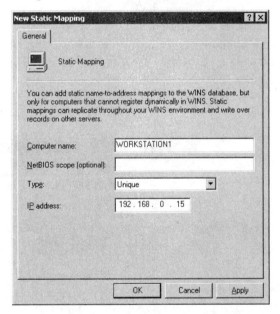

4. If required, enter the NetBIOS scope ID.

5. Use the drop-down arrow to select the type of NetBIOS entry you are creating. If you are creating an entry for a host, leave the default option (Unique) selected.

6. Specify the IP address of the host. Click OK.

Be aware of what can happen if you are using Static Mappings for a DHCP client. If the client's IP address should change, the static mapping must be manually updated. To avoid having to do this, create a client reservation for the host in DHCP so that its IP address remains consistent.

WINS Proxy Agents

In a routed network, resolving NetBIOS names poses a problem, since routers do not forward broadcasts. Forwarding broadcasts can create an abundance of traffic on the network. Also, for clients that do not support WINS, NetBIOS names are resolved using broadcasts. This poses another problem when it comes to resolving the name of a workstation on another subnet.

In situations such as these, a WINS proxy agent can be configured. A WINS proxy agent is a computer on the local subnet that listens for NetBIOS name resolution broadcasts. Once the WINS proxy agent receives a name resolution broadcast, it will forward the request directly to a WINS server on another subnet on behalf of the non-WINS-enabled client and return the results. For name registration requests, the WINS proxy agent will query the WINS server to ensure that the name has not been registered by another workstation.

A computer can be enabled as a WINS proxy agent by editing the local Registry. To do so, edit the HKEY_LOCAL_MACHINE\System\CurrentControlSet\Services\NETBT\Parameters key and change the value of the EnableProxy key to 1 (see Figure 4-14).

FIGURE 4-14

Enabling the
WINS proxy
agent

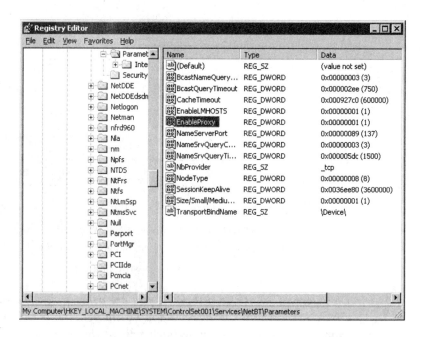

The following steps outline the process that occurs when a non-WINS client broadcasts a name resolution request on a subnet hosting a WINS proxy agent:

1. A non-WINS client sends a NetBIOS broadcast on the local subnet.

2. The WINS proxy agent on the local subnet receives the broadcast and checks to see if it has a mapping for the request in its local cache. If not, the WINS proxy agent queries the WINS server.

3. The WINS server returns the address mapping to the WINS proxy agent.

4. The mapping is placed in the NETBIOS name cache of the WINS proxy client, and the results are returned to the non-WINS client.

INSIDE THE EXAM

The WINS Proxy Agent

For clients that are not WINS enabled, B-node broadcasts are used to resolve hostnames. On a network consisting of a single subnet, this does not pose a problem. However, in routed environments, how do these clients resolve NetBIOS names across routers?

The WINS proxy agent was introduced to address this problem. Once a workstation is enabled as a WINS proxy, it will listen on the local subnet for any B-node broadcasts initiated by non-WINS clients. The WINS proxy sends the requests directly to the WINS server it is configured to use. Since the request is now directed at a specific server on the network, it can pass through the routers.

The WINS proxy agent responds to non-WINS-enabled clients only if it has a mapping for the request in its local cache. So when the WINS proxy receives a B-node name resolution broadcast, it first checks the contents of its cache. If no mapping is found, it sends the request to the WINS server. Once the WINS server responds, the WINS proxy agent will place the results into the cache.

The WINS proxy agent does not initially respond to any requests that it cannot resolve using the contents of the local cache. Thus initially the WINS proxy may not respond to a B-node broadcast. It will respond to the request only once it has a mapping for it within its local cache.

EXERCISE 4-3

Planning for WINS

In the following exercise, you will use the information presented in the scenario to plan a WINS solution.

An organization is in the process of restructuring. Part of the restructuring plan includes the implementation of WINS. The network consists of four different subnets with approximately 300 users. The workstations are running a number of different platforms. Most of the workstations are WINS enabled. There are workstations on Subnet A that are non-WINS clients. Subnet C also hosts a non-WINS-enabled server that all clients must have access to. The solution you implement must support the non-WINS clients. Reliability is also a concern.

1. How many WINS servers are required?
2. How many WINS servers would you recommend?
3. Two of the subnets contain non-WINS clients. How will the WINS implementation allow these clients to resolve NetBIOS names?
4. How can you ensure that all clients can resolve the name of the non-WINS-enabled server on Subnet C?

Configuring WINS Replication

As was discussed earlier in the chapter, a WINS server can be configured to replicate the name registrations within its database with other WINS servers on the network. To do so, the WINS server must be configured with a replication partner.

To configure WINS replication partners:

1. Click Start, point to Administrative Tools, and click WINS.
2. Within the WINS console, right-click the Replication Partners container and click New Replication Partner.
3. In the New Replication Partner dialog box, type in the name or IP address of the WINS server you want to add as a replication partner. Click OK.

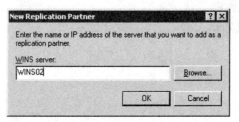

4. The new replication partner now appears in the right pane of the Replication Partners container. Right-click the new replication partner and click Properties. The properties dialog box for the server appears.

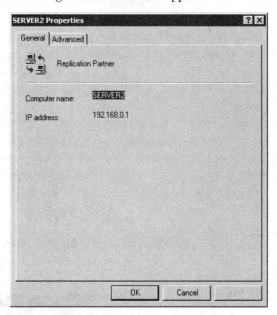

5. Select the Advanced tab. Use the drop-down arrow to select the replication partner type.

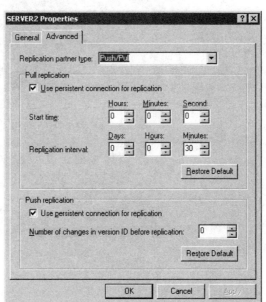

6. The default replication interval is set to 30 minutes.

There are also a number of other options that you can configure in terms of replication. To do so, right-click the Replication Partners container within the WINS console and click Properties (see Figure 4-15).

From the General tab, you have two options. The first option, Replication Only With Partners, is selected by default. This means that replication can occur only between replication partners. By clearing this option, you allow replication to occur with any WINS server, regardless of whether it is a configured replication partner. The second option is used to specify whether static mappings can be overwritten when they conflict with a new name registration or a replica.

You can use the Push Replication tab discussed earlier in the chapter to configure when the WINS server should notify its pull partners. There is also the option to use persistent connections for push replication partners. *Persistent connections* allow a WINS server to keep connections open after replication instead of closing them. This is ideal where WINS servers are connected by high-speed links. Replication can occur more quickly because temporary connections do not need to be reestablished.

Persistent connections were introduced in Windows 2000. Prior to that, WINS servers would close the connection after replication. This meant that each time

FIGURE 4-15

Configuring
replication
partner
properties

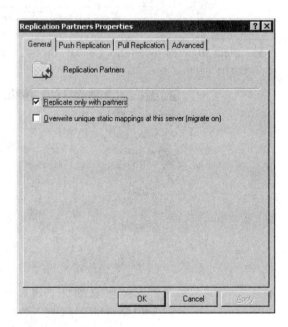

replication occurred, a new connection would first need to be established, requiring processor cycles. Persistent connections are an efficient way of replicating information when WINS servers have high-speed connections between them. They enable a WINS server to keep a connection open after replication is complete. In turn, this means replication can occur more quickly and efficiently.

Using the Pull Replication tab shown in Figure 4-16, you can configure options such as the start time and the replication interval. You can specify the number of times a WINS server should attempt to reestablish a failed connection with a pull partner during replication. You can also configure the WINS server to pull changes at startup and use persistent connections with its push partners.

Using the Advanced tab shown in Figure 4-17, you can configure the WINS server to accept or block records from other WINS servers on the network. The automatic partner replication option enables you to configure replication to occur automatically between WINS servers. When you select this option, the WINS server will automatically configure itself as a replication partner with other WINS servers on the network by broadcasting its presence using the multicast group address of 224.0.1.24. Every WINS server using automatic partner replication will configure itself as both a push partner and a pull partner with other WINS servers on the network.

FIGURE 4-16

Configuring
pull replication
settings

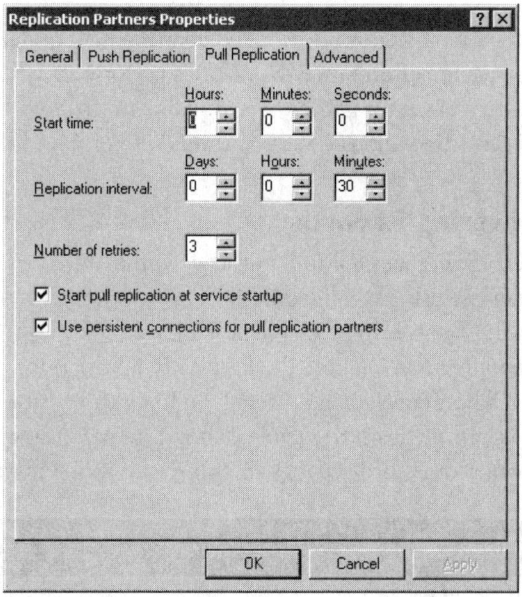

FIGURE 4-17

Configuring
advanced
replication
partner settings

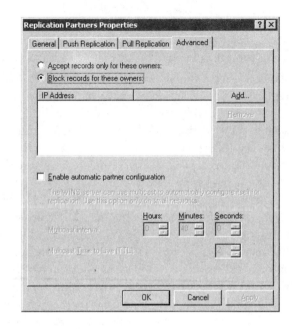

Managing WINS

As with most services installed, management and monitoring tasks should be performed to ensure performance. Most tasks performed will involve the WINS database and can be performed using the tools available in the WINS console. The following section will discuss the various tasks you should perform and the different tools available.

Filtering Records

WINS provides administrators with the ability to search for records within the WINS database using specific criteria. This is extremely useful when there are numerous entries in the database. You can search for records by right-clicking the Active Registrations container and clicking the Display Records option (see Figure 4-18).

When configuring filters, you have three different categories to choose from (as you can see from the three tabs available). You can filter by record mapping, record owner, or record type, as shown in the following table:

Filter Category	Description
Record Mapping	A query can be based on all or part of a NetBIOS name and/or IP address.
Record Owner	A query can be based on the name records for one or more name record owners.
Record Type	A name query can be based on a NetBIOS name record type.

FIGURE 4-18

Using the Display
Records option
to search for
records

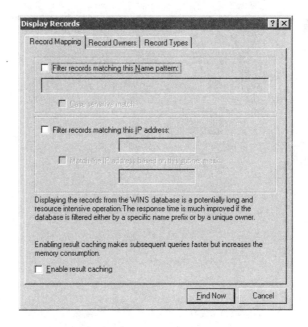

Backing Up and Restoring the WINS Database

Since the WINS database contains the name-to-IP address mappings, you will want to configure the WINS server to periodically back it up. To do so, right-click the WINS server and click Properties. Using the General tab, specify a backup path.

Once the backup location is configured, the Wins_bak folder is automatically created in the location you specified (see Figure 4-19). You can also choose to have the WINS server perform a backup when the server is shut down.

You can also use the Back Up Database option from the shortcut menu to create a single nonrecurring backup of the database.

In the event that the WINS database needs to be restored, you can do so by right-clicking the WINS server, selecting the Restore Database option, and specifying where the backup exists. If you have a backup of the WINS database, you can restore it by right-clicking the WINS server, choosing the Restore Database option, and specifying the location of the backup folder.

If you are trying to restore the WINS database and find that the Restore Database option is not available, this is because the WINS service must be stopped. Once the service is stopped, you will have the option to restore the database.

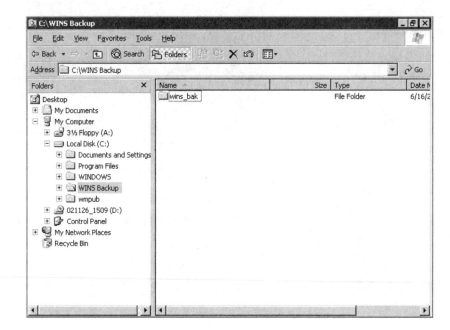

Using Server Statistics

The WINS console provides a quick and simple way to view various server statistics. They can be useful in gathering general performance information as well as for troubleshooting problems. You can view the WINS Server "Server" Statistics by right-clicking the WINS server and choosing the Server Statistics option. Table 4-5 summarizes the various statistics.

Verifying WINS Database

Consistency checking is done to ensure the integrity of the WINS database when there are multiple WINS servers on the network configured for replication. There are two options you can use to verify the consistency of the database: Verify Database Consistency and Verify Version ID Consistency. The Verify Database Consistency option forces the local WINS server to check all names replicated from other WINS servers and compare them with the local versions on the servers that own the records. If necessary, the WINS server will then update its local records. The Verify Version ID Consistency option forces the WINS server to verify that it has the highest version ID for all records it owns among its replication partners.

TABLE 4-5   WINS Server "Server" Statistics

Statistic	Description
Server start time	The date and time that the WINS service was last started
Database initialized	The date and time that static mappings were last imported into the WINS database
Statistics last cleared	The date and time that the server statistics were last reset
Last periodic replication	The last time replication occurred because the replication interval expired
Last manual replication	The last time replication was manually initiated
Last net update replication	The last time replication occurred due to a notification message sent from a push partner to a pull partner
Last address change replication	The last time replication occurred because of an address change message
Total queries (records found)	The number of queries successfully found
Total queries (records not found)	The number of queries that failed because the record was not found
Total releases (records found)	The number of successful releases received from NetBIOS applications being shut down
Total releases (records not found)	The number of failed releases from NetBIOS applications being shut down
Unique registrations (conflicts)	The number of unique name registration requests received that conflicted with an existing record
Unique registrations (renewals)	The number of renewals received for each unique computer name
Group registrations (conflicts)	The number of name registrations received from groups that conflicted with existing records
Group registrations (renewals)	The number of renewals received for group names
Total registrations received	The total number of registration messages received from WINS clients
Last periodic scavenging	The last time the database was scavenged because the renewal interval was reached
Last manual scavenging	The last time the database was manually scavenged by an administrator
Last extinction scavenging	The last time the database was scavenged because the extinction period was reached
Last verification scavenging	The last time the database was scavenged because the verification interval was reached

Tombstoning

Records that are deleted or marked as extinct on one server can cause inconsistencies in the databases of that server's replication partners. For example, a record that was deleted from the database on one server can easily still appear within the database of a replication partner.

Windows Server 2003 supports a feature known as *tombstoning*. Once a record is marked as tombstoned, it is no longer considered to be active on the local WINS server. The record remains within the local database for replication purposes. When a tombstoned record is replicated, all replication partners mark the record as being tombstoned. The record becomes extinct and is eventually removed from the database.

Records within the WINS database can be manually deleted or tombstoned using the following process:

1. Within the WINS console, right-click the Active Registrations container and click the Display Filter option.

2. Use the various filter categories to search for the appropriate record. Click Find Now.

3. In the Details pane, right-click the appropriate record and click Delete.

4. Within the Delete Record dialog box, select one of the following options: Delete The Record Only From This Server or Replicate Deletion Of The Record To Other Servers (Tombstone).

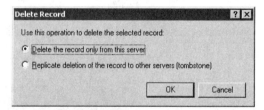

CERTIFICATION OBJECTIVE 4.04

Optimizing WINS

Optimizing WINS falls into two categories. First, what steps can you take to ensure the WINS service is available when it is required? Second, what steps can you take to improve the performance of individual WINS servers? The topic of optimizing WINS servers is briefly discussed in the following sections.

Improving WINS Availability

You can define the availability of a service as the amount of time a service is available when users need it. Ideally, the WINS service should be available whenever it is required. Improving the availability means taking steps to ensure that the WINS service is always available for users on the network when they need to resolve NetBIOS names.

The first way in which the availability the service can be enhanced is by implementing multiple WINS servers and configuring replication. Not only does this improve the availability of the service on a local network, but it can do so for a remote network as well. For example, placing a WINS server within a remote site means the WINS service remains available to users in the event that a connection or router fails.

Another option for increasing availability is to use Windows Clustering. Windows Clustering provides redundancy for a single WINS server and enables immediate recovery for hardware or software failure.

on the
Job

A simple way of improving availability for WINS clients is to configure them with multiple WINS server IP addresses. When the primary WINS server is not available, they can send the request to one of the other configured WINS servers. However, this practice should not be done on the WINS servers themselves. When configuring the TCP/IP properties of a WINS server, let it point only to itself. Since each WINS server must register its own NetBIOS names, this eliminates the possibility of one WINS server owning another's records.

EXERCISE 4-4

Planning for WINS Availability

In this exercise, you will use the information within the scenario to answer the following questions regarding WINS availability.

There are three subnets within the existing network infrastructure. Your implementation plan must enhance the availability of WINS on the network. Subnet A hosts several non-WINS-enabled clients. The remaining clients are all running Windows XP. Subnet C hosts a non-WINS-enabled server that runs a mission-critical application that all users need access to.

1. To eliminate WINS as a single point of failure, how many WINS servers should you plan to implement?

2. In terms of replication, how should replication be configured between the WINS servers?

3. What option do you have for increasing the availability of a single WINS server?

Improving WINS Performance

As mentioned earlier in the chapter, the recommended guideline for implementing WINS is to install two WINS server for every 10,000 clients to ensure adequate performance. There are also steps you can take to improve the performance of a single WINS server. First of all, in terms of hardware, a WINS server should ideally have two processors and a dedicated disk. Also consider using a RAID configuration. Once the WINS servers are installed, you can adjust various configuration settings to improve performance.

- You can adjust the renewal interval to reduce the number of registrations the server must process.
- Have consistency checking performed during off hours, since it is both network and server intensive.
- Limit the number of WINS servers to minimize traffic related to WINS replication.
- Use the various WINS-related counters within System Monitor to monitor server performance.

CERTIFICATION SUMMARY

The Windows Internet Name Service (WINS) is Microsoft's implementation of a NetBIOS name server. It provides a dynamic database of NetBIOS name–to–IP address mappings and provides name resolution services to WINS clients. In a pure Windows 2000 or Windows Server 2003 environment, WINS is not required, although it can still be used. Pre–Windows 2000 clients require NetBIOS to perform various network processes. NetBIOS names or computer names are 16 characters in length, where the first 15 characters identify the workstation and the sixteenth character identifies a specific network service running on the workstation.

A number of different methods can be used to resolve NetBIOS names. The standard resolution methods include broadcasts, NetBIOS name servers, and the NetBIOS name cache. When resolving names, the contents of the cache are always checked first. Microsoft supports three other methods for resolution. They are DNS, HOSTS files, and LMHOSTS files. LMHOSTS files are static text files that contain NetBIOS-to-IP address mappings. The downside of relying on LMHOSTS files for resolution is that they must be manually updated each time changes occur such as the renaming of a workstation.

Before installing WINS, you should take the time to plan the implementation. During this phase, you will need to decide how many WINS servers to install. A general guideline to follow is to install at least two WINS servers for every 10,000 WINS clients. You will also need to decide where the WINS servers should be placed on the network. Your decision will be based on the network connections and how clients are distributed throughout the network. If you install multiple WINS servers, you can configure them as replication partners. By default, when a new replication partner is added, it is configured as both a push partner and a pull partner.

WINS is not installed by default. The service can be installed during the installation of Windows Server 2003, using the Configure Your Server Wizard, or using the Add or Remove Programs applet within the Control Panel. You may be able to leave your WINS server with the default settings, or you can reconfigure it using the WINS console. When it comes to configuring workstations to use WINS, you can do so manually through the properties of TCP/IP or by using DHCP. A WINS proxy agent can also be configured to support non-WINS clients.

To increase the availability of the WINS service, install multiple WINS servers and configure replication between them. You can also increase the availability of a single WINS server using Windows Clustering.

TWO-MINUTE DRILL

Understanding WINS

- ❑ WINS provides a dynamic database of NetBIOS name–to–IP address mappings.
- ❑ NetBIOS names are 16 characters in length, where the first 15 characters identify a workstation and the sixteenth character identifies a network service running on the workstation.
- ❑ WINS resolution consists of four different events: name registration, name renewal, name release, and name resolution.
- ❑ The TTL identifies how long a WINS client can use a NetBIOS name before it must be renewed.
- ❑ Every time a NetBIOS name is resolved, the results are placed within the NetBIOS name cache. Clients will first try to resolve the name using the cache before attempting any other methods of resolution.
- ❑ WINS is required if there are pre–Windows 2000 clients on the network.
- ❑ The three standard resolution methods are broadcast, cache, and NetBIOS name server. Microsoft also includes other methods, such as DNS, HOSTS files, and LMHOSTS files.
- ❑ A WINS client will default to H-node resolution, where the WINS server is queried first. If this fails, a broadcast is used to resolve the name.
- ❑ The entire resolution process for an H-node client occurs in the following order: cache, WINS, broadcast, LMHOSTS, HOSTS, and DNS.
- ❑ An LMHOSTS file is a text file that contains NetBIOS-to-IP address mappings.
- ❑ The #PRE directive indicates that an entry from the LMHOSTS file should be preloaded into the cache.

Planning a WINS Solution

- ❑ Plan to install at least two WINS servers for every 10,000 clients.
- ❑ A pull partner requests database updates from its push partner.
- ❑ A push partner notifies pull partners of updates to its WINS database.

Implementing WINS

❑ WINS clients can be configured manually or dynamically through DHCP.

❑ The 044 WINS/NBNS option identifies the IP addresses of the WINS servers on the network.

❑ The 046 WINS/NBT Node Type option specifies the node type WINS clients will use. The node type indicates the resolution methods used and in what order.

❑ A WINS proxy agent listens for B-node broadcasts and forwards them to its configured WINS server on behalf of the client. The WINS proxy agent can be enabled through the Registry.

❑ By default, WINS servers are automatically configured as both push partners and pull partners when a new replication partner is added.

❑ WINS servers can be configured to accept or block records from other WINS servers on the network.

❑ Persistent connections allow WINS servers to keep connections open after replication is complete. They increase the speed and efficiency of replication because connections do not need to be reestablished each time replication must occur.

❑ Windows Server 2003 supports advanced filtering of records stored in the WINS database. You can filter using three categories: record owner, record mapping, and record type.

❑ A record that is tombstoned is no longer considered active in the WINS database. Tombstoning records eliminates inconsistencies that can occur from records being marked as deleted or extinct.

Optimizing WINS

❑ The availability of WINS can be increase by installing multiple WINS servers and configuring replication as well as by using Windows Clustering.

SELF TEST

Understanding WINS

1. There are two Unix servers on the network, neither of which are running Samba. You want WINS-enabled clients to be able to resolve the names of the Unix servers to IP addresses. The network contains two WINS servers. What should you do?

   A. Install a WINS proxy agent on the network.

   B. Configure static mappings in the WINS database.

   C. Configure the WINS servers as replication partners.

   D. Configure the Unix servers to register their names with the WINS servers.

2. You are configuring the node type for WINS clients using DHCP. You want WINS clients to always send name resolution requests to their configured WINS servers. If this method fails, clients should perform a local broadcast. Which of the following node types should be configured?

   A. B-node

   B. M-node

   C. H-node

   D. P-node

3. Which of the following directives is used within an LMHOSTS file to indicate that an entry should be preloaded into the NetBIOS name cache?

   A. #PRE

   B. #LOAD

   C. #CACHE

   D. #DOM

4. You have enabled WINS on a workstation running Windows XP. The WINS client is configured to use H-node for name resolution. After checking the contents of the NetBIOS name cache, which of the following resolution methods will the client use next?

   A. Broadcast

   B. LMHOSTS

   C. DNS

   D. WINS

5. Joe is the junior network administrator for a small to medium-sized organization. He has been assigned the task of implementing WINS. Due to budget constraints, only one WINS server

will be installed on the network. One of the subnets contains clients that are not WINS enabled. How can you ensure these clients can still resolve NetBIOS names?

A. Enable WINS replication.

B. Install a DHCP relay agent.

C. Configure static mappings for the clients.

D. Install a WINS proxy.

6. Which of the following clients are capable of registering their NetBIOS names with a WINS server? (Choose all correct answers.)

A. Windows NT 4.0

B. Windows 95

C. Windows 98

D. Windows XP

7. There are three WINS servers on the network: WINS01, WINS02, and WINS03. WINS01 is configured as a push/pull partner with WINS02. WINS02 is configured as a push/pull partner with WINS03. The replication interval between WINS01 and WINS02 is 45 minutes. The replication interval between WINS02 and WINS03 is 30 minutes. What is the convergence time?

A. 30 minutes

B. 45 minutes

C. 60 minutes

D. 75 minutes

8. The entire resolution process on a WINS client configured for H-node resolution occurs in what order?

A. Cache, LMHOSTS, WINS, broadcast, HOSTS, DNS

B. Cache, WINS, LMHOSTS, broadcast, HOSTS, DNS

C. Cache, WINS, broadcast, LMHOSTS, HOSTS, DNS

D. Cache, WINS, broadcast, LMHOSTS, DNS, HOSTS

9. John has installed a WINS server on the network. The default settings were not changed after the installation. How long will clients be permitted to use a NetBIOS name before it must be renewed with a WINS server?

A. 12 hours

B. 24 hours

C. 3 days

D. 6 days

Planning a WINS Solution

10. Sean is responsible for implementing a WINS solution for his organization. The network consists of approximately ten subnets. Sean is trying to determine how many WINS servers are required to support this configuration. How many WINS servers must he configure?

    A. 1
    B. 2
    C. 10
    D. 20

11. The database on one of your WINS servers has become corrupt. You configured the WINS server to back up the database to a folder on the local hard drive. When you open the WINS console to restore the database, you notice that the restore option is not available. What is causing the problem?

    A. The WINS service has been stopped.
    B. You are not authorized to perform this procedure.
    C. The WINS service is running.
    D. The backup copy of the database is also corrupt.

12. How can you determine the node type a client is configured to use?

    A. View the properties of TCP/IP through the Network Connections applet.
    B. View the details of the record within the WINS database.
    C. Use the `ipconfig /all` command.
    D. View the 046 WINS/NBT node type option.

Implementing WINS

13. Which of the following sixteenth character identifiers is registered by the workstation service?

    A. <1BH>
    B. <00H>
    C. <06H>
    D. <20H>

14. Which of the following clients requires NetBIOS to perform various network processes?

    A. Windows NT 4.0
    B. Windows 2000
    C. Windows XP
    D. Windows Server 2003

15. You want to increase the amount of time before a record marked as released is marked as extinct. Which of the following values should you change?

    A. Renewal interval
    B. Extinction interval

    C. Extinction timeout

    D. Release interval

16. Mike is the administrator of a Windows Server 2003 network. There are currently five WINS servers on the network. Each server is in a different location. Mike wants to configure the servers so that the convergence time is less than 60 minutes. What should he do?

    A. Configure one server as the central WINS server. Configure all other WINS servers as push/pull partners with the central WINS server. Configure a replication interval of less than 30 minutes.

    B. Configure each server as a push/pull partner with each other server. Configure a replication interval of 30 minutes.

    C. Configure the WINS servers in a circular arrangement. Configure a replication interval of 30 minutes.

    D. Enable automatic partner configuration on all WINS servers. Configure the multicast interval to be 60 minutes.

17. Don is the administrator of a Windows Server 2003 network. He is planning a WINS solution for his company. The network consists of six subnets. A WINS server already exists on Subnet 1. Each subnet hosts both WINS and non-WINS clients. All computers should be able to register and resolve NetBIOS names. What would be the most cost-effective way, requiring the least administrative effort, for Don to accomplish this goal?

    A. Enable a WINS proxy agent on each of the five subnets.

    B. Install a WINS server on each of the remaining five subnets.

    C. Create and configure LMHOSTS files.

    D. Change the node type for all computers on the five subnets.

18. Dave is planning a WINS solution for a medium-sized organization. The network consists of a variety of platforms, including 4 domain controllers running Windows Server 2003, 2 Unix servers, 150 Windows XP Professional workstations, and 50 Windows 2000 Professional workstations. The Samba client is not installed on the Unix servers. Dave's plan must ensure that all Windows clients can resolve the NetBIOS names of the Unix servers. What should he do?

    A. Configure a WINS proxy agent on one of the Windows-based computers.

    B. Configure static mappings for both of the Unix servers.

    C. Install WINS on the Unix servers

    D. Configure static mappings for all of the Windows-based computers.

    E. Place another WINS server on the network.

Optimizing WINS

19. You are planning to deploy WINS for your organization. The network consists of a single subnet. NetBIOS broadcasts are currently used for name resolution. Once a WINS server is installed, which node type will be used by default?

    A. M-node

    B. H-node

    C. B-node

    D. P-node

20. A network consists of several subnets connected using routers. One of the subnets uses NetBIOS broadcasts for name resolution. Users on this subnet are unable to resolve hostnames outside of their local subnet. How can you enable NetBIOS name resolution for these users across all subnets? Select two answers.

    A. Configure LMHOSTS files.

    B. Configure HOSTS files.

    C. Enable a WINS proxy agent on the subnet.

    D. Change the node type to B-node.

LAB QUESTION

FKB International consists of five different subnet locations. Each location has its own IP subnet. Currently, LMHOSTS files are being used for name resolution. Due to the administrative overhead associated with keeping LMHOSTS files up to date, the company has decided to implement a WINS solution instead. Before implementing WINS, you gather the following information to assist in the process:

- The WINS implementation should be fault tolerant.
- Clients must be able to browse resources on all other subnets.
- There are three Unix servers on one subnet that are non-WINS clients. All clients must able to access these three servers.
- WINS is the only name resolution method that should be used. NetBIOS name broadcasts should be eliminated.
- Convergence time should be less than 30 minutes.

Using this information, develop a WINS implementation plan that addresses the following questions:

1. Where should you place the WINS servers? How many WINS servers will be included in the implementation plan?

2. How will you ensure clients can browse resources on all subnets? How will you ensure that clients can access the three Unix servers?

3. How will NetBIOS broadcasts be eliminated on the network?

4. Convergence time must be less than 30 minutes. How will you configure replication between WINS servers?

SELF TEST ANSWERS

Understanding WINS

1. ☑ **B.** Static mappings can be created for clients that do not support WINS, such as Unix clients. This allows WINS clients to resolve the names of the Unix servers to IP addresses. If the Unix servers have Samba installed, they can register their names with a WINS server.

☒ **A** is incorrect because WINS proxy agents listen for B-node broadcasts and forwards them to a WINS server. **C** is incorrect because replication between WINS servers will not enable name resolution of the Unix servers, since no entry for them will exist in the database of either server. **D** is incorrect because Unix does not support WINS.

2. ☑ **C.** When WINS clients are configured for H-node, which is the default, name resolution requests are sent to the WINS servers. If this fails, names can be resolved using a broadcast.

☒ **A** is incorrect because B-node uses a broadcast followed by the LMHOSTS file. **B** is incorrect because M-node uses a broadcast followed by connecting a WINS server. **D** is incorrect because only a broadcast is used for resolution.

3. ☑ **A.** The #PRE directive is used to indicate which entries within the LMHOSTS file should be preloaded into the NetBIOS name cache. These entries are not removed until the workstation is shut down.

☒ **B** and **C** are incorrect because there are no such directives used within the LMHOSTS file. **D** is incorrect because this directive is used to indicate that the entry is for a domain controller.

4. ☑ **D.** When a client is configured to use H-node for name resolution, it will attempt to resolve the name using its configured WINS server if a mapping is not found in the NetBIOS name cache.

☒ **B** and **C** are incorrect because they do not represent the correct name resolution methods used. **A** is incorrect because a broadcast is used only if the WINS servers cannot resolve the request.

5. ☑ **D.** A WINS proxy agent is a computer that listens on the network for B-node name resolution messages and forwards them to its configured WINS server. The WINS proxy agent then returns the results to the client.

☒ **A** is incorrect because there is only a single WINS server on the network. Since the clients are not WINS enabled, they cannot query a WINS server themselves. **B** is incorrect because a DHCP relay agent is used to forward requests for IP addresses to a DHCP server. **C** is incorrect because static mappings would create entries in the database only for non-WINS-enabled clients. They would not permit the clients to query the WINS server to resolve name resolution requests.

6. ☑ **A, B, C,** and **D.** All the clients listed are capable of registering their NetBIOS names with a WINS server.

7. ☑ **D.** The convergence time is calculated by adding the replication intervals. In this case, the convergence time is equal to 75 minutes. This is the amount of time it will take for changes on WINS01 to be replicated to WINS03 and vice versa.

  ☒ **A, B,** and **C** are incorrect because they do not represent the correct value for the total convergence time.

8. ☑ **C.** For an H-node WINS client, the entire resolution process occurs in the following order: cache, WINS, broadcast, LMHOSTS, HOSTS, and DNS.

  ☒ **A, B,** and **D** are incorrect because they do not represent the correct order of name resolution methods used.

9. ☑ **D.** By default, WINS clients must renew their NetBIOS names with the WINS server every six days.

  ☒ **A, B,** and **C** are incorrect because they do not represent the default renewal interval.

Planning a WINS Solution

10. ☑ **A.** There are no requirements for the number of WINS servers that must be installed. Although it is recommended that two servers be installed for fault tolerance, only one WINS server is required.

  ☒ **B, C,** and **D** are incorrect because there are no requirements for the number of WINS servers that must be configured.

11. ☑ **C.** The option to restore the WINS database is available only if the WINS service has been stopped.

  ☒ **A** is incorrect. If the WINS service is stopped, the restore option will be available. **B** and **D** are incorrect because these would not make the restore option unavailable.

12. ☑ **C.** The `ipconfig /all` command will display the node type that a client is configured to use.

  ☒ **A, B,** and **D** are incorrect. Although you can check to see the value configured for the 046 WINS/NBT option, this may not apply to all clients. The remaining two options cannot be used to verify the node type.

Implementing WINS

13. ☑ **B.** The <00H> identifier is registered by the workstation services.

  ☒ **A** is incorrect because <1BH> is registered by domain controllers running as a domain master browser. **C** is incorrect because <06H> is registered by computers running Routing and Remote Access. **D** is incorrect because <20H> is registered by WINS clients running the Server service.

14. ☑ **A.** Windows NT 4.0 requires NetBIOS to perform various network processes.

  ☒ **B, C,** and **D** are incorrect because these clients use hostnames and DNS. However, they provide support for NetBIOS for backward compatibility.

15. ☑ **B.** The extinction interval defines how long before a record marked as released is marked as extinct.

 ☒ **A** is incorrect because the renewal interval defines how long clients can use a NetBIOS name before it must be renewed. **C** is incorrect because the extinction timeout determines how long a record marked as extinct remains in the WINS database. **D** is incorrect because there is no such value.

16. ☑ **A.** By configuring a central WINS server, Mike can make this server responsible for receiving database updates and replicating them to all other WINS servers. A replication interval less than 30 minutes will ensure a convergence time of less than 60 minutes.

 ☒ **B, C,** and **D** are incorrect because each of these options would result in a convergence time of over 60 minutes.

17. ☑ **A.** By enabling a WINS proxy agent, Don can enable clients on the remaining five subnets to register and resolve NetBIOS names.

 ☒ **B** is incorrect because this would not be the most cost-effective method. **C** is incorrect because this would require a large amount of administrative effort to create and maintain LMHOSTS files. **D** is incorrect because changing the node type will not enable clients to register and resolve NetBIOS names.

18. ☑ **B.** If the Samba client is not installed on the Unix servers, they will not register their names with a WINS server. Static mappings must be configured in the WINS database in order for the Windows clients to resolve the names of the Unix servers to IP addresses.

 ☒ **A** is incorrect because a WINS proxy agent enables NetBIOS name resolution for non-WINS clients. **C** is incorrect because the WINS service cannot be installed on a Unix server. **D** is incorrect because Windows-based clients can register their names with the WINS server. The problem lies in resolving the names of the Unix servers, not the Windows-based computers.

Optimizing WINS

19. ☑ **B.** The default node type used for WINS-enabled computers is H-node. Computers will first query the WINS server. If this method of resolution fails, a broadcast is used.

 ☒ **A, C,** and **D** are incorrect because they do not represent the correct node type used by WINS-enabled computers.

20. ☑ **A** and **C.** Configuring LMHOSTS files or enabling a WINS proxy agent will enable clients to resolve NetBIOS names across all subnets.

 ☒ **B** is incorrect because HOSTS files are used to resolve hostnames to IP addresses. **D** is incorrect because changing the node type will not enable clients on the subnet to resolve NetBIOS names of computers on remote subnets.

LAB ANSWERS

1. Ideally, there should be at least one WINS server per subnet. The implementation plan should therefore include a minimum of five WINS servers.

2. By configuring replication between WINS servers, you enable clients to browse resources on all other subnets. Static mappings must be created for the three Unix servers.

3. NetBIOS broadcasts can be eliminated by configuring WINS clients to use P-node for name resolution. This means clients will not perform a broadcast should the WINS server be unable to resolve the resolution request. Clients can be configured to use P-node through DHCP or by editing the Registry of each workstation.

4. One option for replication is to designate one server as the central WINS server (hub and spoke design). The central WINS server is configured as a push/pull replication partner with each of the WINS servers in the branch offices. The replication interval should be less than 15 minutes to ensure that the total convergence time does not exceed 30 minutes.

5

Planning for Network Address Translation

CERTIFICATION OBJECTIVE 5.01

Introduction to NAT

When the Internet first came out, no one knew how quickly it would grow in popularity. It has become a tool used in homes, businesses, and educational institutions. The result of this popularity is a shortage of IP addresses. If you think in terms of a large business, most desktops have Internet access. If it were not for new technologies, each of the desktops would require a public IP address, making it impossible to provide everyone with Internet access.

One of the technologies developed to address this problem is Network Address Translation (NAT). By implementing a solution such as NAT, administrators avoid having to assign each computer on a network a public IP address. Instead, these computers on a network can access the Internet through a single IP address or a limited number of addresses.

Windows Server 2003 includes two technologies that can be used to connect small businesses or home offices to the Internet. Internet Connection Sharing (ICS) and Network Address Translation both provide cost-effective ways to connect multiple computers to the Net. This chapter focuses on NAT and includes a brief discussion on ICS. You will learn the fundamental concepts behind Network Address Translation, the points to consider before implementing it, and how to enable Windows Server 2003 to provide NAT services.

NAT Concepts

As already mentioned, NAT enables you to connect more than one computer to the Internet using a single IP address or limited number of addresses. These are some of the reasons a small business or home office may choose to implement NAT:

- Instead of each workstation having a direct Internet connection, a single connection can be shared among them. This provides a cost-effective method for connecting to the Internet.

- NAT enables you to use one of the private IP address ranges on the private network while still providing access to the Internet.

- A proxy server does not need to be deployed. Instead, NAT can be enabled on a server with an Internet connection. This may be a better solution for smaller businesses and home offices.

NAT was a component included with Windows 2000, but the version of NAT bundled with Windows Server 2003 contains new features. First of all, NAT is integrated with the Basic Firewall service, which combines dynamic and static packet filters to prevent unsolicited traffic from entering the private network. NAT also provides support for L2TP/IPSec connections. This means that L2TP/IPSec VPN connections can now be translated over a NAT interface.

Just as the name Network Address Translation implies, the main service NAT provides is IP address translation. A Windows Server 2003 computer configured for NAT will have at least two interfaces, one connected to the private network and one connected to the Internet. The external interface is assigned the routable IP address (an IP address assigned by an ISP). The interface connected to the private network is by default assigned the IP address of 192.168.0.1. Clients on the private network are also assigned IP addresses from this address range.

NAT consists of three different components that work together to provide Internet connectivity for hosts on the private network:

- **Translation component**   This component is responsible for translating IP addresses and port numbers of the packets as they are forwarded between the internal private network and the Internet.

- **Addressing component**   This component provides computers on the private network with IP addressing information. The NAT server runs a minimal version of DHCP known as the DHCP allocator that assigns each client an IP address, a subnet mask, a default gateway, and the IP address of the DNS server.

- **Name resolution component**   This component receives name resolution requests from clients on the private network, forwards them to the DNS server on the Internet, and returns the results to the client.

As you will see later in the chapter, clients on the private network have their gateways pointing to the NAT server. All Internet requests are routed through the NAT server and appear as though they originated from the same public IP address. The NAT server basically acts on behalf of internal clients. When internal clients access the Internet, NAT receives the request and translates the private IP addresses and the port numbers before forwarding the request to the Internet. The IP address and port number of the internal client are mapped to the external port number and IP address to which the request is made.

Translation Component

When NAT receives a request, it modifies the source IP address, the source port, and the checksum. If additional information must be translated, a NAT editor can be installed. Windows Server 2003 includes NAT editors for the following protocols: FTP, PPTP, ICMP, and NetBIOS over TCP/IP.

All internal requests are mapped to an external request (the internal IP address is mapped to the IP address assigned to the public interface), and the information is kept in a table that is stored in memory. When the response to a request is returned to the NAT server, it uses the mappings stored within the table to determine the internal client to which the response should be returned. NAT supports single or multiple public IP addresses. When a single IP address is used, NAT will translate the port numbers as well as the IP addresses so that requests can be rerouted back to the host on the private network. If NAT is configured with multiple public IP addresses, only the private IP address is translated, not the port number.

Static and Dynamic Mappings   Before you take a look at what actually happens when a NAT server receives a request, you should be familiar with how NAT uses mappings to manage traffic. Each time NAT translates an IP address, an entry is placed in the NAT translation table. This information is used to determine which hosts on the internal network requests initiated from so that the NAT server knows where to return information.

NAT supports two types of mappings: dynamic and static. *Dynamic* mappings are created when a client on the internal private network initiates communication to an Internet location. These mappings are always removed from the translation table after a certain amount of time passes. *Static* mappings are manually created so that traffic initiated from clients on the Internet can be mapped to a specific IP address and port number of a computer on the private network, for example, if you have a web server on the internal network that you want to make available to users on the Internet. Once a static mapping is created, it remains in the translation table.

When NAT receives a request from a client on the private network, NAT changes the private IP address within the packet to that of a public IP address (allocated by an ISP) and also changes the source TCP or UDP port (if a single public IP address is being used). The information is then placed within the translation table. When requests are received on the external interface from Internet clients, the static mappings in the translation table tell the NAT server where the request should be routed or if it should be dropped. Administrators can configure static mappings to specify that certain types of traffic always be routed to a certain computer on the private network. For example, you can have all traffic on the external interface destined for port 80 routed to a web server on the private network.

Inbound and Outbound Traffic   As you will see later in the chapter, when NAT receives a request from a host on the private network, it first checks to see if a mapping exists within the translation table. If there is no mapping, a dynamic one is created. How the mapping is created will depend upon whether you have been assigned a single IP address or multiple addresses.

■ If the NAT server is configured with only a single public IP address, the TCP or UDP port numbers are translated and the source IP address is mapped to the single public IP address.

■ If the NAT server is configured with multiple public IP addresses, it translates the private IP address to one of the available public IP addresses. In this case, the TCP/UDP ports are not translated. If there are no more public IP addresses available, it uses the process outlined in the preceding item.

As already mentioned, static mappings can also be created to allow traffic initiated on the Internet to pass through to the private network. When an Internet-based request is received, NAT first checks to see if a static mapping exists. If there is no static mapping in the translation table matching the request, the packet is dropped. If there is a static mapping, the IP header and the TCP or UDP headers are modified and the packet is forwarded to the private network interface. The only time traffic is permitted to pass to the private network is if a static mapping exists in the translation table or if the traffic was initiated from a client on the private network, which means there would be a dynamic mapping in the translation table matching the request.

NAT Editors   NAT is able to translate the IP address and the UDP and TCP port numbers within the header of a packet. If additional translation is needed, a NAT editor is required. A protocol such as HTTP can be translated because the information is stored within the IP header and the TCP/UDP headers. If translation is required beyond the IP and TCP/UDP headers, NAT editors are required. A NAT editor is an additional software component that can provide translation beyond these headers so that information can pass through the NAT server. Windows Server 2003 provides NAT editors for these protocols:

■ Internet Control Message Protocol (ICMP)

■ Point-to-Point Tunneling Protocol (PPTP)

■ NetBIOS over TCP/IP

■ File Transfer Protocol (FTP)

Addressing Component

Included with NAT is a scaled-down version of the DHCP service known as the DHCP allocator. This component is used to assign IP addressing information to clients on the internal network. By default, NAT will assign clients an IP address from the private address range of 192.168.0.0/24. As you will see later in the chapter, this is one of the main differences between NAT and ICS. With NAT, the range of IP addresses is configurable, so you have the option of using another IP address range if necessary.

The DHCP allocator will assign clients the following parameters:

- IP address
- Subnet mask
- Default gateway
- IP address of the DNS server

The DHCP allocator cannot be used to assign clients any additional parameters, and it supports only a single scope. This means you cannot configure NAT with more than one IP address range. If more than one IP address range is required on the private network, you can disable this component of NAT and install a DHCP server on the private network instead.

Name Resolution Component

NAT also includes a name resolution component. Although NAT does not act as a DNS server itself, it does act as a DNS proxy for clients on the private network. As DNS queries are sent by these clients, NAT receives the requests and forwards them on behalf of the clients to its configured DNS server. Once NAT receives a response, it is returned to the requesting client.

The DHCP allocator assigns clients the IP address of a DNS server. This will be the IP address of the NAT interface connected to the private network.

How NAT Works

The steps that follow outline the process that occurs when NAT receives a request from a client on the private network:

1. The NAT server checks the translation table to determine whether a static or dynamic mapping already exists that matches the request.

2. If no mapping is found, a dynamic mapping is created.

3. If necessary, the appropriate NAT editor in invoked.

4. NAT performs the necessary translations. If multiple public IP addresses exist, the private IP address is translated into a public IP address. If only a single public IP address exists, the IP address as well as the TCP or UDP port number is translated.

5. The mapping is stored within the translation table, and the request is forwarded to the Internet.

6. When the results are returned to the NAT server, it uses the information in the translation table to route the information back to the appropriate client.

For inbound traffic initiated on the Internet, a slightly different process is used for security purposes to protect computers on the local area network from Internet attacks. When an inbound request is received, NAT checks to see if a static mapping exists that matches the request. If there is no mapping, the request is dropped. If a mapping does exist, the TCP/UDP and IP headers are modified and forwarded to the private interface of the NAT server.

So let's take a look at an example of what happens when a client on the private network attempts to access an Internet resource. A small home office has a server running Windows Server 2003 with NAT enabled. The private network is using the default private network address of 192.168.0.0 with a subnet mask of 255.255.255.0. The public interface of the NAT server has been assigned the IP address of w.x.y.z.

1. A host on the private network using the IP address of 192.168.0.5 makes a request for an Internet resource.

2. An IP packet is generated that contains source and destination IP addresses as well as the source and destination port numbers.

3. The IP packet is forwarded to the private interface of the NAT server, where the source port is translated and the source IP address is changed to w.x.y.z.

4. The NAT server stores the information in the translation table, where the source IP address and port number are mapped to the translated IP address and port number.

5. The packet is forwarded to the Internet and the response is returned to the NAT server.

6. NAT checks the translation table to map the public IP address to the IP address of 192.168.0.5. The request is returned to the client on the private network.

NAT Versus Proxy Servers

One of the common methods for connecting private networks to the Internet is to use application-layer proxies such as Microsoft Proxy Server or Microsoft Internet Security and Acceleration Server (ISA).

NAT provides an Internet connectivity solution for nonrouted networks where all users require the same level of Internet access.

NAT itself is not a proxy server. A proxy server can be considered an inspection point between the private network and the Internet. The proxy server will inspect inbound and outbound traffic and permit or deny it according to configured security policies. A proxy can also grant or deny Internet access to groups. On its own, the only thing NAT does is provide translation services. It is not able to inspect packets and grant or deny according to criteria such as protocol, IP address, and group membership.

A product such as ISA server or Microsoft Proxy Server is designed for medium to large organizations, whereas NAT is designed for small to medium-sized networks. A proxy server also functions at the session layer of the OSI model, while NAT functions at the network layer. A proxy server is therefore capable of providing a greater level of security. The only real security provided with NAT is that it masks the IP addresses of hosts on the private network. A proxy server can also support clients that are running protocols other than TCP/IP, such as IPX/SPX, whereas NAT supports only TCP/IP.

Windows Server 2003 now includes a component known as Basic Firewall. You can enable Basic Firewall on a NAT server to secure your private network from unwanted Internet traffic.

One of the main advantages in choosing NAT over an application layer gateway is that the clients do not need to be reconfigured in any way and do not need additional software installed. If you implement a proxy server, you will need to configure the browser settings and possibly install software on the workstations. Of course, another advantage to NAT is cost and administrative overhead. NAT is built in with Windows Server 2003, so no additional hardware or software needs to be purchased. It is also simpler to configure than a proxy server.

NAT and VPN Connections

NAT can also be used with VPN connections. For example, you can place your calling routers behind a server with NAT enabled. Two tunneling protocols can be used for VPN connections: the Point-to-Point Tunneling Protocol (PPTP) and the Layer 2 Tunneling Protocol (L2TP). Since NAT includes an editor for PPTP, it can be successfully translated across a NAT interface.

INSIDE THE EXAM

Using VPN Connections for Increased Security

NAT on its own is an ideal solution for small businesses and home offices where all users require the same access to the Internet. As for controlling access to resources on the private network, once a static mapping is created, NAT on its own does not allow you to secure access on a user-by-user basis.

Take, for example, an organization that wants to restrict access to resources on the private network on a user-by-user basis, meaning some users will have access to resources that others users will not. The problem with using just NAT is that it does not use any authentication. So the workaround is to use VPN connections. Remote users can establish a VPN connection through a NAT server with VPN servers on the private network. Since VPN connections require

authentication, access to resources can be controlled on a user-by-user basis. Also, since the data transferred over a VPN connection is encrypted, another level of security is added.

When configuring VPN connections to work with NAT, you can now use either PPTP or L2TP/IPSec connections. Using a technology known as NAT-T, IPSec packets can now be successfully translated across a NAT interface. Also keep in mind that if you have Windows 2000 or Windows XP VPN clients, you will need to install the L2TP/IPSec NAT update on the workstations.

So in a nutshell, when considering ways in which you can enhance the security of your NAT implementation, consider using VPN connections to take advantage of user-level authentication and data encryption.

With Windows Server 2003, L2TP/IPSec connection can now be successfully translated across a NAT interface. Using NAT-T (IPSec NAT traversal), hosts on a private network behind a network address translator can create L2TP/IPSec connections over a NAT interface. NAT-T is enabled by default on Windows Server 2003.

The problem with using IPSec through NAT is that it does not allow the original IP address to be modified, because any modifications performed on the packet will

e x a m
watch

IPSec NAT-T is supported by the following VPN clients: Windows NT 4.0, Windows 98, Windows ME, and Windows Server 2003. You must *install the L2TP/IPSec NAT-T update on Windows XP and Windows 2000 computers for IPSec to work successfully behind NAT.*

cause the integrity check to fail and the VPN tunnel will not be established. To overcome this problem, a technology known as NAT traversal was developed, whereby the IPSec packet is encapsulated in a UDP/IP header, allowing the IP address and port number to be translated with no need to modify the original IPSec packet.

CERTIFICATION OBJECTIVE 5.02

Implementing NAT

In order to achieve success on the job as well as on the exam, you need to have an understanding of some of the design decisions that need to be made before implementing NAT as well as how to enable and configure it according to the decisions you make. The following section outlines some of the points that need to be considered before implementing NAT as well as the steps involved in enabling and configuring NAT in Windows Server 2003.

Design Decisions

As with most technologies you implement on a network, some preplanning must be done as to how it will be implemented. This holds true when implementing NAT as well. You need to consider a few issues before going ahead and enabling it on a server. Before you choose to implement NAT, keep in mind that it is designed for a small network where all users require the same type of Internet access.

e x a m

ⓦatch

If all users on the private network require the same type of Internet access, then NAT is a possible solution. However, if you need to control access by group membership, then you must consider another product, such as Microsoft Internet Security and Acceleration (ISA).

IP Address Assignment

Every computer on the internal network needs to be assigned an IP address. Since they will not have a direct connection to the Internet, you can use one of the private IP address ranges. By default, the DHCP service included with NAT uses the IP address range of 192.168.0.0 with a subnet mask of 255.255.255.0. You can change this and use one of the other two private ranges of 10.0.0.0 or 172.16.0.0.

You will also need to determine whether the DHCP allocator included with NAT is required. Since it does have limitations—it supports only a single scope and cannot assign clients any optional parameters other than the IP address of the default gateway and DNS server—you may choose to disable this component and install a DHCP server on the private network.

on the Job *One of the nice things about implementing NAT is that it is simple to configure. The clients on the private network only need to be configured with the IP address of the default gateway pointing to the IP address of the NAT server's private interface, whereas implementing a proxy server requires configuring the browser settings as well as other Internet applications.*

Single or Multiple IP Addresses

NAT can support single or multiple IP addresses. The public interface can be assigned a single IP address, or if you've been assigned multiple IP addresses, you will need to configure the public interface with the pool of addresses assigned by the ISP. This will affect only the way in which translation occurs. If multiple IP addresses exist, the port number does not need to be translated. However, with a single IP address, both the private IP address and the port number need to be translated so that NAT can reroute incoming packets to the appropriate host on the network.

As you will see later in the chapter, this is one of the differences between NAT and ICS. ICS only allows the public interface to be configured with a single public IP address.

Allowing Inbound Traffic

Another factor that needs to be considered before enabling NAT is whether there are resources on the private network that need to be made accessible to users on the Internet (such a web server). All return traffic, or traffic that is originally initiated by clients on the private network, is allowed to pass through the NAT server. For Internet-initiated traffic to pass to the private network, you must do the following:

- The computer on the private network hosting the resource that will be made available to Internet users must be configured with a static IP address from the range of IP addresses allocated by the NAT server.
- To avoid any address conflicts, the IP address must be excluded from the range of IP addresses assigned by the NAT server.

■ A static mapping must be configured where a public IP address and port number combination is mapped to the private IP address of the computer and port number.

EXERCISE 5-1

Planning for Network Address Translation

In this exercise, you will use the information provided in the scenario to answer the questions listed here.

You are responsible for planning the Internet connectivity for a small business. Each of the 20 workstations on the private network must be able to access the Internet. The internal network currently uses the private IP address range of 10.0.0.0. All IP addresses are statically configured. Cost has been raised as a concern. The network consists of a single subnet. There is a single domain controller as well as a file and printer server on the network. The business is in the process of developing a web site, which it plans to host on the private network and make available to users on the Internet. You recommend that the workstations share a single connection to a local ISP. With these requirements in mind, answer the following questions.

1. Would you recommend Network Address Translation as an Internet connectivity solution? If so, explain why it is a possible solution.

2. Will NAT support the current addressing scheme? How could NAT simplify the configuration of IP addresses on the private network?

3. What would be the advantages to implementing a DHCP server on the private network as opposed to using the DHCP allocator included with NAT? Would you recommend implementing a DHCP server in this situation?

4. Once the web server is running on the private network, can NAT permit Internet-based traffic to pass through to the private network? If yes, what must be configured?

5. Outline the limitations of NAT. Will these limitations have an impact on this situation?

CERTIFICATION OBJECTIVE 5.03

Enabling and Configuring NAT

Now that you're familiar with how NAT works and some of the points that need to be considered during the planning phase, let's take a look at how NAT is enabled and configured on a computer running Windows Server 2003.

Enabling NAT

NAT is not enabled by default, but you can enable it using either the Routing and Remote Access Snap-in or the Configure Your Server Wizard. How you enable NAT will depend on whether Routing and Remote Access is already enabled on your server. Exercise 5-2 walks you through the process of enabling Routing and Remote Access for NAT services.

EXERCISE 5-2

CertCam 5-2 ON THE CD

Enabling Network Address Translation

In this exercise, you will enable the Routing and Remote Access Service for network address translation.

1. Click Start, point to Administrative Tools, and click Routing And Remote Access.

2. Right-click your server within the console and click Configure And Enable Routing And Remote Access.

3. This launches the Routing and Remote Access Server Setup Wizard. Click Next.

4. From the list of configurations, click Network Address Translation (NAT). Click Next.

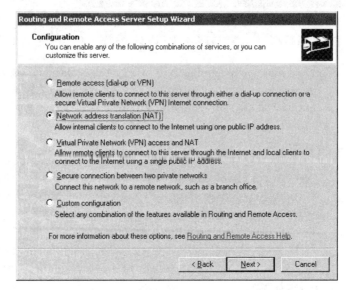

5. From the NAT Internet Connection dialog box, select the interface that will be used to connect to the Internet. You can select an existing connection or create a new demand-dial connection. You also have the option of disabling the Basic Firewall. Click Next.

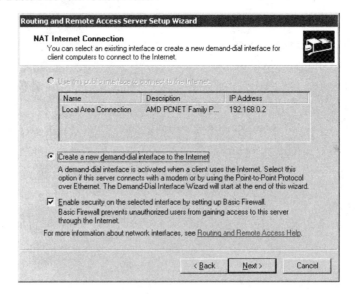

6. Click Next. If you chose to configure a new demand-dial interface, the Demand-Dial Interface Wizard appears and walks you through the process of creating the connection.

7. Click Finish.

In some cases, Routing and Remote Access may already be enabled on your system. If this is the case, you can use the steps that follow to manually enable NAT. Before you begin, verify that the IP address assigned to the internal interface is 192.168.0.1, with a subnet mask of 255.255.255.0 (see Figure 5-1). If you plan to use a different IP address range on the private network, change the IP address accordingly. If necessary, configure a new demand-dial interface within the Routing and Remote Access snap-in.

To manually enable NAT:

1. Click Start, point to Administrative Tools, and Click Routing And Remote Access.

2. Within the console, expand your remote access server, expand the IP Routing container, right-click General and click New Routing Protocol.

FIGURE 5-1

The private interface must be assigned a static IP address

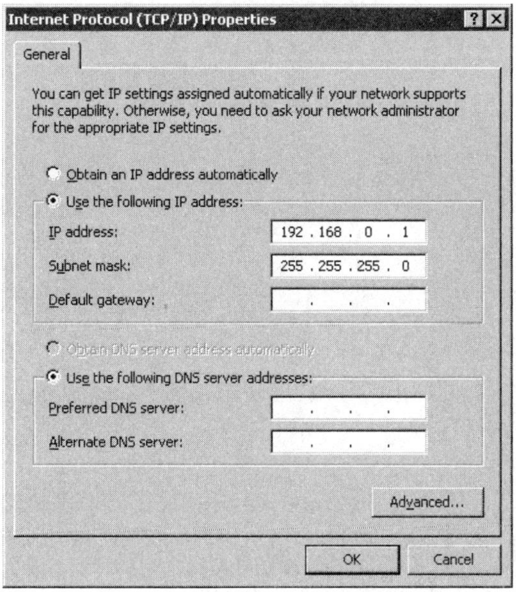

Internet Protocol (TCP/IP) Properties ? X

General

You can get IP settings assigned automatically if your network supports this capability. Otherwise, you need to ask your network administrator for the appropriate IP settings.

○ Obtain an IP address automatically

● Use the following IP address:

IP address: 192 . 168 . 0 . 1

Subnet mask: 255 . 255 . 255 . 0

Default gateway: . . .

○ Obtain DNS server address automatically

● Use the following DNS server addresses:

Preferred DNS server: . . .

Alternate DNS server: . . .

Advanced...

OK   Cancel

3. Select NAT/Basic Firewall. Click OK.

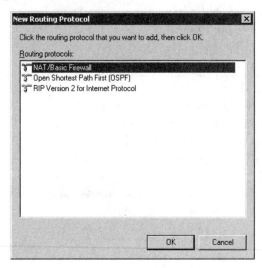

4. Next you must add your private and public interfaces to the NAT protocol. To do so, right-click NAT/Basic Firewall and click New Interface.

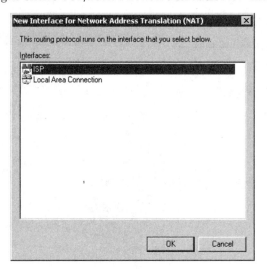

5. Select the interface you want to add and click OK. The Network Address Translation Properties dialog box appears. If the interface connects to the Internet, select Public Interface Connected To The Internet. If you want to protect the public interface, select the option to Enable A Basic Firewall On This interface. If the interface connects to the private network, select Private Interface Connected To Private Network.

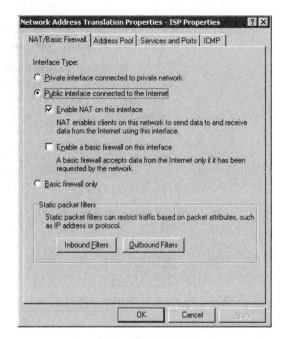

6. Repeat the process outlined in step 5 for both the remaining interface types. Click OK.

Once you've completed these steps, NAT will be enabled on your server. Your next steps will be to configure NAT, if necessary. This will include configuring the public address pool, the DHCP allocator, and the DNS proxy.

Configuring NAT

Once NAT has been installed, it can be configured through the Routing and Remote Access snap-in. The following section looks at the various settings that can be configured for NAT. For example, you may need to configure NAT with a pool of public IP addresses assigned by your ISP, or you may need to change the range of IP addresses being assigned by the DHCP allocator.

Configuring NAT/Basic Firewall Properties

Within the Routing and Remote Access snap-in, you can configure various settings for NAT. To do so, right-click the NAT/Basic Firewall container within the console and select the Properties option (see Figure 5-2).

General Tab   From the General tab shown in Figure 5-2, you can enable or disable logging for NAT. By default, only errors are written to the Windows Server 2003

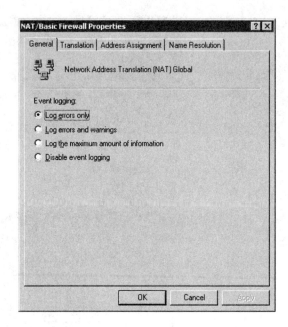

FIGURE 5-2

Configuring
NAT/Basic
Firewall
properties

System log. You can change the logging level by selecting one of the other available options. You can also disable logging altogether.

Translation Tab   As already mentioned earlier in the chapter, NAT stores mapping information within a translation table. You can use the two options available on the Translation tab shown in Figure 5-3 to configure how long TCP and UDP port mappings should remain in the translation table. The default length of time that a TCP mapping remains in the table is 1440 minutes (or 24 hours). UDP mappings are removed after 1 minute. If you make changes to these values, you can use the Reset Defaults button to return them to their original values.

Address Assignment   Using the Address Assignment tab shown in Figure 5-4, you can configure how clients are assigned IP addresses. If there is already a DHCP server on the private network, you will not want to enable the DHCP allocator component of NAT. However, if NAT will assign clients on the private network IP addressing information, select the option to Automatically Assign IP Addresses By Using The DHCP Allocator. You must then specify the range from which clients will be assigned an IP address.

FIGURE 5-3

Configuring how long TCP and UDP port mappings remain in the translation table

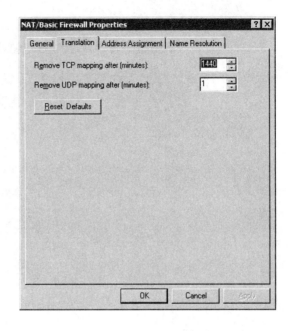

FIGURE 5-4

Enabling DHCP allocator component of NAT

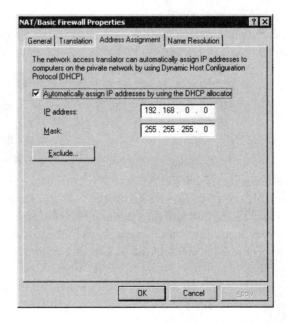

The Excluded
Reserved
Addresses dialog
box

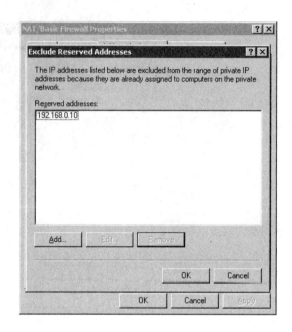

You can use the Exclude button to specify any IP addresses in the address pool that should not be leased to clients (see Figure 5-5)—for example, if you have any computers on the private network that have been assigned static IP addresses. Click Add from the Excluded Reserved Addresses dialog box and type in the IP address (shown next).

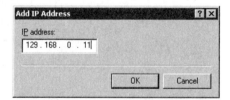

Name Resolution   Using the Name Resolution tab shown in Figure 5-6, you can enable the DNS proxy component of NAT. Doing so means the NAT server will forward name resolution requests on behalf of clients on the private network to a DNS server on the Internet. To enable the DNS proxy component, select the option to resolve IP addresses for Clients Using Domain Name System (DNS). Use the option to Connect To The Public Network When A Name Needs To Be Resolved to specify if demand-dial interface is used to connect to the Internet.

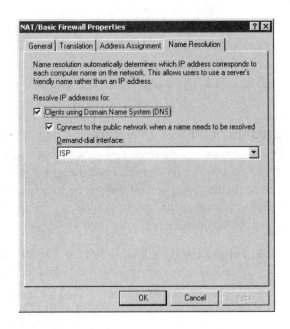

FIGURE 5-6

Enabling the DNS proxy component of NAT

EXERCISE 5-3

Configuring NAT

In this exercise, you will use the Routing and Remote Access snap-in to configure the NAT/Basic Firewall properties.

1. Click Start, point to Administrative Tools, and click Routing And Remote Access.

2. Within the console, right-click NAT/Basic Firewall under the IP Routing container and click Properties.

3. Click the Address Assignment tab. If the DHCP allocator is not already enabled, select the option to Automatically Assign IP Addresses By Using The DHCP Allocator.

4. Leave the default range of 192.168.0.0 as is.

5. Click Exclude. From the Exclude Reserved Addresses dialog box, click Add.

6. Type in **192.168.0.10** and click OK. Click OK again.

7. Select the Name Resolution tab. Ensure that Clients Using Domain Name System is selected.

8. Select the option to Connect To The Public Network When A Name Needs To Be Resolved. Use the down arrow to select your demand dial interface. Click OK.

Configuring NAT Interfaces

Once you have added an interface to NAT, you can configure its properties through the RRAS console. To do so, right-click the appropriate interface and select Properties. The properties dialog box for the private interface contains only a single tab, as shown in Figure 5-7. Using the options available under the interface type, you can choose from one of the following:

- **Private Interface Connected To The Private Network**   Select this option if the interface is physically connected to the private internal network.

- **Public Interface Connected To The Internet Network**   Select this option if the interface is connected to the Internet. If you select this option, you can enable NAT or Basic Firewall. Enabling NAT means only that clients can send and receive data to the Internet. Enabling the Basic Firewall means data from the Internet is accepted only if it was initiated by a client on the private network.

- **Basic Firewall Only**   Select this option if you do not want to enable network address translation but want to protect the interface using Basic Firewall. This means that inbound traffic will be routed only if it originated from the server.

Using the Inbound and Outbound filter buttons, you can configure static packet filters to control the type of traffic that is permitted to pass through the server. Traffic can be restricted by protocol and IP address.

When you are configuring the public interface, you will see three other tabs available along with the NAT/Basic Firewall tab. Using the Address Pool tab shown in Figure 5-8, you can configure the IP addresses for the public interface that have been assigned by an ISP. To do so, click Add; type in the start address, the subnet mask, and the end address; and click OK.

Using the Reservations button, you can reserve a public IP address for use by a computer on the private network. Clicking the Reservations button brings up the Reserve Addresses dialog box, which lists all the addresses currently reserved by computers on the private network. Click Add to reserve a public IP address for a computer on

FIGURE 5-7

Configuring the
properties of the
private interface

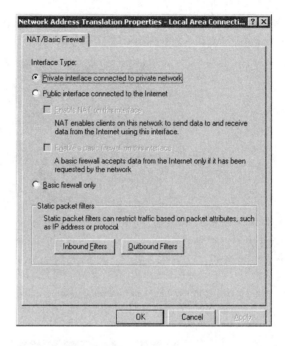

FIGURE 5-8

Configuring the
pool of addresses
assigned by an ISP

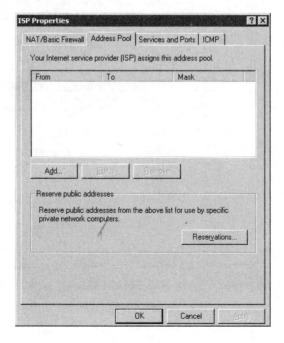

the private network (shown next). To enable Internet traffic to reach the private computer, select the option to Allow Incoming Sessions To This Address.

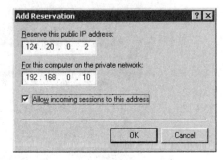

The Services and Ports tab shown in Figure 5-9 is used to specify the services on the private network that will be made available to users on the Internet. For example, if you have an FTP server on the private network, you will need to enable the service from this tab to create an exception for FTP traffic to pass through the server.

Once you enable a service, the Edit Service dialog box appears (see Figure 5-10). You can use the settings to designate the port and IP address that packets should be

FIGURE 5-9

Configuring the services on the private network that will be available to users on the Internet

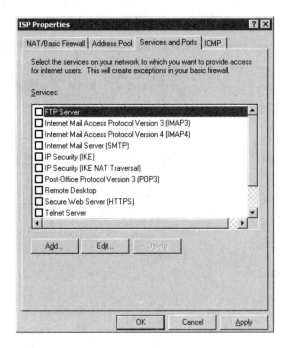

FIGURE 5-10

Configuring the
properties of
the Edit Service
dialog box

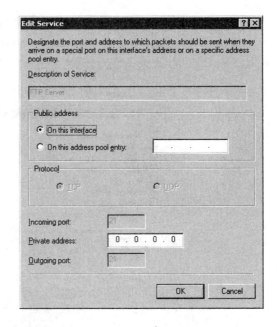

routed to when they are received on the public interface of the server. If the server is assigned a single IP address from an ISP, select the On This Interface option. This means that the incoming IP address is the address assigned to the public interface. If you've been assigned multiple addresses, select the second option, On This Address Pool Entry, and specify the public address pool. Using the private address value, you must specify the IP address of the computer on the private network hosting the service.

Remember that the computer on the private network hosting the service must be configured with a static IP address. You use the Services and Ports tab from the properties dialog box for the public interface to specify the IP address of the computer on the private network.

The ICMP tab allows you to configure how the server will respond to ICMP messages received from Internet users (see Figure 5-11). The Internet Control Message Protocol is used for error reporting and the exchange of status information between two IP hosts. By default, NAT will not respond to any ICMP messages received on the public interface. You can configure which types of ICMP requests NAT will respond to. For example, if you enable Incoming Echo Request, the NAT server will respond to any ping messages received on the public interface.

FIGURE 5-11

Configuring NAT
to respond to
ICMP messages

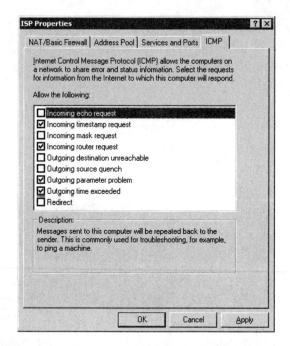

EXERCISE 5-4

Configuring a Static Mapping

In this exercise, you will configure a static mapping using the IP address you excluded in the preceding exercise.

1. Click Start, point to Administrative Tools, and click Routing And Remote Access.

2. Select NAT/Basic Firewall listed under the IP Routing container.

3. In the details pane, right-click the public interface and click Properties.

4. Select the Services And Ports tab.

5. From the list of available services, click Web Server (HTTP).

6. The Edit Service dialog box appears. In the Private address field, type in the IP address you excluded in the preceding exercise (192.168.0.10). Click OK.

7. Click OK to close the properties dialog box for the public interface.

Troubleshooting NAT

Most problems you encounter with NAT will be related to translation, IP address allocation, and name resolution. One of the first places you can look to troubleshoot a problem is the System log (as long as you have enabled logging for NAT/Basic Firewall). Of course, problems can also appear on the client side, where you can also use the System log to troubleshoot the problem. A good way of determining whether the problem is server or client related is to check and see who is affected by the problem. If only some of the workstations on the network are affected, chances are the problem is on the client side. Server-related problems would more than likely affect all workstations on the private network.

You can use these points to assist in troubleshooting NAT-related problems:

- If the hosts on the private network are not receiving an IP address, verify that the DHCP allocator is enabled, using the Address Assignment tab from the NAT/Basic Firewall Properties dialog box.

- If the problem is related to hostname resolution, verify that the DNS proxy component is enabled, using the Name Resolution tab from the NAT/Basic Firewall Properties dialog box.

- Verify that the public interface is configured with the IP address of the DNS servers assigned by the ISP. This can be done using the `ipconfig /all` command.

- If you are using L2TP/IPSec VPN connections behind NAT, verify that the L2TP/IPSec NAT-T update has been installed on any Windows XP and Windows 2000 workstations.

If the problem is related to translation:

- Verify that the interface connected to the Internet is added to the NAT/Basic Firewall routing protocol. In other words, within the Routing and Remote Access console, make sure the public interface is listed in the Details pane when NAT/Basic Firewall is selected.

- Verify that the proper interface type is selected. For the public interface, select the Public Interface Connected To The Internet option. For the internal interface, select the Private Interface Connected To Private Network option.

- Verify that NAT is enabled on the public interface.

- If you are using multiple public IP addresses, verify that you have properly configured the IP address pool.

■ If some applications do not work through NAT, verify the protocol being used by the application. You may need to contact the vendor in regard to how the application works in a translated environment.

■ Verify that the packet filters are not blocking the flow of traffic through the NAT server.

EXERCISE 5-5

Troubleshooting NAT

In this exercise, you will outline some of the steps to take when troubleshooting NAT-related issues.

To date, Windows 2000 clients have been connecting to the head office using PPTP VPN connections. Some clients connect from home offices, and others connect from branch offices. Each of the branch offices uses NAT. For increased security, the company has decided to implement L2TP/IPSec for VPN instead. All the required user and computer certificates have been installed. Once the change is made, some users now report that they are unable to establish a VPN connection with the head office. List the steps you can take to troubleshoot the problem and suggest a possible cause as to why some users are experiencing problems.

CERTIFICATION OBJECTIVE 5.04

Securing NAT

Whenever a network connects to the Internet, a door is opened for attackers. There are always individuals on the Internet looking for ways to exploit security holes. NAT on its own provides some level of security in that it can protect resources on the private network so that they are not available to users on the Internet. However, to enhance the security of your NAT implementation, you can use additional features such as Basic Firewall and packet filtering. These topics will be discussed in the next section.

NAT/Basic Firewall

A new feature of Windows Server 2003 is the Basic Firewall. This component, used to protect your private network from unsolicited inbound traffic, can be enabled on a NAT interface.

When Basic Firewall is enabled on the public NAT interface, it protects the private network using a combination of dynamic and static packet filtering. The source and destination IP addresses of each packet received in the private interface of the NAT servers are recorded within a table. All incoming traffic is compared against the information in the table to determine if it was initiated from a host on the private network. Traffic from the public interface is allowed to pass to the private interface only if there is an entry in the table showing that communication originated from a host on the private network.

on the job

The Basic Firewall service included with Windows Server 2003 cannot block IP version 6 traffic. If this is a requirement, it is recommended that you purchase other software that has this capability.

If the Basic Firewall component is not enabled on the public interface of the NAT server, you can use the steps outlined in Exercise 5-6.

EXERCISE 5-6

Enabling the Basic Firewall

In this exercise, you will enable the Basic Firewall on the public interface.

1. Click Start, point to Administrative Tools, and click Routing And Remote Access.

2. Within the console, click the NAT/Basic Firewall container.

3. Right-click the public interface and click Properties.

4. From the NAT/Basic Firewall tab, select the option to Enable A Basic Firewall On This Interface. Click OK.

Packet Filters

Using the packet filtering capability in Windows Server 2003, you can configure filters to control the types of inbound and outbound traffic that are permitted or denied through a computer running Windows Server 2003. Packet filtering is based on exceptions: you can permit all traffic except that which is prohibited by filters or deny all traffic except that which is permitted by filters. Filters can be configured to restrict traffic by protocol and IP address.

To create a new packet filter:

1. Click Start, point to Administrative Tools, and click Routing And Remote Access.

2. Within the console, select the NAT/Basic Firewall container.

3. Right-click the interface for which you want to configure the packet filters and click Properties. Click either the Inbound Filters button or the Outbound Filters button.

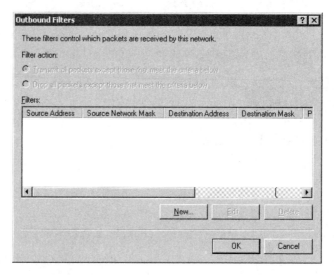

4. Click New to create a new packet filter.

5. Type in the IP address and subnet mask of the source network, and then the IP address and subnet mask of the destination network. Specify the protocol type. Click OK.

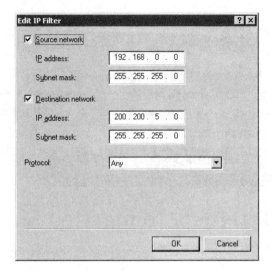

6. Specify the filter action. Select either Transmit All Packets Except Those That Meet The Criteria Below or Drop All Packets Except Those That Meet The Criteria Below. Click OK.

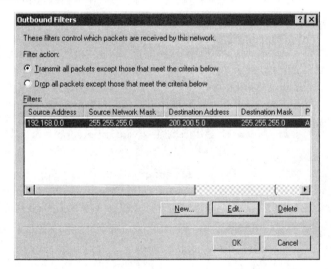

Using the packet filters, an administrator can block or permit traffic originating from any node or subnet going to another node or subnet. The difficulty in this is if you want to block access to a number of Internet sites, you will have to enter several filters.

e x a m

watch
        Packet filters can be applied *filters on the private interface. To restrict*
to the private and public interfaces. To *inbound traffic from the Internet, configure*
restrict outgoing traffic, configure packet *packet filtering on the public interface.*

CERTIFICATION OBJECTIVE 5.05

Enabling Internet Connection Sharing

Windows Server 2003 also includes another technology that can be used to connect multiple computers to the Internet using a single Internet connection. This technology is known as Internet Connection Sharing (ICS). Just as NAT does, ICS enables multiple computers on a local area network to simultaneously access the Internet using a single Internet connection. This technology provides home offices and small businesses with Internet connectivity without added cost, because only one Internet connection is necessary for the entire LAN.

To connect multiple computers on a private network to the Internet using this technology, at least one computer must have an Internet connection with ICS enabled. Enabling ICS is as simple as checking a single box (this is basically the extent of configuring ICS). ICS includes the following components:

- **Network Address Translation component** This component translates the private IP addresses to the public IP address assigned to the public interface.

- **DHCP allocator component** This component provides a simplified version of the DHCP service. The DHCP allocator assigns internal clients IP addresses in the range of 192.168.0.0/24. Unlike under NAT, this IP address range is not configurable.

- **DNS Proxy component** This component resolves DNS names on behalf of clients on the private network. The computer with ICS enabled passes any name resolution requests to the Internet-based DNS server assigned by the ISP.

- **Auto-dial**   An Internet connection with ICS enabled can automatically connect when a client on the private network attempts to access the Internet.

If you are thinking about implementing ICS as a solution for providing Internet access using a single connection, you should keep the following points in mind:

- ICS should not be implemented on networks that have computers, such as domain controllers and DNS servers, configured with static IP addresses. Because ICS will assign clients on the private network an IP address from a nonconfigurable range and no IP addresses can be excluded, enabling ICS may in this case result in IP address conflicts on the private network.
- Once ICS has been enabled on a computer, the IP address of the internal interface will be automatically changed to 192.168.0.1.
- Clients on the private network must be configured to use DHCP. The DHCP allocator will lease them an IP address.
- ICS does support auto-dial. This feature must be enabled for ICS to work with an ISDN or modem connection.

Enabling ICS

ICS is very simple to enable and requires little or no configuration. It is basically a one-step process where you select a single check box. Exercise 5-7 outlines the steps to enable ICS on a computer running Windows Server 2003.

EXERCISE 5-7

Enabling ICS

In this exercise, you will enable ICS on the interface connected to the Internet. Keep in mind that ICS and NAT cannot be enabled on the same computer.

1. Click Start, point to Control Panel, point to Network Connections, right-click the public interface for which you want to enable ICS, and choose Properties.
2. From the properties dialog box, select the Advanced tab.

3. Select the option to Allow Other Network Users To Connect Through This Computer's Internet Connection.

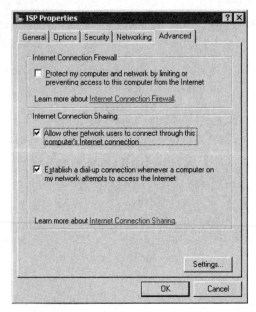

4. To enable auto-dial, select the option to Establish A Dial-Up Connection Whenever A Computer On My Network Attempts To Establish A Connection. This option is enabled by default.

5. Click OK.

Configuring ICS

Once ICS has been enabled, clients on the private network can use applications such as Internet Explorer and Outlook Express as though they had their own direct connection. You may need to further configure ICS to enable various applications, such as NetMeeting, to function through the shared Internet connection. Or if you have services and applications on the private network you want to make available to Internet users (for example, if you host a web server on the private network), you will need to configure ICS.

Applications and services can be configured for ICS using the Settings button located on the Advanced tab used to enable the service. Click the Settings button to display the Advanced Settings properties dialog box (see Figure 5-12). You will see a list of default services that can be enabled. Once you select the check box beside

Configuring
applications and
services to work
with ICS

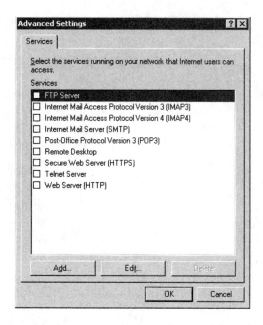

a service, the Service Settings dialog box appears. From here, you can configure the name or IP address of the computer on the private network hosting the service. For example, if you enable FTP, all requests on the public interface on port 21 will be sent to the FTP server on the private network.

If a service is not listed, you can use the Add button. Again, the Service Settings dialog box will appear, where you can type in a description for the service, the name or IP address of the computer on the private network hosting the service, and the external and internal port numbers.

Configuring ICS Clients

Configuring a client to use a shared Internet connection is a relatively straightforward process. You simply configure the TCP/IP properties for the local area connection to automatically obtain an IP address. Also, using the Connection tab from the properties dialog box for Internet Explorer (see Figure 5-13), make sure that the Never Dial A Connection option is selected and the following options on the Local Area Connection Settings dialog box are deselected:

- ■ Automatically Detect Settings
- ■ Use Automatic Configuration Script
- ■ Use A Proxy Server

Configuring the
properties of
Internet Explorer

ICS Versus NAT

This chapter has looked at two different technologies included with Windows Server 2003
that can be used to provide Internet connectivity for hosts on a private network. Both
ICS and NAT are used to allow multiple computers
to share a single Internet connection. Both offer
cost-effective solutions for connecting small
businesses and home offices to the Internet. There
are some distinct differences between the two
services that you should be aware of. Knowing
the differences will assist you in deciding which
of the two technologies will meet your network
requirements. Table 5-1 summarizes the main
differences between ICS and NAT.

*Make sure you are aware
of the differences between ICS and NAT.
Be prepared to answer questions in regard
to choosing one technology over another.*

TABLE 5-1   Differences Between NAT and ICS

Internet Connection Sharing	Network Address Translation
Is enabled using a single check box.	Requires manual configuration.
Hosts on the private network are assigned an IP address from a fixed address range.	Hosts on the private network are assigned an IP address from a configurable address range.
Supports a single public IP address.	Supports multiple public IP addresses.
Does not support a DHCP server on the private network.	Can work with a separate DHC server on the private network.

SCENARIO & SOLUTION

What is the purpose of ICS and NAT?	Both ICS and NAT are used to share a single Internet connection among multiple workstations.
Why would I choose ICS over NAT as an Internet connectivity solution?	ICS can be implemented by selecting a single check box, so it is simpler in terms of administration and configuration. However, it does have some limitations, such as the fact that it supports only a single public IP address, that make it unsuitable for some environments.
I have ICS enabled on a computer running Windows Server 2003. Can I place a web server on the private network and assign it a static IP address?	You can place a web server on the private network, but once it is configured with a static IP address, you may run into address conflicts on the network. ICS does not allow you to exclude specific IP addresses from the address range assigned by the DHCP allocator. NAT, on the other hand, will allow you to do this.
Can I enable NAT and ICS on the same computer?	No. Since NAT and ICS provide the same service, with some distinct differences, you cannot enable ICS and NAT on the same computer.

EXERCISE 5-8

Planning for Internet Connectivity

In this exercise, you will use the information in the given scenario to plan an Internet connectivity solution.

You are the network administrator of a Windows Server 2003 network. There are 40 workstations on the private network running Windows XP. There are also three servers named SRV01, SRV02, and SRV03. Currently, all workstations use APIPA, and there are no plans to implement a DHCP server on the private network. SRV01 is configured with an Internet connection that will be shared among all workstations. The three servers will be configured with static IP addresses. You have been allocated two public IP addresses from the ISP. Internet users must be able to access SRV03. Security is also a concern.

1. Which technology would you implement for the given scenario: ICS or NAT? Explain your answer.

2. How will IP addresses be assigned to clients? Devise an IP addressing plan that will meet the requirements.

3. How will you ensure there are no address conflicts on the private network?

4. Explain how SRV03 will be made available to Internet users.

5. Identify the various ways in which you can secure your implementation.

CERTIFICATION SUMMARY

This chapter looked at two technologies included with Windows Server 2003 used to connect small businesses and home offices to the Internet. Network Address Translation (NAT) and Internet Connection Sharing (ICS) can be used to share a single Internet connection among multiple workstations on a private network. The benefits of this include cost reduction and increased security.

A computer with NAT enabled must have at least two interfaces, one connected to the private network and the other connected to the Internet. Hosts on the private network access the Internet through NAT. When NAT receives an IP packet of the private interface, the IP address and source port are translated and the information is stored within the translation table. Resources on the private network can also be made available to users on the Internet by creating static mappings.

There are several different components to NAT. The DHCP allocator is responsible for assigning hosts on the private network IP addressing information. By default, NAT will assign hosts an IP address from the range of 192.168.0.0/24. This range is also configurable. The DNS proxy component is responsible for forwarding name resolution requests from the private network to the Internet-based DNS server assigned by an ISP. Both of these components can be disabled if necessary.

Before implementing NAT, you must decide upon an addressing scheme. Since the range of IP addresses assigned by the DHCP allocator is configurable, you can use one of the other private address ranges as well. NAT also supports multiple public IP addresses. You may need to configure the address pool for the public interface if you have been allocated multiple IP addresses from an ISP. If you plan to allow inbound traffic, a static IP address will need to be assigned to the computer hosting the service. This IP address must be excluded from the range assigned by the DHCP allocator. Once you have made some basic implementation decisions, NAT can be enabled and configured through the Routing and Remote Access snap-in.

Internet Connection Sharing provides the same service as NAT. It enables you to share a single Internet connection among multiple workstations. There are some very distinct differences between the two technologies. ICS supports only a single public IP address. The range of IP addresses assigned by the DHCP allocator is not configurable, nor can this component be disabled. One of the advantages of ICS over NAT is the ease with which it can be enabled, requiring little or no configuration.

✓ TWO-MINUTE DRILL

Introduction to NAT

❑ NAT is used to share a single Internet connection among multiple workstations.

❑ NAT translates the private IP address to a public IP address and stores the information within a translation table.

❑ If a single public IP address is being used, NAT also translates the source port.

❑ NAT includes the following components: address translation, DHCP allocator, and DNS proxy.

❑ The DHCP allocator is a scaled-down version of DHCP that assigns clients on the private network an IP address in the range of 192.168.0.0/24. The DNS proxy receives name resolution requests and forwards them to the Internet-based DNS server assigned by the ISP.

❑ Using NAT-T, L2TP/IPSec VPN connections can be established through NAT.

❑ Clients on the private network must have their gateway pointing to the private interface of the NAT server.

❑ Once NAT is enabled, the IP address of the private interface is set to 192.168.0.1. This must be changed if you are using a different addressing scheme on the private network.

Implementing NAT

❑ The DHCP allocator included with NAT supports a configurable IP address range. You will need to decide upon an addressing scheme or use the default range of 192.168.0.0/24.

❑ NAT supports multiple public IP addresses. If you are assigned multiple IP addresses from an ISP, the address pool for the public interface must be configured.

❑ Inbound traffic can be permitted by creating static mappings.

Enabling and Configuring NAT

❑ NAT can be enabled through the Routing and Remote Access snap-in.

❑ If Routing and Remote Access is already enabled, you can add the NAT/Basic Firewall protocol.

❑ You can configure the properties of NAT/Basic Firewall as well as the properties of the public and private interfaces.

❑ If there is already a DHCP server on the network, the DHCP allocator can be disabled. The range of IP addresses assigned to clients can also be changed.

❑ The DNS proxy component can be disabled if you do not need NAT to forward name resolution requests to the Internet-based DNS server.

❑ NAT can be configured to respond to various ICMP messages received on the public interface.

❑ If logging is enabled, you can use the System log to troubleshoot NAT-related problems.

❑ Windows 2000 and Windows XP clients require the L2TP/IPSec NAT update in order to use L2TP/IPSec VPN connections behind NAT.

Securing NAT

❑ The Basic Firewall allows inbound traffic only if a static or dynamic mapping exists within the translation table.

❑ Packet filtering can be used to control inbound and outbound traffic by IP address and protocol.

❑ VPN connections can be used to take advantage of user-level authentication and data encryption.

Enabling Internet Connection Sharing

❑ ICS enables a single Internet connection to be shared among multiple workstations.

❑ ICS can be enabled through the properties dialog box of the public interface.

❑ ICS will assign clients on the private network an IP address from the range of 192.168.0.0/24. This range is not configurable.

❑ The DHCP allocator and DNS proxy components included with ICS cannot be disabled.

❑ Static mappings can be created to allow Internet traffic to be routed to a specific computer on the private network.

SELF TEST

Introduction to NAT

1. From the following statements, which are true regarding Internet Connection Sharing (ICS)?

    A. ICS is enabled using the Routing and Remote Access snap-in.

    B. The DHCP allocator included with ICS leases clients an IP address in the range of 10.0.0.0/8.

    C. ICS supports a single public IP address.

    D. The DHCP allocator included with ICS can be disabled.

2. John is planning the Internet connectivity for a remote office. The office will consist of only approximately ten workstations. There is a server on site that hosts the only Internet connection. The network administrator in the remote office has limited experience. With this in mind, which Internet connectivity option should you choose?

    A. Enable NAT on the server.

    B. Add ten more Internet connections for each workstation.

    C. Enable ICS on the server.

    D. Install the DHCP relay component on the server.

3. Which of the following features are included with NAT?

    A. DHCP allocator to assign IP addresses to hosts on the private network

    B. DNS proxy to forward name resolution requests to an Internet-based DNS server

    C. User-based access control to limit access to the Internet resources by group membership

    D. Address translation to map the private IP addresses to a public IP address

4. Bob is planning Internet connectivity for his network. The network hosts three servers that require static IP addresses. There is a computer running Windows Server 2003 that will be connected to the Internet. This will be the only Internet connection. Bob wants to share the Internet connection among the workstations on the private network. What should he do?

    A. Enable ICS using the Routing and Remote Access snap-in.

    B. Enable NAT using the Routing and Remote Access snap-in.

    C. Enable ICS using the properties of TCP/IP for the Internet connection.

    D. Enable NAT using the properties of TCP/IP for the Internet connection.

Implementing NAT

5. NAT is enabled on a computer running Windows Server 2003. The internal network hosts a web server configured with the IP address of 192.168.0.12. The public interface has been assigned the public IP addresses 200.10.10.12. You want to make the web server available to users on the Internet. What should you do?

   A. Configure the web server with a dedicated Internet connection.

   B. Enable NAT on the web server.

   C. Configure HTTP on the public interface of the NAT server to map to the private IP address of the web server.

   D. Map the IP address of the NAT server's private interface to the IP address of the web server.

6. One of the users for your organization has a home office from which he works. He has added two more computers to his home LAN and wants to be able to access the Internet using the existing connection on the third computer. He calls you and asks you how he can enable ICS. Which of the following steps should he perform?

   A. Install the ICS protocol through the Routing and Remote Access snap-in.

   B. Enable ICS using the properties of TCP/IP for the public connection.

   C. Install ICS using the Add or Remove Programs applet.

   D. Install ICS using the Network Connections applet.

7. John is in charge of restructuring the existing network. Users currently connect to the head office using VPN connections through NAT from a branch office. Some users also use VPN connections from home offices. Security requirements have resulted in the implementation of L2TP/IPSec connections instead of PPTP. After the change is made, several users now report they are unable to establish a connection. You discover that this is affecting only Windows XP clients who attempt to connect to the head office behind a NAT server. How can you resolve the problem?

   A. Disable NAT.

   B. Switch back to PPTP, since NAT does not support L2TP/IPSec connections.

   C. Install the NAT-T update on the Windows XP clients.

   D. Configure the properties of Internet Explorer to use a proxy server.

8. Mary is planning the Internet connectivity solution for her small organization. Hosts on the private network currently receive IP addresses from a DHCP server. The DHCP server assigns clients IP addresses within the range of 192.168.0.0/24. With this in mind, how should she proceed?

A. Implement NAT and disable the DHCP allocator.

B. Implement ICS and disable the DHCP allocator.

C. Implement NAT and change the range of IP addresses assigned by the DHCP allocator.

D. Implement ICS and change the range of IP addresses assigned by the DHCP allocator.

9. Which of the following statements are true regarding Network Address Translation?

A. NAT supports only a single public IP address.

B. NAT supports a configurable range of IP addresses assigned by the DHCP allocator.

C. NAT can permit or deny outbound traffic by group membership.

D. NAT can translate L2TP/IPSec connections.

10. An organization is implementing NAT to provide each of its various branch offices with Internet access. After NAT is configured, you discover that clients are unable to resolve fully qualified domain names but can connect to Internet resources using IP addresses. What should you do?

A. Configure an LMHOSTS file on each workstation.

B. Configure each workstation with the IP address of a WINS server.

C. Configure each workstation's gateway to point to the private NAT interface.

D. Configure each workstation with the IP address of the Internet-based DNS servers.

E. Confirm that the DNS proxy is enabled.

11. An organization consists of 50 workstations running Windows XP using APIPA. Five servers on the private network have been configured with static IP addresses. One of the servers hosting the company web site must be accessible to Internet users. Another server has an Internet connection. Jeff has been asked to implement an Internet connectivity solution for the organization that will work with the existing network infrastructure and not impose a large number of changes or costs. What should he do? (Choose all correct answers.)

A. Enable ICS on the server with the Internet connection.

B. Enable NAT on the server with the Internet connection.

C. Enable the DHCP allocator.

D. Exclude the IP addresses that have been assigned to the servers on the private network.

E. Enable HTTP on the public interface and map incoming requests on port 80 to the private IP address and port number of the internal web server.

Enabling and Configuring NAT

12. NAT has been enabled on a computer running Windows Server 2003. The DHCP allocator is also enabled. What is the default range of IP addresses that clients will be assigned?

   A. 10.0.0.0/8
   B. 172.16.0.0/16
   C. 127.0.0.0/8
   D. 192.168.0.0/24

13. NAT was recently enabled on a computer running Windows Server 2003. Users now report than one of their applications is not functioning correctly through the NAT server. All other applications appear to be working normally. What should you do?

   A. Verify that NAT has been enabled on the public interface.
   B. Verify that the address pool has been properly configured.
   C. Verify the protocol being used by the application to see whether there is a NAT editor.
   D. Reinstall the application on all workstations.

14. Which of the following are advantages of implementing ICS over NAT?

   A. ICS is simpler to enable than NAT.
   B. ICS allows more flexibility than NAT.
   C. ICS supports multiple public IP addresses.
   D. ICS requires less configuration than NAT.

15. Once ICS is enabled, what is the default IP address assigned to the private interface?

   A. 192.168.0.1
   B. 10.0.0.1
   C. 172.16.0.1
   D. 127.0.0.1

Securing NAT

16. John has implemented NAT on a computer running Windows Server 2003 to share a single Internet connection between 20 computers running Windows XP professional. Users soon report that they are unable to access the Internet. After investigating the problem you discover that computers on the private network are not receiving IP addresses. What should John do to resolve the problem as quickly as possible?

A. Configure all workstations with a static IP address.

B. Install a DHCP server on the private network.

C. Enable the addressing component of NAT on the private interface.

D. Configure the name resolution component of NAT on the private interface.

Enabling Internet Connection Sharing

17. You are planning to implement NAT to share an Internet connection among computers on the private network. There is a file server on the private network that Internet users need access to. When setting up NAT, which of the following steps will need to be completed to allow access to the file server? Select three correct answers.

   A. Configure the file server as a DHCP client.

   B. Configure the file server with a static IP address.

   C. Disable the addressing component on the NAT server.

   D. Exclude the IP address assigned to the file server from the range of IP addresses assigned by the NAT server.

   E. Configure a special port that maps a public IP address and port number to the private IP address and port number of the file server.

18. Your network consists of three subnets. Subnet 1 hosts a computer running Windows Server 2003 with a direct Internet connection. You want to share the connection between all computers. When configuring the addressing component of the NAT server, how many scopes will it support?

   A. One

   B. Two

   C. Three

   D. Unlimited

19. Which of the following additional components are also included with NAT? Select all correct answers.

   A. DNS service

   B. DNS proxy

   C. DHCP service

   D. DHCP allocator

   E. WINS server

20. NAT has been enabled on a computer running Windows Server 2003. Users on the private network report that they can connect to Internet resources using IP addresses but not using DNS names. What is causing the problem?

    A. Computers on the private network are not configured with the IP address of the Internet-based DNS server.

    B. The name resolution component on the NAT server is disabled.

    C. The DHCP optional parameters have not been configured on the NAT server.

    D. The addressing component on the NAT server is disabled.

LAB QUESTION

FKB Consulting is a small company with a single office. The network consists of 20 computers running Windows XP Professional. APIPA is currently used. There is a server running Windows Server 2003 that has a direct connection to the Internet. Several of the workstations use dial-up networking to access the Internet. The company wants to implement a solution that will share a single Internet connection among all computers so dial-up connections are no longer required. There is a second server on the network that hosts the company's web site. This server must be made available to Internet users. Based on this information, answer the following questions.

    1. How would NAT provide an Internet solution for the company?

    2. List the additional components that are included with NAT.

    3. Which components would need to be enabled on the NAT server to allow computers on the private network to access the Internet?

    4. Outline how the company's web server can be made available for Internet users.

    5. What additional steps can be taken to secure your Internet connectivity solution?

SELF TEST ANSWERS

Introduction to NAT

1. ☑ **C.** ICS supports only a single public IP address. If you have been assigned multiple public IP addresses from an ISP, you will need to use NAT.

    ☒ **A** is incorrect because ICS is enabled through the properties dialog box for TCP/IP. **B** is incorrect because the DHCP allocator leases clients on the private network an IP address from the range of 192.168.0.0/24. **D** is incorrect because the DHCP allocator included with ICS cannot be disabled.

2. ☑ **C.** ICS would be the best choice because it is simple to enable and configure.

    ☒ **A** is incorrect because NAT is more difficult to enable and configure. If the network administrator has limited experience, ICS would be the better solution. **B** is incorrect because adding ten more Internet connections would increase the cost and administrative overhead. **D** is incorrect because the DHCP relay agent is used to forward requests from DHCP clients to a DHCP server.

3. ☑ **A, B,** and **D.** NAT includes the following features: DHCP allocator, DNS proxy, and address translation.

    ☒ **C** is incorrect because NAT does not perform user authentication and therefore cannot control access to Internet resources by group membership.

4. ☑ **B.** Since there are servers on the private network that require static IP addresses, NAT must be used. ICS does not allow you to exclude IP addresses from the range assigned by the DHCP allocator. NAT is enabled through the Routing and Remote Access snap-in.

    ☒ **A** and **C** are incorrect because ICS does not allow IP address to be excluded. Implementing ICS may result in IP address conflicts on the private network. ICS is enabled using the properties of TCP/IP for the Internet connection. **D** is incorrect because NAT is enabled using the Routing and Remote Access snap-in.

Implementing NAT

5. ☑ **C.** To allow Internet users to access the web server on the private network, you must enable the HTTP service on the public interface and map it to the IP address and port number of the web server.

    ☒ **A** is incorrect because this would require getting another Internet connection and assigning the web server a public IP address. **B** is incorrect because NAT is enabled only to share an Internet connection. The web server does not have an Internet connection. **D** is incorrect because Internet requests are received on the public interface.

6. ☑ **B.** ICS can be enabled through the Internet Protocol (TCP/IP) Properties dialog box for the public interface.

    ☒ **A** is incorrect because this is the method used to enable NAT. **C** and **D** are incorrect because these methods cannot be used to enable ICS.

7. ☑ **C.** To allow Windows XP and Windows 2000 VPN clients to establish a tunnel using L2TP/IPSec over a NAT interface, you must install the L2TP/IPSec NAT-T update.
   ☒ **A** is incorrect because this would eliminate the shared Internet connection. **B** is incorrect because NAT does support L2TP/IPSec using NAT Traversal. **D** is incorrect because NAT is not a proxy server and therefore you do not need to configure the properties of Internet Explorer. Also, doing so would not eliminate the fact that L2TP/IPSec connections cannot be translated for Windows 2000 and Windows XP clients without the NAT-T update installed.

8. ☑ **A.** In this situation, NAT would have to be implemented because it allows you to disable the DHCP allocator. This component must be disabled because there is already a DHCP server on the private network.
   ☒ **B** is incorrect because the DHCP allocator included with ICS cannot be disabled. **C** is incorrect because there is already a DHCP server on the private network leasing IP addresses to clients. **D** is incorrect because you cannot configure the range of IP addresses assigned to clients by the DHCP allocator component included with ICS.

9. ☑ **B and D.** The IP address range assigned by the DHCP allocator included with NAT can be changed from the default range of 192.168.0.0/24. NAT can translate L2TP/IPSec packets using NAT traversal.
   ☒ **A** is incorrect because NAT supports multiple public IP addresses by configuring the address pool. **C** is incorrect because NAT cannot limit Internet access by group membership. It's an ideal solution for an environment where all users require the same Internet access.

10. ☑ **D and E.** To enable hostname resolution, configure the workstations with the IP address of the Internet-based DNS servers. Also verify that the DNS proxy has been enabled on the NAT server.
    ☒ **A** is incorrect because an LMHOSTS file is a static text file used to map NetBIOS names to IP addresses. **B** is incorrect because WINS is used to dynamically register NetBIOS names and provide NetBIOS name resolution services. **C** is incorrect because in order to use NAT, workstations must have their gateway pointing to the private interface of the NAT server. This allows them to access the shared Internet connection but does not in itself provide hostname resolution.

11. ☑ **B, C, D, and E.** NAT must be enabled in this situation because ICS does not allow you to exclude IP addresses from the range of addresses assigned by the DHCP allocator. To avoid IP address conflicts, once the DHCP allocator is enabled, the IP addresses assigned to the servers must be excluded. To make the web server available to Internet users, you must enable HTTP on the public Internet so that all requests for port 80 are sent to the web server on the private network.
    ☒ **A** is incorrect because ICS does not allow you to exclude IP addresses from the range assigned by the DHCP allocator.

Enabling and Configuring NAT

12. ☑ **D.** The default range of IP addresses assigned by the DHCP allocator is 192.168.0.0/24

☒ **A** and **B** are incorrect because these do not represent the default range assigned by NAT and ICS. **C** is incorrect because 127.0.0.0 is reserved and cannot be used for anything other than testing purposes.

13. ☑ **C.** For some applications to function through NAT, a NAT editor is required for the protocol being used. Verify which protocol the application uses and contact the vendor to find out how the application can work behind NAT.

☒ **A** and **B** are incorrect because other applications being used are functioning through NAT. **D** is incorrect because if the protocol being used cannot be translated by NAT, reinstalling the application will not correct the problem. A NAT editor will be required.

14. ☑ **A** and **C.** ICS is simpler to enable than NAT; it can be enabled by selecting a single check box.

☒ **B** is incorrect because NAT provides more flexibility than ICS. You can configure the DHCP allocator as well as disable various components. It also supports multiple public IP addresses, whereas ICS supports only one. **D** is incorrect because ICS supports only a single IP address for the public interface, whereas NAT allows you to configure multiple IP addresses using the address pool.

15. ☑ **A.** The IP address assigned to the internal interface once ICS is enabled is 192.168.0.1.

☒ **A, B,** and **C** are incorrect because they do not represent the correct values.

Securing NAT

16. ☑ **C.** By enabling the addressing component, the NAT server can assign computers on the private network IP addresses

☒ **A** and **B** are incorrect because they would require more administrative effort. Enabling the addressing component is the simplest way to solve the problem. **D** is incorrect because the name resolution component is used to resolve DNS queries on behalf of computers on the private network.

Enabling Internet Connection Sharing

17. ☑ **B, D,** and **E.** In order to allow Internet users access to the file server you must configure the server with a static IP and exclude it from the range of addresses assigned by the NAT server. A special port must be created mapping a public IP address and port number to the private IP address and port number of the file server.

☒ **A** is incorrect because the file server requires a static IP address so the NAT server knows where to forward the incoming requests. **C** is incorrect because the addressing component is required in order to assign IP addresses to computers on the private network, unless a DHCP server is being used.

18. ☑ **A.** Nat only supports a single scope.

☒ **B, C,** and **D** are incorrect because the addressing component included with NAT only supports a single scope.

19. ☑ **B** and **D.** NAT also includes an addressing component known as the DHCP allocator that assigns computers on the private network IP addresses. It also includes a name resolution component that forwards name resolution requests on behalf of clients to an Internet-based DNS server.

☒ **A** and **C** are incorrect because NAT does not include these components.

20. ☑ **B.** Clients on the private network are unable to resolve DNS names because the name resolution component included with NAT is disabled.

☒ **A** is incorrect because the NAT server acts as a DNS proxy and forwards requests to an Internet-based DNS server. Therefore clients do not have to be configured with the IP address of the Internet DNS server. **C** is incorrect because optional DHCP parameters cannot be configured on a NAT server. This functionality requires a DHCP server. **D** is incorrect because clients can access Internet resources using IP addresses. This means clients are already configured with IP addresses.

LAB ANSWERS

1. By implementing NAT, the single dedicated Internet connection can be shared among the computers on the private network. This would allow the company to eliminate the existing dial-up connection currently used by various computers.

2. NAT also includes the following components: DHCP allocator, DNS proxy, and the translation component. The DHCP allocator assigns IP addresses to computers on the private network. The DNS proxy forwards DNS queries to the ISP's DNS server. The translation component IP addresses and port numbers of inbound and outbound traffic.

3. The DHCP allocator will be required to assign hosts on the private network IP addresses. The name resolution component must be enabled so clients can resolve hostnames to IP addresses.

4. By creating a special port, a public IP address and port number can be mapped to the IP address and port number of the internal web server. Requests received on the public interface can be sent to the web server on the private network.

5. A NAT implementation can be secured by enabling the NAT/Basic Firewall component and by using packet filtering.

6

Planning, Implementing, and Maintaining Routing and Remote Access

CERTIFICATION OBJECTIVE 6.01

Planning a Routing Strategy

With Routing and Remote Access Service (RRAS), a computer running Windows Server 2003 can be configured as a network router, routing IP packets between networks. This provides businesses with a cost-effective method for interconnecting LANs and WANs. Since the technology is built into the operating system, additional costs for specialized routing hardware are eliminated.

IP Routing

Chapter 1 introduced you to the concept of IP routing and the routing protocols supported by Windows Server 2003. Routing is the process of determining how to send an IP packet from a source host to a destination host. IP routing is possible because each IP packet consists of a source IP address and a destination IP address. Using this information as well as information within the routing table, a router can determine where an IP packet must be sent in order for it to be delivered to the destination host.

Windows Server 2003 supports a number of different routing configurations, including

- Demand-dial routing
- Router-to-router VPNs
- Network Address Translation

Demand-Dial Routing

Routing and Remote Access allows a computer running Windows Server 2003 to be configured as a demand-dial router. With this configuration, the router can initiate a connection to a remote network to deliver a packet to a remote site.

Demand-dial routing can significantly reduce the cost associated with connecting to networks. It enables an organization to use dial-up telephone lines to route traffic instead of having to use leased lines. The connection is established only when it is required and will also be disconnected if it remains idle for a configured amount of time.

Demand-dial routing supports the use of demand-dial filters and dial-out hours. By configuring demand-dial filters, an administrator can specify the type of traffic that can initiate the connection. Using dial-out hours, an administrator can further restrict when the connection can be used.

Demand-dial routing supports both on-demand and persistent connections. Cost will be a major concern when deciding which type of connection to use. If the connection is time-sensitive, meaning it cannot remain connected 24 hours a day, you should implement an on-demand demand-dial connection. This can be done by configuring an idle-disconnect time. If the link can remain connected 24 hours a day—for example, if the link is used to connect to another router by dialing a local number—you can implement a persistent demand-dial connection.

e x a m
ⓦ a t c h
If you are implementing routing protocols with demand-dial routing, keep in mind that OSPF cannot be used with   *nonpersistent connections. If you are using on-demand connections, it is recommended that you implement static routing.*

Demand-dial connections can be one-way initiated or two-way initiated. With a one-way-initiated connection, one router is configured as the calling router and the other is configured as the answering router that accepts incoming connections. connection with a router in a head office (in what is also known as a hub-and-spoke design). With a two-way-initiated connection, both routers can initiate and accept connections. This means either router is capable of establishing a demand-dial connection.

Router-to-Router VPN

Traditionally, packets are routed between routers that have a point-to-point connection. With the Internet growing as such a popular tool, however, packets can also be routed between routers using what is referred to as a router-to-router VPN connection. The benefit of this configuration is that long-distance WAN links can be replaced by links to a local ISP. For example, routers in remote offices can be connected by dialing into a local ISP and then creating a virtual connection across the Internet using a tunneling protocol. Windows Server 2003 supports two tunneling protocols: PPTP and L2TP (each of which will be discussed later in the chapter). If you choose to implement L2TP/IPSec, with certificate authentication, a PKI infrastructure must be put into place.

With a router-to-router VPN, you can also use either persistent or on-demand connections. Persistent connections require that both routers have a permanent connection to the Internet, meaning they can be left in a connected state. With on-demand connections, the answering router is configured with a permanent Internet connection.

The calling router is configured with two on-demand connections, one that connects to the ISP and one that establishes a virtual connection with the answering router.

Again, router-to-router VPNs can use static or dynamic routing. If the connections being used are on-demand, it is recommended that you implement static routes.

Network Address Translation

Using a technology known as Network Address Translation (NAT), a single Internet connection can be shared among multiple workstations. Once NAT is enabled on a computer running Windows Server 2003 using the Routing and Remote Access snap-in, workstations on a private network can access the Internet using this computer's Internet connection. As the NAT server receives requests, it translates the private IP address into a public IP address (refer to Chapter 5 for detailed information on how to plan and implement NAT).

Selecting Routing Protocols

As mentioned in Chapter 1, a routed network can use static or dynamic routing. With static routing, the routing tables must be updated manually. This solution can be viable for small networks where the network topology rarely changes.

To implement dynamic routing, a routing protocol must be used. Windows Server 2003 supports two routing protocols: Routing Information Protocol (RIP) and Open Shortest Path First (OSPF). To effectively implement IP routing, you should be aware of the type of environment each protocol is best suited for.

You can refer to Chapter 1 for more detailed information on RIP and OSPF.

RIP for IP

RIP for IP enables routers to dynamically exchange routing information, thereby eliminating the need for administrators to manually update the routing tables when changes to the network topology occur. When deciding whether to implement RIP as the routing protocol, keep the following points in mind:

- RIP is best suited for small to medium-sized organizations with no more than 50 networks.

- It is difficult to scale for large networks, as RIP has a maximum hop count of 15. Therefore, any networks that are more than 15 hops away are considered to be unreachable.

- RIP works well for those networks that contain multiple paths between any two endpoints.

■ RIP is also well suited for those environments where the network topology tends to change over time—where, for example, new networks are added or existing ones are removed.

OSPF

Like RIP, OSPF provides for dynamic routing by allowing routers to share routing information. When deciding whether to implement OSPF as your network routing protocol, keep the following points in mind:

■ OSPF is designed for large environments that consist of more than 50 networks.

■ It is more difficult to implement, configure, and administer than RIP.

■ OSPF is suitable for environments that consist of multiple paths between two endpoints.

■ It is also well suited to those environments where the network topology tends to change.

CERTIFICATION OBJECTIVE 6.02

Introduction to Remote Access

Windows Server 2003 includes the Routing and Remote Access Service, which allows you to configure a computer as a remote access server, allowing users to dial in or use VPN connections to remotely access the private network. The Routing and Remote Access Service included with Windows Server 2003 offers the following new features and enhancements:

■ **Support for preshared keys with L2TP/IPSec connections** For connections using L2TP/IPSec, a remote access server can be configured to use a preshared key instead of certificates.

■ **Basic Firewall** NAT can now be integrated with the Basic Firewall component, which provides dynamic packet filtering, thereby increasing security.

■ **L2TP/IPSec connections over NAT** Using a technology known as NAT traversal, L2TP/IPSec connections can now be translated over a NAT interface.

How Remote Access Works

Remote access is a technology that enables a computer to connect to a network from a remote location, for example, a roaming user connecting to an organization's private network from a home office to access shared files. The remote access client connects to a remote access server using some method of WAN connectivity such as the telephone line. The remote access server authenticates the user and authorizes the connection attempt. Once a connection request has been granted, the remote access user can typically perform all the same tasks that can be performed with a LAN connection such as accessing web servers, shared resources, and e-mail.

Windows Server 2003 supports two different methods of remote access connectivity:

- **Dial-up remote access**   Client computers typically use the telephone line to create a direct connection to a port on a remote access server.
- **VPN remote access**   Client computers typically create a connection to an ISP using the telephone line or other WAN connectivity method and then create a virtual connection with a remote access VPN server using the Internet as a transport medium.

Elements of Dial-Up Remote Access

With a dial-up remote access solution, client computers normally use the telephone line to establish a direct connection with a server that has remote access enabled. A remote access dial-up solution will consist of the following components (see Figure 6-1):

- **Remote access server**   The computer running Windows Server 2003 with remote access enabled. The remote access server authorizes and authenticates connection requests and forwards packets between the remote access client and the private network.
- **Remote access client**   The remote access client establishes a PPP connection with the remote access server using a modem and a telephone line. Windows Server 2003 supports the following remote access clients: Windows XP, Windows 2000, Windows ME, Windows 98, Windows NT 4.0, UNIX, and Macintosh.
- **WAN connectivity**   Both the client and the server require dial-up equipment and some form of WAN connectivity to establish a connection.
- **Remote access protocols**   A remote access protocol is required to establish a remote access connection between the client computer and the server. The primary remote access protocol used for dial-up remote access is the Point-to-Point Protocol (PPP).

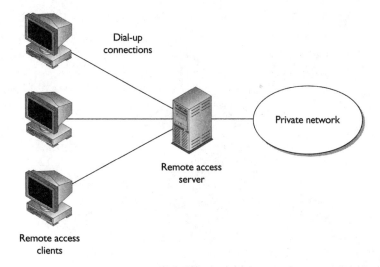

FIGURE 6-1

A dial-up remote
access solution

Dial-up
connections

Private network

Remote access
server

Remote access
clients

■ **LAN protocols** A LAN protocol is required for the client computer to access resources on the private network once a connection is made with the remote access server. Windows Server 2003 remote access supports two LAN protocols: TCP/IP and AppleTalk.

Elements of VPN Remote Access

With a remote access VPN solution, client computers establish a connection with an IP-based network, usually the Internet, then create a virtual connection with a remote access server using a tunneling protocol. A remote access VPN solution will consist of the following elements (see Figure 6-2):

■ **VPN client** This is the computer that establishes a VPN connection with a remote access server using a tunneling protocol.

■ **VPN server** This is the computer running Windows Server 2003 that accepts incoming VPN connections and forwards packets between the VPN client computer and the private network.

■ **Tunneling Protocols** Windows Server 2003 supports two tunneling protocols: the Layer Two Tunneling Protocol (L2TP) and the Point-to-Point Tunneling Protocol (PPTP).

■ **Internet** This is the medium used to connect the VPN client with the VPN server. It can be any IP-based network, with the Internet being used most often.

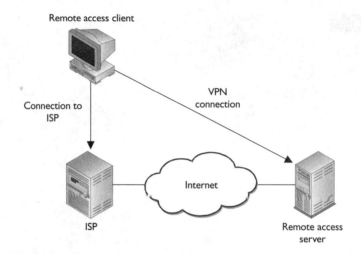

FIGURE 6-2

A VPN remote
access solution

CERTIFICATION OBJECTIVE 6.03

Planning for Remote Access

Before you enable remote access, you should take the time to plan the implementation.
Once you have decided on a remote access method, your main concern will be planning
for security and ensuring that the remote access infrastructure is secure.

Selecting a Remote Access Method

Windows Server 2003 supports two different remote access methods: dial-up and VPN.
You will need to evaluate the advantages and disadvantages of each remote access
method to determine which one will best suit your needs.

With a dial-up solution, remote access clients connect to a remote access server
using a telephone line. The remote access server requires at least one modem or
multiport adapter as well as a telephone line or other form of connectivity. If the
remote access clients require access to resources on the private network, the remote
access server must also be configured with a LAN connection. The remote access client
simply requires a modem and a telephone connection. When determining whether
to use a dial-up remote access solution, consider the advantages and disadvantages
outlined in Table 6-1.

TABLE 6-1 Advantages and Disadvantages of a Dial-Up Remote Access Solution

Advantages	Disadvantages
Connections are inexpensive to implement on the remote access client.	Hardware required on the remote access server can be expensive.
Dial-up connections are relatively inexpensive.	Data transmission rates are generally slow.
They provide a reliable remote access solution.	Dial-up remote access does not scale well as the number of remote access users increases.
They are relatively simple to implement.	A connection can be unreliable, depending on the location of the remote access user.

The second option for remote access connectivity is to implement a VPN remote access solution. To provide users with remote access via the Internet, the remote access VPN server is normally configured with a permanent Internet connection. Again, if users require access to the private network, the server must also have a LAN connection. The VPN client must have a modem or network adapter as well as Internet connectivity using the phone line or other WAN connectivity method. A VPN solution also requires the use of a tunneling protocol. The remote access client and the remote access server must be configured to use PPTP or L2TP (keep in mind that the client and the server must be configured to use the same tunneling protocol). Table 6-2 summarizes the advantages and disadvantages of implementing a remote access VPN solution.

TABLE 6-2 Advantages and Disadvantages of a VPN Remote Access Solution

Advantages	Disadvantages
The Internet can be used to transport data, possibly reducing the cost associated with long-distance dial-up charges.	Performance can be impacted because data must be tunneled.
A private connection is not required between a remote access client and a remote access VPN server.	The remote access server and remote access client must support the same tunneling protocol (PPTP or L2TP).
This solution is more scalable than a dial-up remote access solution.	Since packets are being transmitted over the Internet, there is a greater security risk, even though data is encrypted.

Planning for Dial-Up Remote Access

As already mentioned, RAS can provide remote connectivity for dial-up or VPN connections. You must consider a number of issues before implementing RAS for dial-up users. Doing so can help eliminate implementation problems.

IP Address Assignment   When a remote access client dials into a remote access server, the client must be assigned an IP address. There are two options for assigning IP addresses to remote access clients. One option is to configure the RAS server with a static range of IP addresses to lease to remote access users. If you use this method, consider the IP addressing scheme currently implemented on the network. If there is a DHCP server on the private network, ensure that the static address range does not overlap with a scope configured on the DHCP server, as this could lead to address conflicts. If the static address range is different from that on the private network, ensure that the network routers are configured with the necessary routes to that address range so that traffic destined to any remote access clients is sent to the remote access server.

The second option is to use DHCP to assign IP addresses to remote access clients. In this case, the remote access server obtains IP addresses from a DHCP server on the private network to lease to clients when they establish a PPP connection.

Incoming Ports   You will need to consider the maximum number of remote access clients that will be dialing in at any given time and ensure that the RAS server can support this. More than likely, your remote access server will be configured with a modem bank and multiple phone lines. Once the hardware is installed, ensure that the ports are all enabled to allow remote access.

Remote Access Policies   Remote access policies allow an administrator to control remote access connections. For example, policies can be used to determine which users have remote access permission. Before implementing policies, you need to determine the administrative approach you will use. In terms of remote access permissions, they can be controlled through the policy or through the properties of each user account. Controlling access through each user account provides a decentralized model, while using policies to control access centralizes administration.

For example, an administrator may decide to implement a decentralized approach and configure the properties of each user account to either Allow access or Deny access. A policy must still exist, but the permissions of the policy would be set to

INSIDE THE EXAM

Remote Access and the DHCP Relay Agent

A remote access server can be configured with a static range of IP addresses to lease to clients, or it can obtain IP addresses from a DHCP server on the private network to lease to clients. When a dial-up client establishes a PPP connection with a remote access server, it is assigned an IP address. However, clients are not provided with any optional IP parameters that may be used on the private network when the PPP connection is established. For example, if there is a DNS server on the network, clients will not be provided with its IP address when a PPP connection is established.

Once Windows XP, Windows Server 2003, and Windows 2000 clients have been assigned an IP address, they send a DHCPInform message to the remote access server requesting additional parameters such as the IP address of the name server being used on the private network. These messages need to be sent to the DHCP server on the private network. So in order for the remote access server to be able to forward the DHCPInform messages to the DHCP server, the remote access server must have the DHCP relay agent component enabled.

The DHCP relay agent component can be enabled within the Routing and Remote Access snap-in. Once the DHCP relay agent component is enabled on the remote access server, remote access clients will be able to obtain additional IP parameters used on the private network. The remote access server is able to forward the DHCPInform messages to the DHCP server and return the results back to the remote access client.

deny remote access (as you will see later in the chapter, when you configure remote access policies, permissions configured for a user account override those within a remote access policy). On the other hand, to centralize administration of remote access permissions, an administrator may choose to configure user accounts, so access is controlled through the remote access policies. The policy permissions would then determine whether a user is permitted remote access.

If there are multiple remote access servers on the network, each server must be configured with at least one remote access policy, or else you can centralize the administration of policies by using Internet Authentication Service, in which case, the policies are stored on the server running IAS. This server is then responsible for the authentication and authorization of connection attempts.

Planning for VPN Access

A virtual private network (VPN) enables you to connect to a remote server using a public network such as the Internet. Once a connection to the Internet is established, the remote access client creates a connection to the remote access VPN server using a tunneling protocol. The tunnel provides secure communications between the remote access client and the private network over the Internet. One of the biggest advantages to implementing VPNs for remote access is cost. Users can dial into a local ISP and then create a virtual connection to a remote access VPN server, as opposed to dialing directly into the RAS server and possibly having to incur long-distance charges. As with implementing a dial-up remote access solution, some preplanning is required before implementing remote access VPN.

Tunneling Protocols   Windows Server 2003 supports both the Point-to-Point Tunneling Protocol (PPTP) and the Layer Two Tunneling Protocol (L2TP). Both protocols are installed by default. PPTP and L2TP both provide encryption of data. With PPTP, encryption is built into the protocol and uses MPPE 40-bit to 128-bit encryption, whereas L2TP uses IPSec or DES to encrypt data , supporting key lengths between 56-bit (DES) to 128-bit (3DES). When deciding which protocol to implement, keep the following points in mind:

- PPTP can be used with a variety of dial-up clients, including Windows 95, Windows 98, Windows NT 4.0, Windows ME, Windows 2000, and Windows XP.

- L2TP is supported by Windows 2000 and Windows XP clients. Windows 98, Windows ME, and Windows NT 4.0 also support the protocol with the L2TP/IPsec VPN client installed.

- L2TP provides computer-level and user-level authentication and requires a PKI infrastructure or the use of a preshared key for authentication.

- PPTP provides user-level authentication using any of the following authentication protocols: EAP, CHAP, MS-CHAP, SPAP, and PAP.

| **TABLE 6-3** | Differences Between PPTP and L2TP |

PPTP	L2TP
Uses PPP to encrypt data	Data is encrypted using IPSec.
Can encrypt IP, IPX, and NetBEUI traffic	Can encrypt only IP traffic.
Supports only IP-based networks	Can encapsulate traffic on a variety of networks, including ATM, Frame Relay, and X.25.
Supports a variety of platforms	Supported by Windows 2000 and Windows XP. L2TP/IPSec VPN client required by Windows 98, Windows ME, and Windows NT 4.0.

Table 6-3 summarizes the various differences between the protocols; it may assist in deciding which protocol to implement.

on the **Job**

It is recommended that you use computer-level authentication with L2TP/IPsec. If you do, a PKI infrastructure is required to issue certificates to VPN servers and VPN workstations.

Certificates

When implementing L2TP/IPSec VPN connections, you can use computer certificates or a preshared key for authentication. For a higher level of security, it is recommended that you implement computer certificates for authentication. Doing so requires a PKI infrastructure to issue certificates to the VPN servers as well as the VPN workstations. Before implementing remote access VPN, you will need to consider whether certificates are required, and if so how they will be issued and installed.

EXERCISE 6-1

Planning for Remote Access

In this exercise, you will use the information presented in the scenario to plan a remote access solution.

The Bayside Corporation is expanding its Sales department. Sales staff will now be required to travel throughout the U.S. to attract new customers and maintain contact with existing ones. All members of the sales staff will require remote access to the company's network while traveling. They need to be able to access a database server as well as the company's internal web server. You have been asked to recommend a remote access connectivity strategy for Bayside. What method of connectivity would you recommend to Managers of the Bayside Corporation and why? Explain why you would choose one remote connectivity method over another.

CERTIFICATION OBJECTIVE 6.04

Implementing Remote Access

Once you have gone through the planning phase and determined your remote access solution, the next step will be to enable and configure the routing and remote access service on those computers that will provide remote access to client computers. The service can be enabled and configured using the Routing and Remote Access console.

Enabling Remote Access

Remote access can be enabled on a computer running Windows Server 2003 in one of two ways: you can use the Configure Your Server Wizard, or you can use the Routing and Remote Access console. Exercises 6-2 and 6-3 outline the steps involved when using the Routing and Remote Access snap-in to enable dial-up remote access and VPN remote access.

EXERCISE 6-2

Enabling Dial-Up Remote Access

In this exercise, you will enable dial-up Remote Access on a computer running Windows Server 2003.

1. Click Start, point to Administrative Tools, and click Routing and Remote Access.

2. Within the Routing and Remote Access console, right-click your server and click Configure And Enable Routing and Remote Access. This launches the Routing and Remote Access Server Setup Wizard. Click Next.

3. From the list of configurations, select Remote Access (Dial-Up Or VPN). Click Next.

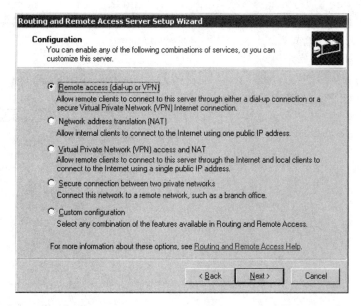

4. Select the methods clients can use to gain remote access. You can choose VPN or Dial-Up. Select Dial-Up and click Next.

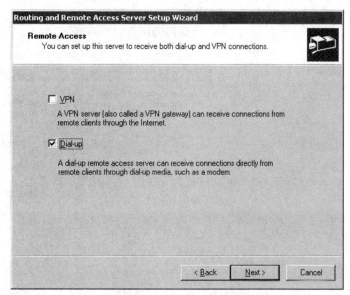

5. From the IP Address Assignment dialog box, select how you want remote access clients to receive an IP address. You can have a DHCP server on the private network assign IP addresses or you can configure a pool of addresses on the RAS server. Click From A Specified Range. Click Next.

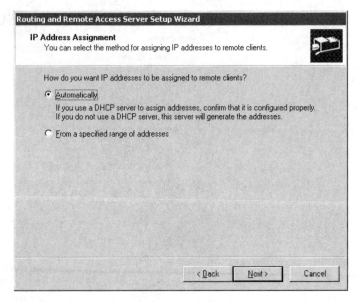

6. From the Address Assignment Range dialog box, click New to configure a new address range. Type in the start and end IP addresses. Click OK. Click Next.

7. Click No, Use Routing And Remote Access To Authenticate Connection Requests. Click Next.

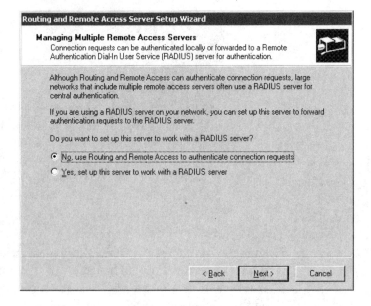

8. Click Finish. A message will appear informing you that the DHCP relay agent must be configured on the remote access server to support the relaying of DHCP messages between remote access clients and a DHCP server on the private network. Click OK.

You can refer to Chapter 2 for step-by-step instructions on how to enable the DHCP relay agent on a computer running Windows Server 2003.

EXERCISE 6-3

Enabling VPN Remote Access

This exercise will walk you through the steps involved in enabling a computer running Windows Server 2003 for VPN remote access.

1. Click Start, point to Administrative Tools, and click Routing And Remote Access.
2. Within the console, right-click your server and select Enable And Configure Routing And Remote Access. This launches the Routing and Remote Access Server Setup Wizard. Click Next.
3. From the list of configurations, select Remote Access (Dial-Up Or VPN). Click Next.
4. Select VPN and click Next.

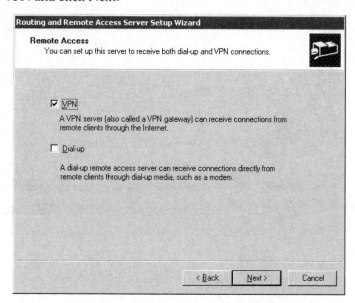

5. From the VPN Connection dialog box, select the interface that is connected to the Internet. Click Next.

6. From the IP Address Assignment dialog box, select Automatically to have the VPN server obtain IP addresses from a DHCP server on the private network. Alternatively, select From A Specified Range Of Addresses to use a static IP address range. Once the IP address range is configured, click Next.

7. Select whether to use a RADIUS server for authentication and authorization. For this exercise, click No, Use Routing And Remote Access To Authenticate Connection Requests. Click Next.

8. Click Finish.

Once remote access has been enabled, there are a number of properties that you can configure at the server level (see Figure 6-3). Table 6-4 summarizes the various tabs and configurable options.

FIGURE 6-3

Configuring the properties of a remote access server

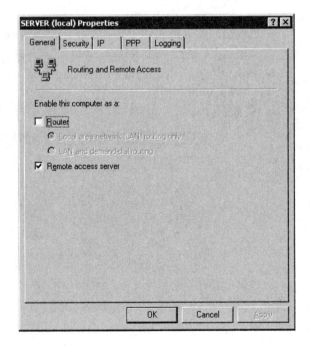

TABLE 6-4	Properties of a Remote Access Server

Tab	Description
General	Used to enable a server as an IP router, a remote access server, or both.
Security	Used to configure the Authentication and Accounting methods as well as a preshared key for L2TP connections.
IP	Used to enable IP routing and remote access and demand-dial connections. You can also specify how clients are assigned IP addresses: from a static pool or using DHCP.
PPP	Used to enable multilink, LCP, and software compression. These must be enabled at the server level before they can be configured for a remote access policy.
Logging	Used to specify the types of events to log. The default is to log errors and warnings only.

Inbound Connections

Windows Server 2003 supports two different dial-up protocols: the Point-to-Point Protocol (PPP) and the Serial Line Internet Protocol (SLIP). PPP has become the industry-standard communication protocol. It supports a number of different protocols over a dial-up connection, including TCP/IP, IPX/SPX, and NetBEUI.

SLIP, on the other hand, is a legacy protocol that is normally used to connect to UNIX systems. Keep in mind that Windows Server 2003 supports SLIP only for outbound connections. It does not support dial-up connections using this protocol. One of the major problems with using SLIP is its lack of security. For example, it sends passwords in clear text.

You can configure the PPP protocol using the PPP tab from the remote access server's properties dialog box (see Figure 6-4). From here, you can enable multilink connections, which allow multiple phone lines to be combined into a single logical connection to increase available bandwidth. Multilink is used in conjunction with the Bandwidth Allocation Protocol (BAP), which allows connections to be added and dropped dynamically as bandwidth requirements change. For example, if a client is configured to use multilink, when the bandwidth requirements reach a specific level, the client can send a BAP request for an additional link. Two other protocols that can be enabled from the PPP tab are the Bandwidth Allocation Control Protocol (BACP) and the Link Control Protocol (LCP). These protocols work together to elect a favored peer when multiple BAP requests are received.

FIGURE 6-4

Configuring the
Point-to-Point
Protocol

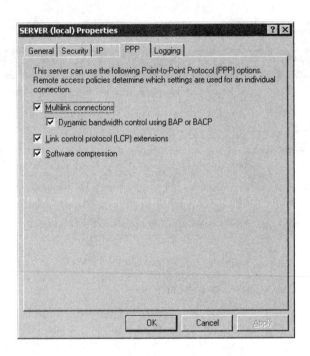

FIGURE 6-4

Configuring the
Point-to-Point
Protocol

on the
Öob

Keep in mind that if you want to enable multilink in a remote access policy, it must first be enabled at the server level using the PPP tab.

Once remote access is enabled, a number of ports are automatically created for incoming connections. You can configure them using the Ports container within the Routing and Remote Access snap-in (see Figure 6-5). As you can see, several ports are created for PPTP and L2TP connections as well as for any modems installed.

You can configure additional ports by selecting the port and clicking Configure. If the device supports multiple ports, using the Maximum Ports setting, you can increase the number of available ports (see Figure 6-6). You can also configure the ports for inbound use only or for inbound and outbound use. For a remote access server, make sure that inbound use is selected to enable the port to accept incoming connections from remote access clients. If the server is being used for demand-dial routing as well, select the Demand-Dial Routing Connections (Inbound And Outbound) option.

FIGURE 6-5

Configuring ports

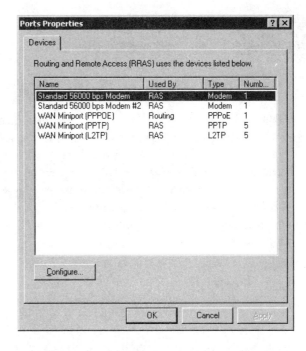

FIGURE 6-6

Configuring the
Maximum Ports
setting

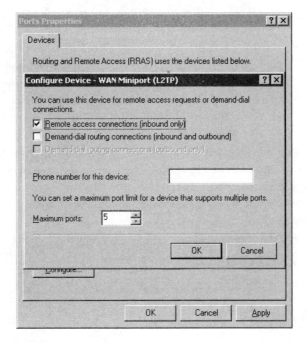

CERTIFICATION OBJECTIVE 6.05

Ensuring Remote Access Security

Enabling remote access opens the door for remote access users to access the private network from a remote location. When considering remote access, the topic of security is bound to arise. How can you provide certain clients with remote access while denying others? How can you ensure secure connections between remote access clients and remote access servers? How can you ensure data security?

Remote access supports a number of features that allow administrators to address the issues of remote access security. These features include remote access policies, authentication, and data encryption.

Remote Access Policies

Remote access policies play a crucial role in remote access security. They enable an administrator to control which users and groups are allowed remote access permissions and to control the properties of the connection, such as the encryption and authentication protocols used and the time of day users are allowed remote access.

If you recall from Windows NT 4.0, remote access was controlled through the properties of each user account. Windows 2000 introduced remote access policies as a method of providing administrators with much more control over remote access.

Using remote access policies, remote access connection attempts can be granted or denied according to a number of different criteria. For example, administrators can specify the day and time that remote access is permitted as well as the group that the policy applies to. Once a connection attempt is granted, it can be further controlled by defining encryption settings and maximum session times.

After remote access has been enabled, two remote access policies are created by default; they are listed within the Remote Access Policies container (see Figure 6-7). Additional policies can be created if necessary.

In order for remote access clients to connect to a remote access server, there must be at least one remote *access policy configured. If no policy exists, remote access users will not be able to connect.*

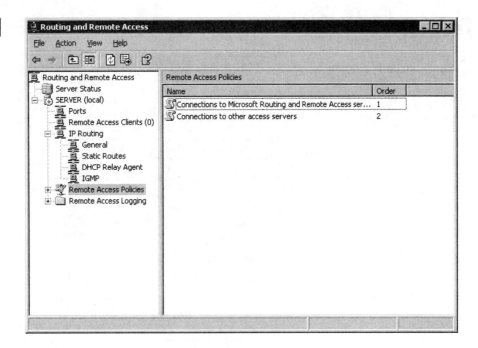

FIGURE 6-7

The default
remote access
policies

Remote Access Policy Elements

A remote access policy is basically a set of rules that are used to configure connection restrictions. Each remote access policy consists of three different elements:

- Conditions
- Permissions
- Profile

Conditions The first element of a remote access policy is the conditions. These are various settings configured by an administrator that are evaluated against the initial connection attempt by a remote access user. When a user attempts to access a remote access server, the properties of the connection attempt must match the conditions of at least one remote access policy. Table 6-5 outlines the various policy conditions that can be configured (see Figure 6-8).

Permissions The remote access permissions determine whether a user is permitted or denied remote access. Permissions can be controlled through the properties of a user

FIGURE 6-8

Conditions that
can be configured
for a remote
access policy

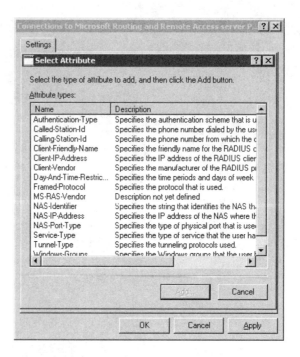

TABLE 6-5   Remote Access Conditions

Condition	Description
Authentication-Type	The type of authentication method used by the client. Authentication methods include CHAP, EAP, MS-CHAP, and MS-CHAP v2
Called-Station-ID	The phone number of the network access server (NAS)
Calling-Station-ID	The phone number from which the remote access user dials in
Client-Friendly-Name	The friendly name assigned to the RADIUS client that is requesting authentication
Client-IP-Address	The IP address of the RADIUS client
Client-Vendor	The vendor of the network access server (NAS) requesting authentication
Day-and-Time-Restrictions	The day of the week and time of day that the connection is permitted
Framed-Protocol	The protocol used for framing incoming packets (for example, PPP or SLIP)
NAS-Identifier	This is the name of the network access server (NAS)
NAS-IP-Address	The IP address of the NAS

TABLE 6-5	Remote Access Conditions *(continued)*
Condition	**Description**
NAS-Port-Type	The type of media that is used by the client
Service-Type	The type of service that the client is requesting
Tunnel-Type	The tunnel type being used by the requesting client (PPTP or L2TP)
Windows-Groups	The groups to which the requesting client must belong

account and through a remote access policy, keeping in mind that the account properties override the settings within the remote access policy.

When configuring the properties of a user account, you have three options available from the Dial-in tab (see Figure 6-9). The remote access permissions for a user account can be set to Allow Access, Deny Access, or Control Access Through Remote Access Policy. Selecting one of the first two options allows you to explicitly grant or deny remote access to a user.

FIGURE 6-9

Configuring the
dial-in properties
of a user account

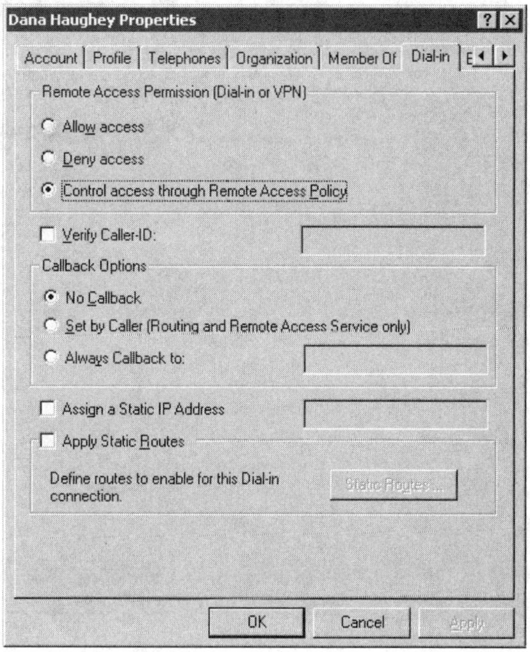

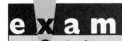

The permissions assigned using the dial-in properties of a user account will override those settings within a remote access policy. For

example, if the permissions of the policy allow access but the properties of the user account deny access, the connection attempt is denied.

If you select the third option to control access through the policy, the policy settings will determine whether a user is granted remote access. Using the policy, you can either Grant Remote Access Permission or Deny Remote Access Permission (see Figure 6-10).

on the

Ⓙo b

If the option to Control Access Through Remote Access Policy is grayed out, verify that your domain functional level is Windows Server 2003. This option is not available when the domain functional level is set to Windows 2000.

FIGURE 6-10

Configuring permissions of a remote access policy

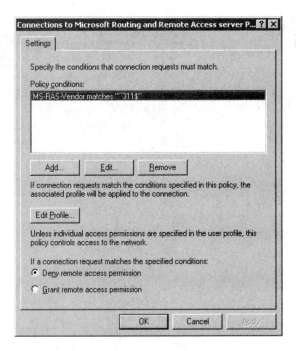

Profile   The profile of a policy determines the properties of a connection attempt. Once a connection attempt has been authorized, these are the properties that are then applied to the connection. You can configure the profile settings by right-clicking a policy within the Remote Access Policies container, clicking Properties, and selecting the Edit Profile button. Profile settings include the following (see Figure 6-11), each of which is summarized in Table 6-6:

- Dial-in Constraints
- IP
- Multilink
- Authentication
- Encryption
- Advanced Settings

Various settings can also be configured through the properties of a user account. Again, the settings you configure must match the connection attempt or it will be denied. Using the Dial-in Constraints tab from the account properties dialog box,

FIGURE 6-11

Configuring the profile settings of a remote access policy

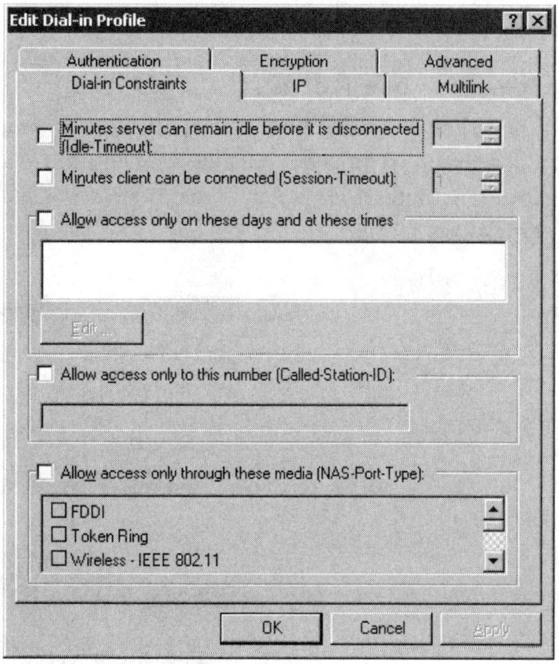

| TABLE 6-6 | Remote Access Profile Settings |

Profile Settings	Description
Dial-in Constraints	Used to configure the Idle-Timeout and Session-Timeout values, the day and time restrictions, as well as number and media restrictions.
IP	Used to specify how remote access clients are assigned IP addresses and to configure inbound and outbound packet filters.
Multilink	Used to enable and configure multilink connections and the Bandwidth Allocation Protocol (BAP).
Authentication	Specifies the various authentication methods that can be used by remote access users.
Encryption	Specifies the levels of encryption that can be used by remote access clients.
Advanced Settings	Used to specify additional connection parameters.

you can configure the callback options. For example, you can configure a specific number that the remote access server will call the user back at, thereby limiting where the user can gain remote access from. You can also configure a static IP address for the client as well as configure static routes that will be applied to the connection (see Figure 6-12).

How Remote Access Policies Are Evaluated

When planning for remote access policies, it is important that you have a thorough understanding of how the policies' elements are evaluated during the connection process. Remote access policy elements are evaluated in the following order: conditions, permissions, profile.

| FIGURE 6-12 |

Configuring static routes for a remote access client

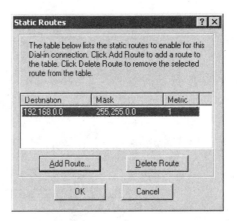

When a remote access user attempts a connection, the RAS server first evaluates the connection attempt against the conditions of the policy. If the conditions of the policy are not met, the connection attempt by the user is denied. For example, if the conditions specify that the remote access user must be a member of the Sales group, this condition must be met or the connection attempt is denied. If multiple policies exist, they are evaluated in the order that they appear within the Remote Access Policies container until the conditions of a policy are met.

If the conditions of a policy are met, the permissions of the policy and the permission configured for the user account are evaluated. If the dial-in permissions for the user account are set to Deny Access, the connection attempt is rejected (regardless of whether the policy permissions grant access). If the policy dial-in permission is set to Deny Access, the connection attempt will be rejected. If the policy is used to Control Access, the connection attempt is granted or denied according to the permissions configured in the policy.

If the user has been granted remote access permission, the policy evaluation process continues by evaluating the connection attempt against the profile settings and the user account properties. If the settings match the connection attempt, remote access is permitted.

The following steps outline the policy evaluation process:

1. A user attempts to establish a connection. The connection attempt is evaluated against the conditions of the first policy (if multiple policies exist). The conditions of each policy are evaluated until a match is found.

2. If the connection attempt does not match the conditions of any policy, it is rejected. If the connection attempt does match the conditions of a policy, the evaluation process continues.

3. Next the permissions are evaluated. If the user's account properties grant access, the profile settings are evaluated. If the user's account properties deny access, the connection attempt is rejected.

4. If access is controlled through the policy permission, access is either granted or denied according to the permission settings.

5. If the user's account properties grant access or if the policy permissions grant access, the profile settings and the properties of the user account are evaluated.

6. If the connection attempt matches both the account settings and the policy profile settings, the connection attempt is granted.

7. If the connection attempt does not match the account settings and the policy profile settings, the connection attempt is rejected.

on the **Job**

Knowing how the elements of a remote access policy are evaluated can make troubleshooting remote access much simpler.

Planning for Remote Access Policies

Before configuring a remote access policy, you need to decide upon the various settings that will be required. This means you will need to determine the conditions, permissions, and profile settings that need to be configured. When planning for policy settings, keep the following points in mind:

- The initial connection attempt is compared against the conditions of a policy. Choose the condition attributes that you want the connection attempt to match. If multiple policies exist, the conditions of at least one policy must be met or the connection attempt will be rejected. Also, the policies are evaluated in the order that they appear within the Remote Access Policies container.

- The permissions can be set through the account properties and through the remote access policy. If the user is granted remote access, the profile settings of that policy are evaluated. You can centralize the administration of permissions by controlling access through the remote access policies. It is also generally easier to apply remote access permissions to groups than to individual users.

- When configuring the profile settings for a policy, keep the topic of security in mind. Consider using only MS-CHAP v2 and EAP for authentication methods. If at all possible, avoid using PAP, since the passwords are sent in clear text. Also, configure the highest level of encryption possible. This will be determined by the platforms being used by the remote access users.

EXERCISE 6-4

CertCam 6-4 ON THE CD

Planning for Remote Access Policies

In this exercise, you will plan for remote access policies using the information presented in the scenario.

Bayside has several temporary employees that work from home offices. These individuals have been hired to work on a company project. All of the users require remote access to a server on the private network where they post data to share with other users working on the same project.

These temporary employees require certain remote access restrictions. They should be permitted remote access only during weekday business hours (8 A.M. to 5 P.M.).

All idle sessions should be disconnected after 20 minutes. Since there are 30 employees working on the project, you want to grant all 30 users remote access permissions with as little administrative effort as possible. The restrictions put in place should not interfere with the remote access capabilities of full-time employees. How will you plan the remote access policy implementation for these employees?

Authentication Methods

Authentication is the process of verifying credentials. In terms of remote access, authentication occurs when a remote access client sends its credentials to a remote access server for verification. A user's credentials are sent to the remote access server through use of an authentication protocol. Windows Server 2003 supports a number of different protocols that can be used to authenticate remote access clients. The protocols supported include

- Password Authentication Protocol (PAP)
- Shiva Password Authentication Protocol (SPAP)
- Challenge Handshake Authentication Protocol (CHAP)
- Microsoft Challenge Handshake Authentication Protocol (MS-CHAP)
- Extensible Authentication Protocol (EAP)

Password Authentication Protocol

The Password Authentication Protocol (PAP) is generally the least secure of all the authentication protocols. When a user authenticates using PAP, the username and password are sent in clear text, meaning they are not encrypted. Therefore, it is not recommended that this authentication protocol be used. PAP is most often used to connect to legacy Unix systems that do not support more secure authentication protocols.

Shiva Password Authentication Protocol

The Shiva Password Authentication Protocol (SPAP) is an authentication protocol used by Shiva remote access servers. It is supported by Windows Server 2003 for Shiva clients. Windows clients also use the protocol to authenticate to a Shiva LAN Rover. SPAP uses a two-way encryption algorithm to encrypt the password, and therefore it is more secure than PAP. However, the problem with SPAP is that once the password has been encrypted, it is always encrypted in the same way. An Internet attacker could easily capture the encrypted password and use it to authenticate with the remote access server.

Challenge Handshake Authentication Protocol

The Challenge Handshake Authentication Protocol (CHAP) is an industry-standard authentication protocol. Unlike SPAP and PAP, CHAP does not send the credentials across the network. Instead, CHAP uses a challenge-response where the Message Digest 5 (MD5) is used to encrypt the response. CHAP can be used to authenticate non-Windows clients. If your network supports only Windows-based clients, consider using MS-CHAP instead. Windows Server 2003 supports CHAP so that it can authenticate dial-up clients running non-Microsoft platforms.

Microsoft Challenge Handshake Authentication Protocol

The Microsoft Challenge Handshake Authentication Protocol (MS-CHAP) version 1 is Microsoft's version of CHAP that is used to authenticate Windows-based clients. It also uses a challenge-response with nonreversible encryption of the password. Windows Server 2003 also includes MS-CHAP version 2, which provides a stronger level of encryption than version 1 and provides separate encryption keys for sending and receiving.

ⓦatch *MS-CHAP is supported only by workstations running Windows 98, Windows NT 4.0, Windows 2000, Windows XP, and Windows Server 2003.*

Extensible Authentication Protocol

The Extensible Authentication Protocol (EAP) is an extension to the Point-to-Point Protocol that provides support for other authentication methods such as smart cards. The authentication mechanism used is negotiated between the remote access client and the remote access server. In order for authentication to occur, both the client and the server must support the same authentication method. If used with smart cards, this protocol requires a PKI infrastructure. Windows Server 2003 by default supports the following EAP methods:

- EAP-MD5 Challenge
- Protected EAP (PEAP)
- Smart Card

Enabling Authentication Methods

Remote access policies will determine the authentication methods that must be used by remote access clients. Before an authentication protocol can be enabled within a policy, it must be enabled at the server level. To do so, right-click your remote access server within the Routing and Remote Access console and click Properties. Using the Security tab, select the Authentication Methods tab (see Figure 6-13). Select the methods the remote access server can use to authenticate requesting clients and click OK.

Once the authentication protocols are enabled at the server level, you can configure the authentication methods for the remote access policies. This can be done by right-clicking a remote access policy within the Remote Access Policies container and clicking Properties. From the General tab, click the Edit Profile button and select the Authentication tab (see Figure 6-14). Enable those authentication protocols available for that remote access policy and click OK. Table 6-7 outlines the differences between the various authentication protocols.

FIGURE 6-13

Enabling authentication methods on a remote access server

FIGURE 6-14

Enabling
authentication
methods for a
remote access
policy

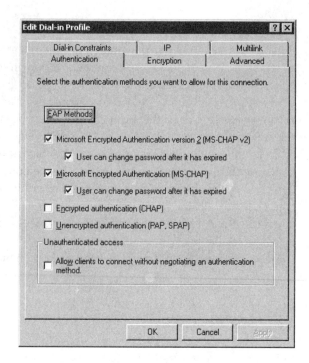

TABLE 6-7   Remote Access Authentication Protocols

Authentication Protocol	Description
PAP	• Password-based • Provides no encryption • Used only if the remote access client does not support any other authentication methods
SPAP	• Password-based • Used to authenticate Shiva clients or the Shiva LAN Rover remote access server
CHAP	• Password-based • Provides encrypted authentication • Supported by a variety of platforms, including Macintosh and Unix
MS-CHAP	• Password-based • Provides encrypted authentication • Supported by Windows 98, Windows ME, and Windows NT 4.0

TABLE 6-7	Remote Access Authentication Protocols *(continued)*
Authentication Protocol	**Description**
MS-CHAP version 2	• Password-based • Provides mutual authentication • Supported by Windows 2000, Windows XP, and Windows Server 2003 • Can be used for dial-up and VPN remote access
EAP-MD5	• Password-based • Provides encrypted authentication • Supports dial-up authentication only
PEAP	• Certificate and password-based • Used for authentication of wireless clients
EAP-TLS	• Certificate based • Provides mutual authentication • Uses certificates or smart cards for authentication • Supported by dial-up and VPN remote access

Encryption Methods

You can add another level of security to your remote access implementation by using various *data encryption* methods to secure data being sent between a remote access server and a remote access client. Windows Server 2003 supports two types of encryption:

■ **Microsoft Point-to-Point Encryption (MPPE)**   MPPE uses 40-bit, 56-bit, and 128-bit encryption keys to encrypt data. MPPE can be used with PPP or PPTP VPN connections and is used by EAP-TLS and MS-CHAP to encrypt authentication information.

■ **IP Security (IPSec)**   IPSec is used to encrypt data for L2TP VPN connections. It uses the Data Encryption Standard (DES) and the Triple Data Encryption Standard (3DES).

Enabling Encryption Methods

Unlike authentication methods, encryption methods are enabled only through the remote access policies, which you can access by clicking the Edit Profile button from the remote access policy's properties dialog box and selecting the Encryption tab (see Figure 6-15). You can select any of the following options:

- **Basic Encryption**   Uses IPSec 56-bit DES or MPPE 40-bit data encryption
- **Strong Encryption**   Uses IPSec 56-bit DES or MPPE 56-bit data encryption
- **Strongest Encryption**   Uses IPSec Triple DES (3DES) or MPPE 128-bit encryption
- **No Encryption**   Allows remote access clients to connect without using any form of data encryption

If the No Encryption option is the only one selected, any attempts by remote access clients to connect using data encryption will be rejected.

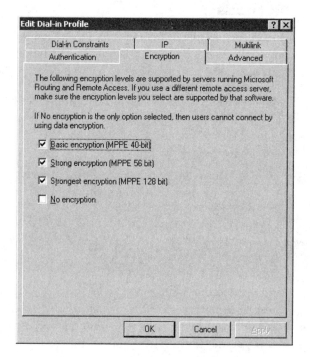

FIGURE 6-15

Configuring encryption methods for a remote access policy

EXERCISE 6-5

Creating a New Remote Access Policy

In this exercise, you will create a new remote access policy.

1. Within the Routing and Remote Access console, right-click the Remote Access Policies container and click New Remote Access Policy. This launches the New Remote Access Policy Wizard. Click Next.

2. Specify how you want to set up the policy. You can use the wizard or create a custom policy. Leave the default option selected. Type in a name for the policy. Click Next.

3. Select the remote access method for which you want to create the policy. Select Dial-Up and click Next.

4. From the User or Group Access dialog box, specify whether to grant access to individual users or groups. Keep in mind that user permissions override group permissions. Click Add, type in the name of an existing group (for example, Domain Users), and click Check Names. Click OK. Click Next.

5. Select the method of authentication: EAP, Microsoft Encrypted Authentication version 2, or Microsoft Encrypted Authentication. Click Next.

6. Select the policy encryption levels. Click Next.

7. Click Finish.

Other Security Options

Along with implementing secure authentication methods and data encryption, there are a number of other options available that can be used to increase the security of a remote access implementation. Some of these options include

- Network Access Quarantine Control
- Caller-ID
- Remote Access Account Lockout

Network Access Quarantine Control   Network Access Quarantine, a new feature in Windows Server 2003, protects the private network by placing any remote access connections in a quarantine mode so that network access is limited. Only when it has been determined that the connection meets the organization's requirements or when a connection is brought into accordance with certain criteria, will the remote access connection be removed from quarantine mode. This way, if any computer configurations do not meet the requirements of the organization, such as if antivirus software is not installed or is disabled, they will be restricted from accessing the network.

Caller ID   Using the caller-ID feature, administrators can limit the locations from which a user can gain remote access. For example, users can be allowed remote access only from home offices. The benefit of this is an increase in security; however, it restricts users to dialing in from only a single location.

Caller ID can be configured through the dial-in properties of a user account. When a remote access client dials into a remote access server, if the number that client is calling from does not match the number specified through the account properties, the connection attempt is denied.

on the **Job**   *In order to implement caller ID, the dial-up equipment must also support this feature.*

Remote Access Account Lockout   Using the remote access account lockout feature, an administrator can specify how many failed logon attempts can occur before a remote access user's account is locked out. Consider implementing this feature when using remote access VPN, since an Internet attacker may be trying to gain access by guessing the password to a valid user account.

on the **Job**   *The remote access user account lockout feature is separate from the account lockout option configured in a group policy.*

When implementing remote access account lockout, you must determine two variables: how many failed logon attempts before the account is locked out and how often the failed attempts counter is set back to 0. For example, if the number of failed logon attempts is set to 3, after a remote access user's third failed attempt to log on, the account will be locked out. The reset counter will determine how long before the number of failed logon attempts is set back to 0.

The remote access account lockout feature is enabled using the Registry (it is disabled by default). To enable remote access, you must change the MaxDenial value found under the HKEY_Local_Machine\System\CurrentControlSet\Services\ RemoteAccess\Parameters\AccountLockout subkey (see Figure 6-16). To configure the

FIGURE 6-16

Enabling the
remote access
account lockout
feature

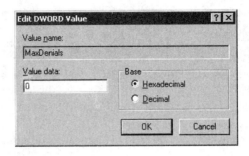

amount of time that must pass before the failed attempts counter is reset, edit the
ResetTime value found under the same Registry subkey. The default value for
the ResetTime is 48 hours, or 2880 minutes (see Figure 6-17).

on the
job

*If you are planning to implement the remote access account lockout feature,
it must be enabled on the computer that authenticates the remote access
users. If remote access servers are configured as RADIUS clients, edit the
Registry of the IAS server responsible for authenticating remote access clients.
If no RADIUS server is used, enable this feature on each remote access server.*

Internet Authentication Service

As your network infrastructure increases in size, multiple remote access servers may be
required. In order to centralize various functions related to remote access, you may choose
to implement a RADIUS server. A RADIUS server centralizes the authentication of
remote access users as well as centralizing storage of remote access accounting information
(see Figure 6-18).

Windows Server 2003 includes its own version of a RADIUS server, known as
Internet Authentication Service (IAS). IAS can be installed using the Add or

FIGURE 6-17

Configuring the
failed attempts
counter

SCENARIO & SOLUTION

When planning for security, which authentication protocol should be used?	Whenever possible, use EAP-TLS with smart cards for the strongest authentication. Otherwise, choose MS-CHAP v2, if the remote access clients support this protocol.
How can I increase security for a dial-up remote access solution?	By configuring the strongest authentication protocol supported by remote access clients and by implementing data encryption.
How can I increase security for a remote access VPN solution?	Again, you will want to choose the strongest authentication protocol and, if possible, use L2TP/IPSec. Along with encryption, L2TP/IPSec connections provide data integrity, confidentiality, and authentication of the sender.
Can I use IPSec for dial-up remote access clients?	When a connection is established, MPPE is used for encryption between the remote access client and the remote access server. You can implement IPSec, such that after the PPP connection has been established, data sent between the remote access client and hosts on the private network will be encrypted using IPSec.

Remove Programs applet within the Control Panel (you will learn how to install and configure the service later in the chapter). With IAS, a server can be configured as a RADIUS server and a RADIUS proxy. When a computer is configured as a RADIUS server by installing IAS, remote access servers can forward authentication requests

Internet
Authentication
Service and
Remote Access
Servers

Internet authentication server

Remote access servers

from remote access clients to the IAS server, which then becomes responsible for authenticating connection requests. IAS provides a number of benefits, including centralizing user authentication and administration of remote access policies and centralizing the storage of auditing and accounting information collected from the remote access servers. When IAS is installed, the remote access server can be configured as a RADIUS client. You can do this while enabling remote access or afterward by editing the properties of the remote access server. Once a remote access server is configured as a RADIUS client, remote access requests are forwarded to the IAS server and local remote access policies are no longer used. The server running IAS provides authentication, auditing, and accounting services for RADIUS clients.

When configured as a RADIUS proxy, an IAS server can forward authentication and accounting information to other RADIUS servers on the network. The IAS server functions as a message router and forwards messages to another specified RADIUS server or client. Connection request processing rules are configured to tell the IAS server where to forward the authentication request messages. Keep in mind that an IAS server can function as a RADIUS server and a RADIUS proxy. Depending on the connection request processing rules configured, some connection requests can be authenticated and others can be forwarded to another server.

Be prepared to encounter exam questions pertaining to Internet Authentication Service and when it would be a viable solution.

How IAS works

A remote access server can be configured as a RADIUS client. When a computer running Windows Server 2003 is running IAS, the following process occurs when a RADIUS client receives a connection request from a remote access client:

1. A remote access server receives a connection request from a remote access client.

2. If the remote access server is configured as a RADIUS client, an Access-Request message is created and sent to the IAS server.

3. The IAS server evaluates the Access-Request message.

4. The connection attempt is evaluated against the conditions of the remote access policies.

5. The user's credentials are verified and the dial-in properties for the user's account are obtained from a domain controller.

6. The IAS server determines if the user has been granted remote access permission through the user's account properties and the settings of the remote access policy.

7. If the user has permission, the profile settings of the policy and the dial-in settings of the user account are evaluated against the connection attempt.

8. An Access-Accept message is sent to the remote access server if the connection attempt has been granted. An Access-Reject message is sent if the connection attempt is not authorized.

9. The remote access server completes the connection attempt if the user has been authorized.

10. An Accounting-Request message is sent to the IAS server once the connection has been completed where it is logged.

An IAS server can also be configured to act as a RADIUS proxy that forwards connection requests to other servers according to the connection request processing rules. When IAS is configured as a RADIUS proxy, it will receive Access-Request messages from RADIUS clients and forward them to the appropriate RADIUS server according to the connection processing rules that have been configured.

Remote Access Policies and IAS

Remote access policies can be stored locally on each remote access server. This means that a connection attempt to a specific remote access server is subject to the local policies. The other option is to administer remote access policies from a server running IAS. Once a remote access server is configured to use an IAS server, remote access policies can no longer be configured locally. The benefit of this is that remote access policies for multiple remote access servers can be administered from a central location.

Installing IAS

Internet Authentication Service can be installed using the Add or Remove Programs applet within the Control Panel. To install IAS on a computer running Windows Server 2003:

1. Click Start, point to Control Panel, and select Add Or Remove Programs.

2. Click Add/Remove Windows Components.

3. From the list of Windows components, select Networking Services. Click the Details button.

4. From the list of networking services subcomponents, select Internet Authentication Service. Click OK.

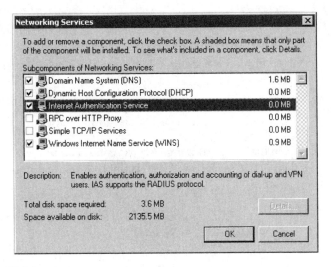

5. Click Finish.

Once IAS is installed, you can administer it using the Internet Authentication Service console found within the Administrative Tools. You will also need to configure the remote access servers as RADIUS clients to the IAS server. To do so:

1. Right-click your remote access server within the Routing and Remote Access console and click Properties.

2. From the properties dialog box, select the Security tab and change the Authentication provider to RADIUS Authentication.

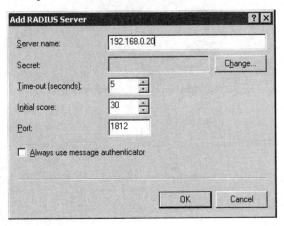

3. Click the Configure button.

4. From the RADIUS Authentication dialog box, click Add.

5. Type in the name or IP address of the server running IAS. Click OK. Click OK again.

6. From the Security tab, change the Accounting provider to RADIUS Accounting.

7. Repeat the process outlined in step 5 to specify the server running IAS that will maintain the accounting information for the remote access server.

On the server running IAS, you must add the remote access server as a RADIUS client. This can be done within the Internet Authentication Service console. Use the following steps to add a remote access server as a RADIUS client:

1. Click Start, point to Administrative Tools, and click Internet Authentication Service.

2. Within the console, right-click RADIUS Clients and select New RADIUS Client to launch the New RADIUS Client Wizard.

3. Type in a friendly name for the client as well as the IP address or DNS name of the remote access server. Click Next.

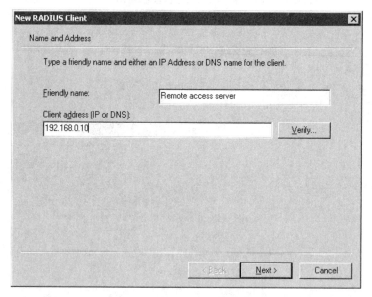

4. Specify any additional information and click OK.

5. The new RADIUS client will appear within the RADIUS Clients container.

EXERCISE 6-6

Planning for Remote Access Security

In this exercise, you will use the information in the scenario to plan security for a remote access implementation.

Riverside Corporation has asked you to plan the security for its remote access dial-up solution. Members of the Managers group require remote access from their home offices. All workstations are currently running Windows XP Professional. There are plans to implement smart cards within the next year. Your security plan should address the following requirements:

- The strongest authentication level is required.
- Remote access clients should be restricted to accessing the private network from home offices only.
- Remote access accounts should be locked out after three failed logon attempts.
- Remote access should be permitted only during business hours.
- Data encryption is critical.

Using these criteria, put together a remote access security plan that will meet all the requirements.

CERTIFICATION OBJECTIVE 6.06

Troubleshooting Remote Access

A number of different problems can arise with remote access. For example, a remote access client is unable to authenticate with a remote access server, or a remote access client can successfully establish a remote access connection but is not able to access any resources on the private network. As problems arise, chances are you will not be able to determine the cause of each one and its solution immediately without some further investigation. An efficient network administrator will be familiar with the various tools that can be used for troubleshooting and how to use them. The following section will discuss some of the tools that can specifically be used for troubleshooting remote access problems.

Logging

Windows Server 2003 supports two types of logging for troubleshooting remote access: event logging as well as authentication and accounting logging. Information stored within log files can provide valuable information when it comes to troubleshooting. Log files are often a good starting point for determining what is causing a problem to occur.

Event Logging

With *event logging*, events are written to the system log and can be viewed using the Event Viewer. By default, event logging is enabled for remote access. The types of events that are logged include warnings and errors. You can choose which events to log using the Logging tab from the remote access server's properties dialog box (see Figure 6-19).

Authentication and Accounting Logging

You can also enable authentication and accounting logging, which is separate from event logging. This type of logging, used to monitor and track remote access usage and

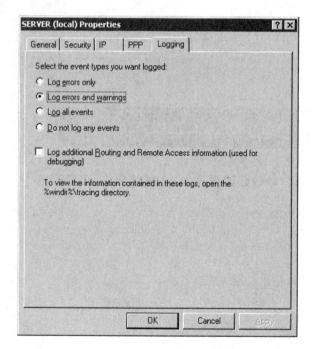

FIGURE 6-19

Configuring event logging for remote access

authentication attempts, can be extremely helpful when troubleshooting failed remote access authentication attempts. If the remote access server is configured for Windows Authentication or Windows Accounting, the log files are by default stored locally in the systemroot\System32\Logfiles directory. You can configure the type of information to log using the following procedure:

1. Click Start, point to Administrative Tools, and click Routing and Remote Access.

2. Click the Remote Access Logging container.

3. Right-click the Local File within the details pane and click Properties.

4. From the Local File Properties dialog box, select the information you want to log.

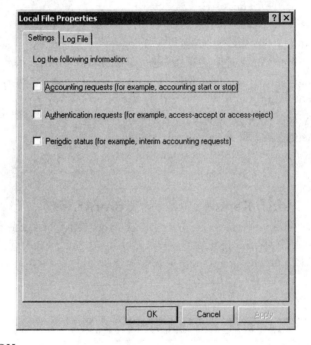

5. Click OK.

Remember that if you are using an IAS server, you also have the option of logging the authentication and accounting information to a central location.

INSIDE THE EXAM

More on Authentication Logging

Using authentication logging can provide invaluable information for troubleshooting. If there are multiple remote access servers on the network, it can also simplify administration by storing the logs in a central location on a server running IAS.

When you configure logging, you can specify the different types of requests that you want logged. When you enable the logging of authentication requests, the following information is collected and stored within the log file:

■ Authentication requests: All authentication requests received by the remote access server

■ Authentication accepts and rejects: All authentication requests sent from the IAS server to a RADIUS client indicating whether the request is granted or denied

So how would this information assist you with troubleshooting? One of the most common problems that can occur with remote access is that a remote access client is denied access. When a rejected connection attempt is logged, the entry also specifies the name of the remote access policy that rejected the connection attempt. This gives you a good starting place in determining what configuration settings are causing the connection attempt to be rejected (especially if you have multiple remote access policies configured).

netsh Remote Access Commands

The netsh command-line utility can be used to view and modify the network configuration of a local or remote computer. Using the netsh RAS command, you can configure and troubleshoot a remote access server. Table 6-8 summarizes the various netsh RAS contexts that can be used.

CERTIFICATION SUMMARY

Using Routing and Remote Access, a computer running Windows Server 2003 can be configured as a network router and a remote access server. Windows Server 2003 supports the remote access service that enables client computers to connect to a private network from a remote location such as a home office. The two remote access methods supported are dial-up remote access and VPN remote access.

When planning for remote access, you will need to determine which remote access solution will best meet your organization's needs. For both solutions, you can use a

TABLE 6-8	Netsh Commands Used for Remote Access

Context	Description
netsh ras	Used to administer remote access servers.
netsh ras diagnostics	Used to view diagnostic information.
netsh ras IP	Used to view and configure IP-related information such as configuring the static range of IP addresses on a remote access server.
Netsh ras AAA	Used to view and configure the authentication, accounting, and auditing database for an IAS server.

DHCP server or configure the remote access server with a static range of IP addresses to assign remote access clients when they establish a connection. If you decide to implement a remote access VPN, a tunneling protocol is required. Windows Server 2003 supports the Point-to-Point Tunneling Protocol (PPTP) and the Layer Two Tunneling Protocol (L2TP). Both solutions also require remote access policies. A decentralized approach can be used in which each remote access server is configured with at least one remote access policy, or a centralized model can be used in which policies are stored on a server running IAS.

Remote access policies play a crucial role in remote access security. A remote access policy consists of conditions, permissions, and profile settings. In order for a connection request to be granted, the request must match the conditions, permissions, and profile settings of a remote access policy. Permissions can be controlled through the user account properties and through the remote access policies.

Authentication is the process of verifying a user's credentials. Windows Server 2003 supports the following authentication protocols: PAP, SPAP, CHAP, MS-CHAP, and EAP. Encryption ensures the security of information being sent between the remote access client and the remote access server. Windows Server 2003 supports MPPE and IPSec encryption technologies.

Windows Server 2003 includes its own version of a RADIUS server known as Internet Authentication Service (IAS). IAS can be installed using the Add or Remove Programs applet within the Control Panel. With IAS, a server can be configured as a RADIUS server and a RADIUS proxy. When remote access servers are configured as RADIUS clients, they forward authentication requests to a server running IAS. The IAS server is then responsible for authenticating remote access connection requests. An IAS server can also be configured as a RADIUS proxy, forwarding connection requests to another server according to the connection processing rules that are configured.

TWO-MINUTE DRILL

Planning a Routing Strategy

❑ Using the Routing and Remote Access snap-in, a computer running Windows Server 2003 can be configured as a network router.

❑ Windows Server 2003 supports demand-dial routing, router-to-router VPNs, and Network Address Translation.

❑ On-demand connections should use static routing rather than dynamic routing.

❑ OSPF does not support nonpersistent connections.

Introduction to Remote Access

❑ Remote access enables a client computer to access a private network using a WAN connection.

❑ Windows Server 2003 supports two different remote access connectivity solutions: dial-up remote access and VPNremote access.

Planning for Remote Access

❑ A remote access server can be configured with a static range of IP addresses to lease to remote access clients, or it can be configured to obtain IP addresses from a DHCP server on the private network.

❑ The DHCP relay agent must be enabled on the remote access server to forward DHCPInform messages between a remote access client and a DHCP server.

❑ Remote access policies provide administrators with a way of restricting remote access connections.

❑ A VPN solution requires a tunneling protocol. Windows Server 2003 supports the Point-to-Point Tunneling Protocol (PPTP) and the Layer Two Tunneling Protocol (L2TP).

❑ PPTP has encryption built in and uses MPPE 40-bit to 128-bit encryption. It is supported by a variety of platforms.

❑ L2TP uses IPSec to encrypt data and uses DES with supported key lengths between 56 bits (DES) and 128 bits (3DES). It is supported by Windows 2000 and Windows XP. Windows 98, Windows ME, and Windows NT 4.0 will support it if running the L2TP/IPSec VPN client.

❑ When implementing L2TP/IPSec, certificates or a preshared key can be used for authentication.

Implementing Remote Access

❑ Remote access can be enabled using the Routing and Remote Access console.

❑ The authentication and accounting methods determine if the remote access server authenticates connection requests or if they are forwarded to a RADIUS server and where the accounting information is maintained.

❑ Windows Server 2003 supports two different dial-in protocols: the Point-to-Point Protocol (PPP) and the Serial Line Internet Protocol (SLIP). SLIP is supported only for outbound connections.

❑ Multilink allows multiple phone lines to be combined into a single logical connection.

❑ The Bandwidth Allocation Protocol (BAP) works with multilink so that additional connections can be added and dropped as bandwidth requirements change.

Ensuring Remote Access Security

❑ A remote access policy consists of conditions, permissions, and profile settings. At least one remote access policy must exist or all connection attempts will be rejected.

❑ In order for a connection request to be granted, the connection request must match the settings of at least one remote access policy.

❑ Remote access permission can be controlled through the properties of a user account or through a remote access policy. Permissions configured for a user account override those configured within a policy.

❑ Windows Server 2003 supports a number of authentication protocols, including PAP, SPAP, CHAP, MS-CHAP, MS-CHAP version 2, and EAP.

❑ PAP is the least secure authentication protocol because credentials are sent to the remote access server unencrypted. MS-CHAP version 2 is supported only by Windows 2000, Windows Server 2003, and Windows XP.

❑ Windows Server 2003 supports two encryption methods: MPPE and IPSec.

❑ Microsoft Point-to-Point Encryption (MPPE) uses 40-bit, 56-bit, and 128-bit encryption keys to encrypt data. MPPE can be used with PPP or PPTP VPN connections. It is used by EAP-TLS and MS-CHAP to encrypt authentication information.

❑ IPSec is used to encrypt data for L2TP VPN connections. It uses the Data Encryption Standard (DES) and the Triple Data Encryption Standard (3DES).

❑ Remote Access Account Lockout can be enabled to limit the number of failed logon attempts before an account becomes locked out.

❑ Internet Authentication Service can be installed on a computer running Windows Server 2003 to centralize the authentication of connection requests and the logging of information.

❑ With IAS, a server can be configured as a RADIUS server and a RADIUS proxy.

Troubleshooting Remote Access

❑ With event logging, events are written to the System log and can be viewed using the Event Viewer. By default, event logging is enabled for remote access.

❑ Authentication and accounting logging are used to monitor and track remote access usage and authentication attempts.

SELF TEST

Planning a Routing Strategy

1. John is the network administrator in charge of planning a remote access solution. Several users will be dialing into a remote access server from various locations. All the workstations are running Windows XP. When planning for authentication protocols, which of the following should you choose?

   A. PAP

   B. CHAP

   C. MS-CHAP

   D. MS-CHAP version 2

2. FKP International is implementing a remote access solution. All users require remote access. Members of the Sales group should have no day and time restrictions. All other users should be permitted remote access only during business hours. How can this be accomplished?

   A. Configure the properties of each user account with the appropriate day and time restrictions.

   B. Configure two remote access policies. Configure the conditions of one remote access policy with day and time restrictions.

   C. Configure a single remote access policy. Configure the conditions of the policy with day and time restrictions.

   D. Configure a single remote access policy. Configure the profile settings with day and time restrictions.

Introduction to Remote Access

3. A remote access user reports being unable to establish a remote access connection. Tom, the network administrator, suspects there is a conflict with the remote access policies. What tool should Tom use to determine which policy is rejecting the remote access connection attempt?

   A. Network Monitor

   B. Event logging

   C. Authentication and accounting logging

   D. System Monitor

4. Riverside has an existing remote access server. Due to an increase in the number of remote access clients, two additional remote access servers are being added to the infrastructure. Mary, the network administrator, wants to centralize authentication and accounting information. Which of the following should Mary implement?

A. Routing and Remote Access

B. IIS

C. IAS

D. ISA

5. Bill is planning a remote access solution for a small company. Members of the Managers group all require remote access. Smart cards are being implemented for all remote access computers. With this in mind, which authentication protocol will you plan to implement?

A. PAP

B. CHAP

C. MPPE

D. EAP

Planning for Remote Access

6. Mark has recently implemented a remote access solution. His boss is concerned about security and hackers attempting to log on with a user's credentials and attempting to guess the password. What can Mark do to eliminate this security risk?

A. Configure the account lockout feature within the remote access policy.

B. Enable account lockout through a group policy.

C. Enable the remote access account lockout feature through the Registry.

D. Enable the remote access account lockout feature for each user account.

7. Members of the Sales group require remote access to the company's client database when they are traveling. Each mobile computer is configured with a smart card. The company's remote access server has a T1 connection to an ISP. Which of the following remote access solutions would you implement?

A. A VPN remote access solution using PPTP

B. A dial-up solution using PPP

C. A VPN solution using L2TP/IPSec

D. A dial-up solution using SLIP

8. Which of the following remote access authentication protocols requires a PKI infrastructure?

A. EAP-TLS

B. MS-CHAP v.2

C. CHAP

D. SLIP

9. Which of the following protocols can be used to establish a VPN tunnel with a Windows Server 2003 remote access VPN server? (Choose two correct answers.)

   A. PPP

   B. PPTP

   C. L2TP

   D. IPSec

Implementing Remote Access

10. Jim is planning to implement remote access for his medium-sized organization. Remote access clients are all running Windows XP Professional. These clients need to be assigned optional TCP/IP parameters when they establish a remote access connection. Which of the following should you include in your implementation plan?

    A. DHCP

    B. IPSec

    C. DHCP relay agent

    D. DNS

11. John is configuring the encryption settings on his remote access server. The remote access clients support only 40-bit encryption. Which of the following options should he select?

    A. Basic

    B. Strong

    C. Strongest

    D. No encryption

12. A remote access server has been configured. Mike is testing the configuration from his home computer running Windows 2000. He establishes a remote access connection but is unable to access computers on other subnets using their computer name. What should Mike do to fix the problem?

    A. Configure the properties of his user account to allow remote access.

    B. Enable the DHCP relay agent on the remote access server.

    C. Configure the remote access server to assign remote access clients optional TCP/IP parameters.

    D. Configure the remote access policy to allow remote access.

13. Sean in planning a remote access solution for a medium-sized company. Thirty users will require VPN access. A group already exists for these 30 users called VPN_Users. How can Sean ensure that only members of this group will have VPN remote access?

    A. Configure the profile of the remote access policy so that it applies only to the VPN_Users group.

    B. Grant each of the 30 users remote access permission through the properties of their user accounts.

    C. Configure the conditions of the profile so that it applies only to the VPN_Users group.

    D. Grant the VPN_Users group remote access permission through the properties of the group account.

Ensuring Remote Access Security

14. Which of the following correctly defines the order in which remote access policy elements are evaluated?

    A. Conditions, permissions, profile

    B. Permissions, conditions, profile

    C. Profile, permissions, conditions

    D. Conditions, profile, permissions

15. John wants to implement 56-bit encryption for all remote access clients. Which option should he enable when configuring encryption settings for the remote access policy?

    A. Basic

    B. Strong

    C. Strongest

    D. No encryption

16. David is the administrator of a Windows Server 2003 network. The current infrastructure consists of 8 subnets. All subnets are connected using Windows Server 2003 RRAS servers. Non-persistent demand-dial connections have been configured. David does not want to manually update routing tables. He wants to configure password authentication between routers. Which of the following should he implement?

    A. Static routes

    B. RIP V2

    C. ICMP

    D. OSPF

17. Greg is the junior administrator of a Windows Server 2003 network. He is in charge of configuring remote access policies. All users on the network require remote access. All users should have the same remote access security requirements except the Administrators group. How should you configure RRAS?

    A. Within the RRAS console, create two groups, one for Administrators and one for Users. Create two policies and use the Windows Group condition to apply each policy to the appropriate group.

    B. Create two groups within Active Directory Users and Computers. Configure a single remote access policy. Use the Windows Group condition to specify which policy settings will apply to which group.

    C. Within the RRAS console, create two groups, one for Administrators and one for Users. Create one policy and use the Windows Group condition to specify which policy settings should apply to which groups.

    D. Create two groups within Active Directory Users and Computers. Configure two remote access policies. Use the Windows Group condition to apply each policy to the appropriate group.

18. Mark is the administrator of a Windows Server 2003 network. He is adding 5 remote access servers on to the company network. He wants to create a single remote access policy once for all remote access servers. What should he do?

    A. Create a single remote access policy. Replicate the policy to the remaining RAS servers.

    B. Place the RAS servers within the same OU. Configure a single remote access policy and apply it to the OU through a Group Policy Object.

    C. Configure a single remote access policy. Use the Security Configuration and Analysis Tool to apply the settings to all RAS servers.

    D. Configure a single remote access policy on a server running IAS. Configure each RAS server as a RADIUS client.

Troubleshooting Remote Access

19. Which of the following encryption levels will be used when Basic encryption is enabled through a remote access policy?

    A. MPPE 56-bit

    B. MPPE 40-bit

    C. MPPE 128-bit

    D. IPSec 56-bit DES

20. Which of the following encryption levels will be used when Strong encryption is enabled through a remote access policy?

   A. MPPE 56-bit

   B. MPPE 40-bit

   C. MPPE 128-bit

   D. IPSec 56-bit DES

LAB QUESTION

FKP International is deploying routing and remote access; members of the Sales department require remote access to client information when they are traveling; several other users also require remote access from home offices. Currently, mobile users are running Windows XP. Members of the Sales department should have no restrictions configured. All other users should only be permitted to dial in during the business hours of 9 A.M.–6 P.M. Since multiple remote access servers are being deployed, you want to centralize the administration of them. Based on this information, provide the answers to the following questions.

1. How many remote access policies are required and why?

2. How can you ensure that the appropriate policy is applied to the appropriate group?

3. When configuring remote access policies, which authentication method should you implement?

4. Members of the Sales department often travel out of local dialing range. What option is available to ensure they do not incur the long distance charges?

5. How will remote access administration be centralized?

SELF TEST ANSWERS

Planning a Routing Strategy

1. ☑ **D.** Although MS-CHAP version 2 is supported only by Windows 2000, Windows XP, and Windows Server 2003, of the protocols listed, it provides the highest level of security.

   ☒ **A** is incorrect because PAP provides no encryption. **B** and **C** are incorrect. Although either of these protocols can be used, MS-CHAP version 2 is more secure than CHAP and MS-CHAP.

2. ☑ **B.** By configuring two separate policies, you can use the Windows group condition to apply policies to different groups. Two policies will need to be created, one for the Sales group and one for all other users. You can then configure the day and time restrictions for the remote access policy that will be used for all other users.

   ☒ **A** is incorrect because day and time restrictions cannot be configured through the user account properties. **C** is incorrect because a single policy with day and time restrictions would prevent the Sales group from accessing the private network during all hours. **D** is incorrect because two policies are required. Also, the day and time restrictions are configured by editing the conditions of the policy, not the profile settings.

Introduction to Remote Access

3. ☑ **C.** By enabling authentication and accounting logging, you can determine which remote access policy is rejecting a connection attempt.

   ☒ **A** is incorrect because this tool is used to capture and analyze network traffic.
   B is incorrect because the event log tracks messages generated by the remote access service when logging is enabled. **D** is incorrect because the System Monitor is used to track the real-time performance of system components.

4. ☑ **C.** Internet Authentication Service (IAS) is used to centralize authentication and accounting information for remote access servers.

   ☒ **A** is incorrect because remote access is configured to allow client computers to access the private network from remote locations. **B** is incorrect because IIS is a web service. **D**, which is ISA (the Internet Security and Acceleration Service), is used for firewall and caching purposes.

5. ☑ **D.** The Extensible Authentication Protocol (EAP) must be used for smart card authentication.

   ☒ **A** and **B** are incorrect because PAP and CHAP do not support smart cards. Both are password-based authentication protocols. **C** is incorrect because MPPE is used for encryption.

Planning for Remote Access

6. ☑ **C.** The remote access account lockout feature can be enabled through the Registry.
☒ **A** is incorrect because remote access account lockout cannot be enabled through a remote access policy. **B** and **D** are incorrect because these methods cannot be used to enable the remote access account lockout feature. Also, the account lockout option configured through a group policy is for domain logons and is therefore separate from the remote access account lockout feature.

7. ☑ **C.** To avoid the remote access clients' having to incur long-distance charges to dial directly into the remote access server, a VPN remote access solution should be implemented. Since the users are configured with smart cards, you should implement L2TP/IPSec.
☒ **B** and **D** are incorrect because a dial-up solution may result in the remote access users having to incur long-distance charges to access the remote access server. **A** is incorrect because L2TP/IPSec is required for smart card logons.

8. ☑ **A.** In order to use EAP-TLS, a PKI infrastructure is required.
☒ **B, C,** and **D** are incorrect because these authentication protocols do not require a PKI infrastructure, as they are password-based.

9. ☑ **B** and **C.** PPTP and L2TP are the two tunneling protocols supported by Windows Server 2003.
☒ **A** is incorrect because PPP is used to establish a dial-up connection with a remote access server. **D** is incorrect because IPSec is used for encryption.

Implementing Remote Access

10. ☑ **C.** The DHCP relay agent must be enabled on the remote access server for the DHCPInform messages to be forwarded to the DHCP server on the private network. This allows remote access clients to be assigned optional TCP/IP parameters after establishing a remote access connection.
☒ **A** is incorrect because installing DHCP alone does not allow remote access clients' computers to be assigned optional parameters. The remote access server needs to be able to forward the DHCPInform messages between the remote access client and the DHCP server on the private network. **B** is incorrect because IPSec is used for encryption. **D** is incorrect because it is used to resolve hostnames to IP addresses.

11. ☑ **A.** Basic encryption uses MPPE 40-bit encryption.
☒ **B** is incorrect because Strong encryption uses MPPE 56-bit or IPSec 56-bit DES encryption. **C** is incorrect because Strongest encryption uses IPSec triple DES or MPPE 128-bit encryption. **D** is incorrect because this option means no encryption is used.

12. ☑ **B.** The remote access client must be configured with the IP address of the name server on the private network. Therefore, the DHCP relay agent must be configured on the remote access server so that the remote access client computer can be assigned the IP address of the name server.

☒ **A** and **C** are incorrect because the client has already established a remote access connection and therefore permissions are not the problem. **D** is incorrect because the remote access server cannot be configured to assign clients optional TCP/IP parameters. It can only forward the DHCPInform messages to the DHCP server when the DHCP relay agent is enabled.

Ensuring Remote Access Security

13. ☑ **C.** Using the Windows Group option, you can configure the conditions of the remote access policy so that it applies only to members of the VPN_Users group.

☒ **A** is incorrect because this option must be configured through the conditions of the policy, not the profile settings. **B** is incorrect. Configuring the Windows Group option by editing the conditions of the policy ensures that only members of the VPN_Users group are allowed VPN access. **D** is incorrect because you cannot grant remote access permissions through a group's properties dialog box.

14. ☑ **A.** Policy elements are evaluated in the following order: conditions, permissions, and profile settings.

☒ **B, C,** and **D** are incorrect because they do not represent the correct order in which policy elements are evaluated.

15. ☑ **B.** Strong encryption uses MPPE 56-bit or IPSec 56-bit DES encryption.

☒ **A** is incorrect because Basic encryption uses MPPE 40-bit encryption. **C** is incorrect because Strongest encryption uses IPSec Triple DES or MPPE 128-bit encryption. **D** is incorrect because this setting requires no encryption between the remote access client computer and the remote access server.

16. ☑ **B.** RIP V2 can be used with non-persistent connections. It also supports password authentication between routers.

☒ **A** is incorrect because using static routes means the routing tables will have to be updated manually. **C** is incorrect because OSPF does not support non-persistent connections. **D** is incorrect because ICMP is not a routing protocol. It is a protocol used for diagnostics and error reporting.

17. ☑ **D.** Two groups must be configured within the Active Directory Users and Computers console. Two separate policies must be configured. The Windows Group condition can be used to apply each policy to the appropriate group.

    ☒   A is incorrect because groups cannot be created within the RRAS console. **B** and **C** are incorrect because multiple policies are required if each group of users require different settings.

18.   ☑   **D.** In order to apply a single policy to a group of RAS servers, the policy must be centrally configured on a computer running IAS. The RAS servers can then be configured as RADIUS clients.

    ☒   **A, B,** and **C** are incorrect because remote access policies cannot be deployed using any of these methods.

Troubleshooting Remote Access

19.   ☑   **B, D.** When Basic encryption is enabled, MPPE 40-bit or IPSec 56-bit is used.

    ☒   **A** and **C** are incorrect because they do not represent the correct values.

20.   ☑   **A, D.** When Strong encryption is enabled, MPPE 56-bit or IPSec 56-bit encryption is enabled.

    ☒   **B** and **C** are incorrect because they do not represent the correct values.

LAB ANSWER

1.   Two remote access policies are required—one for the Sales group and one for all other users.

2.   By configuring the Windows Group option within the policy, you can specify which group of users a remote access policy should be applied to.

3.   Since all workstations are running Windows XP, you can just use MS-CHAP version 2. All other authentication protocols can be disabled.

4.   One solution would be to configure VPN connections for these users. This allows them to access the company network across the Internet instead of dialing directly into the remote access server.

5.   Administration of remote access servers can be centralized by implementing IAS.

7

Planning and Maintaining Network Security

Securing Private Networks

Networks have become a crucial way for organizations to share and transfer information. With this comes a concern about security. Companies need to ensure that information remains confidential and only the necessary parties have access to it.

Part of a network administrator's job is to ensure data security to eliminate the possibility of security breaches. Not planning for and implementing security precautions can open the door to a number of different attacks in which unauthorized individuals gain access to data that should remain secure. Table 7-1 outlines some of the common attacks that can occur.

One of the ways in which you can protect against these various attacks is by implementing the Internet Protocol Security Protocol (IPSec). IPSec is a suite of protocols that work together to protect information transferred between hosts. The data is encrypted on the sending computer and decrypted on the receiving computer.

Implementing IPSec will protect data from interception and manipulation. It also eliminates the possibility of hackers intercepting a packet between a source and destination computer and inserting changed packets into the data stream (known as anti-replay). The following sections will look at how IPSec works and some of the issues to consider when planning for IPSec, as well as how to configure an IPSec policy.

Introduction to IPSec

The purpose of IPSec is the secure communications between hosts on a network or between networks, for example, by requiring hosts to authenticate and data to be encrypted. IPSec provides a way to ensure that sensitive data is unreadable by attackers as it is being sent between two hosts. The following section will look at the various IPSec components and how they work together to secure communications between hosts.

on the **job**

In order for an IPSec implementation to be effective, a strong authentication strategy must be in place. Since IPSec secures communications between two trusted hosts, however, if a hacker is able to become "trusted," IPSec provides no security.

TABLE 7-1 Common Internet Attacks

Attack	Description
Eavesdropping	This type of attack occurs when an attacker gains access to the data paths and is able to read traffic as it travels between hosts.
Data modification	This is basically an extension to eavesdropping. Once the data has been read, the attacker modifies it without the sender's or receiver's knowledge.
Identity spoofing	On an IP-based network, computers are normally identified by IP addresses. With identity spoofing, an attacker falsely assumes an IP address to appear as though they were a trusted source.
Denial of service (DoS)	With this type of attack, an attacker gains access to the private network. Once access is gained, a number of different attacks can be performed to prevent normal use of a computer or network.
Sniffer	With this type of attack, a program or device is used to capture and read network data.
Password-based	With this type of attack, an attacker uses a valid username and tries various password combinations to gain unauthorized access to a computer or network.

IPSec Components

Three different components work together to provide IPSec functionality. Each component performs a specific function to ensure secure communications. These components include

- IPSec policy agent
- ISAKMP/Oakley Key Management Service
- IPSec driver

IPSec Policy Agent   The *IPSec Policy Agent* resides on each computer running Windows Server 2003. This component is responsible for retrieving policy information required by other IPSec components. If the computer is a member of a domain, the IPSec policy agent will retrieve policy information from Active Directory. This is done when the computer starts up, at preconfigured intervals, or manually using the gpupdate command. Policies are retrieved from the local Registry if the computer is not a domain member.

ISAKMP/Oakley Key Management Service   Before two hosts can securely exchange data, they must agree on the various security parameters to use. This agreement, known as a security association (SA), is the responsibility of the ISAKMP/

Oakley Key Management Service. The method of generating an SA and key exchange is known as the Internet Key Exchange (IKE).

The security association is a combination of a shared key, a security protocol, and a security parameters index (SPI). The SPI is a unique identifier used to distinguish the various SAs that may exist on a receiving computer.

The Internet Key Exchange consists of two phases: Phase 1, or Main Mode Negotiation, and Phase 2, or Quick Mode SA. During Phase 1, a secure authentication channel is established between hosts. The following parameters are negotiated during this phase:

- Encryption algorithm
- Authentication algorithm
- Authentication method
- Diffie-Hellman group used for keying material

During the second phase, the SA is negotiated between the two hosts on behalf of the IPSec drive. The process results in two separate SAs being negotiated, one for inbound communication and one for outbound communication. The two hosts exchange the following information:

- IPSec protocol (AH or ESP)
- Hash algorithm (MD5 or SHA1)
- Encryption algorithm (3DES or DES)

IPSec Driver   The IPSec driver is responsible for matching inbound and outbound traffic against the IP packets filter list received from the IPSec Policy Agent. The IPSec driver monitors inbound and outbound traffic. Using the filters within the IPSec policy, it will secure the appropriate outbound traffic and verify and decrypt inbound traffic.

How IPSec works

The following steps outline how IPSec works between two hosts on the same network:

1. David launches an application from his computer, WRK01, which must send data to Greg's computer, WRK02.

2. The IPSec driver on WRK01 informs the ISAKMP/Oakley service that secure communications between the two hosts are required.

3. A shared key and SA (security association) is established by the ISAKMP/Oakley on WRK01 and WRK02.

4. The shared key and SA are passed to the IPSec driver on each computer.

5. The IPSec driver on WRK01 uses the key to encrypt the data and sends it to WRK02.

6. When WRK02 receives the data, the IPSec driver decrypts the information and forwards it to the appropriate application.

Transport Mode and Tunnel Mode

IPSec can operate in two different encryption modes: transport mode and tunnel mode, with the default being transport mode. *Transport mode* is used for host-to-host communication such as between a client and a server. This mode is normally used to secure end-to-end communications, for example, between a client and a server on the same network. In *tunnel mode*, the IP payload as well as the IP header is encrypted. This mode is typically used for interoperability with gateways and for computers that do not support VPN connections using L2TP/IPSec and PPTP.

Understanding IP Security Policies and Rules

IP Security policies are simply a set of rules that define when and how secure communications occur. The settings of the policy tell the IPSec driver when to secure outbound traffic as well as the encryption and authentication methods to use. Each IPSec policy consists of various elements such as an IP filter list and filter actions.

IP Security Policy Elements

An IPSec policy consists of rules that determine when and how traffic is secured. Each policy consists of various configurable settings allowing an administrator to customize policies to meet specific security needs. Each IPSec policy consists of the following elements:

- IP filter lists
- IP filters
- Filter actions
- Authentication methods
- Tunnel endpoints
- Connection type

IP Filter Lists   The IP filter list consists of one or more IP packet filters. The filter list defines the type of traffic that the filter actions will apply to. In other words, the IP filter list specifies which type of traffic will be affected by the rule (see Figure 7-1). For example, filter actions can be applied to all IP traffic as defined in the IP filter list.

FIGURE 7-1

The IP filter list of
an IPSec policy

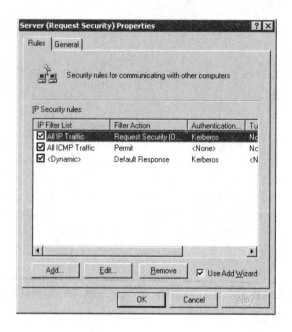

As you will see later in the chapter, Windows Server 2003 includes predefined IPSec policies with predefined settings. There are two predefined IP filter lists that can be used within an IPSec policy:

- **All ICMP Traffic**   This includes all ICMP traffic sent and received from the computer.
- **All IP Traffic**   This includes all IP traffic (except multicast and broadcast traffic) sent and received by the computer.

IP Filters   The *IP filters* define specific types of inbound and outbound traffic that should be secured. Each IP filter consists of the following settings:

- The source and destination IP addresses of a packet. An address can be the IP address of a specific host, a DNS name, or the IP address of a subnet.
- The protocol being used. By default, all protocols are included in a filter. However, you can customize this by selecting individual protocols.
- The source and destination ports. By default, an IP filter includes all TCP and UDP ports. You can customize an IP filter to apply to specific UDP or TCP ports.

You can configure IP filters using the IP Filter List button from within the properties dialog box for the IPSec policy (see Figure 7-2).

FIGURE 7-2

Configuring IP
filters within an
IPSec policy

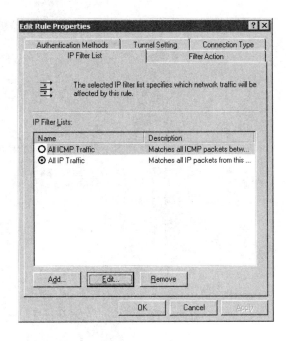

Filter Actions   The *filter action* determines what happens when an IP packet matches a filter within the IP filter list. The filter action can permit unsecured communication, block unsecured communication, or negotiate security. If the filter action is to negotiate security, you can also specify the security methods used along with their order of preference.

Filter actions can be configured using the Filter Action tab from the Edit Rule Properties dialog box (see Figure 7-3). The three predefined filter actions that can be used within a policy include

■ **Permit**   This action permits unsecured communications.

Request Security   With this filter action, the security method is set to negotiate security. The host will attempt to negotiate secure communications but still allow any inbound unsecured communications to initially pass through (known as passthrough). This policy also allows non–IPSec aware clients to still communicate with the computer (known as fallback).

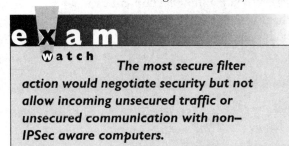

The most secure filter action would negotiate security but not allow incoming unsecured traffic or unsecured communication with non–IPSec aware computers.

FIGURE 7-3

Configuring the
filter action

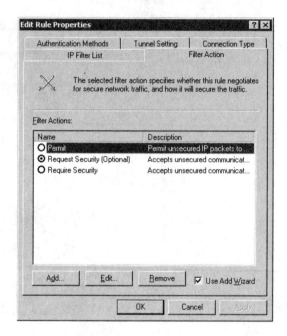

- **Require Security**   With this filter action, the security method is set to
  negotiate security. It does allow initial inbound traffic to pass through without
  being secured; however, unsecured communications with non–IPSec-aware
  clients is not allowed.

Authentication Methods

An IPSec policy also specifies the types of authentication methods that can be used.
The authentication methods specify how the two parties can identify themselves to one
another. In order for two hosts to successfully authenticate, they must have a common
authentication method. If not, secure communication will fail. You can configure
the authentication methods using the Authentication Methods tab from the Edit Rule
Properties dialog box (see Figure 7-4). When planning for authentication methods,
consider using multiple methods so that a common method can be established between
two hosts. The authentication methods that can be used include

- Kerberos
- Preshared key
- Public key certificates

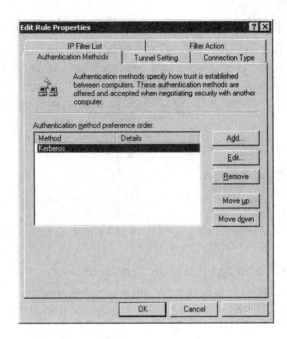

FIGURE 7-4

Configuring the
authentication
methods for an
IPSec policy

Kerberos   This is the default authentication method used, as it is the default
authentication protocol in Windows Server 2003. This method can be used
to authenticate any client from the same domain or a trusted domain that is running
the Kerberos V5 protocol.

Public Key Certificates   Public key certificates provide the most secure
authentication method and are ideal in nontrusted environments, for remote access,
for access involving the Internet, and for those computers that do not use Kerberos V5.
This method does require a PKI infrastructure, as each computer requires two keys:
a public key and a private key.

Preshared Key   With this authentication method, the two hosts use a shared
secret key for authentication. When the two parties negotiate security, the information
is encrypted using the shared secret key. The two parties use the same key, so if the
receiver can decrypt the information, authentication is achieved. If you are considering
using this method of authentication, keep in mind that the shared key is stored in
plain text within the IPSec policy.

Tunnel Endpoints

This setting of an IPSec policy will determine whether traffic is being tunneled and, if so, the IP address of the tunnel endpoints. You can configure this setting using the Tunnel Settings tab from the Edit Rule Properties dialog box (see Figure 7-5). When you are configuring the tunnel endpoints, keep in mind that the tunnel endpoint for outgoing traffic will be that of the tunnel peer, whereas the tunnel endpoint for incoming traffic will be the IP address of the local computer.

Connection Types

This setting of an IPSec policy specifies what connection types the rule will apply to (see Figure 7-6). You can configure the rule to apply to all network connections, the local area network (LAN), or the remote access connection.

Choosing an IPSec Protocol

IPSec uses two different authentication protocols to provide data security. The two protocols are Authentication Header (AH) and Encapsulating Security Payload (ESP). Both protocols are discussed next.

Authentication Header (AH)   Authentication Header (AH) provides data security for an entire IP packet, including the IP header and the data payload. It

FIGURE 7-5

Configuring the tunnel endpoints

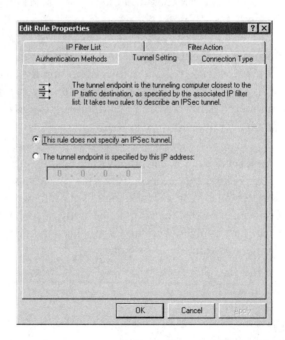

provides integrity, authentication, and anti-replay. AH ensures the data has not been modified, but unlike ESP, it does not provide confidentiality. AH provides data integrity and authentication through the *integrity check value (ICV)*. The sender calculates a hash value known as the ICV. The receiver then calculates the hash and checks it against the ICV to verify integrity. This ensures the data has not been modified and that the sender was the one who sent the packet. Anti-replay is achieved through the use of sequence numbers. It ensures that a packet is received only once.

Encapsulating Security Protocol (ESP)   The Encapsulating Security Protocol (ESP) provides authentication, integrity, and anti-replay along with confidentiality. Unlike AH, ESP protects only the IP payload (unless tunnel mode is being used). Through encryption, ESP provides confidentiality of the data being sent.

Default Security Policies

Windows Server 2003 includes three predefined IP Security policies, each configured with predefined IP filter lists and filter actions (see Figure 7-7). These policies are chiefly intended to provide administrators with an example. They can be used as is; however, if modifications to the settings are required, it is recommended that you create a new policy.

FIGURE 7-6

Configuring the connection types a rule applies to

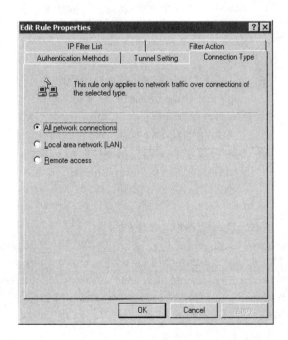

FIGURE 7-7

Windows Server
2003 default IP
Security policies

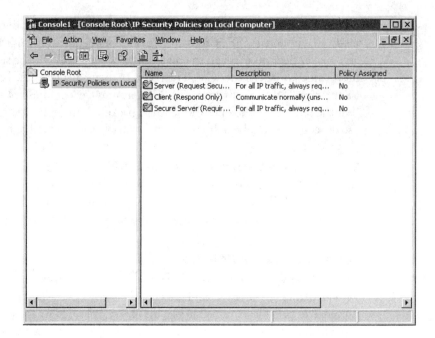

- **Client (Respond Only)**   With this policy, a computer will only respond to requests for secure communications from another computer. It will not attempt to secure any other communications. This policy is normally used by workstations so that they can respond to any requests for secure communications from a server.

- **Server (Request Security)**   With this policy, the host will attempt to negotiate the highest level of security (authentication and encryption). This policy is normally used in mixed-mode environments that have clients that do not support IPSec, which means nonsecure communications are permitted.

- **Secure Server (Require Security)**   This policy is normally used on hosts that require secure communications. This means any requests for nonsecure communications are denied.

Client (Respond Only) Policy   A computer configured to use this policy will respond to any requests it receives to secure communications from another computer. The policy therefore allows both secure and nonsecure communications. In other words, this policy specifies that the computer use nonsecure communications unless otherwise requested to use secure communications. The Client (Respond Only) policy has the following predefined settings configured:

- **IP Filter List** <dynamic>
- **Filter Action** Default Response Rule
- **Authentication Method** Kerberos
- **Tunnel Setting** None
- **Connection Type** All network connections

Server (Request Security) Policy   This policy is ideal in situations where communications should be secured but support for non–IPSec aware clients is required. With this policy, initial inbound traffic is accepted unsecured (passthrough) but the computer then attempts to request security for any additional communications with the sending computer. The policy also supports fallback, which means communications with non–IPSec aware clients is permitted. The Server (Request Security) policy uses the following predefined settings:

- Rule 1
  - **IP Filter List** All IP Traffic
  - **Filter Action** Request Security (Optional)
  - **Authentication Method** Kerberos
  - **Tunnel Setting** None
  - **Connection Type** All network connections
- Rule 2
  - **IP Filter List** All ICMP Traffic
  - **Filter Action** Permit
  - **Authentication Method** N/A
  - **Tunnel Setting** None
  - **Connection Type** All network connections

- Rule 3
  - **IP Filter List** <dynamic>
  - **Filter Action** Default Response Rule
  - **Authentication Method** Kerberos
  - **Tunnel Setting** None
  - **Connection Type** All network connections

Secure Server (Require Security) Policy This policy is ideal for those servers that require secure communications at all times. The settings of this policy require all inbound and outbound traffic to be secured. This policy contains the following predefined settings:

- Rule 1
  - **IP Filter List** All IP Traffic
  - **Filter Action** Require Security
  - **Authentication Method** N/A
  - **Tunnel Setting** None
  - **Connection Type** All network connections
- Rule 2
  - **IP Filter List** All ICMP Traffic
  - **Filter Action** Permit
  - **Authentication Method** Kerberos
  - **Tunnel Setting** None
  - **Connection Type** All network connections
- Rule 3
  - **IP Filter List** <dynamic>
  - **Filter Action** Default Response Rule
  - **Authentication Method** Kerberos
  - **Tunnel Setting** None
  - **Connection Type** All network connections

exam

watch   *The default policies all use   an intranet, since Kerberos can be used*
Kerberos as the authentication method and   only between members of the same domain
are therefore meant for communication on   or a trusted domain.

How IPSec Policies Are Applied

Once IPSec policies are configured, they can be applied in six different ways:

- **Computer startup**   When a computer starts up, the IPSec driver is loaded and reads the local Registry to determine what actions it should take. The behavior of the IPSec driver is determined by the startup mode of the IPSec service.

- **Persistent policy**   Persistent policies are configured using the `netsh` command. These policies can be used to secure a computer when a local policy or Active Directory–based policy is not available. They are used to secure a computer during the transition from computer startup to when a local or Active Directory–based policy is applied. Persistent policies override both local and Active Directory–based policies.

- **Active Directory–based policy**   IPSec policies can be assigned by applying a Group Policy Object to a site, domain, or Organizational Unit. IPSec policy settings will be applied to all computers within the container to which the Group Policy Object is applied.

- **Directory cache policy**   When IPSec policies are applied through Active Directory, a copy of the policy is stored locally. In the event that a computer cannot connect to the domain, the cache copy of the policy is applied.

- **Local computer policy**   Each computer running Windows 2000, Windows XP, and Windows Server 2003 maintains a local computer policy. If a computer is not a member of a domain, the local IPSec policy can be used to secure communications. In this case, the IPSec policy is stored on the local computer.

- **netsh dynamic mode policy**   Using the `netsh ipsec` dynamic command, you can configure IPSec rules that take effect immediately. However, once the IPSec service is stopped, any rules configured using this method are lost and no longer applied.

Creating IPSec Policies

IPSec policies can be created using the `netsh` command or by using the IP Security Policy Management snap-in. You can open the IP Security Policy Management snap-in using the following steps. Exercise 7-1 walks you through the process of creating a new IPSec policy.

1. Click Start, click Run, and type **mmc**.

2. From the File menu, select Add/Remove Snap-in.

3. Click Add. From the list of available stand-alone snap-ins, select IP Security Policy Management. Click Add.

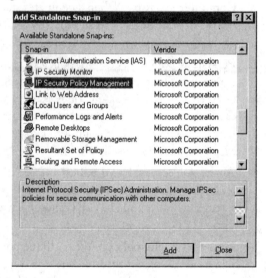

4. From the Select Computer Or Domain dialog box, select Local Computer. Click Finish.

5. Click Close. Click OK.

EXERCISE 7-1

Creating an IPSec Policy

In this exercise, you will use the IP Security Policy Management snap-in to create a new IPSec policy.

1. Click Start, click Run, type **mmc**, and click OK.

2. Click File and select Add/Remove Snap-in.

3. Click Add. From the list of available stand-alone snap-ins, select IP Security Policy Management. Click Add.

4. From the Select Computer Or Domain dialog box, select Local Computer. Click Finish.

5. Click Close. Click OK.

6. Right-click IP Security Policies On Local Computer and select Create IP Security Policy. This launches the IP Security Policy Wizard. Click Next.

7. Type in a name and description for the policy. Click Next.

8. From the Request For Secure Communications dialog box, leave the default option of Activate The Default Response Rule selected.

9. From the Default Response Rule Authentication Method dialog box, you can configure the type of authentication method for the policy. Leave the default option of Active Directory Default (Kerberos V5 Protocol) selected. Click Next.

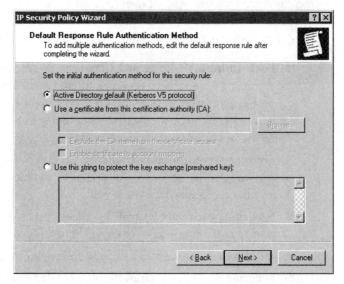

10. Click Finish. If the Edit properties option is selected, the properties dialog box for the new policy will appear, allowing you to further configure the various settings.

11. Once a policy is created, it can be assigned by right-clicking the policy and selecting the Assign option.

Planning for IPSec

As with most technologies, prior planning is required to ensure all the requirements are met and the technology is properly implemented. Since IPSec can have an impact on performance, you must decide what areas require security and then determine how the security requirements can be met. When planning for IPSec, keep the following points in mind:

- Determine those clients and servers on the network that require IPSec.
- Determine how IPSec policies will be applied.
- Determine the authentication methods that will be used.
- Determine the settings required for each IPSec policy.

Determining Where Security Is Required

When planning for IPSec, one of the first things that must be determined is where security is required. Since IPSec does have an impact on performance, you may not want to secure all network communications between all hosts on a network. The following list outlines some of the situations in which IPSec is recommended:

- **Packet filtering**   IPSec uses IP packet filtering to permit, block, or negotiate communications. Packets can be filtered according to IP address range and protocols, as well as TCP and UDP port numbers. Since IPSec is not really a firewall, it can be used with technologies such as NAT and ICF to further restrict inbound and outbound traffic.
- **Securing server-to-server traffic**   IPSec can be used to secure communications between two servers or two subnets. For example, it can secure traffic between a web server and a database server.
- **Securing host-to-server traffic**   IPSec can be used to secure client-to-server traffic. You can also restrict those clients that are allowed access to the server.
- **VPN connections**   L2TP/IPSec can be used to secure VPN connections.
- **Securing gateway-to-gateway tunnels**   IPSec in tunnel mode can provide security between two endpoints when one does not support IPSec.

on the job   *Keep in mind when you are planning to deploy IPSec that it does utilize the CPU. On computers and servers that have sufficient resources, this should not be too much of a concern. However, for servers that already provide a number of network services, encrypting and decrypting data can impact server performance.*

You also need to consider the role a computer plays when planning for IPSec. Some server roles may require a higher level of security than others. For example, a remote access server may require a higher level of security than a web server on the private network.

Planning for IP Security Policies

Once you have determined those areas that require secure communications, you are ready to begin planning for IPSec policies. One of the first things to consider is where IPSec policies will be applied. For example, if IPSec is being configured for a group of computers, you may want to apply the policy at the Organizational Unit level. In any case, IPSec policies can be applied at any of the following levels. Where you apply an IPSec policy will be determined by which computers the policy settings need to apply to. IPSec policies can be applied at the following levels and are applied in the following order:

- Local
- Site
- Domain
- Organizational Unit

When planning how to apply IPSec policies, keep in mind that domain membership will have an impact on where policies can be retrieved from. If the computer is a member of a Windows Server 2003 domain, policies can be stored locally or within Active Directory. For computers that are not members of a domain, such as a stand-alone server, policies can be configured locally or imported from another computer.

Determining Policy Settings

Once you have determined the areas of the network that require security and how the IPSec policies will be applied, the final step will be to create the IPSec policies and configure the policy settings to meet the various security requirements.

INSIDE THE EXAM

Active Directory–Based Policies

As already mentioned, one of the ways in which policies can be applied is through Active Directory. A policy can be applied to a site, to a domain, or to an Organization Unit. All computers within the container to which the policy is applied will be affected by the policy settings.

One of the strategies you can use when applying policies through Active Directory is to apply a policy at the domain level and also at the OU level. The domain-level policy can be used to establish a baseline of security for all computers within the domain. Additional IPSec policies can then be configured at the OU level to provide higher levels of security for areas of a network that may be more sensitive than others. Remember when multiple policies exist, an OU-level policy will override a domain-level policy. Also, when configuring policies with broad IPSec settings, it is generally easier in terms of administration to apply them at the highest possible level of the Active Directory hierarchy, such as the domain level.

For example, computer accounts can be grouped into two different Organizational Units, one for servers and one for workstations. A separate policy can be configured for the Server OU to enforce a higher level of security. Workstations will be affected by the domain-level policy that enforces a baseline of security. Since the policies configured at the OU level override those configured at the domain level, computers within the Server OU will be affected by the policy configured at this level.

By default, policies are inherited from parent container to child container. For example, a policy applied at the domain level would affect all Organizational Units within that domain. You can, however, change the default behavior of how policies are applied using GPO permissions, No Override, and Block Inheritance. When a GPO is created, all users are assigned the Apply group policy permission. This permission applies all the policy settings to authenticated users. So if you want to exempt a user or group from being affected by the policy settings, you can simply remove this permission.

If multiple policies exist, they are applied in the following order: local, site, domain, Organizational Unit. This means that policy settings applied to an OU will override those applied at the domain level. This is the default behavior but can be altered using the Block Inheritance and No Override options. Enabling the Block Policy Inheritance option for a container such as an OU means that any policies configured at a higher level in the hierarchy will not be inherited. On the other hand, setting the No Override option on a GPO means that any policy settings configured at a lower level in the hierarchy cannot override them.

There are two methods by which you can go about implementing IPSec policies. First, you can create the IPSec policies first and then configure the filter lists and filter actions (this process is outlined in Exercise 7-1). Or you can first configure the filter lists and filter actions, then create the IPSec policies. The filter lists and actions you create are shared among all IPSec policies. You can use the following steps to create and manage any IPSec filter lists and filter actions:

1. Within the IP Security Policy Management snap-in, right-click IP Security Policies On Local Computer or IP Security Policies On Active Directory (depending on how policies are being applied) and select Manage IP Filter Lists And Filter Actions.

2. From the Manage IP Filter Lists tab, click Add to create a new IP filter. Click Edit to change the settings of an existing IP filter.

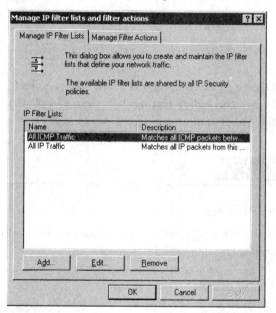

3. From the Manage Filter Actions tab, Click Add to configure a new filter action or Edit to change the properties of an existing one.

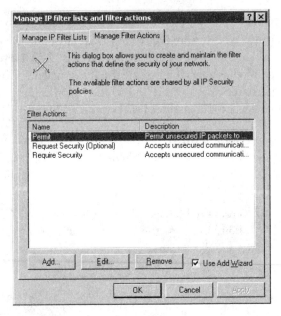

on the
Job

Once a policy is configured with the required settings, it must then be assigned before the policy settings will take effect. This can be done by right-clicking the policy and selecting the Assign option.

EXERCISE 7-2

Planning IPSec Policies

In the following exercise, you will use the information in the given scenario to plan the implementation of IPSec policies.

DKP International has hired you to assist in the deployment of IPSec policies. The company currently has a single Active Directory domain. All workstations are running Windows XP Professional and Windows 2000 Professional. All workstations are members of the DHP International domain. All servers within the domain are running Windows Server 2003.

Members of the Finance department access sensitive client information stored on a member server. The company is currently concerned about an attacker or unauthorized user gaining access to the information. The company wants to require secure communications between these workstations and the member server. Drawing on this information, devise an IPSec policy plan that will meet the security requirements. In your plan, explain which of the default policies should be assigned and why, how policies should be deployed, and the authentication method that should be used.

Wireless Network Security

Over the past few years, many advances have been made in the area of wireless networking. Wireless networking is used to establish wireless connections across short and long distances. For example, mobile users can use wireless networking technologies to access e-mail using cellular phones. In any case, implementing wireless networking also raises concerns about security. Without careful planning and consideration and ensuring that authentication authorization mechanisms are in place, a user with a wireless network adapter may be able to gain access to a private network.

SCENARIO & SOLUTION

Why is it recommended that a preshared key not be used for authentication?	This authentication method is supported mainly for interoperability. It is not recommended because it stores the shared key in plain text.
Which of the authentication methods provides the highest level of security?	Certificate-based authentication provides the highest level of security, followed by Kerberos.
Should I use the IPSec policies included with Windows Server 2003?	The policies can be used, although they are provided as more of an example. Also, the policies are designed to secure intranet traffic. So if you need to secure Internet-based traffic, a new policy should be configured.
What is the benefit of using a persistent policy?	Persistent policies add another level of security to your IPSec implementation. Persistent policies are beneficial because they secure a computer in the event that a local Active Directory policy is not available, for example, if a policy becomes corrupt.

Security Options

There are a number of benefits that can be achieved from implementing wireless networking technologies. However, before these benefits can be fully achieved, a strong security foundation must be put into place. Wireless networking is more susceptible to attack than a traditional wired network. Authentication and encryption are required to protect from such things as unauthorized access and eavesdropping. The following sections will look at the various security mechanisms that can be used to secure wireless networks.

802.11 Wireless Equivalent Privacy

The 802.11 Wireless Equivalent Privacy (WEP) standard defines encryption for wireless networks. WEP provides security on wireless networks by encrypting data sent between a client and a server. WEP encrypts data using the RC4 cipher stream with either 40-bit or 128-bit encryption levels. It also provides data integrity by including an integrity check value (ICV) in the wireless frame.

802.1x Authentication

The 802.1x standard is an industry standard used for authentication on Ethernet networks and 802.1 networks (wireless networks). It uses the Extensible Authentication Protocol (EAP) during the authentication process. With EAP, the exact authentication method can be negotiated between a client and a server. EAP can use certificates, smart cards, and credentials for authentication.

With EAP, you can choose any of the following authentication methods:

- **EAP-Transport Layer Security (TLS)**   This method uses certificates for server authentication. Users and computers are authenticated using certificates or smart cards.

- **Protected EAP (PEAP) with EAP MS-CHAP version 2**   This method uses certificates for server authentication. Users authenticate using credentials (usernames and passwords). This method is easiest to deploy.

- **Protected EAP (PEAP) with EAP-TLS**   This method uses certificates for server authentication. Credentials are used to authenticate users. This method provides the highest level of security.

on the job   *PEAP with TLS is more secure than EAP-TLS because it also encrypts the user's certificate information.*

802.11 Authentication and Verification

The 802.11 Authentication and Verification standard defines how identities are verified and authenticated on a wireless network. It defines two authentication subtypes: *open systems* and *shared key*. Identity verification is achieved through open systems through a message exchange between the wireless client and the network access point. Authentication is achieved using a shared key. If an initiator has knowledge of a shared secret, that initiator is considered to be authenticated.

Wireless Network Policies

Windows Server 2003 enables you to define wireless network policies within a Group Policy Object and store them within Active Directory. Doing so allows administrators to centralize the administration of wireless networks. By deploying wireless network policies, you can configure various wireless settings for users, enable 802.1x authentication, and specify the networks users can connect to.

Creating Wireless Network Policies

Using the Group Policy Editor, you can create a wireless network policy for your organization. You can apply the policy through a GPO at the various levels of an Active Directory hierarchy (site, domain, OU). Keep in mind, however, that only one wireless network policy can exist at any layer in the Active Directory hierarchy. Use these steps to create a new wireless network policy:

1. Open the appropriate Group Policy Object.
2. Expand Computer Configuration, Windows Settings, Security Settings.
3. Right-click Wireless Network (802.11) Policies and click Create Wireless Network Policy. Click Next.
4. Type in a name and description for the policy. Click Next.
5. Click Finish. The properties dialog box for the new policy will appear, from which you can configure the settings.

From the General tab for the wireless network policy, you can configure a number of different settings (see Figure 7-8). From here, you can configure the name and description for the policy as well as how often the computer will poll Active Directory for changes to the policy (the default is 180 minutes). Using the Network access list, you can specify the type of wireless network that clients can access. The Use Windows

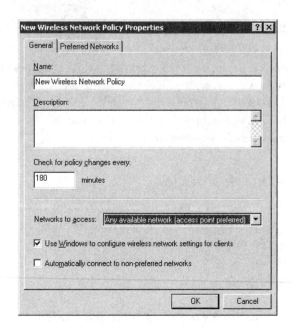

To Configure Wireless Network Settings For Clients option is selected by default. This means that when a client accesses a wireless network, the network adapter settings will automatically be configured to match those of the network. To enable clients to connect to wireless networks not listed on the Preferred Networks tab, select the option to Automatically Connect To Non-Preferred Networks.

From the Preferred Networks tab (see Figure 7-9), you can add, edit, and change the order of preferred networks (preferred networks are those that wireless clients can connect to). Clicking the Add button allows you to configure a new preferred network (see Figure 7-10).

Using the Network Properties tab, you can configure a name and description for the preferred network and specify the key settings, if a network key is required. The IEEE 802.1x tab can be used to enable the 802.1x authentication standard and configure the authentication methods (see Figure 7-11). Table 7-2 summarizes the various settings available.

FIGURE 7-9

Using the
Preferred
Network tab
of a wireless
network policy

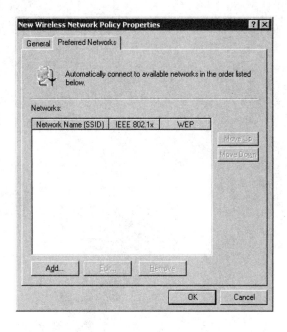

FIGURE 7-10

Adding a new
preferred
network

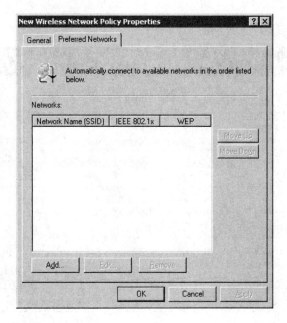

FIGURE 7-11

Using the
IEEE 802.1x
tab of a wireless
network policy

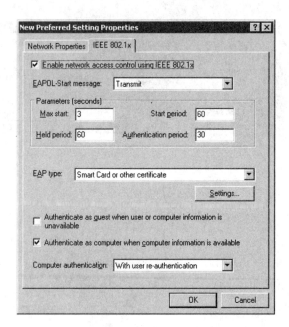

TABLE 7-2 IEEE 802.1x Settings

Setting	Description
Enable network access control using IEEE 802.1x	Selecting this option enables 802.1x authentication.
EAPOL start messages	Used to specify the transmission behavior of EAPOL start messages. Below that you can configure various settings such as the Start period and Held period.
EAP type	Used to configure the EAP type to be used on wireless networks. Options include Smart Card or other certificate or Protected EAP (PEAP).
Authentication as guest when user or computer information is unavailable	Allows users to attempt authentication if user and computer information is not available.
Authenticate as computer when computer information is available	Allows the computer to authenticate to the network if a user is not logged on.
Computer authentication	Used to specify how the computer should authenticate.

CERTIFICATION OBJECTIVE 7.03

Secure Network Administration

One of the topics that falls under network administration is that of remote administration. The benefits of being able to use various technologies to remotely administer workstations and servers are numerous and can include a decrease in time and cost associated with administering a network. For example, if an organization has remote sites, a network administrator does not necessarily have to visit the location to troubleshoot technical problems. Instead, some of the troubleshooting can be done remotely. Windows Server 2003 includes two technologies that can be used for remote administration: Remote Assistance and Remote Desktop for Administration.

Of course, using remote administration technologies can open the door for attackers, as once you have remote access to a system, you can gain access to local resources and network resources. When implementing remote administration technologies, security must also be considered.

Planning for Remote Assistance

Administrators are always looking for more efficient ways to troubleshoot problems as they arise, especially if there are a large number of end users on the network or if there are branch offices that do not have local administrators. Remote Assistance is a tool included with Windows Server 2003 that enables administrators and other support persons to remotely assist users with computer problems. Using Remote Assistance, the expert or assistant can remotely view a user's desktop and even remotely take control of a desktop if permission has been granted.

on the job

One of the main benefits to using Remote Assistance is that administrators or other support personnel do not need to be physically sitting at a computer to assist a user in troubleshooting problems.

How Remote Assistance Works

When a user is experiencing technical problems, they can send an invitation for remote assistance to an administrator or other support personnel. An invitation for remote assistance can be sent using Windows Messenger and via an e-mail message. Depending on how Remote Assistance is configured, an administrator can also offer help to a user without being first explicitly invited. The remote assistance process basically occurs in three steps:

1. A user sends a remote access invitation using Windows Messenger or using an e-mail message.

2. The invitation is accepted and a window appears on the assistant's computer displaying the user's desktop.

3. The assistant can view the user's desktop. Interaction with the desktop can occur only if the user enables the Allow Expert Interaction option.

on the Job

Remote Assistance can be used on the local network and across the Internet. If you are using it behind a firewall, make sure that TCP port 3389 is opened.

Securing Remote Assistance

If the proper permissions have been granted, an expert or assistant is capable of taking over another user's desktop and performing all functions the user can perform. This would include accessing information stored on the computer as well as accessing network resources. Although Remote Assistance is a great tool for troubleshooting, this can raise security concerns. The following section will look at some of the ways in which you can secure a remote access implementation.

Group Policy   Group policies can be used to limit those users that can ask for remote assistance as well as those users who can offer remote assistance. Within a group policy there are two options that can be enabled: Solicited Remote Assistance and Offer Remote Assistance. The settings can be found by navigating to the following container: Computer Configuration | Administrative Templates | System | Remote Assistance (see Figure 7-12).

The Solicited Remote Assistance option is used to specify whether users can ask for remote assistance, and if the assistant is allowed to view their desktop or take control as well. To configure the settings, double-click the Solicited Remote Assistance option (see Figure 7-13).

To allow users to ask for remote assistance, it must first be enabled. Once it is enabled, you can specify whether assistants can view remote desktops or also take control by selecting one of the following options: Allow Helpers To Remotely Control The Computer or Allow Helpers To Only View The Computer. The Maximum ticket time is used to specify the maximum duration time for a Remote Assistance ticket. You can also specify the method for sending e-mail messages asking for remote assistance.

FIGURE 7-12

Using Group
Policy to allow
remote assistance

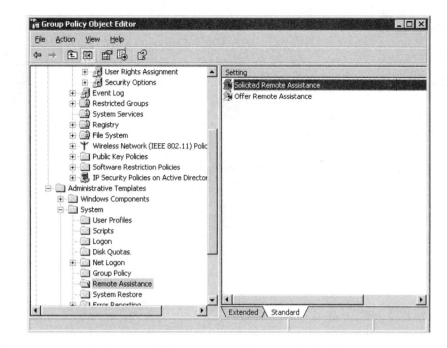

FIGURE 7-13

Configuring
Solicited Remote
Assistance

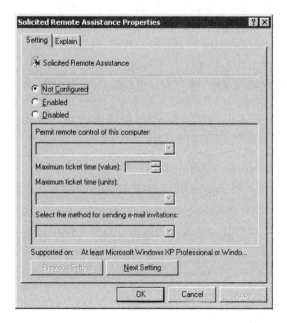

FIGURE 7-14

Configuring the
Offer Remote
Assistance option

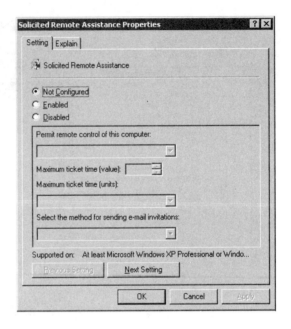

The second option, Offer Remote Assistance, is used to configure whether an assistant can offer remote assistance without first being explicitly asked by a user (see Figure 7-14). Once this option is enabled, you can then specify the type of control assistants have. Selecting the Show button allows you to configure a list of helpers (or assistants).

Local Security   An administrator also has the option of turning Remote Assistance off on a local computer. Doing so means that any user who logs onto the computer will not be able to send requests for remote assistance. You can turn off Remote Assistance on a computer running Windows XP using the following steps:

1. Click Start, and select Control Panel.

2. Within the Control Panel, locate and double-click the System applet.

3. From the System Properties dialog box, select the Remote tab.

4. Under Remote Assistance, enable or disable the option to Allow Remote Assistance Invitations To Be Sent From This Computer.

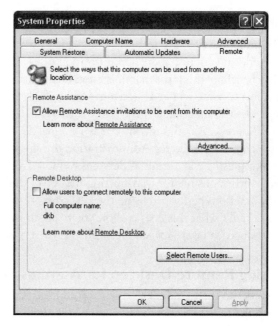

5. If Remote Assistance is enabled on the computer, select the Advance button to specify if assistants are permitted to remotely control the local computer. You can also specify how long Remote Assistance invitations remain open.

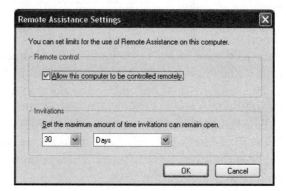

Using Terminal Services for Remote Administration

Terminal Services is another tool that can be used for remote assistance. Through the use of thin-client software, a workstation can act as a terminal emulator. The user interface is transmitted to the client. The user can then perform various functions that are processed on the terminal server.

Remote Desktop for Administration

Terminal Services is a technology included with Windows Server 2003. It can be used to perform various remote administration tasks by remotely connecting to a computer. The benefit of this is that administrators do not need to be physically seated at a computer in order to administer it. This in turn can save both time and money. Windows Server 2003 provides this functionality through the Remote Desktop for Administration component. In Windows 2000, this was known as Terminal Services on Remote Administration Mode.

Remote Desktop for Administration provides you with remote access to a server desktop using the Terminal Services Remote Desktop Protocol (RDP) on port 3389. RDP is responsible for transmitting the server desktop to the client and transmitting any functions performed using the keyboard or mouse back to the server for processing. Essentially, what this does is allow you to administer a server from a remote computer as though you were logged on locally at the server.

Using Remote Desktop for Administration

In order to use Remote Desktop for Administration, you must first have a connection with the remote computer and also be running the client software. A connection can be established across a local area network, using a dial-up connection, or via a VPN connection. The client software (known as Remote Desktop Connection) is automatically installed on computers running Windows XP and Windows Server 2003. It is accessible from the Start menu under the All Programs | Accessories | Communications container.

For security purposes, users are not permitted to establish a remote desktop connection. Only members of the Administrators group are permitted to do so. All other users must be granted permission. This can be done by adding the necessary users to the Remote Desktop Users group. Remember that once a user establishes a remote desktop connection, they can perform a number of administrative tasks, which means it is important to plan which users require this right.

Finally, in order for connections to be established with a server, the option to Allow Users To Connect Remotely To Your Computer must be enabled (using the System applet within the Control Panel). This option is disabled by default on computers running Windows Server 2003.

CERTIFICATION OBJECTIVE 7.04

Troubleshooting Network Security

Once IPSec policies are in place, administrators will want to ensure that communications are actually being secured. As problems arise, administrators must also know how to troubleshoot them or at least what tools are available to help determine the problem so that network security is not compromised. The IP Security Monitor tool can be used to both monitor network communications and troubleshoot IPSec-related problems when they occur. Another tool that can be used to troubleshoot network security is Resultant Set of Policy. It allows an administrator to verify the IPSec policy settings that are assigned to a computer. The following section will look at both IP Security Monitor and Resultant Set of Policy and how they can be used to troubleshoot network security.

IP Security Monitor

As you saw earlier in the chapter, IPSec is a suite of protocols used to secure communications between two hosts. The IP Security Monitor utility included with Windows Server 2003 can be used to validate that secure communications are indeed taking place where required. The tool can also be used to troubleshoot IPSec-related problems. IP Security Monitor provides information such as the IPSec policy that is currently active and whether a secure communication channel is being established between computers.

on the
job

If you are using IP Security Monitor, keep in mind that it can be used to monitor only computers that are running Windows XP and Windows Server 2003. You cannot use it to monitor IPSec on a computer running Windows 2000.

The version of IP Security Monitor included with Windows Server 2003 has many enhancements and new features that were not included with the version included with Windows 2000. Here are some of the new enhancements:

- IP Security Monitor can be used to view IPSec statistics on the local computer or a remote computer.
- IP Security Monitor will display information about the policy that is currently active on the computer.
- IP Security Monitor now displays both Main Mode and Quick Mode statistics.
- The rate at which the information is refreshed can be customized.
- Administrators can search for specific types of information based on source and destination IP addresses.

e**x**a m
w a t c h
    Make sure you are familiar with IP Security Monitor before taking the exam. Since it now has many new enhancements and features not *found in the versions included with Windows 2000, you can expect to encounter exam questions relating to the topic.*

Using IP Security Monitor

In Windows 2000, the IP Security Monitor program was launched using the `ipsecmon.exe` command. With Windows Server 2003, IP Security Monitor is launched as a Microsoft Management Console. To open the IP Security Monitor snap-in, perform the following steps:

1. Click Start and click Run.

2. Type **mmc** and click OK.

3. From the File menu, click Add/Remove Snap-in.

4. From the Add/Remove Snap-in dialog box, click Add.

5. From the list of available snap-ins, select IP Security Monitor and click the Add button. Click Close.

6. Click OK.

As already mentioned, IP Security Monitor can be used to view IPSec statistics on a local computer or on a remote computer. To view the statistics on another computer, right-click the IP Security Monitor container within the console and click Add Computer. Browse for the computer you want to add or type in the appropriate computer name.

The IP Security Monitor container will either display the name of the local computer or the remote computer that you are connected to. By expanding the computer, you will see three containers: Active Policy, Main Mode, and Quick Mode. Selecting the Active Policy container displays information about the policy that is currently applied to the computer. It includes the following information:

- **Policy Name**   This lists the name of the IPSec policy that is currently active on the computer.

- **Policy Description**   This option displays the description assigned to the policy when it was created.

- **Policy Last Modified**   This option displays when the policy was last modified. It is available only if local policies are being used.

- **Policy Store**   This option displays the storage locations for the active IPSec policy.

- **Policy Path**   This option specifies the Lightweight Directory Access Protocol path to the IPSec policy.

- **Organizational Unit**   This option specifies the Organizational Unit to which the group policy has been applied.

- **Group Policy Object Name**   This option specifies the name of the Group Policy Object to which the IPSec policy is applied.

You'll notice two other containers listed under your server within the IP Security Monitor console: Main Mode and Quick Mode. Clicking either of these containers displays a number of other containers. In any case, you can use these different options to monitor communications between hosts. A multitude of statistics are available that can be used to monitor IPSec communications.

Resultant Set of Policy

A new tool introduced in Windows Server 2003 is known as Resultant Set of Policy (RSoP). It's an addition to the Group Policy utility that can be used to view the IPSec policy settings on a computer. You can use the tool to troubleshoot policy issues or to test the results of a policy change. To use RSoP, you must first open the Resultant Set of Policy snap-in. The tool allows you to run two different types of queries: logging mode queries and planning mode queries.

TABLE 7-3   gpresult Command-Line Switches

Option	Description
/s *computer*	Specifies the name or IP address of the remote computer.
/u *domain\user*	Runs the command using the account specified.
/p *password*	Specifies the password associated with the user account specified with the /u switch.
/user *target username*	Specifies the user for which the RSoP data is gathered.
/scope {user	computer}	Specifies whether to display user or computer results.

You can also use the `gpresult` command-line tool to view policy settings and the Resultant Set of Policy for a computer or user. Table 7-3 summarizes the various switches available with the command.

Logging Mode Queries

Logging mode queries are performed to view all the IPSec policies that are currently assigned to a computer. This is extremely useful when there are multiple policies configured that may be affecting a computer. The results will display which policies a computer is affected by, the precedence of each policy, and the settings for the IPSec policy that is being applied to the computer. Exercise 7-3 walks you through the process of using RSoP to perform a logging mode query.

EXERCISE 7-3

Using Resultant Set of Policy to Perform Logging Mode Queries

In this exercise, you will use the Resultant Set of Policy utility to view IPSec policy settings.

1. Click Start, click Run, type **mmc**, and click OK.

2. Click File and select Add/Remove Programs.

3. From the Add/Remove Snap-in dialog box, click Add.

4. From the Add Standalone Snap-in dialog box, scroll through the list of available snap-ins and select Resultant Set Of Policy. Click Add. Click Close. Click OK.

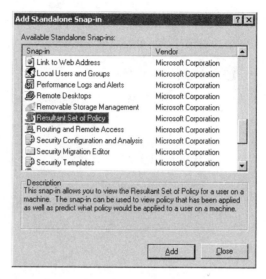

5. From the Action menu, select Generate RSoP Data. This launches the Resultant Set of Policy Wizard. Click Next.

6. From the Mode Selection dialog box, you can select the mode you want to use. Leave the default mode (Logging Mode) selected. Click Next.

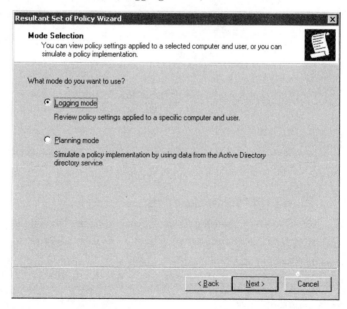

7. The next dialog box enables you to select the computer for which you want to display IPSec policy settings. Select This Computer, if not already selected. Click Next.

8. From the User Selection dialog box, you can specify what settings you want to display. You can display results for the current user logged on, results for a specific user, or computer settings only. Leave the default option of Current User selected. Click Next.

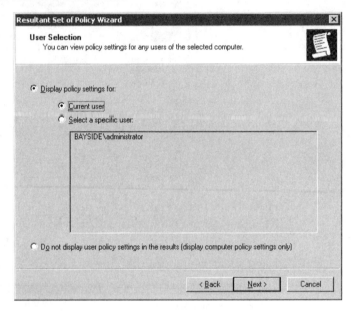

9. Review the Summary of Selections and click next.

10. Once the wizard has completed gathering the required information, click Finish.

11. You can view the IPSec policy settings by navigating to the User Configuration | Windows Settings | Security Settings | IP Security Policies On Local Computer container.

Planning Mode Queries

When used in planning mode, RSoP can be used to simulate the impact of policy settings under various circumstances. This can assist an administrator in capacity planning, growth planning, and reorganization. Table 7-4 summarizes the advanced options available in planning mode. These are the various circumstances under which policy settings can be evaluated.

TABLE 7-4   Planning Mode Options

Option	Description
Slow Network Connection	This advanced option will simulate a slow network connection when performing the query. This allows you to see how a policy will behave when applied across a slow network connection.
Loopback Processing	This simulation will apply the settings within the computer policy to any user that logs on. This allows you to determine how these users will be affected. Two options available are Replace and Merge. The Replace option will replace the policy settings normally applied to the user with those in the computer's policy. The Merge option will combine the policy settings normally applied to the user with those configured in the computer's policy.
Site	This option allows you to specify a site other than the one in which the query is being run.
Alternate Active Directory Paths	This option allows you to simulate different Active Directory paths for the user or computer.
Computer Security Groups	This option can be used to simulate the results of a user's or computer's belonging to various security groups.
WMI Filters	This option allows WMI filters to be included in the query.

EXERCISE 7-4

Using Resultant Set of Policy to Perform Planning Mode Queries

1. Within the Resultant Set of Policy snap-in, select Generate RSoP Data from the Action menu. This launches the Resultant Set of Policy Wizard. Click Next.

2. From the Mode Selection dialog box, you can select the mode you want to use. Select Planning Mode. Click Next.

3. From the User And Computer Selection dialog box, you can choose the user account, computer, or container for which you want to simulate the settings.

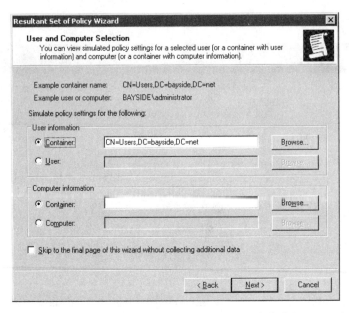

4. Under Computer Information, select Computer and click Browse. Locate your computer and click OK. Click Next.

5. From the Advanced Simulation Options dialog box, you can select any optional parameters. Click Next.

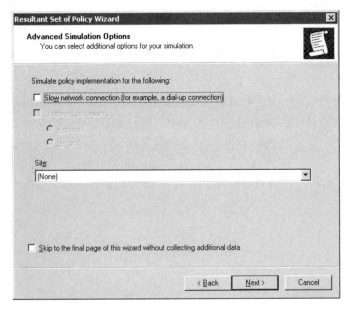

6. From the Alternate Active Directory Paths dialog box, you can configure an Active Directory path other than the current one. Click Next.

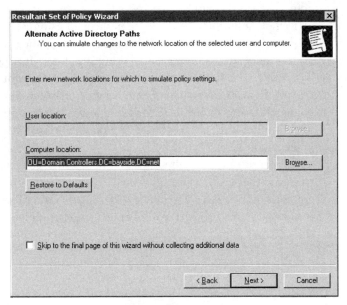

7. Using the Computer Security Groups you can simulate the results of the user or computer belonging to different security groups. Click Next.

8. Review the Summary of Selections and click Next. Click Finish.

9. The results of the query are displayed in the RSoP console.

CERTIFICATION SUMMARY

This chapter began by introducing you to the IP Security Protocol. IPSec can be used to secure communications between hosts. IPSec policies can be assigned locally or through Active Directory to define what type of traffic should be secured and the methods used to secure it. When implementing IPSec, you must first determine what areas of your network require security. You can then plan how IPSec policies will be assigned, the authentication methods that will be used, and the various policy settings such as IP filter lists and filter actions.

Wireless networking is used to establish wireless connections across short and long distances. A number of standards have been developed to secure communication over wireless networks, for example, the 802.1x authentication standard. Wireless network policies can be deployed through Active Directory, allowing you to centralize the administration of wireless networks.

Remote administration can be performed using Remote Assistance or Remote Desktop for Administration. With Remote Assistance, a user can send an invitation for assistance to support personnel using Windows Messenger or via an e-mail message. The helper or assistant can view the user's desktop or interact if permission has been granted. Remote Desktop for Administration enables a workstation to act as a terminal emulator. Using RDP, the desktop of a server is transmitted to a workstation. Any actions input using the keyboard or mouse are transmitted back to the server for processing.

IP Security Monitor allows you to monitor IPSec communications between hosts to ensure that traffic is being secured. It provides information about which policy is currently active on a computer. It also displays Main Mode and Quick Mode statistics. Resultant Set of Policy (RSoP) can be used to troubleshoot policy assignment and simulate the impact that various policy settings will have on a user or computer.

✓ TWO-MINUTE DRILL

Securing Private Networks

❑ IPSec is a suite of protocols used to secure communications between hosts.

❑ The three components of IPSec are the IPSec Policy Agent, ISAKMP/Oakley Key Management Service, and the IPSec driver.

❑ The IPSec Policy Agent retrieves policy information for use by other IPSec components.

❑ The ISAKMP/Oakley Key Management Service negotiates security parameters between hosts.

❑ The IPSec driver monitors and secures inbound and outbound traffic.

❑ IP Security policies consist of rules that define when and how secure communications should occur.

❑ Filter actions determine what happens when an IP packet matches a filter within the filter list.

❑ IPSec supports the following authentication methods: Kerberos, preshared key, PKI certificates.

❑ Windows Server 2003 includes three IPSec policies designed to secure intranet traffic: Client (Respond Only), Server (Request Security), Secure Server (Require Security).

Wireless Network Security

❑ 802.1x is an industry standard used for authentication on Ethernet networks and 802.1 networks (wireless networks). The 802.1x standard uses the Extensible Authentication Protocol (EAP) during the authentication process.

❑ The 802.11 Wireless Equivalent Privacy (WEP) standard defines encryption for wireless networks. WEP provides security on wireless networks by encrypting data sent between a client and a server.

❑ The 802.11 Authentication and Verification standard defines how identities are verified and authenticated on a wireless network. It defines two authentication subtypes: Open Systems and Shared Key.

❑ Wireless network policies can be deployed through Active Directory.

Secure Network Administration

❑ Remote assistance enables support personnel to remotely assist users with computer problems.

❑ A helper (or assistant) can remotely view the desktop if permission has been granted.

❑ An invitation for remote assistance can be sent using Windows Messenger or via an e-mail message.

❑ Using group policy, an administrator can control which users are permitted to ask for remote assistance and which users can provide remote assistance.

❑ Remote Assistance can be disabled locally using the System applet within the Control Panel.

❑ Remote Desktop for Administration included with Windows Server 2003 replaces the Terminal Services on Remote Administration Mode included with Windows 2000.

Troubleshooting Network Security

❑ IP Security Monitor can be used to validate that communications between hosts is being secured.

❑ IP Security Monitor displays information about the Active Policy. It also displays Main Mode and Quick Mode statistics.

❑ Resultant Set of Policy (RSoP) can be used to troubleshoot policy issues or simulate the impact different settings will have on a computer or user.

SELF TEST

Securing Private Networks

1. Which of the following IPSec components are responsible for negotiating security parameters with another host?

   A. ISAKMP/Oakley

   B. IPSec driver

   C. IPSec Policy Agent

   D. IPSec policy

2. David is the administrator for a Windows Server 2003 network. He has been asked to implement an IPSec policy on one of the file servers. The policy should request security but allow communications with non–IPSec aware clients. Which of the following policies should he assign?

   A. Client (Respond Only)

   B. Server (Request Security)

   C. Secure Server (Require Security)

   D. Secure Client (Request Security)

3. Jim has just configured a new IPSec policy. The policy contains the settings that will apply to all file servers within the domain. The policy settings are contained within a GPO applied to an OU. Once the policy is configured, what must Jim do?

   A. Restart the servers.

   B. Apply the new IPSec policy.

   C. Use the `gpupdate` command to apply the policy settings.

   D. Assign the new IPSec policy.

   E. Assign the GPO.

Wireless Network Security

4. A file server on the network hosts confidential financial information that is accessed by members of the Finance department. You want to ensure that the server communicates with only those clients that support IPSec. No unsecured communications should be allowed. Which of the following policies should be assigned to the server?

   A. Server (Request Security)

   B. Client (Respond Only)

    C. Server (Request Security)

    D. Secure Server (Require Security)

5. Which of the following IPSec policy components determines whether specific types of traffic are secured, blocked, or permitted?

    A. Filter action

    B. IP filter list

    C. IPSec driver

    D. IP filter

6. Which of the following correctly defines the order in which IPSec policies are applied?

    A. Local, domain, site, OU

    B. Local, site, domain, OU

    C. Local, OU, site, domain

    D. Domain, OU, site, local

7. Dan is planning the implementation of IPSec. He wants to ensure that policy settings are applied during the transition from computer startup to when the local policy is applied. What should he do?

    A. Configure a directory cache policy

    B. Configure an Active Directory–based policy

    C. Configure a persistent policy

    D. Configure a `netsh` dynamic mode policy

8. Several IPSec policies have been configured. Mary wants to determine which policy is currently active on one of the web servers. What should she do?

    A. Display the properties for TCP/IP.

    B. Display the IPSec statistics through the IP Security Policy Management snap-in.

    C. Open the IP Security Monitor snap-in.

    D. Open the Windows Event Viewer.

9. Mary wants to test the impact that a change in policy settings will have on a group of users. What should she do?

    A. Make the policy change and use IP Security Monitor to view the results.

    B. Use Resultant Set of Policy in logging mode to view the impact the changes will have.

    C. Use Security Configuration and Analysis in logging mode to view the impact changes will have.

    D. Use Resultant Set of Policy in planning mode to view the impact changes will have.

Secure Network Administration

10. Mike is the junior administrator for a Windows Server 2003 network. He is configuring secure communications between two member servers. He locally assigns each server the Client (Respond Only) policy. However, he notices that communication between the two servers is not being secured. What is causing the problem?

   A. The policies must be assigned through Active Directory.

   B. Active Directory is not installed.

   C. Both servers are assigned the Client (Respond Only) policy.

   D. The policy has not been applied.

11. You are planning the deployment of IPSec on your network. Communications between two stand-alone servers must be secured. When configuring the IPSec policy, which authentication methods can be used? Select two answers.

   A. Kerberos

   B. MS-CHAP version 2

   C. Preshared key

   D. Certificates

Troubleshooting Network Security

12. IPSec consists of which two security protocols?

   A. EAP

   B. AH

   C. RDP

   D. ESP

13. Which of the following authentication methods can be used with IPSec?

   A. MS-CHAP

   B. Kerberos

   C. Certificates

   D. MS-CHAP version 2

   E. Shared Key

14. Which of the following authentication methods are used by the 802.1x authentication standard?

   A. EAP-TLS

   B. PEAP-MSCHAP version 2

   C. PEAP-TLS

   D. PEAP-MSCHAP

15. John is planning the implementation of Remote Assistance on his company network. Only members of the Help Desk group should be able to provide remote assistance to users. How should he proceed?

   A. Add the Help Desk group to the Administrators group.

   B. Add the Help Desk group to the Remote Assistance group.

   C. Configure a Remote Assistance policy on the local computers.

   D. Deploy a Remote Assistance policy through a GPO.

LAB QUESTION

You have been asked to assist FKP Consulting in reorganizing certain areas of their existing network infrastructure. The main goal is to increase the current level of security throughout the network. Management would like all communications between the company database server and the financial group to be secured at all times. Another file server on the network hosts some confidential information. However, some clients using Windows 95 require access to the data. Managers are also concerned about remote administration and security. Help Desk currently uses Remote Assistance to troubleshoot problems when appropriate. However, Management would like to look for ways in which this can be more securely implemented. Given this information, answer the following questions:

1. How should IPSec policies be deployed? Why?

2. Which of the default IPSec policies would you apply? Why?

3. When configuring the authentication methods within the IPSec policies, which authentication method would you choose? Explain your answer.

4. How can you use group policy to secure Remote Assistance within a domain?

5. A specific server on the network hosts confidential data. For security purposes, no users should have remote assistance capabilities on this server. How can you ensure this?

SELF TEST ANSWERS

Securing Private Networks

1. ☑ **A.** The ISAKMP/Oakley Key Management Service is responsible for negotiating the security parameters with another host.

   ☒ **B** is incorrect because the IPSec driver monitors inbound and outbound traffic to determine which traffic must be secured based on policy rules. **C** is incorrect because the IPSec policy agent is responsible for retrieving policy information.

   D is incorrect because IPSec policies are used to define which type of traffic requires security and how it should be secured.

2. ☑ **B.** By assigning the Server (Request Security) policy, David assures that the server will always try to secure communications but will also allow nonsecure communications with non–IPSec aware clients.

   ☒ **A** is incorrect because this policy configures a computer to respond to requests for security. **C** is incorrect because this policy would not allow communication with non–IPSec aware clients. **D** is incorrect because this is not a default policy included with Windows Server 2003.

3. ☑ **D.** After a new IPSec policy is configured, it must be assigned. This can be done by right-clicking the policy and selecting the Assign option.

   ☒ **A, B,** and **E** are incorrect because they do not represent the correct method for assigning an IPSec policy. **C** is incorrect because the `gpupdate` command is used to update policy settings after they have been changed. The IPSec policy must be assigned before the settings will be applied through a GPO.

Wireless Network Security

4. ☑ **D.** In order to ensure that no unsecured communications are permitted, the server must be configured with the Secure Server (Require Security) policy. This policy does not allow communications with non–IPSec aware clients.

   ☒ **A** is incorrect because this policy permits communications with non–IPSec aware clients. **B** is incorrect because assigning this policy means the server would respond only to requests for secure communications. **C** is incorrect because this is not a default policy included with Windows Server 2003.

5. ☑ **A.** The filter action determines whether specific types of traffic are blocked, permitted, or secured.

   ☒ **B** and **D** are incorrect because IP filters and IP filter lists are used to define the type of traffic that a policy will apply to. **C** is incorrect because the IPSec driver uses policy settings to determine which inbound and outbound traffic should be secured.

6. ☑ **B.** IPSec policies are processed in the following order: local, site, domain, and Organizational Unit. This means that local policies are overwritten by Active Directory–based policies.
   ☒ **A, C,** and **D** are incorrect because they do not represent the correct order in which policies are applied.

7. ☑ **C.** Persistent policies can be applied to secure a computer during the transition from computer startup to when the local policy is applied.
   ☒ **A** is incorrect because directory cache policies are created automatically. Policies settings are cached locally in the event that the computer is unable to access the network. **B** is incorrect because Active Directory policies can be created to apply settings to different users and computers throughout the network. **D** is incorrect because dynamic mode policies are created to apply policy rules immediately. However, once the IPSec service is restarted, these settings are removed.

8. ☑ **C.** The IP Security Monitor tool will display which IPSec policy is currently active on a computer.
   ☒ **A, B,** and **D** are incorrect because these tools cannot be used to determine which IPSec policy is currently active on a computer.

9. ☑ **D.** By using Resultant Set of Policy in planning mode, you can test to see what kind of impact various policy settings will have on users and computers.
   ☒ **A** and **B** are incorrect because these tools cannot be used to perform this task. **D** is incorrect because RSoP must be run in planning mode, not logging mode, to simulate the impact of various policy changes.

Secure Network Administration

10. ☑ **C.** Since both servers are configured with Client (Respond Only), communications between the two hosts will never be secured. This policy configures a computer to only respond to security requests, never request them.
    ☒ **A** and **B** are incorrect because Active Directory is not required to implement IPSec policies. **D** is incorrect because IPSec policies are not applied but rather assigned.

11. ☑ **C and D.** In this scenario, you can use either preshared key or certificates for authentication.
    ☒ **A** is incorrect because Kerberos authentication can be used only between hosts that are members of the same domain or a trusted domain. **B** is incorrect because IPSec does not use MS-CHAP for authentication.

Troubleshooting Network Security

12. ☑ **B and D.** IPSec consists of the following security protocols: AH and ESP. These protocols provide authentication, confidentiality, integrity, and encryption.

☒   C is incorrect because EAP (Extensible Authentication Protocol) allows for arbitrary authentication where two hosts can negotiate on the exact authentication method. **A** is incorrect because RDP (Remote Desktop Protocol) is used to transfer information between a terminal server and a workstation.

13. ☑ **B, C,** and **E.** IPSec supports the following authentication methods: Kerberos, certificates, and preshared keys.

    ☒ **A** and **D** are incorrect because IPSec does not support these authentication methods.

14. ☑ **A, B,** and **C.** The 802.1x authentication standard uses EAP-TLS, PEAP-TLS, and PEAP-MSCHAP version 2.

    ☒ **D** is incorrect because this standard does not support MS-CHAP version 1.

15. ☑ **D.** By configuring a Remote Assistance policy and deploying it through a GPO within Active Directory, you can limit which users can use Remote Assistance.

    ☒ **A, B,** and **D** are incorrect because these methods cannot be used to perform the given task. Adding users to the Administrators group would give them administrative permissions throughout the domain. There is no such group known as the Remote Assistance group. Remote Assistance policies are applied through Active Directory, not locally.

LAB ANSWER

1. IPSec policies should be deployed through Active Directory.

2. In order to ensure that communication between the database server and hosts is always secured, the Secure Server (Require Security) policy should be assigned to the server. This ensures that the server will always require secure communications. The workstations can be configured with the client (respond only). The additional file server should be assigned the Server (request security) policy. This way, the server will attempt secure communications but still permit communications with those clients that do not support IPSec.

3. Since communication is occurring only between computers within the same domain, the Kerberos authentication method can be used.

4. By configuring a Remote Assistance policy through a Group Policy Object, you can control which users can request and offer remote assistance.

5. Remote Assistance can be disabled locally on a computer using the System applet within the Control Panel.

8

Planning, Implementing, and Maintaining Server Availability

CERTIFICATION OBJECTIVES

CERTIFICATION OBJECTIVE 8.01

Planning for High Availability

For those businesses running mission-critical applications or services that require a high level of availability, Windows Server 2003 Enterprise Edition and Windows Server 2003 Datacenter Edition offer solutions to meet these business needs. Both platforms offer clustering technologies to help avoid server, application, or service downtime. Through Network Load Balancing and the Cluster service, businesses can increase the availability of applications and services and ensure that they remain available to users.

Introduction to the Cluster Service

A *cluster* is a group of computers working together as if it were a single computer. This allows access and management of the cluster as a single unit. Each server within a cluster is referred to as a *node*. The idea behind implementing a cluster is to increase the availability of certain applications and services. The nodes within a cluster will continuously communicate with one another to monitor status. A node can detect when another node in the cluster fails, at which point it can take over the services and applications to ensure availability.

Cluster Components

Several different components make up a cluster. These components work together to provide high availability for services and applications. The different cluster components can be placed into two general categories: hardware components and software components.

Hardware Components   Specialized hardware is required to implement a cluster. Before the Cluster service will function, this hardware must be properly installed and configured. All servers, also referred to as nodes, in a cluster must be able to communicate with the other nodes within the same cluster. In order to provide high availability, nodes must be able to determine when other nodes on the cluster fail so that they can resume responsibilities when a failure does occur. Through the use of specialized hardware, this communication between nodes is possible. The Cluster service supports two different hardware components for connecting nodes: Small Computer System Interface (SCSI) and Fibre Channel (both of which must be PCI).

SCSI is a general interface that allows a computer to be connected to many different types of devices. SCSI devices can be either internal or external devices, but all of the devices need an interface to communicate with the PC. This is what the SCSI adapter is for.

The SCSI adapter is a controller card similar to the IDE and floppy controller that controls IDE hard disks or the floppy drive in a PC. The SCSI adapter is used to control the SCSI devices attached to it. It also allows information to pass from the PC bus to the SCSI bus and vice versa. The SCSI adapter sends signals to the SCSI devices that contain their own controller that carries out the command of the adapter on the device.

SCSI adapters and SCSI devices receive information from each other through an identification process. Each SCSI device, including the adapter, must be assigned a unique ID. Although each device and adapter will be preconfigured with a default SCSI ID, the ID will more than likely need to be changed. The device or adapter with the highest SCSI ID has higher priority than the devices with a lower SCSI ID.

on the
() o b

When you are configuring the SCSI IDs, keep in mind that each device connected to the same SCSI adapter or on the same SCSI bus must have a unique ID. If not, the devices will not function properly.

Since a SCSI hard drive is faster than a standard IDE hard drive and will allow for faster performance, SCSI hard drives are used for clustering (they are also standard in most servers). Using SCSI hard drives as opposed to IDE helps to ensure that the disk subsystem does not become a bottleneck on a server.

As already mentioned, nodes within a cluster share a common hard drive or multiple hard drives. This is so that the nodes can all access shared data required to continue servicing client requests when one of the nodes within the cluster fails. When a node fails, the other node will continue the functions of the failed node by taking control of the shared drive(s) where the data is stored. The shared disk resource where the cluster database is stored is called the *quorum resource*. In every cluster, there must be at least one quorum resource.

The shared drives are the location of shared applications and folders. The shared applications are installed from all nodes to the shared resource, using the same configuration. This will allow for one node to continue services of another failed node. The shared resources must have the same drive letters on all nodes. This can be changed in the Computer Management Utility under the Disk Management option.

A newer type of connectivity to external devices that has emerged in the last few years is Fibre Channel. Fibre Channel is a technology that allows signals to be transmitted to the devices over fiber optic cable. This allows for a faster connection speed to and from the devices as well as the ability to place these devices in separate buildings in case of natural disaster.

Fibre Channel allows for not only the transmission of SCSI commands but also the transmission of video and network. Fibre Channel depends on Fibre Channel hubs or Fibre Channel switches to connect PCs and devices together. There can be 126 devices on a Fibre Channel chain. Fibre Channel chains are actually loops like in a ring network.

Devices can all be connected to a hub, to a switch, or from device to device. If the devices are all connected to a hub or a switch, they can be hot-swappable without disrupting the whole Fibre Channel loop, as hot-swapping would if the devices were connected from one to another.

There are differences in the setups for SCSI and Fibre Channel. SCSI has cable length limitations of 3 meters, but Fibre Channel can have 30 meters between devices (with distances totaling 10 km). Data rates on the SCSI chain are 20 MBps, and Fibre Channel supports up to 1 GBps. Fibre Channel can also use copper cabling or even twisted pair with some reduction of functionality.

All Fibre Channel devices have what is called a Gigabit Interface Converter (GBIC), which is a plug-in module that is specific to the type of cable being plugged into the device (note that there are different types of fiber optic cable). The GBIC will convert electrical signals to optical signals and vice versa.

The specific GBIC required can be placed in a hub, switch, or external device, or even in the Fibre Channel adapter on a server or workstation. This modularization allows for easier upgrade; if the cabling changes, then only the module needs replacing, not the whole adapter (or even the hubs and switches).

Software Components   Once the hardware portion of the cluster is implemented, then the actual components need setting up in the operating system itself. This is the portion of the cluster that will make it specific to the requirements and application used in your setup. These components are the basis of how the applications will be managed by the cluster. The software components of a cluster are listed here:

- **Resources**   These are logical entities that are controlled by the cluster. These resources can be active on only one node of the cluster at any given time.

- **Dependencies**   Dependencies are when one resource depends on another resource for functionality. If any resource should fail, then so would any resource that depends upon the resource that failed. For example, the DHCP service would depend upon the physical disk and IP address. Should either of these two resources fail, so would the DHCP service.

■ **Groups**   A *group* is a collection of *resources*. If a resource within a group fails, the entire group will fail over to another node (depending on the failover settings configured for the group). A group can be owned by only one node at a time. If one or all resources fail, then the group as a whole will change ownership, not individual resources.

■ **Failover**   *Failover* is the process of a group being moved from one node to another when a resource fails within the group. Groups can be set to retry the failed resource a certain number of times before the group is moved to the other resource.

■ **Failback**   Failback is the process of moving a group back to the original cluster node when it comes back online. For example, if Node A should fail, its groups can fail over to Node B. Once Node A comes back online, groups can be configured to failback to the original node.

■ **Quorum Resource**   The Quorum Resource is the shared disk for the cluster that holds the database of cluster information. The database information contains data necessary to recover the cluster. The Quorum Resource must be a physical disk resource. This allows for any node to have control of the Quorum Resource to update the node's local database in case of corruption. If a node joins a cluster, but no other node is active, then the node can still join the cluster, instead of making a new cluster, by retrieving the database information.

How Clustering Works

In a cluster configuration, the nodes can detect one another's status and availability. This is one of the most important features of the Cluster service. The communication between cluster nodes is crucial to the availability of the resources. The ongoing communication between the nodes allows the Cluster service to monitor the status and availability of the nodes as well as the status of cluster resources. It uses this information to determine when resources need to fail over to another cluster member.

RPC   RPC (Remote Procedure Call) is a communication mechanism by which applications can make a call on a remote computer and is the mechanism by which cluster nodes communicate. It uses IPC (interprocess communication) mechanisms to call program functions on remote computers. RPC is synchronous in nature, which means that there must be a reliable high-speed network connection between the two computers. When a call is made on a remote system, a response is required. With RPC, a server can act as a client and make a remote procedure call on another network server. Due to the synchronous nature of RPC, the client will then wait for a reply containing the results of the procedure's execution. The Cluster service uses RPCs for node-to-node communication and to monitor the status of cluster resources. It allows a cluster component on one node to make a call to a cluster component on another node.

Resource Monitor   One of the most important functions of the Cluster service is its ability to monitor the status of cluster resources. At least one resource monitor resides on each cluster node and is responsible for monitoring the status of each cluster resource using Remote Procedure Calls (RPCs). It tracks resource status by polling the cluster resources at certain intervals. Through RPCs, the resource monitor checks the status of resources using two different polling intervals, "LooksAlive" poll intervals and "IsAlive" poll intervals.

- "LooksAlive" poll intervals are simple checks that the Resource Manager performs on a resource to determine if it is still running.
- "IsAlive" poll intervals are more thorough checks used to determine the status of a resource (online or offline).

The resource monitor passes the information to the Resource Manager. The Resource Manager then uses the information to initiate certain actions such as restart or failover. The RPC service on each cluster node needs to be running so that the status of each resource can be monitored.

Heartbeats   The Cluster service is constantly monitoring the health of the network and the nodes by sending heartbeat messages to other nodes in the cluster. Heartbeat messages generated by the Node Manager on each cluster member are used to monitor the online status of cluster members. Heartbeat messages are exchanged between the cluster nodes at regular intervals of 1.2 seconds. The heartbeat messages are exchanged using UDP (User Datagram Protocol) port 3343.

Node Manager   The Cluster service is composed of several components that are each known as managers. One of these components is known as the Node Manager. The primary responsibility of the Node Manager is to track the status of other nodes in the cluster and to pass the information on to the Resource Manager. The Node Manager runs on each cluster member and maintains a list of all other nodes within the cluster. The Node Managers on each cluster member communicate with each other through heartbeat messages. The Node Manager on each node tracks the status of the other cluster members by generating heartbeat messages and waiting for a reply. The Node Manager is also responsible for responding to any heartbeat messages it receives from the other cluster members. If the Node Manager on one of the cluster members fails to respond to a heartbeat message, it is assumed to be offline.

A cluster node can basically be in one of three states as listed here:

- **Offline**   A node that is in an offline state may not be running, the Cluster service itself may not be started, or the service may have failed on startup and not be responding to heartbeat messages.

- **Online**   A node that is in an online state is a fully functional member of the cluster. It can own groups and resources and is producing or responding to heartbeat messages.

- **Paused**   A node that is in a paused state is still a functioning member of the cluster. The only difference between a node that is online and one that is paused is that a paused node cannot own any resource groups. A node that is in a paused state still responds or generates heartbeat messages.

Recovering from Cluster Node Failure

If a node in the cluster becomes damaged due to a failure such as a hard disk failure or to corrupt or missing system files or cluster registry entries, you can use the Automated System Recovery (ASR) disk set to restore the failed node (automated system recovery is discussed later in the chapter). In order to use the recovery process outlined here, you must have created the ASR floppy and backup media using the Windows Server 2003 Backup utility. To recover a failed cluster node:

1. Restart the computer using the Windows Server 2003 installation CD.
2. During the text mode portion of setup, press F2.
3. Insert the ASR floppy disk when prompted.
4. Follow the onscreen instructions. Once the restore process is complete, the node can rejoin the cluster.

As already mentioned earlier, the Quorum Resource is crucial to the cluster. If the quorum data becomes corrupt, it can be restored using the Backup utility. Once you start the restore process, select the option to Restore The Cluster Registry To The Quorum Disk And All Other Nodes. Doing so will stop the Cluster service on the local computer and restore the cluster configuration information. Once the computer is restarted, the service will be stopped on all other nodes. The quorum data will be restored to the quorum disk and all other nodes within the cluster. You can then proceed to restart the service on the remaining cluster nodes.

Planning for the Cluster Service

With proper implementation, the Cluster service can provide an effective solution for increasing the availability of mission-critical services and applications. Before going ahead and implementing a clustering solution, prior planning is required. This ensures the technology is implemented in a way that meets a company's requirements and helps the actual installation process to go much more smoothly. Prior planning eliminates the need of having to make last-minute decisions during the installation. When planning for the Cluster service, some of the points to consider include

- Choosing the cluster model to implement
- Planning the failover and failback policies to be used
- Planning the private network used for cluster communication
- Choosing the applications to run on a cluster

Choosing a Cluster Model

A cluster can be implemented using different models. The models range in complexity from a single-node cluster to a multiple-node cluster. The various models include

- Single-node cluster
- Hot standby
- High-availability model

on the
job

These are three of the cluster models that can be implemented. There are other variations of these models that can be implemented.

Single-Node Cluster   This model has only a single node in the cluster. There is no failover ability for the applications. This model will provide for ease of administration to manage resources and the groups. Also, with configuration of the groups and resources, if a group or resource fails, the server can attempt to automatically restart the group or resource. The single-node cluster model also provides for future scalability by adding a second node to provide fault tolerance. The availability of applications in this model is a little higher than normal, but not much. If the server hardware should fail, then all resources are offline to clients.

Hot Standby   In this model, one node is a spare in case of failure of the other node. In other words, one node remains idle while the other services client requests. This model will run all of the groups on one node, with the other node sitting idle ready to assume responsibility should the first node fail. This allows for one server with a lot of processing power, and the other node has just enough to manage the groups that are failed over until the original node comes back online. The second node does not have to be inferior hardware; the two can be equal in processing power, depending on how critical the resource is to the organization to keep functioning.

For example, if Node A is running a critical SMTP service in Group 1 and Node B is running no groups, and Node A fails, then Node B starts the Group 1 and will run Group 1 until Node A comes back online (if failback is enabled), Node B fails, or Group 1 is moved back to Node A manually.

This model provides for very high availability for mission-critical applications for an organization.

High-Availability Model   In this model, each node controls some of the resources; for instance, each node may have a group for balancing processing loads. The servers should each have the same hardware to provide for the ability to handle both groups if one node fails.

For example, if Node A is running Group 1 and Node B is running Group 2, then in case of a node failure, each node should be able to handle the processing load of its group and the group of the other node. If Node A fails, then Node B should have the processing power to run both Group 1 and Group 2.

This model provides for high availability and is best suited for file and print sharing.

Planning a Failover and Failback Strategy

Failover occurs when an application or service running on one node fails. When this occurs, the application or service can be restarted on another node in the cluster. Before you implement a cluster, you should decide how you want failover to occur between cluster nodes. For example, if there are more than two nodes in a cluster, you can specify which nodes a resource can fail over to by specifying a possible owner list.

What you need to consider is whether you want an application or service to preferentially run and which nodes in the cluster you want it to fail over to. When determining this, consider the hardware and current load already placed on other cluster nodes. If an application or service fails over to another node in the cluster, that node must have the hardware and performance level to run the resource.

When considering failover, you must also think about the topic of failback. This occurs when a resources is moved back to the original node once it is detected to be online again. For example, if the original node is more equipped to run the application or service, you may want to configure a failback policy so that the resource will immediately fail back to the original node when it comes back online.

Planning the Private Network

Each cluster member will need at least one PCI network adapter. The recommended configuration is to have two network adapters per node to connect to the network, as using one network adapter per node creates a single point of failure. One network adapter will be used to connect the cluster members to the public network (client-to-cluster communication). This adapter will carry the client-to-cluster traffic. The second network adapter will be used to connect the cluster members to a private network (node-to-node communication). The private network will consist of only the cluster members, and the adapters on the private network will carry traffic only between the two cluster members.

You will also need to determine how IP addresses will be assigned to the cluster nodes. A DHCP server can assign the IP addresses, or they can be static. Keep in mind that if you use a DHCP server to assign IP addresses to your cluster nodes, this becomes a single point of failure. In other words, if the DHCP server becomes unavailable, so may the cluster nodes. To eliminate this single point of failure, consider assigning each of the network adapters a static IP address.

Choosing Applications for Clustering

First of all, you will need to determine which applications and services are critical to the operation of a business. These are the ones you will want to configure in a cluster environment to ensure availability. Next, you need to determine which applications and services can actually be installed in a cluster environment. Some applications and services cannot be installed in a cluster. These are the criteria that an application must meet in order to take advantage of the failback capabilities:

- The application must use TCP/IP. Any applications that use IPX/SPX or NetBEUI will not be supported. For example, Exchange uses TCP/IP and therefore can function within a cluster.

- The applications must be able to specify where the data is stored. In order to fully take advantage of failover, the data should be stored on the shared disks.

- Client applications must be able to recover from temporary failure. If the client loses connectivity for a few moments as failover occurs, it should be able to re-establish connectivity.

Applications can be grouped into two categories: cluster aware and cluster unaware. Applications that are cluster aware support the Cluster API. This means the applications can register with the Cluster service to receive status and notification information. A cluster-aware application can still be used within a cluster and fail over as long as it meets the criteria listed.

Introduction to Network Load Balancing

Network Load Balancing is the ability to cluster up to 32 servers to act as one server. This type of clustering is not the same as the clustering covered in the preceding section. With Network Load Balancing, there are multiple servers with the same services installed. These servers can then be accessed by a large number of clients, with the requests being balanced between the multiple servers.

The services used with Network Load Balancing are web services (WWW and FTP), terminal services, streaming media services, virtual private network (VPN) services, and other mission-critical applications. This allows for multiple servers to be used to offer these resources for clients and have the ability to offer the clients the best service by connecting them to the least busy server.

For example, if a company had several servers (a maximum of 32 per cluster) running its company Internet site (each server hosting a copy of the same web pages), as a large number of users on the Internet access the company's web site, they will be directed to the least busy server, which will answer their request for a web page. This will allow all of the clients to have a fast answer to their request for the web pages they require rather than all of the clients accessing one server and having to wait for their requests to be fulfilled by the overburdened server.

How Network Load Balancing Works

When a client accesses a Network Load Balanced cluster, each node receives the packet being sent from the client. Each node compares the incoming packet to its port rules and uses them to determine whether it should accept or reject the packet. Once a node has accepted a packet, it must then determine if another node has the same port rule set and if the node is online. If it is the only node with the port rule or the only one with the port rule that is online, it processes and responds to the packets sent by the client. If the node is not the only node online with the required port rule to accept a packet, then the node with the highest handling priority (or the lowest value) will process and respond to the packet.

Now if all nodes are set for Multiple Hosts Filtering Mode, then as traffic comes from the clients, each node runs an algorithm based on client IP address, the port the packet is destined for, and other information to determine which node will manage the packet. The algorithm used to determine which node will manage the client request is the Statistical Mapping Algorithm.

All nodes of the Network Load Balanced cluster will communicate with one another through multicasting or broadcasting to the cluster name. All nodes receive the packet and will determine which nodes are online or offline and also which nodes have been added to or left the cluster. Once this has been determined, the Unique ID is determined for each node to see if the priorities have changed; this will determine if a different node is now supposed to be managing all of the default traffic. Once all the nodes agree, this is called convergence. Once convergence has been achieved, an entry will be written to the Event log on each node in the System log with an Event ID of 29.

A problem with Network Load Balancing is that smart hubs, or those that act like switches, will keep track of the IP address of the PC attached to the physical ports of the hub. This way, it can send a packet destined for an IP address to its specific port on the hub. This causes problems with nodes that are using only one network adapter, since the hub will track only one address and will not be able to manage the same IP address on multiple hub ports. You will have to make sure that the hub will support multiple addresses on one individual hub port and one IP address on multiple hub ports.

Network Load Balancing Monitor

Windows Server 2003 comes with a tool that can be used to create and manage Network Load Balancing clusters from a single computer. The utility is known as the Network Load Balancing Monitor. The Network Load Balancing Monitor can be used to perform the following tasks:

- Create new clusters.
- Add new hosts to a cluster. This in turn enables NLB on the remote computer and allows you to remotely configure its parameters.
- Remove hosts from a cluster.
- Configure the properties of the cluster and individual cluster hosts.
- Replicate cluster configuration information to other hosts.
- Troubleshoot cluster problems.

on the job *The Network Load Balancing Monitor can be installed on a computer running Windows XP. This allows you to remotely configure and manage Windows Server 2003 computers with Network Load Balancing enabled.*

WLBS Cluster Control Utility

The Network Load Balancing control utility can be used to manage and control Network Load Balancing once it is configured. The utility can be used on a local cluster node or used from a remote computer that has connectivity (LAN or WAN) with the cluster hosts. The syntax for the command is nlb *command [remote options][/h]*. Table 8-1 summarizes some of the parameters that can be used with the command.

exam

⚙atch *WLBS.exe has been replaced by NLB.exe (Network Load Balancing control utility).*

TABLE 8-1	NLB.exe Command-Line Parameters

Parameter	Description
Suspend	Suspends all cluster operations until the resume command is issued.
Resume	Resumes all cluster operations after they have been suspended.
Start	Starts cluster operations.
Stop	Stops cluster operations.
Drainstop	Disables all new traffic handling. Current connections are maintained, but no new connections are accepted.
Ip2mac	Disables the media access control corresponding to the specified cluster name or IP address.
Params	Displays information about your current Network Load Balancing configuration.
Display	Displays extensive information about your current Network Load Balancing configuration, cluster state, and past cluster activity.

Planning for Network Load Balancing

Like the Cluster service, Network Load Balancing requires a certain amount of prior planning as well. For example, you must do some capacity planning to determine the number of hosts that are required. Planning for NLB includes

- Choosing an NLB model
- Performing a risk assessment
- Capacity planning

Choosing an NLB Model

There are basically four different NLB models for single or multiple adapters running in unicast or multicast mode. Multicast refers to sending a packet to multiple hosts, whereas unicast refers to sending a packet to a single host. The four models include

- Single adapter in unicast mode
- Multiple adapters in unicast mode
- Single adapter in multicast mode
- Multiple adapters in multicast mode

Single Adapter in Unicast Mode   This NLB model is the simplest and least expensive to implement. With this model, each host is configured with a single network adapter card that is configured to run in unicast mode. The main disadvantage to this model is that network performance may be compromised. The single network adapter card has to carry normal network traffic as well as traffic between hosts in the cluster.

Multiple Adapter in Unicast Mode   With this model, each host is configured with multiple network adapters that are running in unicast mode. This model tends to be preferred over all others. A disadvantage, however, is the slight increase in cost to purchase multiple adapters for each server. The advantage is that one adapter can be connected to a private network to handle load-balancing traffic, while the other adapter can be used for client-to-server traffic only.

Single Adapter in Multicast Mode   With this model, each server is configured with a single network adapter that is running in multicast mode. This model is preferred over using a single adapter in unicast mode because it allows for regular communication between load-balanced servers. However, routers must support multicasting, and performance may still be degraded because both the client-to-server traffic and server-to-server traffic are going through a single adapter.

Multiple Adapters in Multicast Mode   With the model, each server is configured with multiple network adapters that are running in multicast mode. Again, there is an increase in cost because multiple network adapters must be purchased and some routers may not support multicasting. On the other hand, client-to-server and server-to-server traffic can be segmented, thereby improving performance.

INSIDE THE EXAM

More on Network Load Balancing

Network Load Balancing can operate in two different modes: unicast and multicast. In order to choose an NLB model, you should be aware of the difference between the two. In unicast mode, the media access control (MAC) address of the cluster is assigned to the server's network adapter. In other words, the built-in MAC address is replaced by the cluster's MAC address. In multicast mode, both the MAC address assigned to the cluster and the built-in MAC address are used.

Risk Assessment

One of the main purposes of NLB is to increase availability of services and applications. However, a Network Load Balancing cluster is effective only if single points of failure are eliminated. For example, not taking steps to protect your cluster from power outages (installing a UPS) can result in the entire cluster going offline. A good implementation plan would identify these single points of failure so that they will not impact the performance of a cluster. Table 8-2 outlines some other common points of failure and solutions that can be implemented to avoid them.

on the Job

When you are planning for the Cluster service, you should also perform a risk assessment and use the information summarized in Table 8-2 to identify and eliminate single points of failure.

Capacity Planning

When planning for Network Load Balancing, you need to determine how many clients can access a server with the services and be able to run the applications with few or no access problems. Then determine your anticipated number of clients and divide the number of anticipated clients by the number of clients that accessed a single server with no problems. Round the number up and that will be the number of nodes you will require in your Network Load Balancing cluster. If the number of clients anticipated becomes greater, then add servers to keep the cluster performance at an acceptable level. Always make sure the nodes will be able to handle the extra load placed upon them if one server should fail.

TABLE 8-2   Some Single Points of Failure and Recommended Solutions

Point of Failure	Solution
DHCP	Assign static IP addresses to all interfaces on the cluster nodes.
Disks	Implement hardware- or software-level RAID for the private disks. Use hardware-level RAID on the shared disk/disks.
Hardware failure	Always ensure there are spare parts on hand such as controller cards and drives.
Power outages	UPS devices should be used to provide power in case of power failures.
Routers/hubs/etc.	Have spare components on hand; implement redundant routes.
Network cards	Configure each cluster node with at least two network cards.
Authentication	Make the cluster nodes domain controllers in their own domains so that they do not become dependent on an external server for authentication.

Once you have determined the number of servers that will be in the cluster, you can then look specifically at the hardware that will be required. This will be based on the type of applications that will be running on the server and the number of clients that will be accessing them. For example, some applications may be hard disk intensive, while others are CPU intensive.

EXERCISE 8-1

Planning for the Cluster Service

The Cluster service is used to increase the availability of mission-critical applications and services. However, a cluster is not a fail-proof solution. Any single point of failure on the network can impact the performance of a cluster and as a result make the clustered applications and services unavailable to users. In this exercise, you will list the many single points of failure on a network that may impact a cluster. Discuss how they can impact a cluster and how they can be eliminated.

CERTIFICATION OBJECTIVE 8.02

Identifying System Bottlenecks

A bottleneck can occur when a system resource or component is not operating efficiently, is performing slowly, or is not large enough. In other words, a component is not performing as it should under a given load and therefore is impacting the overall performance of a system. For example, the disk subsystem may be too slow on a file server, or there may be insufficient RAM. The only way to pinpoint bottlenecks on a system is to regularly monitor server performance.

Introduction to Monitoring Server Performance

Part of regular server maintenance should include monitoring server performance. Once you are familiar with how a server behaves under a certain load, system bottlenecks will be much easier to detect before they begin to seriously degrade server performance. The following section will look at how you can monitor performance on a computer running Windows Server 2003 and some of the key system components that should be monitored on a regular basis.

System Monitor

Windows Server 2003 includes a tool called System Monitor that can be used to monitor the real-time performance of system components, services, and applications on a local or remote computer. System Monitor can be used to perform the following tasks:

- Collect real-time performance data for system components, services, and applications.
- Configure what aspects of each component you want to monitor.
- Control which users are able to view performance data locally or across the network by using the Performance Monitor Users and the Performance Log Users groups.
- View real-time data.
- Save data in a log file for later analysis.
- Display captured data in various forms such as a graph or histogram.
- Create monitoring configurations that can be used on other computers.

System Monitor allows you to monitor the performance of hardware, services, and applications installed on a computer. You can further define what you want to collect performance information on through the following:

- **The type of data you want to collect**   Different services, applications, and hardware are represented as performance objects. Each performance object has its own set of performance counters. The counters determine what aspects of a particular object you want to monitor. If multiple instances of an object exist (such as two network interfaces), you can select which instance to monitor.

- **Where the data will be collected from** You can use System Monitor to gather statistics about the local computer, or you can use it to monitor remote computers.

- **How the data will be collected** The sampling parameters allow you to define manual sampling, on-demand sampling, or automatic sampling.

Using System Monitor System Monitor is automatically installed with Windows Server 2003. To open the Performance console, click Start, point to Administrative Tools, and click Performance. You will find the System Monitor utility within the Performance console (see Figure 8-1). When System Monitor is initially opened, three counters are monitored by default. These are

- **Memory** Pages/Sec
- **Physical Disk** Avg. Disk Queue Length
- **Processor** % Processor Time

on the
Job

The performance objects that can be monitored will vary from computer to computer depending on the components that are installed.

FIGURE 8-1

The Performance
console

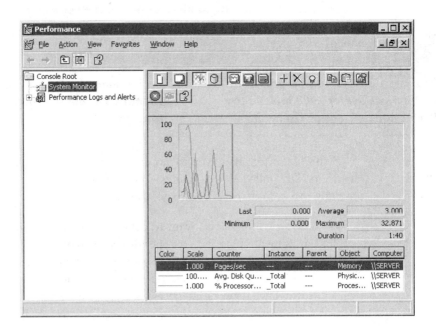

Chances are you will want to monitor other performance objects and counters. To add a counter to System Monitor:

1. Click Start, point to Administrative Tools, and click Performance.

2. Right-click the System Monitor details pane and click Add Counter or click the Add button on the toolbar (represented by a plus sign).

3. To monitor the local computer, select Use Local Computer Counters. To monitor another computer on the network, click Select Counters From Computer and specify the computer name or IP address.

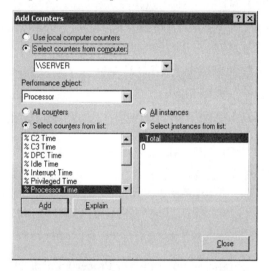

4. Use the Performance Object box to select the specific object you want to monitor. Once you select an object, the related counters are displayed.

5. Select All Counters to monitor all counters related to the performance object. To select specific counters, click Select Counters From List. Click each counter you want to monitor and click Add. You will also notice an Explain button that provides information about the various counters.

6. To monitor all instances associated with a counter, select All Instances. Otherwise, click Select Instances From List and select the instance to monitor.

7. Click Close.

Before you can perform the procedure just outlined, you must be a member of the Administrators group, the Performance Logs Users group, or the Performance Monitor Users group. Alternatively, you can delegate a user account the necessary permissions.

Adding a User to the Performance Monitor Users Group

In this exercise, you will create a new user account and add it to the Performance Monitor Users group.

1. Click Start, point to Administrative Tools, and click Active Directory Users And Computers.

2. Right-click the Users container, point to New, and click User.

3. Type in a first name and a last name for the new user. Type in the user logon name. Click Next.

4. Enter a password for the user account. Click Next.

5. Click Finish.

6. Click the Builtin container. In the details pane, right-click Performance Monitor Users and click Properties.

7. Click the Members tab and click Add.

8. Enter the name of the user account you created in step 3. Click OK. Click OK to close the group's properties dialog box. The new user will now have permission to gather statistics using System Monitor.

From the System Monitor Properties dialog box, you can further customize the settings. To do so, click the Properties button located on the toolbar. Using the General tab, you can configure how you want to view the data (graph, histogram, or report), the display elements, and the counter values for a report or histogram (see Figure 8-2). Using the Sample Automatically Every option, you can define the sampling interval (the default value is every 1 second). This determines the rate at which statistics for counters are refreshed.

Using the settings available on the Source tab, you can specify where data should be displayed from (see Figure 8-3). You have three options: you can view the values for the current activity displayed, for data stored in an existing log file, or for data stored in an SQL database. For example, you can save data you collect to a log file and view the information at a later date. The remaining tabs can be used to further customize how information is displayed within System Monitor.

FIGURE 8-2

Using the
General tab
to customize
System Monitor

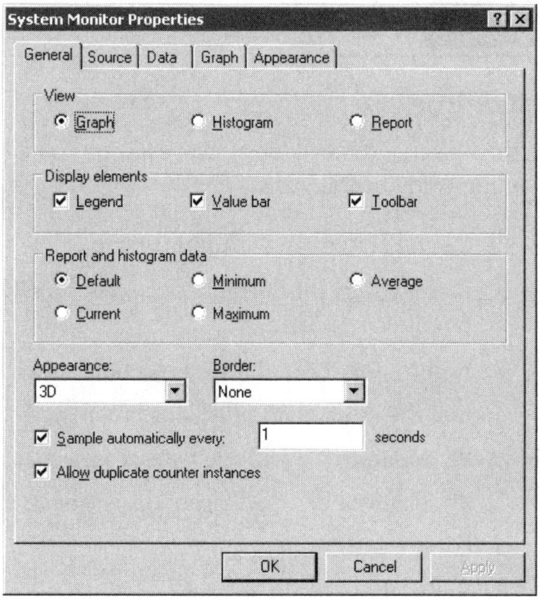

FIGURE 8-3

Using the Source
tab to specify
where data is
displayed from

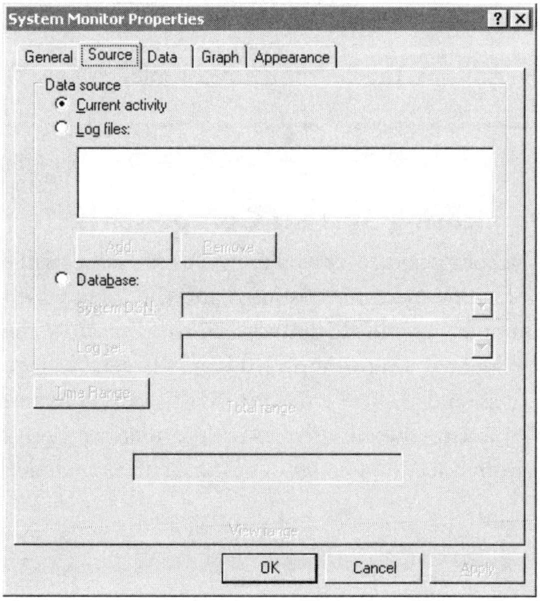

EXERCISE 8-3

Using System Monitor

In this exercise, you will use System Monitor to monitor the performance of a computer running Windows Server 2003.

1. Click Start, point to Administrative Tools, and click Performance.

2. From within the Performance console, select the System Monitor icon if it is not already selected.

3. Right click the graph in the details pane and click Add Counters.

4. Use the Add Counters dialog box to add the following counters:

   ■ **Memory**   Available Bytes, Page Faults/sec, Page Reads/sec, Page Writes/sec

   ■ **Paging File**   %Usage, %Usage Peak

5. Click Close.

6. Right-click the graph again and select Properties.

7. From the System Monitor Properties dialog box, click the General tab.

8. Change the amount of time that the statistics are gathered to 5 seconds. Click OK.

9. Close the Performance console.

Monitoring System Components

The components that you monitor on a server will of course depend upon what services and applications are installed and the role the server is playing on the network. For example, you may focus more on the disk subsystem when monitoring a file server as opposed to monitoring an Exchange server. On top of this, there are four different areas that should always be monitored on a server as part of the server maintenance routine. Monitoring these four areas on a regular basis can help you establish a baseline of performance for a server. These four areas include

■ Memory

■ Processor

■ Disk

■ Network

Memory   Inadequate RAM is one of the areas that can severely impact server performance. Yet it is also one of the least expensive ways of increasing server performance. Since RAM plays such an important role in server performance, it should be monitored on a regular basis. The two most important counters that you should monitor are

- **Pages/sec**   This counter can give an administrator an overall idea of how memory is working (both physical and virtual). The value of this counter indicates the number of pages being moved between RAM and the paging file per second. If this value is continually over 75%, RAM may be a bottleneck on the server.
- **Available Bytes**   This counter simply indicates the amount of RAM waiting to be used. If this counter is continually low, the RAM may need to be upgraded.

Processor   Probably the most important hardware component within a server is the processor. Everything a server does requires processor time. When monitoring the System object, the two counters you should pay close attention to are

- **% Total Process Time**   This provides an indication as to how much processor time is spent executing nonidle threads.
- **Processor Queue Length**   This counter indicates the length of the processor queue. A value that is continuously over 4 may indicate that the processor needs to be upgraded or additional processors added.

Disk   When monitoring the disk, you will want to gather performance information for both the logical disk and the physical disk. The counters that should be monitored regularly include

- **Logical Disk: % Free Space**   This counter will display the amount of free space for a partition. You should be monitoring the system partition at a minimum.
- **Logical Disk: % Disk Time**   This counter measures the amount of time that a disk is busy servicing read/write requests. A value that is continuously over 80% would indicate that an upgrade may be necessary.
- **Physical Disk: Avg. Disk Queue Length**   This counter provides an indication as to the amount of disk activity. If this value is continuously over 4, an upgrade may be required.

Network   Although there are a number of tools available to monitor network performance, System Monitor can be used to gather some basic statistics as to how a server is responding on a network.

- **Network Interface: Output Queue Length**   A value over 3 would indicate a bottleneck.
- **Redirector: Network Errors/sec**   This value indicates the rate at which unexpected errors are occurring. A high value would indicate a serious communication problem.

on the
Job   *Numerous counters are available within System Monitor, and it is almost impossible to know what each is for. If you highlight a specific counter, you can click the Explain button and an explanation about the counter will appear.*

CERTIFICATION OBJECTIVE 8.03

Monitoring Network Services

Over time, a number of changes can take place that can impact an existing network. Networks can increase in size, new shares added, and new applications and services installed. Part of maintaining a network includes monitoring network services to ensure they continue to perform at an acceptable level as a network changes and grows.

Network administrators must ensure that the network continues to perform efficiently over time. By monitoring network services, you can gather information that can be used for troubleshooting, for capacity planning, to establish a baseline that can help identify changes in performance over time, and for putting together performance level reports. Several tools included with Windows Server 2003 can be used to monitor network services. These tools include Network Monitor, Event Viewer, and Service Dependencies.

Network Monitor

Network Monitor is a tool included with Windows Server 2003 that can be used to monitor and log network activity. The statistics gathered can be used to manage and optimize network traffic by identifying unnecessary protocols and misconfigured workstations, as well as detecting problems with network applications and services. Some of the features included with Network Monitor include

- **Display filters**   Display filters allow you to view specific data from a capture according to the criteria you specify.
- **Capture filters**   Capture filters allow you to state criteria to specify the type of data that should be captured.
- **Triggers**   Triggers enable certain actions to be performed depending on the content of a packet.

Network Monitor consists of two components:

- **Network Monitor Driver**   This component is responsible for capturing the frames traveling to and from a network adapter.
- **Network Monitor Tools**   The Network Monitor Tools provide the ability to view and analyze the data captured by the Network Monitor Driver.

You can use Network Monitor to capture performance data remotely. To do so, install the Network Monitor Driver on the computer you want to monitor. On your workstation, install the Network Monitor Tools. The tools are required because you need to be able to view and analyze the data that is captured.

Installing Network Monitor

By default, Network Monitor is not installed. It is a relatively simple process, however, to add it. You can use these steps to install Network Monitor, keeping in mind that installing Network Monitor automatically installs the Network Monitor Driver:

1. Click Start, point to Control Panel, and click Add or Remove Programs.
2. Click Add/Remove Windows Components.
3. Within the Windows Component Wizard, select Management And Monitoring Tools, and click the Details button.

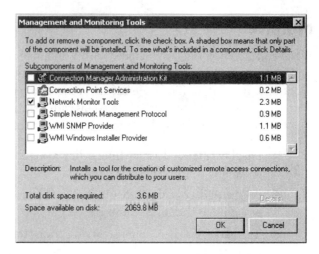

4. Select the Network Monitor Tools check box. Click OK.

5. Click Next. Click OK.

Since Network Monitor can be used to view information about packets being sent across a network, Network Monitor should be used only by authorized users. To prevent unauthorized users from running the utility, Network Monitor can display other instances running on the network. It will display information such as the computer name, where the instance is installed, and the user currently logged onto the computer.

In some cases you may want to install only the Network Monitor Driver. Installing the driver enables you to capture traffic traveling to and from a network interface. However, there is no utility installed to view the captured data. Therefore, you would need to use an application such as SMS to view the captured data. This is useful when you want to capture traffic from multiple computers and view the captures data from a central location. To install the Network Monitor Driver component only, perform the following steps:

1. Within the Network Connections applet, right-click the Local Area Connection and choose Properties from the pop-up menu.

2. From the properties dialog box for the Local Area Connection, click Install.

3. In the list, click Protocol and then click Add.

4. Within the Network Protocol dialog box, click the Network Monitor Driver.

5. Click OK.

Using Network Monitor

After installing Network Monitor, a shortcut to launch the console is added to the Administrative Tools menu. To open Network Monitor, click Start, point to Administrative Tools, and click Network Monitor. When the Network Monitor console is first opened, four panes are displayed within the console (see Figure 8-4). The Graph pane displays the network activity in a bar chart. The Session Stats pane displays information about individual sessions established with the computer. The Station Stats pane displays statistics about the sessions in which the server is participating in. The Total Stats pane provides you with a summary of the statistics since the capture was started.

To start using Network Monitor, you must first start a capture. To do so, click the Start option from the Capture menu. Once a capture is started, all frames going to and from the computer are captured. To view the captured data, click the Stop And View option from the Capture menu. Network Monitor displays all the frames captured during the capture period within a Summary window. You can view specific information about a frame by selecting it within the Summary window (see Figure 8-5).

FIGURE 8-4

The Network
Monitor console

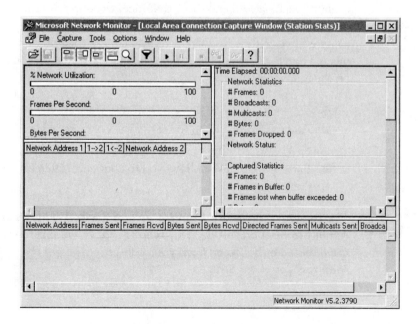

FIGURE 8-5

Viewing detailed
information
about a frame

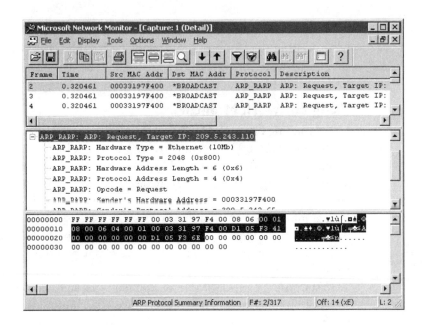

Capture Filters Once a capture is started, Network Monitor captures all frames. During a lengthy capture, a large number of frames may be captured. You can configure a capture filter to define a set of criteria that must be met. Network Monitor will examine each packet, and those that meet the criteria are captured. This allows an administrator to use Network Monitor to capture specific types of traffic. To configure capture filters within Network Monitor, choose the Filter option from the Capture menu. From the Capture Filter dialog box (see Figure 8-6), you can create filters based on the following criteria:

- **Protocol** Used to specify the protocol or specific protocol properties.
- **Address Pairs** Used to specify the computer addresses from which frames should be captured.
- **Pattern Matches** Allows you to configure different variables that captured frames should meet.

The version of Network Monitor included with Windows Server 2003 does not run in promiscuous mode. This means that it will intercept only packets that are directed either to or from your computer. To get the full version of Network Monitor, you need SMS.

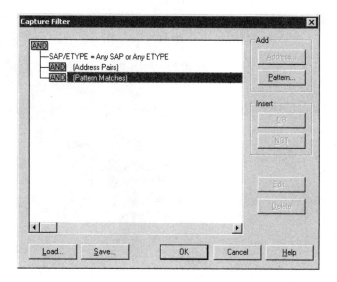

FIGURE 8-6

Configuring
a capture filter

Display Filters   Network Monitor makes it easy for administrators to filter captured traffic according to the criteria you specify. For example, if you want to view all captured packets for a specific protocol, you can configure a display filter. To configure a display filter, select the Filter option from the Capture menu after you have run Network Monitor and captured the network traffic.

Triggers   Using triggers, certain actions can be performed when specific criteria defined by an administrator are met. Network Monitor will examine the contents of each packet. Any captured packets that meet the defined conditions will trigger a specific action to be taken. To configure a trigger, click the Capture menu and click Trigger (see Figure 8-7). When the trigger criteria are met, you can have any of the following actions occur:

■ The computer will beep.

■ Network Monitor will stop capturing frames.

■ A command-line program will be executed.

FIGURE 8-7

Configuring
a trigger

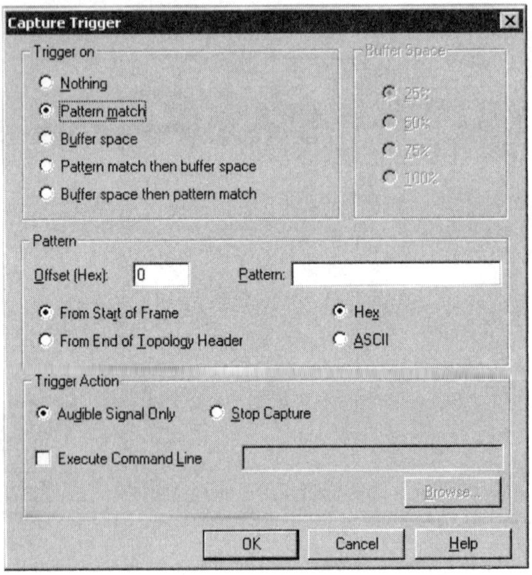

Event Viewer

The Windows Server 2003 Event Viewer is used to view the contents of various log files. Every computer running Windows Server 2003 has three default log files: Application, System, and Security. Depending on the role the server is configured in, there may also be additional log files. For example, a server running the DNS service will also have a DNS log, or a computer configured as a domain controller will also contain two additional log files: the File Replication service log and the Directory Service log. The various logs available for viewing within the Event Viewer include

- **Application**   Events generated by applications and programs running on the computer.
- **Security**   Events generated as outlined in the audit policy. For example, if unsuccessful logon attempts are being audited, any failed logon attempts are recorded in the security log.
- **System**   Events generated by Windows system components.
- **Directory Service**   Events generated by Active Directory. This log file is available only on computers running Active Directory.

- **File Replication Service** Events generated by the Windows File Replication service. This log is available only on those computers running Active Directory.
- **DNS Server** Events generated by the DNS service. This log file is available only on those computers running DNS.

You can open the Event Viewer console by clicking Start, pointing to Administrative Tools, and selecting Event Viewer (see Figure 8-8).

Once you select one of the available log files, the entries are displayed within the right pane (see Figure 8-9).

Interpreting Events

Each event contains detailed information that can be useful when troubleshooting various problems. You can view more information about an event by double-clicking it within the details pane. The event header information is summarized in Table 8-3.

Different types of events can be recorded within a log file. The types of events recorded will depend on the log file you are examining. There are five possible event types that can be recorded. They are summarized in Table 8-4.

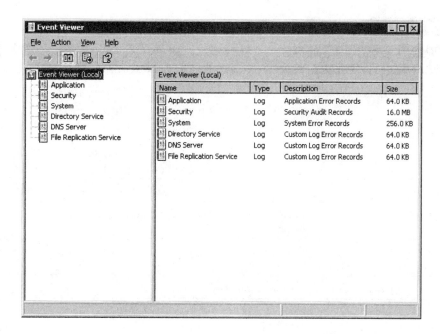

FIGURE 8-8

Windows Server 2003 Event Viewer

FIGURE 8-9

Viewing the
contents of
a log file

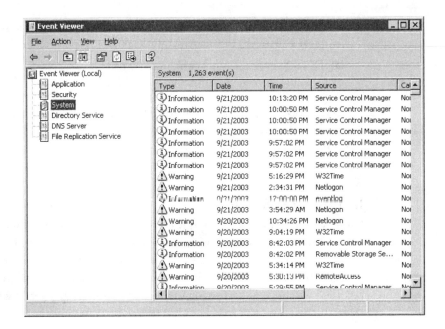

TABLE 8-3   Information Logged for Each Event

Information	Description
Date	The date when the event occurred.
Time	The specific time of day that the event occurred.
User	The name of the user under which the event occurred.
Computer	The name of the computer the event occurred on. Normally, this is the local computer unless you are viewing the contents of a log file on a remote computer.
Source	The component that generated the event. This can be a program or a system component.
Event	This is a number identifying the event that has occurred. This can be used by support personnel to troubleshoot the event.
Type	This defines the type of event. The system and application logs define an event as a warning, error, or information.
Classification	This defines the classification of the event by the event source.

TABLE 8-4   Event Types Logged Within Event Viewer

Event Type	Description
Information	Describes a successful event.
Warning	Indicates that an event occurred that may lead to a significant problem.
Error	A significant problem has occurred.
Success Audit	Indicates that an audited event successfully occurred.
Failure Audit	Indicates that an audited event was unsuccessful; for instance, a failed logon attempt occurred.

on the job   *Success and Failure audit entries are found only within the Security log.*

EXERCISE 8-4

Using the Event Viewer

In this exercise, you will use the Event Viewer to monitor system components and services.

1. Click Start, point to Administrative Tools, and click Event Viewer.
2. Select the System log. The contents are displayed in the details pane.
3. Scroll through the log entries. Locate an event with a yellow exclamation mark.
4. Right-click the event and select Properties.
5. Document the following event information where applicable:
   - Date
   - Time
   - Type
   - User

- Source
- Category
- Event ID

6. If possible, access the Microsoft web site to find information relating to the event corresponding to the event ID.

Service Dependencies

A service is a component that runs on a computer, providing an operating system feature such as event logging or error reporting. Some services may have other services dependent upon them or may be dependent upon another service in order to start. When a service fails, it can be useful to know which services it is dependent upon to verify that those services are started. Or when stopping and starting services, it is important to know if any other services will be affected by the action.

Using Service Dependency

As just mentioned, some services running on a computer may be dependent on other services, which means the service will not start until any services it is dependent upon are started. Windows Server 2003 provides administrators with a quick way of determining those services that another is dependent upon or that depend upon others. Using the Services console, you can quickly determine a service's dependencies. To do so, use the steps outlined here:

1. Click Start, point to Administrative Tools, and click Services. This opens the Services console.

2. Right-click the appropriate service and click Properties.

3. From the service's properties dialog box, click the Dependencies tab. The Dependencies tab will list those services that it is dependent upon and the services that are dependent upon it.

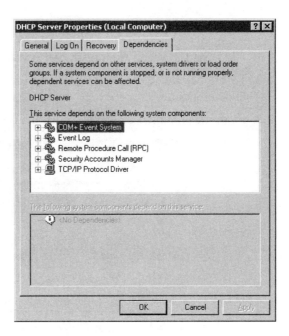

Before you attempt to stop a service, it is a good idea to verify which services are dependent upon it to determine if any other services will be affected.

Use Service Recovery Options to Diagnose and Resolve Service-Related Issues

Windows 2000 introduced the ability to configure Service Recovery options. Service Recovery options allow an administrator to specify certain actions to occur when a service fails to start. They enable you to specify what actions should be taken if or when a service fails. For example, if a service suddenly fails, you can have the computer restarted.

There are three service recovery actions that can be configured to occur. By default, when a service fails, no action is taken. The three actions that can occur include

■ Restart the service

■ Run a program

■ Restart the computer

You also configure when you want these actions to occur. A recovery action can be performed when a service initially fails for the first time, when it fails for a second time, and for any subsequent failures.

To configure recovery options:

1. Click Start, point to Administrative Tools, and click Services.

2. Right-click the service that you want to configure recovery options for and click Properties.

3. From the properties dialog box, click the Recovery tab.

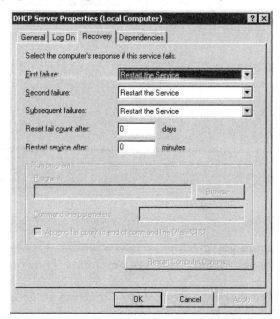

4. To configure a recovery action, click the arrow beside First Failure. Select one of the available options. If you choose to run a program, specify the program to run as well as any command-line parameters.

5. Repeat step 4 to configure recovery actions for second and subsequent failures.

6. Click OK.

CERTIFICATION OBJECTIVE 8.04

Implementing a Backup and Recovery Strategy

Earlier in the chapter, you were introduced to two different ways in which to increase the availability of network services and applications. However, neither of these solutions is meant to take the place of regular backups. Every company needs to have a strong backup and recovery strategy to protect against things such as hard drive failure and data corruption.

Windows Server 2003 includes a backup utility that can be used to back up and restore files and folders on FAT and NTFS partitions. The version of Backup included with the operating system allows you to perform the following tasks:

- Back up folders and files
- Restore folders and files
- Schedule when backups should occur
- Create an Automated System Recovery set
- Back up the System State Data
- Back up data from remote storage

Backup Types

When you are planning a backup strategy, one of the first things you must do is decide what type of backup you want to perform. Windows Server 2003 enables you to perform five different types of backups:

- **Copy** This type of backup simply copies the folders and files you have selected to the backup media. It does not alter the archive bit and therefore does not interrupt any normal or differential backups.

■ **Daily** This backup type will copy the selected files and folders that have changed during the day to the backup media. It uses the archive bit attribute to determine if files and folders have changed.

■ **Differential** Once a folder or file changes, the archive bit is reset. A differential backup will copy all those files and folders that have changed to the backup media but does not reset the archive bit. A differential backup will back up files and folders since the last normal or incremental backup.

■ **Incremental** This backup type backs up only the folders and files that have been added or changed since the last backup. An incremental backup will back up files and folders changed since the last normal or incremental backup and reset the archive bit.

■ **Normal** This backup type copies all the selected files and folders to the backup media. As files and folders are copied to the backup media, the archive bit is removed.

on the
Ü o b

Normally, when you are implementing a backup strategy, you will plan to perform a normal backup followed by incremental backups, or else a normal backup followed by differential backups. The former strategy reduces the time to perform routine backups but increases the amount of time it takes to restore data. The latter strategy increases the amount of time to perform routine backups but decreases the amount of time to perform a restore.

Using Windows Backup

The Backup program can be used to back up folders and files, restore folders and files, and create an Automated System Recovery set. The Backup program is installed by default with Windows Server 2003. To launch the Backup program and create a new backup job:

1. Click Start, point to All Programs | Accessories | System Tools, and click Backup.

2. From the Backup and Restore Wizard, click Advanced Mode. If you want the wizard to walk you through the process of configuring a backup, do not select the Advanced Mode option.

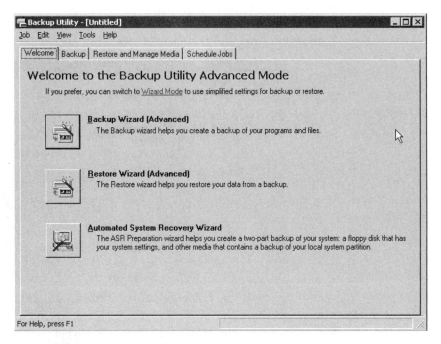

3. Click the Backup Wizard (Advanced). Click Next.

4. Specify the items you want to back up. You can back up everything on the local computer, selected data, or the System State Data. Click Next. If you

chose to back up selected data, the next dialog box will allow you to choose the folders and files to back up. Click Next.

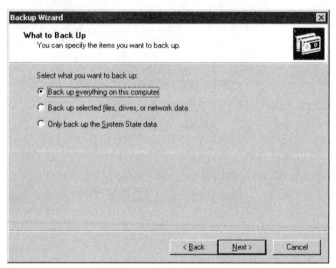

5. Specify the backup type, destination, and backup name. Click Next.

6. To configure advanced options, select the Advanced button. Click Next.

7. From the Type Of Backup dialog box, select the type of backup you want to perform. Click Next.

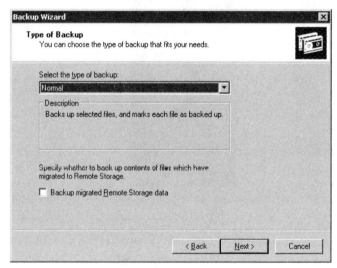

8. Select the additional options to configure, including Verify After Backup, Use Hardware Compression, Disable Volume Shadow Copy. Click Next.

9. Specify whether to overwrite existing data on the backup media and whether to restrict access to the data. Click Next.

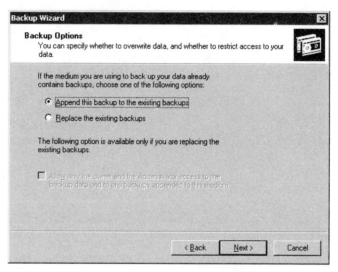

10. The next dialog box allows you to configure when you want to run the backup. You can run it immediately or use the Set Schedule button to specify when the backup should run.

11. Click Finish.

Volume Shadow Copy

Normally, when a backup takes place, any files that are currently open will not be backed up. With a volume shadow copy, those files that would not normally be backed up during the backup process can be copied to the backup media. A volume shadow copy creates a copy of a volume and exact copies of files (including those that are open). This ensures that those files that have changed during the backup process are still copied. These are the benefits of a volume shadow copy:

- Files can still be written to during the backup. For example, an application can still write information to a database.
- Users can still access files during a backup.
- Backups can be performed at any time without locking users out.

SCENARIO & SOLUTION

Can I back up the folders and files on a remote computer?	Yes. You can back up the folders and files on a remote computer if you have the appropriate permissions on that computer. However, the System State Data cannot be backed up remotely. You can back up the System State Data only on the local computer.
Which users or groups have permission to perform backups?	If you are a member of the administrators group or the backup operators group on a local computer, you can back up local folders and files. If you are a member of the administrators group or backup operators group on a domain controller, you can back up any local folders and files on any computer in the domain or in a trusted domain. Also a user with explicit permissions, such as the owner or any user with read, read and execute, modify, or full control NTFS permissions for a file, can back it up.
I am concerned about a user accessing the information stored on the backup media. How can I increase security?	You can restrict access to folders and files stored on the backup media by selecting the option to Allow Only The Owner And The Administrator Access To The Backup Data in the Backup Job Information dialog box. Once this option is selected, only the administrator or the person who created the backup can restore the data.

on the job

Volume Shadow copy is enabled by default. It can be disabled by selecting the Disable Volume Shadow copy option from the Advanced dialog box for an individual backup job.

Shadow Copies of Shared Folders

The Volume Shadow Copy (VSC) service is new in Windows Server 2003. VSC works by taking a snapshot of a shared folder once the service has been enabled. The snapshot will consist of an image of the contents of the folder at any given time. The purpose behind VSC is to enable quick recovery of a deleted file instead of having to restore the file from backup media (which can be a lengthy process). Creating shadow copies of shared folders provides the following benefits:

■ It provides a quick way to recover a file that has been accidentally deleted.

■ It allows you to easily recover a file that has been inadvertently overwritten.

■ It provides a way of comparing different versions of the same file.

on the **job**

Keep in mind that volume shadow copies of a shared folder are in no way meant as a replacement for performing regular backups.

Planning for Shadow Copies of Shared Folders   The main consideration when planning for shadow copies of shared folders is where the copies will be stored and the amount of free space that will be used. Shadow copies can be stored on the same volume, or you can specify a different volume. The default amount of space used is 10 percent of the volume being copied (the minimum amount of space that can be specified is 100MB). Once the storage limit is reached, the oldest shadow copies will be overwritten with the new ones. If you change the location to a separate volume, you should increase the maximum storage limit to the amount of available space.

When considering the amount of free space to use for volume shadow copies, also consider the number of files that will be copied, the size of the files, and the frequency with which files change.

Enabling Shadow Copies   Shadow copies can be enabled through the properties dialog box of a volume. Simply right-click on a volume within the My Computer console and click Properties. From the properties dialog box, select the Shadow Copies tab (see Figure 8-10). Select the Enable button to enable shadow copies for the selected volume. By selecting the Settings button, you can configure where the shadow copies will be stored, configure the maximum storage limit, and configure a schedule. By default, two shadow copies are created per day, one at 7 A.M. and another at 12 P.M. This can be changed by clicking the Schedule button.

Automated System Recovery

The Automated System Recovery (ASR) feature can be used in case of system failure. The disk can be used to recover a system when all other options have been tried, such as booting into Safe Mode and the Last Known Good Configuration. You can create an ASR set within the Backup program. The wizard will back up the System State Data, system services, and all disks that are associated with the operating system components. It creates a disk that can be used to restore the system in the event of failure.

If you ever need to recover a system, you can press F2 during the text mode portion of setup and insert the ASR set. The ASR will use the information on the floppy disk

FIGURE 8-10

Enabling shadow
copies

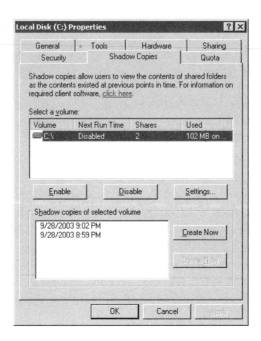

to restore the disk signatures, volumes, and partitions on the disks needed to restart the system. It installs a minimal version of Windows and immediately starts to restore from backup using the disk set created with the ASR wizard.

ASR is a very useful tool when it comes time to restoring a system. Before you can use this feature, however, you must have run the ASR wizard to create the Automated System Recovery set. Doing so should become a part of regular server maintenance. Also, whenever major changes are made to a server, you should run the ASR to create an updated disk set.

CERTIFICATION SUMMARY

Windows Server 2003 includes two technologies that can be used to increase the availability of services and applications: the Cluster service and Network Load Balancing. A cluster is a group of computers working together as if they were a single computer. This allows access and management of the cluster as a single unit. Each server within a cluster is referred to as a node. The idea behind implementing a cluster is to increase the availability of certain applications and services. Network Load Balancing is the ability to cluster up to 32 servers to act as one server. This type of clustering is not the same as the clustering covered in the preceding section. With Network Load Balancing, there are multiple servers with the same services installed. These servers can then be accessed by a large number of clients that will be balanced between the multiple servers.

In order to ensure that system components, services, and applications continue to perform under a given workload, you should monitor server performance on a regular basis. Windows Server 2004 includes a utility known as System Monitor that can be used to monitor the real-time performance of various components. You can also have performance data collected into a log file or a database for later analysis. When you are monitoring a server, the four components that should be included are memory, disk, processor, and network.

Windows Server 2003 also includes a number of other utilities that can be used for monitoring purposes. Network Monitor can be used to gather statistics on network traffic. The Event Viewer can be used to monitor the activity of an operating system and its various services and applications. The Services applet within the Control Panel can be used to monitor service dependencies and configure recovery options.

To ensure that you can recover from data loss, it is important to have a backup and restore strategy in place. Windows Server 2003 includes the Backup utility that can be used to back up folders, files, and System State Data. You can also use it to create an Automated System Recovery set to recover from system failure.

✓ TWO-MINUTE DRILL

Planning for High Availability

❑ A cluster is a group of computers working together as if they were a single computer. This allows access and management of the cluster as a single unit. Each server within a cluster is referred to as a node.

❑ There are two types of hardware components that allow the nodes to communicate and share information: Small Computer System Interface (SCSI) and Fibre Channel (both of which must be PCI).

❑ When a node fails, the other node will continue the functions of the failed node by taking control of the shared drive(s) where the data is stored. The shared disk resource where the cluster database is stored is called the Quorum Resource. In every cluster, there must be at least one Quorum Resource.

❑ Dependencies are when one resource depends on another resource for functionality. If any resource should fail, then so would any resource that depends upon the resource that failed.

❑ Failover is the process of a group being moved from one node to another when a resource fails within the group. Failback is the process whereby a group fails over to another node in the cluster; when the original node comes back online, the group will be moved back to the original node.

❑ The Cluster service is constantly monitoring the health of the network and the nodes by sending heartbeat messages to other nodes in the cluster.

❑ With Network Load Balancing, there are multiple servers with the same services installed. These servers can then be accessed by a large number of clients that will be balanced between the multiple servers.

❑ Windows Server 2003 comes with a tool that can be used to create and manage Network Load Balancing clusters from a single computer. The utility is known as the Network Load Balancing Monitor.

❑ When planning for the Cluster service and Network Load Balancing, you must identify and eliminate single points of failure by installing a UPS to protect the cluster from power outages.

Identifying System Bottlenecks

❑ Bottlenecks occur when a component is unable to perform under a given workload and therefore impedes server performance.

❑ Windows Server 2003 includes the System Monitor utility that can be used to monitor system components, applications, and services.

❑ The four major system components that should be monitored are network, disk, memory, and processor.

❑ You can use the Performance Logs Users group or the Performance Monitor Users group to control those users that can use System Monitor.

Monitoring Network Services

❑ Using a tool called Network Monitor, which is included with Windows Server 2003, you can monitor and log network activity and then use the information to manage and optimize traffic.

❑ Event Viewer can be used to view the contents of various event logs. By default, a computer running Windows Server 2003 typically has three logs listed within the Event Viewer: Application, System, and Security.

❑ Service recovery options enable you to specify what actions should be taken if or when a service fails. The actions include restarting the system, restarting the service, and running a program.

Implementing a Backup and Recovery Strategy

❑ The Backup utility included with Windows Server 2003 can be used to back up and restore folder and files as well as create an Automated System Recovery set.

❑ The five different types of backup include normal, incremental, differential, daily, and copy.

SELF TEST

Planning for High Availability

1. You are responsible for designing and implementing a cluster configuration for your company, which is running several mission-critical applications that must maintain a high level of availability. Since the availability of the cluster is dependent on the configuration of the network, you plan to eliminate as many points of failure as possible. Your company has also expressed its expectations for the cluster.

   Required result:

   - Eliminate the cluster hardware as a single point of failure.

   Optional results:

   - Eliminate domain membership as a point of failure.
   - Eliminate IP addressing as a single point of failure.

   Proposed solution:

   - Implement hardware-level RAID on the shared disks; implement software-level RAID on the private disks in each node.
   - Configure each node with two network adapters: one for "internal cluster communication" and the other for "all communications."
   - Assign static IP addresses to all adapters on each cluster node.
   - Configure the nodes as member servers in an existing domain with one domain controller.

   Does the proposed solution

   A. Meet the required and all optional results?
   B. Meet the required and one optional result?
   C. Meet only the required result?
   D. Meet neither the required result nor the optional results?

2. What is the maximum number of servers that can operate in a Network Load Balanced cluster?

   A. 2
   B. 4
   C. 16
   D. 32

3. Which of the following protocols can be used for Network Load Balancing?

    A. IPX/SPX

    B. NetBEUI

    C. TCP/IP

    D. AppleTalk

4. If a resource fails, what happens to the group it is in?

    A. It is renamed.

    B. It is deleted.

    C. It will cause the whole group to fail.

    D. It will fail back.

5. Which two of the following types of devices can be used to connect the nodes in a cluster to a shared device?

    A. IDE

    B. SCSI

    C. EIDE

    D. Fibre Channel

6. David is configuring the service recovery options for one of the services running on a Windows Server 2003 domain controller. Which of the following actions can be taken if a service fails? (Choose all correct answers.)

    A. The service can be restated.

    B. The computer can be rebooted.

    C. The services that it is dependent upon can be restarted.

    D. A message can be sent to users logged onto the server that the service has failed.

    E. An e-mail message can be sent to the network administrator.

    F. A program can be run automatically.

7. Greg is the junior network administrator of a Windows Server 2003 network. He has been asked to use Network Monitor to gather statistics. He wants to gather statistics on only certain types of traffic. What should he do?

    A. Configure a display filter.

    B. Configure a capture filter.

    C. Configure a packet filter.

    D. Configure an alert.

8. Don needs permission to view real-time data as it is captured using System Monitor. He should be capable of performing this task from the server or from his workstation. What should you do?

A. Add his user account to the Performance Log Users group.

B. Add his user account to the Administrators group.

C. Add his user account to the Performance Monitor Users group.

D. Add his user account to the Domain Admins group.

9. Mike has configured service recovery options on a computer running Windows Server 2003 so that if a service fails, the computer will automatically attempt to restart it. A network service running on the computer has stopped. However, the computer is unable to restart the service. Mike reboots the server, but the service will not start. What should Mike do?

A. Configure the service recovery options to attempt to restart all service dependencies if the service fails to start.

B. Use the Dependencies tab to verify that all service dependencies are started.

C. Continue to reboot the server.

D. Use Event Viewer to determine if all service dependencies are currently running.

10. Which of the following backup types will back up all the files and folders that have changed but not reset the archive bit?

A. Incremental

B. Copy

C. Normal

D. Differential

11. Don is the network administrator for a Windows Server 2003 network. He is using Network Monitor to capture and analyze network traffic for a web server on the network. He is configuring a trigger within the Network Monitor console. Which of the following actions can be configured within Network Monitor when the criteria of a trigger are met?

A. The computer will beep.

B. The computer will shut down.

C. The computer will reboot.

D. A command-line program will execute.

E. The capture will stop.

F. An e-mail will be sent to an administrator.

Identifying System Bottlenecks

12. Dave is monitoring the DHCP servers on the network. He wants to view all the packets going to and from each of the servers from his workstation. Which of the following is required to do this?

    A. Network Monitor tools

    B. System Monitor

    C. Network Monitor Driver

    D. Event Viewer

13. Which of the following backup types back up all the files and folders that have changed and resets the archive bit?

    A. Copy

    B. Incremental

    C. Differential

    D. Normal

Monitoring Network Services

14. John is preparing to install a new service pack on one of the domain controllers. Before he does this, he wants to back up everything on the server without interfering with the regular backup. What type of backup should he perform?

    A. Normal

    B. Copy

    C. Incremental

    D. Differential

Implementing a Backup and Recovery Strategy

15. John performs a normal backup on Sunday. Monday through Thursday evening, he performs incremental backups. On Friday morning, the server crashes and data must be restored. From which backup media will John have to restore?

    A. Sunday only

    B. Sunday through Thursday

    C. Thursday only

    D. Sunday and Friday

LAB QUESTION

In this lab, you will use the information in the given scenario to answer the questions outlined.

You are the network administrator for Good Nature, Inc. The company, which manufacturers and sells bath products, is completely Internet based. Customers can place an order through one of the company's web servers and the orders are processed the same day. All client information is stored within a company database. The company is currently receiving a few hundred orders a day.

1. You have been asked to implement a solution that will increase the availability and improve the performance for the company web server. What would you suggest?

2. List as many single points of failure as you can that may affect a network load balanced cluster along with their possible solutions.

3. The company's database is configured in a cluster. Your manager is concerned about the application running on the second node in the cluster because it does not have the same hardware as the original node. What should you tell him?

4. Your manager has also asked you to implement a backup strategy that will reduce the time it takes to back up folders and files. What type of strategy would you recommend?

SELF TEST ANSWERS

Planning for High Availability

1. ☑ **B.** The proposed solution meets the required result and one of the optional results. Configuring the cluster nodes as member servers in an existing domain makes them dependent on the network for authentication. To eliminate this as a point of failure, the cluster nodes should be configured as domain controllers within their own domain.
☒ Therefore, **A**, **C**, and **D** are incorrect.

2. ☑ **D.** Network Load Balancing supports a maximum of 32 nodes per cluster.
☒ **A**, **B**, and **C** are incorrect because these options do not represent the correct values.

3. ☑ **C.** The only protocol that can be used for Network Load Balancing is TCP/IP.
☒ **A**, **B**, and **D** are incorrect. The nodes of the Network Load Balance cluster can run other protocols with TCP/IP, but the packets received that are not TCP/IP will not be load balanced.

4. ☑ **C.** If a resource on one cluster node fails, the entire group will fail over to another node in the cluster.
☒ **A** and **B** are incorrect; a group that a resource belongs to is neither renamed nor deleted if the resource fails. Answer **D** is incorrect because failback occurs when a group's preferred node comes online after failover has occurred.

5. ☑ **B** and **D**. SCSI or Fibre Channel devices can be used to connect cluster nodes to a shared device.
☒ **C** and **D** are incorrect because these devices cannot be used to connect nodes to the shared device.

6. ☑ **A**, **B**, and **F**. The three actions that can be taken when a service fails include restarting the service, restarting the server, or automatically running a program.
☒ **C**, **D**, and **E** are incorrect because these actions cannot be configured to occur when a service fails.

7. ☑ **B.** Configuring a capture filter instructs Network Monitor to capture only data that meets the criteria you specify.
☒ **A** is incorrect because display filters are configured after a capture to filter data according to the criteria specified. **C** is incorrect because packet filters are used to control inbound and outbound traffic on a computer. **D** is incorrect because alerts are used to notify an administrator that an event has occurred.

8. ☑️   **C.** Adding his user account to the Performance Monitor Users group will give him permission to perform the required tasks.
    ☒   **A, B,** and **D** are incorrect because adding the user account to any of these groups will give him more permissions than are required to perform the tasks.

9. ☑️   **B.** Some services require other services to be first running before they can be started. You can use the Dependencies tab from the service's properties dialog box to verify service dependencies.
    ☒   **A** is incorrect because this is not a configurable action. **C** is incorrect because rebooting the server continuously will not restart the service. **B** is incorrect because the Event Viewer does not list service dependencies.

10. ☑️   **D.** A differential backup will copy only those folders and files that have changed. However, it does not reset the archive bit.
    ☒   **A** is incorrect because an incremental backup resets the archive bit. **B** is incorrect because a copy backs up all files and folders without interfering with the archive bit. **C** is incorrect because a normal backup will back up all files and folders and reset the archive bit.

11. ☑️   **A, B,** and **E.** A trigger action can include having the computer beep, having the computer shut down, and having the capture stop.
    ☒   **C, D,** and **F** are incorrect because a trigger cannot be configured to perform any of these actions.

Identifying System Bottlenecks

12. ☑️   **A.** The Network Monitor tools are required in order to view the captured data.
    ☒   **B** and **D** are incorrect because these tools are not used to monitor all network traffic from a computer. Answer **C** is incorrect because the Network Monitor Driver captures the traffic but does not provide the GUI to view it.

13. ☑️   **B.** A incremental backup will copy only those folders and files that have changed. It also resets the archive bit.
    ☒   **C** is incorrect because a differential backup does not reset the archive bit. **A** is incorrect because a copy backs up all files and folders without interfering with the archive bit. **D** is incorrect because a normal backup will back up all files and folders and reset the archive bit.

Monitoring Network Services

14. ☑️   **B.** A copy simply copies the folders and files you have selected to the backup media. It does not alter the archive bit and therefore does not interrupt any normal or differential backups.
    ☒   **C** is incorrect because an incremental backup resets the archive bit. **D** is incorrect because a differential backs up all files and folders that have changed and does not reset the archive bit. **A** is incorrect because a normal backup will back up all files and folders and reset the archive bit.

Implementing a Backup and Recovery Strategy

15. ☑ **B.** You must restore from Sunday through Thursday's backup media. Since incremental backups are being performed, each day's tape will contain new changes; therefore, you will have to restore from each tape.

☒ **A** and **C** are incorrect because these options would not restore all the required data. Answer **D** is incorrect because a backup was not performed on Friday.

LAB ANSWER

1. Network Load Balancing. This technology is used to increase the availability of multiple servers running the same services (such as the World Wide Web service). Client requests are then balanced across all the servers.

2. Some of the possible points of failure include

   - **DHCP**   Assign static IP addresses to all interfaces on the cluster nodes.

   - **Disks**   Implement hardware- or software-level RAID for the private disks. Use hardware-level RAID on the shared disk/disks.

   - **Hardware failure**   Always ensure there are spare parts on hand such as controller cards and drives.

   - **Power outages**   UPS devices should be used to provide power in case of power failures.

   - **Routers/hubs/etc.**   Have spare components on hand; implement redundant routes.

   - **Network cards**   Configure each cluster node with at least two network cards.

   - **Authentication**   Make the cluster nodes domain controllers in their own domains so that they do not become dependent on an external server for authentication.

3. Implement a failback policy so that the database can be configured to move back to the original node once it comes back online. This way, the database is running only on the second cluster node when the original is offline.

4. Answers may vary. A possible solution would be to perform a normal backup once a week. An incremental backup can be performed in the remaining weekdays. By performing an incremental backup, you can reduce the time it takes to back up folders and files each day, because only the changes for each day are copied to the backup media.

9

Planning and Implementing Server Roles and Security

CERTIFICATION OBJECTIVES

9.01	Selecting the Appropriate Operating System	9.03	Planning Security for Server Roles
			Two-Minute Drill
9.02	Planning a Secure Baseline Installation	Q&A	Self Test

CERTIFICATION OBJECTIVE 9.01

Selecting the Appropriate Operating System

Part of planning for server roles and security is being able to select the appropriate operating system for a specific environment or server role. Windows Server 2003 includes different platforms, each with its own set of unique features. You should be aware of these features as well as any limitations in order to choose the platform to best meet your needs.

Versions

As with the Windows 2000 platforms, Microsoft has released different versions of the Windows Server 2003 operating system. Windows Server 2003 includes the following family of products:

- Windows Server 2003 Standard Edition
- Windows Server 2003 Enterprise Edition
- Windows Server 2003 Web Edition
- Windows Server 2003 Datacenter Edition

Organizations today have a very diverse set of requirements. Vendors need to deliver platforms that are capable of performing a variety of functions. The Windows Server 2003 platforms are very versatile in their design, allowing them to perform in a variety of network environments and function in a variety of different server roles, including

- Mail server
- File and print server
- Web server
- Application server
- RAS/VPN server
- Terminal server
- DHCP/WINS/DNS server
- Domain controller

All four of the Windows Server 2003 platforms provide four core technologies. They are all designed to provide dependability, productivity, security, and connectivity through their standard features. While maintaining these four core technologies, each platform has unique features and has been built with a different network environment in mind.

The following sections will outline the key differences between the products and the environments they are designed for. Understanding the capabilities of each platform will ensure you select the operating system that will best meet the needs of your organization.

Standard Edition

Windows Server 2003 Standard Edition is designed to meet the needs of smaller organizations. It provides a high level of availability and all the features needed to meet the needs of workgroups, branch offices, and departments. It offers solutions for file and printer sharing, centralized management through Active Directory, secure Internet connectivity, and web services. It offers a certain level of scalability, supporting two-way symmetric multiprocessing and up to 4GB of RAM.

For organizations needing to achieve the highest level of availability, Enterprise Server or Datacenter Server would be the ideal choice.

Web Edition

Windows Server 2003 Web Edition is specifically designed for those small organizations or departments needing to build and host web applications and web services. The functionality behind Web Server is targeted toward ISPs and developers to provide web services. The technology of Web Server incorporates ASP and the .NET framework, allowing web developers to easily build and deploy web applications and services.

The Web Edition's functionality is not intended to go beyond that of a member server and does not equal the full functionality of a server operating system. For example, while Web Edition can be a member of a domain, it cannot run Active Directory. So for organizations looking for more functionality from their server operating system, one of the other Windows Server 2003 platforms should be considered.

Enterprise Edition

Many organizations today are running critical line-of-business applications, messaging applications, and e-commerce web sites that are crucial to their day-to-day operations. In other words, these applications and services need to be up and running. Any downtime or decrease in performance can in the end mean a loss of business or revenue. The features and capabilities of Windows Server 2003 Enterprise Edition help organizations address the issue of high availability and scalability.

Windows Server 2003 Enterprise Edition is designed for medium to large organizations. It has all the features of Standard Server with additional features targeted for businesses requiring a high level of availability and the ability to scale applications up and out as demands increase.

Scalability or "scaling up" can be achieved by adding more horsepower to a server as demands increase. One of the ways in which Enterprise Edition addresses scalability is through Enhanced Symmetric Multiprocessing (SMP). To increase server performance, you can "scale up" by adding up to a maximum eight processors. Enterprise Server also includes enhanced memory capabilities, allowing you to add up to 8GB of memory.

To provide high availability and fault tolerance for mission-critical applications, services, and data, Enterprise Edition supports server clusters through Cluster Service. Cluster Service provides a means of connecting multiple servers, up to eight nodes, together to work and appear as a single system. Cluster Service provides high availability by automatically detecting when an application or service fails and automatically restarting it on another cluster member. Downtime from failed applications and services can be as little as a few seconds and go unnoticed by users.

DataCenter Edition

Windows Server 2003 Datacenter Edition is designed for large enterprises requiring the highest level of server performance. It is by far the most powerful operating system out of the four Windows Server 2003 platforms, offering the highest level of scalability, reliability, and availability.

Unlike the other version of Windows Server 2003, Datacenter Edition cannot be purchased on its own. The operating system comes preloaded on a system that has been certified by Microsoft, meaning the hardware has been put through the stress tests for proven reliability. This would only make sense—why would you install a platform built for the highest reliability on hardware that is unreliable? For maximum uptime, reliability must be built into the hardware and the software.

Windows Server 2003 Enterprise Edition and Windows Server 2003 Datacenter Edition both support clustering. **This feature is not available in Windows Server 2003 Standard Edition or the Web Edition.**

Some of the features that set Datacenter Edition apart from the other operating system versions are its support for 32-way symmetric multiprocessing and up to 64GB of RAM (the 64-bit version is capable of supporting 64 processors and 128GB of RAM). It includes a technology known as hyperthreading, which allows a processor to execute multiple threads simultaneously, thereby increasing performance.

CERTIFICATION OBJECTIVE 9.02

Planning a Secure Baseline Installation

Windows Server 2003 includes many new enhancements that make it more secure than its predecessors. However, there are still many options that can be configured to increase the security of the systems on your network.

Securing a system should start with the installation of the operating system. The base installation of Windows Server 2003 can be made more secure by implementing the practices outlined in the following section. Once you have determined the steps to include when performing a baseline installation, it should become standard security practice when adding any new systems to the network. The following section will discuss these topics as they pertain to securing a system running Windows Server 2003:

■ Performing a secure baseline installation

■ Securing a baseline installation

■ Securing the system

■ Critical updates

■ Maintaining system security

Performing a Baseline Installation

Securing a system begins with the initial installation of the operating system. A system may be vulnerable to exploits (until the service packs and critical updates have been installed). If at all possible, the first step you should take in performing a secure baseline installation is to disconnect the system from the network. Now, this may not be possible in some cases. Network connectivity may be required to perform a remote installation of the operating system or to access service packs and updates from a network share. If network connectivity is required, you should at a minimum ensure that the system is not accessible from the public Internet.

Aside from the physical security, there are also a number of other ways to secure the operating system during the initial installation. These options will be discussed in the following sections.

File System

When you install Windows Server 2003, you have the option of selecting the type of file system with which to format the system partition. You can choose either FAT or NTFS (see Figure 9-1). Since FAT does not support many of the features of NTFS, such as file-level security and encryption, a production server should never be configured with a FAT partition (the system partition and any partitions that will host shares or other data). Therefore, during the installation you should select one of the options allowing you to format with NTFS.

Minimizing Components

One of the mistakes administrators can make is to install unnecessary components. For example, having Microsoft File and Printer sharing on a system when it is not required can leave a system vulnerable, especially if the proper permissions are not configured. Previous versions of Windows, including Windows NT 4.0 and Windows 2000, both allowed you to customize the installation by adding additional components.

FIGURE 9-1

Selecting the file system to use when installing Windows Server 2003

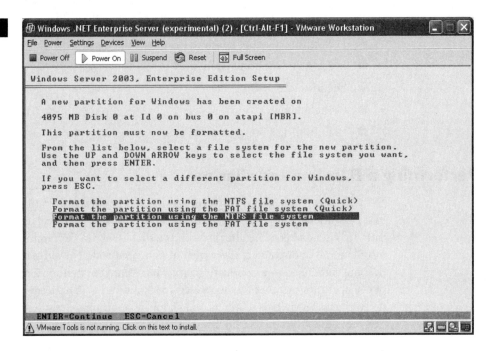

e x a m

ⓦatch   *Since the installation process has slightly changed in Windows Server 2003, it is important that you remember for the exam*

that for security purposes and to reduce vulnerabilities, optional components cannot be added until after setup is complete.

Microsoft has recognized this as being a security risk. Therefore, the installation of Windows Server 2003 reduces the number of vulnerabilities by installing only certain core components. Administrators no longer have the option during the installation to add optional components such as DHCP or Internet Information Services. Any optional components required can be added after the installation is complete.

e x a m

ⓦatch   *With previous versions of Windows, it was recommended that you configure a complex password for the Administrators account during the installation of the operating system. Windows Server 2003 no longer*

allows noncomplex passwords. As you configure the password for the Administrators account during the installation, an error message will appear if the password does not meet the complexity requirements.

Securing a Baseline Installation

Once the operating system has been installed, you can make it much more secure by installing the latest service packs and updates. During this phase of performing a baseline installation, you should complete the following steps:

- Install the latest service packs (although as of this writing, no service packs have yet been released for Windows Server 2003).
- Install the critical updates that apply to the system (for example, if you are running IIS, make sure the updates for this software are installed as well).
- Install the latest version of Internet Explorer. Also ensure that it is secured with the latest service packs and updates.

on the **Job** *Administrators often connect to the Internet from a network server when configuring or troubleshooting a system. Therefore, you should ensure that all the latest updates for Internet Explorer have been installed.*

Services Packs and Updates

Microsoft releases service packs for its various software packages, such as operating systems and applications, so that updates can be easily distributed. To obtain a service pack, administrators can connect to Microsoft's web site and download the service pack they wish to install. Service packs are intended to fix known issues with an operating system, keep the product up to date, and introduce new features. Service packs can include any of the following:

- Updates to the operating system
- New administrative tools
- Drivers
- Additional components

on the **Job** *It is not uncommon for several service packs to be released over time for a single operating system. Keep in mind when using service packs that they are cumulative, so any new service packs contain all the fixes in the previous service packs, along with new updates.*

Most organizations opt to keep up to date and install the latest service packs on their servers. Because service packs often contain fixes for known security issues for an operating system, applying the latest service pack is an important step in creating a secure baseline installation for servers. On the other hand, there are risks and vulnerabilities associated with introducing a new service pack. Therefore, before going ahead and deploying them as soon as they are released, you should plan to install them in a test environment first. This point holds true for deploying critical updates as well.

Between the releases of service packs, Microsoft releases updates, which are used to temporarily patch a specific problem with an operating system. One of the issues associated with installing updates is that they are developed and released rather quickly and, therefore, are not tested thoroughly. So installing the update can, in turn, have a negative impact. It is important to evaluate the updates released by Microsoft to determine whether they are necessary. If a particular vulnerability does not apply to your server, the patch should not be applied.

When service packs and updates are deployed, they should first be deployed within a test environment so that you can evaluate the impact on the server before installing it in the production environment.

INSIDE THE EXAM

Those Darn Administrator's Passwords

If you have taught technical courses, you have probably wondered why students are always told to use "password" as a password for the Administrators account. How many times have students gone through lab exercises being directed to log on using the word "password"? Although it makes it easier for beginners to remember, it's not good practice out in the real world but is a major security threat. And how many of those students walk away from a course using the word "password" as their actual password?

First and foremost, the Administrators account should be renamed, and second, a more complex password should be used. One of the nifty new features you'll come across when you install Windows Server 2003 is the little warning box that will pop up if you type in the word "password" when configuring the password for the Administrators account. This would be an ideal time to stop students in their tracks and remind them that in the real world, this is not acceptable practice. In fact, if you try, setup will not continue until you provide a password that meets the new password complexity requirements.

Securing the System

Once you have completed the steps just outlined, you should have a functioning system that is fairly secure. Your next step in creating a secure baseline installation will be to customize the system settings to meet your specific security needs. The following section will look at some of the configuration changes that can be made to a base installation to increase overall security.

Antivirus Software

Most organizations now support online communication. Almost all systems will have access to the Internet and e-mail applications. Although this does facilitate communication and collaboration, it also sparks a major security concern. Online communication makes it easier for attackers to introduce viruses and worms into a private network. Therefore, when securing a new system, it is essential that antivirus software be installed.

INSIDE THE EXAM

Hfnetchk.exe Utility

You can use the Hfnetchk.exe utility to determine the updates that might be required for your server. When the command-line utility is run, it scans the system to determine the operating system, service packs, and programs installed. It then determines the security patches available for your system given the components running. Hfnetchk.exe displays the updates that should be installed to bring the system up to date.

You can run Hfnetchk from Windows NT 4.0, Windows 2000, Windows XP systems, or Windows Server 2003; it will scan either the local system or remote systems for patches available for the following products:

- Windows NT 4.0, Windows 2000, Windows XP, Windows Server 2003

- Internet Information Server 4.0 and 5.0
- SQL Server 7.0 and 2000 (including Microsoft Data Engine)
- Internet Explorer 5.01 and later
- Exchange 5.5 and later
- Office 2000 and later
- Windows Media Player 6.4 and later

The system requirements to run the utility and perform a local computer scan include

- Windows NT 4.0, Windows 2000, Windows XP, Windows Server 2003
- Internet Explorer 5.0 or later (an XML parser is required; one is included with Internet Explorer 5.0)

The Workstation and Server services must be started.

on the *Once antivirus software is installed, you must ensure that it is up to date with the latest signature files. This would fall under the category of maintaining server security.*

Disabling Services

When you install Windows Server 2003, several default services are enabled. Many of these services will not be required and should be disabled. For example, the DHCP client will not be required if the server is configured with a static IP address. You can view the default services on a computer running Windows Server 2003 by clicking Start, pointing to Administrative Tools, and clicking Services (see Figure 9-2).

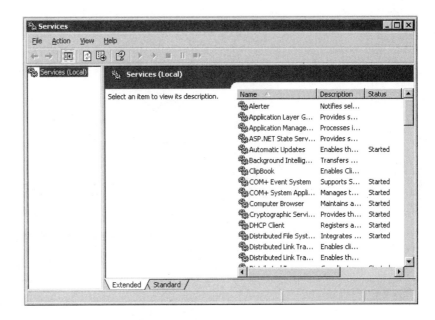

FIGURE 9-2

The Services
console

Any services that are not required should have their status set to disabled. To do so, right-click the appropriate service within the Services console and click Properties. From the properties dialog box, change the startup type for the service to Disabled. You will also notice that the startup type can be set to Manual. This option is not recommended for services that are not required, because the service can still be started by another program when required.

EXERCISE 9-1

Disabling the Indexing Service Using the Services Snap-in

In the following exercise, you will use the Services console to change the startup type for a service.

1. Click Start, point to Administrative Tools, and click Services.

2. Scroll through the list of services till you locate the Indexing Service. (Also notice the services installed by default and which of them are now disabled.)

3. Right-click the Indexing Service and click Properties.

4. From the General tab, use the arrow by the Startup Type drop-down box and select disabled. Click OK.

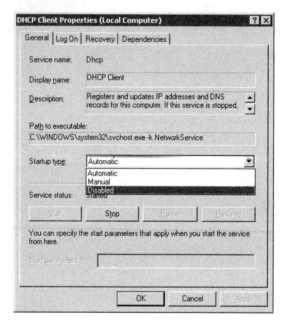

File Permissions

File permissions are another way in which security can be increased. Permissions can be configured on shared folders and files as well as system files. In previous versions of Windows, the system files were not adequately protected and therefore permissions had to be changed in order to secure a system.

Windows Server 2003 now does a much better job of protecting the system files. By default, the Users group is assigned Read, Read and Execute, and List Folder Contents permissions to the root directory. The Users group also does not include the anonymous SID, protecting folders and files from unauthorized access.

Password Policy

A *password policy* is an excellent way of strengthening the security on a local system or within a domain. A password policy defines settings such as the frequency at which users must change their password or the minimum length for passwords. The base installation does not have a secure password policy configured (see Figure 9-3), so this is one of the

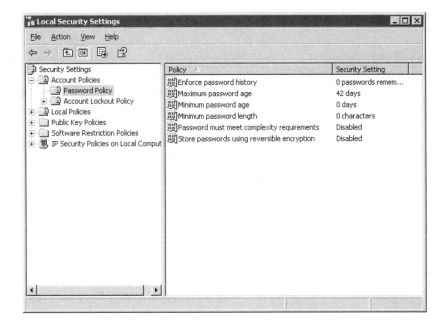

FIGURE 9-3

Windows
Server 2003
default password
policy settings

things you should do when securing a system. Table 9-1 outlines the various settings within a password policy, the default settings, and the settings recommended by Microsoft.

TABLE 9-1

Recommended
Password Policy
Settings

Password Policy Setting	Default Value	Recommended Value
Enforce password history	0	24 passwords remembered
Maximum password age	42 days	42 days
Minimum password age	0	2 days
Minimum password length	0	8 characters
Password must meet complexity requirements	Disabled	Enabled
Store passwords using reversible encryption	Disabled	Disabled

FIGURE 9-4

Windows Server
2003 default
account lockout
policy settings

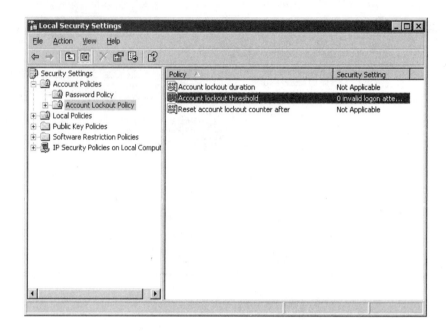

Account Lockout Policy

The account lockout feature enables an administrator to define an acceptable number
of failed logon attempts before an account is disabled. The benefit of this feature is that it
prevents attackers from using a valid user account to gain unauthorized access by guessing
the associated password.

The base installation of Windows Server 2003 does not have an account lockout
policy defined (see Figure 9-4), which means an attacker can attempt to gain access
using a brute-force attack. So defining an account lockout policy should be included
when securing the baseline installation. Table 9-2 outlines the account lockout policy
settings, showing the default values as well as the recommended values.

TABLE 9-2   Recommended Account Lockout Policy Settings

Account Lockout Policy Setting	Default Value	Recommended Value
Account lockout duration	Not applicable	30 minutes
Account lockout duration	0	3–5 failed attempts
Reset account lockout counter after	Not applicable	30 minutes

Auditing

Auditing, a security tool that allows an administrator to track specific events as they occur, is an extremely important feature when securing a system. Any audited events that do occur are written to the Security log, which can be viewed using the Windows Event Viewer. You can use the information within the Security log to determine when attacks are occurring (auditing is covered in greater detail in Chapter 10). Table 9-3 lists the events that can be audited in Windows Server 2003, as well as the events that are by default audited with the base installation (see Figure 9-5).

on the **(j) o b** *It is not recommended that you enable auditing for all events. Auditing of events does consume system resources and can therefore have an impact on system performance. Its also causes the Security log to grow rather large, which means events will either be overwritten or the log emptied on a regular basis.*

Critical Updates

Critical updates are released by Microsoft to address security loopholes and other faults found in Windows or other Microsoft applications such as Outlook, Internet Explorer, and Internet Information Service. Microsoft posts the updates on the Windows Update site where users and administrators can readily access them.

The base installation of an operating system does not have any of the critical updates installed. You may have some of the updates readily available to apply immediately

TABLE 9-3	Audit Policy Setting	Default Value
Default Audit Policy Settings	Audit account logon events	Success
	Audit account management	No auditing
	Audit directory service access	Success
	Audit logon events	Success
	Audit object access	No auditing
	Audit policy change	No auditing
	Audit privilege use	No auditing
	Audit process tracking	No auditing
	Audit system events	No auditing

FIGURE 9-5

Windows Server
2003 default audit
policy settings

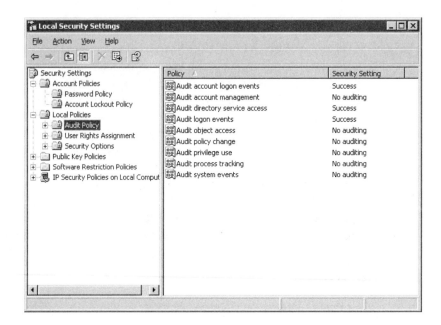

after the installation. However, once you complete the installation, it is generally a good idea to access the Windows Update site to verify that all the latest updates have been applied.

Using Windows Update

Microsoft makes it relatively simple for administrators and users to determine the latest updates that should be installed on a system. Critical updates for Windows and other applications are posted to the Windows Update site, where they are readily available for download. You can access the Windows Update site by clicking Start, pointing to All Programs, and selecting Windows Update (see Figure 9-6).

Once you reach the Windows Updates web site, you can click the Scan For Updates link. Windows Updates will scan your system and list the critical updates that have been found. By selecting the Review And Install link, you can view the list of updates and select which ones you want to install.

on the
job

Those updates that are deemed to be critical to the operation of a system are automatically selected for install. These updates provide security fixes to keep your system and network secure.

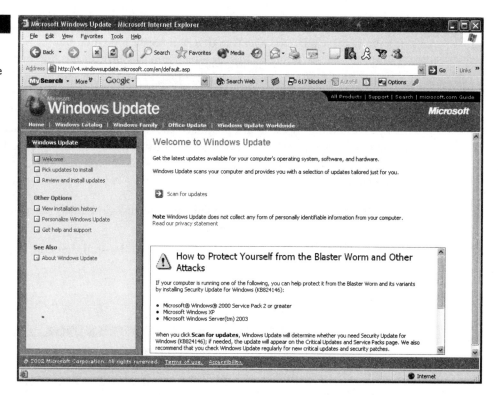

FIGURE 9-6

The Windows Update web site

Maintaining System Security

Once you have secured a computer by performing the various tasks outlined in the preceding sections, your server should be protected against common attacks. However, your efforts to secure it should certainly not stop there. Without a sound ongoing maintenance program in place, a system can become vulnerable to new forms of attacks. The following section will discuss some of the ways in which the security of your system can be maintained over time.

Automatic Updates

As already mentioned earlier, Microsoft will release critical updates for its various platforms and applications (such as Internet Information Service). In order to maintain security, it is important that a system is kept up to date with the latest critical updates. Automatic Updates is a feature that will notify you when new critical updates are available on the Windows Updates site. Furthermore, by using Automatic Updates, you can configure Windows to automatically download and install available updates (see Figure 9-7).

By default, computers running Windows Server 2003 are enabled for automatic updates. When updates are posted to the Windows Update web site, they are automatically downloaded and you are notified that they are ready to be installed. You can change the default behavior of Automatic Updates and select one of the remaining two options:

- Notify me before downloading any updates and notify me again before installing them on my computer.

- Automatically download the updates, and install them on the schedule I specify.

FIGURE 9-7

Configuring
Automatic
Updates

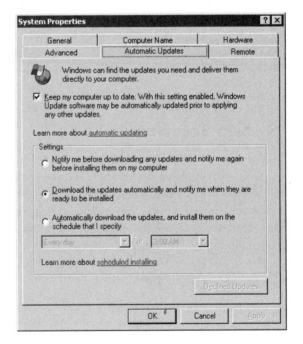

When it comes to deploying automatic updates, another technology you can use is Software Update Services. This free tool from Microsoft allows updates to be downloaded onto a server on your private network. You can then test the updates and approve them before they can be deployed to computers. Software Update Services will be discussed in Chapter 10.

EXERCISE 9-2

Configuring Automatic Updates

In this exercise, you will configure Automatic Updates so that they are automatically downloaded and installed on the schedule specified.

1. Click Start, point to Control Panel, and click System.

2. From the System Properties dialog box, click the Automatic Updates tab.

3. Select the third setting: Automatically Download The Updates, And Install Them On The Schedule I Specify.

4. Using the drop-down arrows, configure the updates to occur every Sunday at 12:00 A.M.

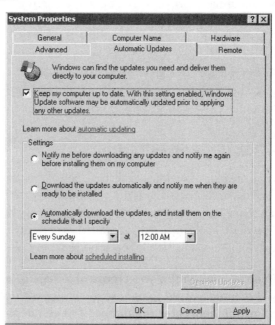

SCENARIO & SOLUTION	
Why is the importance of performing a secure baseline installation?	The importance of it is to increase security within your organization. The initial installation of Windows Server 2003 can be made more secure by following certain practices. These practices should become standard throughout your organization.
What is the difference between a service pack and a critical update?	Service packs contain updates, new drivers, and new components, and they fix issues related to known security loopholes. Between the releases of service packs, Microsoft releases updates, which are used to temporarily patch a specific problem with an operating system.
How can I determine what updates my system needs?	You can visit the Windows Updates web site. From there, you can perform a scan of your system. The results will list the critical updates that are missing from your system.

Analyzing Security Configurations

Maintaining security should also entail scanning current security configurations to identify areas in which security can be improved. One of the tools you can use to perform this task is known as the Microsoft Baseline Security Analyzer (MBSA is discussed further in Chapter 10). MBSA will scan a system for missing updates and misconfigurations that may leave a system vulnerable to attacks. Of course, you should plan to run this tool when you are initially securing a new system. Afterward, plan to occasionally use the tool to scan your systems to verify and detect missing updates.

Deploying a Baseline Installation

After creating a baseline installation, one of the things you can do to ensure that all new systems are configured with the same security settings is to create an image of the system. The same image can then be deployed to new systems as they are added to the network. One of the tools included with Windows Server 2003 that can facilitate this is called the Remote Installation Preparation (RIPrep).

on the
●job *Keep in mind that if you create an image of a secure baseline installation, you will eventually need to update the image with any new service packs and updates or install them after the image has been deployed.*

Remote Installation Preparation

RIPrep can be used not only to image an operating system, but applications and configuration settings can be included in the image as well. In terms of TCO, RIPrep provides an efficient and very fast way of deploying a fully configured desktop onto a system (both servers and workstations).

To use RIPrep, two computers are required: a reference computer that you intend to image and a Remote Installation Server (RIS) to host the images. Once the reference computer is configured, the RIPrep utility is used to image the computer and copy the image to an RIS server on the network. Images are then deployed from the RIS server to the target workstations.

Before you decide to use RIPrep to image a computer, keep the following points in mind:

■ RIPrep can image only a single disk and a single partition, so the operating system and all required applications must reside on one partition.

■ None of the files on the reference computer can be encrypted.

■ Once an image has been created and copied to the RIS server, it cannot be modified.

■ The images created using RIPrep can be deployed only from a RIS server.

So with that in mind, your first step in creating an image is to configure the reference computer exactly the way you want the target computers to be configured. After the operating system is installed, configure any components and settings and install any service packs and applications. Before running RIPrep, make sure you copy the local administrators profile into the default user profile so that all the settings you've just configured are applied when a user logs onto a target computer.

on the *As with any images you create, it's generally good practice to test the* **Job** *computer before creating the image to make sure everything works as it's supposed to. Imagine deploying an image to several target computers only to discover that settings are incorrect or applications don't function as they are supposed to.*

Your next step, once the reference computer is configured to your satisfaction, is to begin the imaging process, which entails running the RIPrep utility. Unlike Sysprep, this utility is run across the network from a RIS server, which obviously means a RIS server must be installed and configured before any images are created. You can run the utility by typing in the UNC, for example, **\\RISserver\REMINST\Admin\ I386\RIPrep.exe**. The RIPrep Wizard will walk you through the process of creating the image; it accomplishes the following tasks:

- It removes all unique settings such as the SID and computer name.
- It copies the image to the RIS server.
- It creates an answer file called RIPrep.sif and associates it with the image.

Once the image is copied to the RIS server, it can be deployed to the target workstations. This process is covered in the next section.

exam

ⓦatch *The disk capacity of the target computer must be equal to or greater than that of the reference computer. If the disk capacity is greater,* *RIPrep will by default format the entire volume, unless you change the RIPrep.sif so that the usewholedisk parameter is set to "no."*

Remote Installation Services

Windows Server 2003 includes a utility called Remote Installation Services (RIS). This is probably the most powerful tool for deploying operating systems because of its flexibility, the operating systems it supports, and its overall ease of use.

The version of RIS that ships with Windows Server 2003 can be used to deploy any of the following operating systems:

- Windows Server 2003 (all versions)
- Windows XP
- Windows 2000 Server (all versions)
- Windows 2000 Professional

Overview of RIS

When you use RIS, computers connect to the RIS server during the boot phase and begin the installation of the operating system across the network. The operating system can be installed by using the installation files on the source CD or by using images created with RIPrep (which was outlined in the preceding section).

For you to use RIS to deploy operating systems, the following requirements must first be met:

- There must be an NTFS partition on the RIS server separate from the boot and system partitions to store images.
- There must be a DHCP server on the network to assign remote clients and IP addresses.
- A DNS server must be available on the network for clients to locate Active Directory services.
- Active Directory must be installed, as it's required by the RIS servers.

The requirements on the client side are fairly straightforward. They must obviously meet the minimum requirements to install the operating system, they must have a network card that conforms to the PXE specifications, and the BIOS must be configured to boot from the network card.

on the job *If you are using RIPrep images, set the BIOS to boot from the floppy drive instead of the network card.*

CERTIFICATION OBJECTIVE 9.03

Planning Security for Server Roles

Servers can play a number of different roles on a network. For example, one server may be configured as a domain controller and another may be running DNS. Security configurations for a server will largely depend on the role a server is configured in. Previous chapters have discussed some of these server roles and how to secure them. However, one of the roles not discussed is that of a web server. Since Windows Server 2003 can be configured as a web server by installing Internet Information Services, you should be familiar with some of the ways in which IIS can be secured. The following section will look at planning security for various server roles and how to use the Security Configuration and Analysis utility to deploy different security configurations.

Securing a Web Server

Once you have performed all the steps outlined earlier in the chapter to configure a secure baseline installation, you will have a secure system. However, when Internet Information Services (IIS) is installed, your secure system once again becomes vulnerable to attacks. After you install IIS and before you place the web server in the production environment, there are a number of steps you can take to further secure the system.

IIS Updates

Probably the most important step in ensuring the security of your web servers is to install all the latest updates for IIS. IIS is known for its many vulnerabilities, so if security is a concern (which it should be), this is the easiest way to ensure web server security.

Again, using the tools discussed earlier in the chapter can assist an administrator in making sure a web server has all the latest updates installed. Using Windows Update and the Microsoft Baseline Security Analyzer will help you in keeping your web server up to date and secure.

IIS Lockdown Wizard

The IIS lockdown tool can be used to instantly configure a system that is running IIS. It also monitors all incoming requests to the web server so that only those requests that match the rules configured by an administrator are allowed to pass. The security implication of this is that only valid requests are responded to. An administrator can create rules to filter traffic by factors such as content and length.

URL Scan

The IIS lockdown tool installs the URLscan, which is an ISAPI filter used to screen incoming requests received by a web server. The purpose of URLscan is to reduce the risk of Internet attacks. With URLscan installed, the security of a server running IIS can be increased. It is also recommended that you further configure the default filters and customize them to meet your specific security requirements.

Controlling Anonymous Access

When IIS is installed, two additional user accounts are created: IUSR_*computername* and IWAM_*computername* (where *computername* is the local computer name assigned to the web server). These user accounts are used by anonymous users to gain access to the web server. If anonymous access is enabled, you can use these two user accounts and customize the permissions for IIS-related folders and files to control anonymous access.

on the
Job

When you are configuring permissions, it is extremely important that these two user accounts not be assigned permissions to any resources other than those within a web site.

In order for anonymous users to gain access, anonymous access must be enabled for the web site (the default web site automatically has anonymous access enabled). The following steps outline how you can disable anonymous access. Doing so means only those users with valid user accounts will be able to access the web site.

1. Click Start, point to Administrative Tools, and click Internet Information Services (IIS) Manager.

2. Right-click the web site for which you want to disable anonymous access and click Properties.

3. From the properties dialog box, select the Directory Security tab.

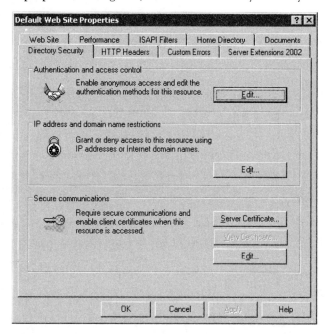

4. Click the Edit button under Authentication And Access Control.

5. To disable anonymous access, clear the check box beside the Enable Anonymous Access option.

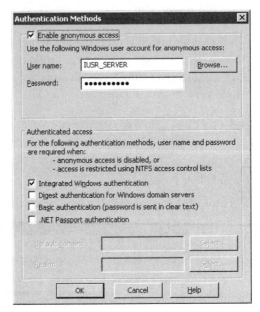

IIS Log Files

The IIS log files contain valuable information about any attempted attacks against your web server. The log files are by default stored in the c:\Windows\System32\Logfiles\ <*servicename*> directory. If a malicious user wanted to, they could gain access to the directory to delete the log files as a means of covering their tracks. To prevent this from happening, it is recommended that you configure the permissions (or verify them) on the directory so that only the administrator and the System account have full control. All other users require only Read and Read and Execute permissions to the directory.

IIS Logging

Logging is crucial in determining when your web site is being attacked. By default, logging in IIS 6.0 is enabled. If not, you can use the steps outlined here to enable it:

1. Click Start, point to Administrative Tools, and click Internet Information Services (IIS) Manager.

2. Right-click the web site for which you wish to enable logging and click Properties.

3. From the Web Site tab, select the option to Enable Logging.

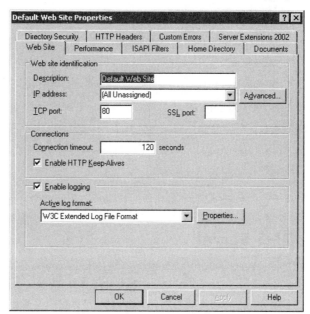

4. To specify the types of events to log, click the Properties button and select the Advanced tab.

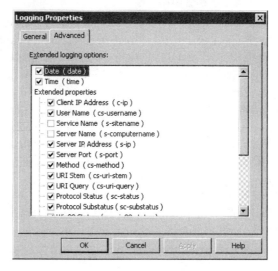

5. Select the appropriate advanced options and click OK.

When configuring the advanced logging options, it is recommended that you enable these options as a minimum:

- Client IP Address
- User Name
- Method
- URI Stem
- HTTP Status
- User Agent
- Server IP Address
- Server Port

Securing a DNS Server

DNS servers are crucial within a Windows Server 2003 environment because it is required by Active Directory. Not only that, clients will require DNS to correctly resolve hostnames to IP addresses. Therefore, it is important to take certain precautions to ensure the security of your DNS servers.

DNS Vulnerabilities

Most Internet-based servers, including DNS servers, may be susceptible to Denial of Service (DoS) attacks. In such cases, an attacker can flood a server with invalid information, thereby slowing it down or taking it completely offline.

Another security risk that DNS servers are susceptible to is zone poisoning or cache poisoning. Poisoning can occur in two ways. First, when the dynamic update feature is enabled, an attacker can essentially add a record to the zone file that is pointing to any location they choose. Or alternatively, an attacker can update the DNS cache on a DNS server with a bogus record, again pointing to any location they choose.

Zone transfers also pose a security threat for your DNS infrastructure. If you recall from Chapter 3, a zone file contains the resource records for a particular portion of the DNS namespace. Through zone transfers, the file is transferred from one DNS server to another. The problem with this is if a DNS server is configured to allow any other DNS server to initiate a zone transfer, an attacker from outside the local network may be able to transfer the zone file.

Securing DNS

By default, the DNS server service is protected from poisoning so that attackers are unable to place malicious data in the DNS cache. The Secure cache against pollution option, which is enabled by default, ensures this. If for some reason this option is not enabled, you can do so using the Advanced tab from the DNS server's properties dialog box.

Dynamic updates allow DNS clients to automatically update their own host records with a DNS server. As mentioned previously, the problem with this is that unauthorized users may be able to perform updates. If you plan to use dynamic updates, you should ensure that the zone is configured only for secure updates, so that only those authenticated users can update the zone file. You can verify using the General tab from the zone's properties dialog box that it is configured for secure updates only.

Finally, you can address the issue of unauthorized zone transfers by restricting which DNS servers are authorized to initiate them. From the properties dialog box for the zone file, select the Zone Transfers tab. Select Only To Servers Listed or Only To The Following Servers on the Name Servers tab and specify the IP addresses of the DNS servers that are permitted to initiate zone transfers.

DHCP Servers

Like DNS servers, DHCP servers provide a critical service on a network. The role of a DHCP server is to lease IP addresses and other parameters required for network connectivity. The loss of a DHCP server can wreak havoc on a network if precautions are not taken as clients can lose the ability to communicate on the network. Due to their important role on a network, DHCP servers can definitely be the target of security attacks. Therefore you need to take additional steps to secure your DHCP implementation and ensure clients can still obtain IP addresses in the event an attack does occur.

DHCP Vulnerabilities

DHCP servers can be the target of a Denial of Service (DoS) attack. This may be performed by an attacker outside of the private network or by a malicious user on the private network. For example, configuring an existing workstation with the same IP address as that of the DHCP server will result in IP address conflicts. Or flooding the request buffer on a DHCP server with invalid requests thereby losing its ability to respond to valid requests. If the DHCP server is unavailable, clients can end up losing their ability to communicate on the network.

Securing DHCP

Aside from protecting the network from such external attacks, you can implement a DHCP solution that will take the possibility of a DoS attack occurring into account. To ensure that clients can still obtain an IP address, multiple DHCP servers should be configured. Again you can use the 80/20 rule discussed in Chapter 2 to effectively utilize multiple DHCP servers on the network. By putting this rule into practice, DHCP clients will still be able to lease an IP address should one of the DHCP servers fail.

on the
() o b
With the 80/20 rule, one DHCP server is configured with 80 percent of the IP address for a subnet and another DHCP server is configured with the remaining 20 percent. In the event that one DHCP server goes offline, DHCP clients can still obtain a valid IP address from the other DHCP server. This is a simple, cost-effective way of securing your DHCP implementation.

Monitoring events is one of the most effective ways in which you can determine when security breaches may be occurring. By default, a DHCP server will log certain events to the Windows Server 2003 System log. However, you can configure a DHCP server to log much more detailed events. You can do so using the General tab from the properties window for a DHCP server (found within the DHCP console).

on the
() o b
By default, Server Operators and all authenticated users have read access to the DHCP audit logs. There is no reason why all users should have access to this information, so you should edit the ACL for the %systemroot%\system32\ dhcp folder. For increased security, only network administrators should have access to the DHCP audit logs.

Security Configuration and Analysis

Windows Server 2003 makes it simple to deploy security configurations. A security template holds a number of security settings that Microsoft considers to be appropriate for a server, domain controller, or workstation. Windows Server 2003 comes with several predefined sample security templates. Each of the templates contains security settings for different levels of security, depending on the type of server the template is applied to. For example, you can apply the highsecdc.inf template to all domain controllers in an environment requiring a high level of security. The templates can be used as is or can be customized to meet the specific security needs of an organization. Security templates can be used to configure the following settings within a local security policy or a group policy:

- Account policies
- Local policies
- Event log
- Restricted groups
- System services
- Registry
- File system

Using the Default Security Templates

The predefined security templates included with Windows Server 2003 can be viewed using the Security Templates snap-in. To view the default security templates, perform the following steps:

1. Click Start | Run and type **MMC**. Press ENTER.

2. From the File menu, click Add/Remove Snap-In. From the Add/Remove Snap-In dialog box, click Add.

3. Scroll through the list of available snap-ins. Select Security Templates and click Add. Click Close.

4. Click OK.

5. Within the management console, expand Security Templates and click the default container. The preconfigured security templates are listed in the right pane.

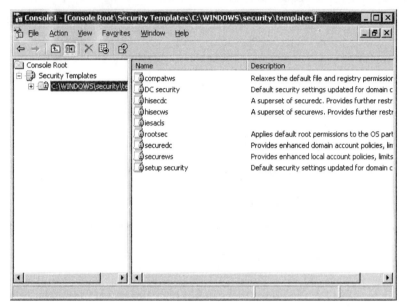

By default, the following security templates are stored within the %systemroot%\security\templates directory:

- **Setup Security**   This template is created during the installation of Windows Server 2003 and contains the default security settings applied during the installation of the operating system. You should not change the settings within this template, because it can be used to reapply default security settings.

- **Compatible (compatws.inf)**   This template relaxes security so that members of the Users group can run applications that are not a part of the Designed for Windows Logo Program. The default permission allows only members of this group to run applications that are part of the Windows Logo group. Instead of adding members to the Power Users group, permissions can be relaxed so that members of this group can run the necessary applications.

- **Secure (secure*.inf)**   This template modifies security settings that impact the operating system and network protocols such as the password policy, account policy, and various Registry settings. It also removes all members from the Power Users group.

■ **Highly Secure (hisec*.inf)**   This template increases the security of the parameters defined within the secure template. This template also removes all members from the Power Users group.

The Designed for Windows Logo Program helps customers identify those products that have been tested with the operating system.

Analyzing Security with the Security Configuration and Analysis Tool

Windows Server 2003 includes a tool known as the Security Configuration and Analysis tool. Using this tool, you can analyze the current security state of a server or workstation by comparing the existing settings against an existing template. By performing a security analysis on a regular basis, administrators can ensure that a server or workstation continues to meet the security requirements of an organization. Over time, discrepancies can occur in the security configuration of a server or workstation. The analysis pinpoints any discrepancies, allowing an administrator to resolve any security conflicts that exist. After an analysis is run, the results are displayed for review.

EXERCISE 9-3

CertCam 9-3 ON THE CD

Security Configuration and Analysis

In this exercise, you will use the Security Configuration and Analysis tool to analyze the current security settings on a computer running Windows Server 2003 against those within an existing template.

 1. Click Start, Run, and type **MMC**. Press ENTER.

 2. From the File menu, click Add/Remove Snap-In. From the Add/Remove Snap-In dialog box, click Add.

 3. Scroll through the list of available snap-ins. Select Security Configuration And Analysis, and click Add. Click Close and then click OK.

 4. Within the management console, right-click Security Configuration And Analysis, and click Open Database.

5. Type a new filename to create a new database, or select an existing database.

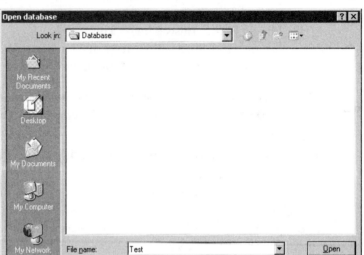

6. If you are creating a new database, select an existing template and click Open.

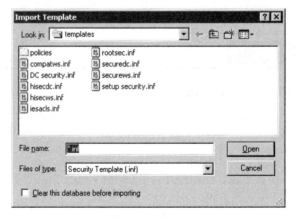

7. Within the Details pane, right-click Security Configuration And Analysis, and click Analyze Computer Now.

8. Specify the path for the error log, or use the default location. Click OK. The system security settings are analyzed.

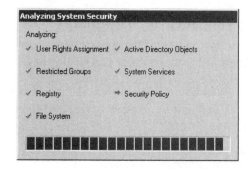

9. After the security settings have been analyzed, double-click Security Configuration And Analysis within the Details pane.

Any security settings that do not match those within the security template are marked with a red X (see Figure 9-8). As you can see in the figure, the values configured on the computer for the minimum password age and minimum password length do not match the values defined within the database.

FIGURE 9-8

Viewing the security analysis results

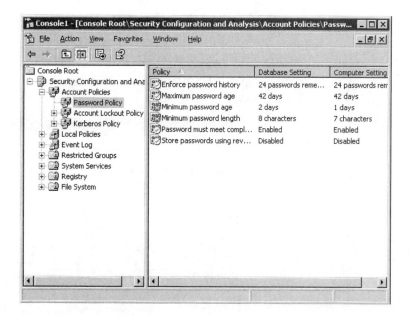

Applying Security Templates

A security template can be applied in two ways: locally or through a group policy. To apply a security template to a local policy, perform the following steps:

1. Within the Security Configuration and Analysis console, right-click Security Configuration And Analysis, and click Open Database.

2. Type a name for the database and click Open.

3. From the Import Template dialog box, select a template and click Open.

4. Right-click Security Configuration And Analysis, and click Configure Computer Now. The security settings are immediately applied to the local computer.

To import a security template for a domain or organizational unit, perform the following steps:

1. Click Start | Administrative Tools, and select Active Directory Users And Computers.

2. Right-click the domain or organizational unit for which you want the security settings applied, and click Properties.

3. From the properties dialog box, select the Group Policy tab.

4. Click Edit to edit an existing group policy, or click New to create a new group policy.

5. In the group policy console, under Computer Configuration, expand Windows Settings and right-click Security Settings. Click Import Policy.

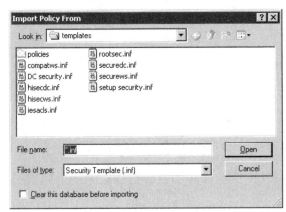

6. Select the security template that you want to import and click Open.

Security settings on a domain controller are automatically refreshed every five minutes. Security settings on a workstation or server are automatically refreshed every 90 minutes with a random 30-minute offset.

Once you make changes to any security settings, you can force an immediate refresh using the gpupdate command. When the command is used on its own, it will automatically refresh any user and computer settings that have changed. Using the command with the /target switch allows you to specify whether computer or user settings are refreshed. Using the /force switch means all settings are refreshed, regardless of whether or not they were changed. The gpupdate command replaces the secedit command in Windows 2000. On Windows Server 2003, the secedit command does not work.

Creating Custom Templates

The predefined security templates can be applied as is. However, they can also serve as a starting point for configuring security. Any of the predefined templates can be customized to meet the specific security requirements of an organization.

To customize an existing template, perform the following steps:

1. Open the Security Templates snap-in. Expand the Security Templates container.

2. Click the default path folder. In the right pane, right-click the security template that you want to modify and click Save As.

3. Type a new name for the security template and click Save.

The newly created template will appear within the right pane. To modify the security settings, double-click the new template. Any of the settings contained within the template can be modified by right-clicking an attribute and selecting Properties. For example, to configure a password history, right-click the Enforce Password History option from within the Password Policies container for a security template and click Properties. Select the option to Define This Policy Setting In The Template and configure a value.

If you do not want to customize one of the existing security templates and would rather define an entirely new template, you can do so again using the Security Templates snap-in. To do so, right-click the default path location within the Security Templates snap-in and click New Template. Type in a name and description for the template, and click OK. The new template is displayed within the right pane, from which you can begin configuring the security settings.

CERTIFICATION SUMMARY

In this chapter, you learned about the four operating systems in the Windows .NET Server family of platforms. Each one is built on the core technologies of Windows 2000 and has its own set of unique features. Windows .NET Standard Server is designed for small organizations and departments, while Enterprise Server and Datacenter Server having built-in capabilities making them suitable choices for large enterprise environments requiring a high level of availability, reliability, and scalability. Web Server is very specific in its design and doesn't contain many of the advanced features included with the other three versions.

The chapter then went on to look at performing a secure baseline installation. This begins with the installation of Windows Server 2003. During the install, as well as after, there are a number of configuration changes that can be made to make your system more secure. A system is also not considered secure until the latest service packs and updates have been installed. A lot of time and effort can go into a secure baseline. In order to maintain this level of security, you can use the Windows Updates web site to download the latest updates for your system. You can also use the Microsoft Baseline Security Analyzer to verify that all the required updates are installed.

Microsoft includes the Security Configuration and Analysis utility, which can be used to analyze the current security settings on a system. This is useful in verifying that the security settings haven't changed over time. If they have, the utility will pinpoint any discrepancies. Security templates can be used to configure specific security settings and import them onto a system (either locally or through group policy). Security templates can be configured for various server roles. Each time a new system is added to the network, the appropriate security template can be applied. This procedure reduces administration and allows you to easily deploy standard security configurations.

✓ TWO-MINUTE DRILL

Selecting the Appropriate Operating System

❑ Windows .NET Server includes Standard Server, Web Server, Enterprise Server, and Datacenter Server.

❑ Web Server can only be a member server within a domain.

❑ Enterprise Server and Datacenter Server support clustering technology.

❑ Datacenter Server is not available "out of box."

Planning a Secure Baseline Installation

❑ If at all possible, the first step you should take in performing a secure baseline installation is to disconnect the system from the network.

❑ During the installation, you should format the system partition using NTFS. It includes features such as file-level security that FAT does not.

❑ Only the required services and applications should be installed on a system. Those services not required should be disabled.

❑ All systems should be configured with the latest service packs and updates to make them more secure.

❑ Various policy settings, such as a password policy and audit policy, should be configured as part of a secure baseline.

❑ Automatic update is a feature that allows you to easily keep your system up to date with the latest critical updates.

❑ Microsoft Baseline Security Analyzer can be used to determine the updates that need to be installed on a system as well as any misconfigurations that exist, making the system vulnerable to attacks.

Planning Security for Server Roles

❑ Probably the most important step in ensuring the security of your web servers is to install all the latest updates for IIS.

❑ The IIS lockdown tool should be used to secure a web server.

❑ The IIS lockdown tool installs the URLscan, which is an ISAPI filter used to screen incoming requests received by a web server. The purpose of URLscan is to reduce the risk of Internet attacks.

❑ A security template holds a number of security settings that Microsoft considers to be appropriate for a server, domain controller, or workstation.

❑ Windows Server 2003 comes with several predefined sample security templates. Each of the templates contains security settings for different levels of security based on the type of server the template is applied to.

❑ Windows Server 2003 includes a tool known as the Security Configuration and Analysis tool. Using this tool, you can analyze the current security state of a server or workstation by comparing the existing settings against an existing template.

❑ The gpupdate command replaces the secedit command in Windows 2000. On Windows Server 2003, the secedit command does not work.

SELF TEST

Selecting the Appropriate Operating System

1. You want to have Windows automatically check for critical updates and install them on a set schedule. What tool can you use to configure this?

   A. Automatic Downloads

   B. Windows Update

   C. Automatic Update

   D. Windows Downloads

2. Which of the following operating systems includes clustering technologies? (Choose all that apply.)

   A. Windows .NET Standard Server

   B. Windows .NET Web Server

   C. Windows .NET Enterprise Server

   D. Windows .NET Datacenter Server

3. You are adding a new Windows .NET Server to your network infrastructure. The existing network already has two domain controllers running Windows .NET Standard Server. Due to an increase in organization growth, another domain controller is being added. You carefully select server hardware that exceeds the recommended requirements and install Windows .NET Web Server. You soon discover that you are unable to install Active Directory. What is causing the problem?

   A. You cannot install Windows .NET Standard Server and Windows .NET Web Server on the same network.

   B. The server doesn't meet the hardware requirements to install Active Directory.

   C. Windows .NET Web Server does not support Active Directory.

   D. You are not logged on as administrator.

4. Mary is concerned that some of the servers on the network no longer meet the security requirements outlined by her organization. Different network administrators often troubleshoot problems and make configuration changes while doing so. She wants to verify the current security settings and compare them against the initial template used to configure new servers. What tool can she use?

   A. IP Security Monitor

   B. Security Configuration and Analysis

   C. Network Monitor

   D. Security Templates

Planning a Secure Baseline Installation

5. Mary is implementing a secure baseline for all new servers configured on the network. She wants each server to be configured with a standard set of security settings. What is the simplest way for Mary to configure the security settings on all new servers to be identical?

    A. Mary must manually configure the settings on each server.

    B. Mary can create a security template using the Security Templates snap-in with all the required security settings and deploy it through a GPO.

    C. Mary can use the Security Configuration and Analysis tool to create a new template with all the required security settings.

    D. Mary can use Software Updates Services to configure each new server with the required security settings.

6. Diane is the network administrator for a Windows Server 2003 network. There are five servers being added to the network. She wants each server to be configured with the same security settings. What is the most efficient way for Diane to accomplish this task?

    A. Create a new template using the Security templates snap-in. Deploy the template to all servers using Software Updates Services.

    B. Create a new template using the Security Templates tool. Deploy the template through a group policy object.

    C. Create a new template using the Security Configuration and Analysis Tool and deploy it through a group policy object.

    D. Manually configure the local security settings on each server.

7. Felicia is the network administrator for a Windows Server 2003 network. There are several junior network administrators employed. Felicia suspects that changes have been made to the security settings on several servers. There is a standard security template that all new servers are configured with. What tool can Felicia use to verify the current security settings against those within the original template?

    A. Security Templates

    B. Active Directory Users and Computers

    C. Security Configuration and Analysis

    D. Microsoft Baseline Security Analyzer

8. John has just obtained his MCSE and is the new network administrator for a small company. All servers are currently running Windows Server 2003. John has just been notified that a new service pack is available. What should he do before installing the new service pack?

    A. Read the documentation to learn how to install the service pack.

    B. Notify any users connected to the servers that the servers will be offline for a period of time.

C. Take all servers off the network.

D. Install the service pack in a test environment.

9. Doug is the network administrator of a Windows Server 2003 network. He has created a security template that is applied to all new servers that are added to the network. To verify security settings, Doug runs the Security Configuration and Analysis tool on a member server. He wants to ensure that the security settings currently configured are the same as those in the security template. Once the analysis is complete, he notices several of the settings appear with a red X beside them. What does this mean?

A. It indicates that the security settings configured match those configured within the security template.

B. It indicates that the security settings correspond to the type of role the server is configured for.

C. It indicates that the security settings are not required for the role the server is configured for.

D. It indicates that the security settings configured do not correspond to those within the security template.

Planning Security for Server Roles

10. Mary is the network administrator of ICI International. There is a GPO configured for all domain controllers. Mary has just made changes to the security settings in the GPO by applying a new security template. What is the default interval that the security settings are automatically refreshed?

A. 5 minutes

B. 15 minutes

C. 60 minutes

D. 90 minutes

11. Mary is the network administrator of ICI International. There is a GPO configured for all member servers. Mary has just made changes to the security settings in the GPO. What is the default interval that the security settings are automatically refreshed?

A. 5 minutes

B. 15 minutes

C. 60 minutes

D. 90 minutes

12. A new member server is being added to the network. To increase security, you are configuring a security template that will be used for future installations. When configuring the password policy, what is the recommended value for the password length?

A. 0

B. 6

    C. 8

    D. 12

13. You are planning to deploy a security template to workstations within your network. Users need to be able to run programs that are not part of the Designed for Windows Logo Program. Which of the following should you choose?

    A. compatws

    B. hisecdc

    C. securews

    D. securedc

14. You are creating a security template that will be deployed to all member servers within the organization. To increase security, you configure a password policy. Which of the following is the recommended value for the minimum password age?

    A. 2 days

    B. 20 days

    C. 42 days

    D. 60 days

15. Due to a recent security breach, John has been asked to increase security for all member servers. He creates a new security template and applies the template to the member servers using a group policy object. He wants the changes propagated immediately. What should he do?

    A. Nothing. Changes made to the security settings are refreshed immediately.

    B. Use the secedit command to update the security settings.

    C. Nothing. He must wait for the 90-minute interval to pass for the new security settings to be applied.

    D. Use the gpupdate command to update the security settings.

LAB QUESTION

You are the senior network administrator for a large organization. Lately you have noticed that many of the organization's member servers are all configured differently. For security purposes, you would like to create a standard outlining how new member servers will be configured. In your plan, outline how administrators will perform secure baseline installations. Discuss the ways in which you can increase the security of a base installation of Windows Server 2003. Also include in the plan ways in which the security of the member servers can be maintained over time.

SELF TEST ANSWERS

Selecting the Appropriate Operating System

1. ☑ **C.** Using Automatic Updates, you can configure Windows to automatically download updates and install them according to a schedule.

    ☒ **A** and **D** are incorrect because these tools do not exist in Windows .NET Server. **B** is incorrect because Windows Update itself cannot be used to configure how and when updates occur.

2. ☑ **C** and **D.** They both support clustering technologies.

    ☒ **A** and **B** are incorrect because neither of the two operating systems support clustering technologies.

3. ☑ **C.** You cannot install Active Directory on a computer running Web Server.

    ☒ **A** is incorrect because Standard Server and Web Server can coexist on the same network. **B** is incorrect because the hardware exceeds the requirements to install the operating system. Therefore, if Active Directory were supported, it would successfully install. **D** is incorrect because you must be an administrator to log on locally to the server. If the user is already logged on, this option is eliminated.

4. ☑ **B.** The Security Configuration and Analysis tool can be used to analyze the current security settings of a computer and compare them against the settings within an existing template.

    ☒ **A** is incorrect because IP Security Monitor is used to troubleshoot and monitor IPSec communications. **C** is incorrect because Network Monitor is used to capture and analyze network traffic. **D** is incorrect because the Security Templates snap-in is used to configure existing templates and create new ones.

Planning a Secure Baseline Installation

5. ☑ **B.** Mary can use the Security Templates snap-in to create a new template with the required security settings. The template can then be imported when new servers are configured.

    ☒ **A** is incorrect because although this is a viable solution, it is not the most efficient one. It will require configuring the same settings on each server. **C** is incorrect because this tool cannot be used to create new templates. **D** is incorrect because SUS is used to deploy software updates to clients.

6. ☑ **B.** The Security Templates snap-in is used to configure new security templates. Once the template is configured, it should be deployed through a group policy object.

    ☒ **A** is incorrect because software update services cannot be used to deploy security templates. It is used to deploy Windows updates. **C** is incorrect because the Security Configuration and Analysis tool cannot be used to create new templates. **D** is incorrect. Although this solution would work, it is not the most efficient, as it entails configuring the same security settings on multiple servers.

7. ☑ **C.** The Security Configuration and Analysis tool can be used to compare the existing security settings configured on a computer with those in a security template. The results will show any discrepancies that exist between those settings configured on the computer and those configured within a template.

    ☒ **A** is incorrect because the Security Templates snap-in is used to create and configure the security templates. **B** is incorrect because Active Directory Users and Computers snap-in is used to manage objects within Active Directory, such as user accounts, groups, and computers. **D** is incorrect because Microsoft Baseline Security Analyzer is used to scan a computer to determine which updates are missing. It also identifies any misconfigurations that may leave a system vulnerable to attacks.

8. ☑ **D.** Installing a service pack on a new system can have adverse affects. Therefore it is always good practice to install a service pack within a test environment before deploying it in the production environment.

    ☒ **A** is incorrect. Although you should always read the documentation included with any new software you install, a service pack should always be deployed within a test environment before installing it on production servers. **C** and **D** are incorrect. If a server is going to be offline, users should be notified if they will be affected. However, this is not the first step to take when deploying a service pack. Also, all servers within a network infrastructure should never be taken offline at the same time.

9. ☑ **D.** Once an analysis has been completed, you can view the results. Any security settings that do not match those configured within the template are marked, making them easily identifiable.

    ☒ **A**, **B**, and **C** are incorrect because they do not represent the correct answers as to why the red X appears after performing an analysis of the local security settings against those within a templates.

Planning Security for Server Roles

10. ☑ **A.** Security settings on a domain controller are automatically refreshed every 5 minutes. Once changes to the security settings have been made, they can be refreshed manually or you can wait for the five-minute interval to elapse and they will be refreshed automatically.

    ☒ **B**, **C**, and **D** are incorrect because they do not represent the correct interval at which security settings are automatically refreshed on a domain controller.

11. ☑ **D.** Security settings on a member server will be automatically refreshed at 90-minute intervals.

    ☒ **A**, **B**, and **C** are incorrect because these do not represent the correct interval at which security settings on a member server are automatically refreshed.

12. ☑ **C.** The recommended password length when configuring a password policy is 8 characters.
☒ **A, B,** and **D** are incorrect because they do not represent the recommended value when configuring the password length for a password policy.

13. ☑ **A.** The compatws template relaxes security so that members of the Users group can run applications that are not a part of the Designed for Windows Logo Program. The default permission allows only members of this group to run applications that are part of the Windows Logo group. Instead of adding members to the Power Users group, permissions can be relaxed so that members of this group can run the necessary applications.
☒ **C** is incorrect because the highsecws template will not allow users to run these applications. **B** and **D** are incorrect because these templates contain security settings that are designed for systems configured as domain controllers.

14. ☑ **A.** When tightening the security of a base installation by configuring a password policy, the recommended value for the minimum password age is two days.
☒ **B, C,** and **D** are incorrect because these do not represent the correct recommended values for this setting.

15. ☑ **D.** Using the gpupdate command, security settings can be manually refreshed and immediately propagated.
☒ **A** and **C** are incorrect because changes made to security settings are automatically refreshed at 90-minute intervals on member servers. **B** is incorrect because this is the command used in Windows 2000 to manually refresh security settings.

LAB ANSWER

Answers may vary. Your plan should include a description of the various configuration changes that can be made to the base installation of Windows Server 2003, both during the installation and after the installation. You should outline the installation of service packs and critical updates as well as why they are important. The documentation should list the various policy settings that should be changed and their recommended values.

The maintenance plan should include a description of how the servers will be maintained. This can be done using the Automatic Updates feature of Windows Server 2003 and also the Microsoft Baseline Security Analyzer utility. Also, a security template should be defined with the required policy settings. The template can then be applied to each new member server that is added to the network in order to standardize security settings throughout the network.

10

Planning, Implementing, and Maintaining a Security Infrastructure

CERTIFICATION OBJECTIVES

Planning for Certificate Services

Security has become an important topic in today's world of computing. Therefore, there needs to be a secure method of passing information between hosts and ensuring that the host you are communicating with is indeed who they say they are. One of the most secure ways of doing this is through the use of digital certificates.

When it comes to implementing digital certificates, organizations have the option of using a third party (commercial company) to issue their digital certificates. An alternative to this is implementing Certificate Services, included with Windows Server 2003. Certificate Services facilitates the creation of a Public Key Infrastructure (PKI) allowing data to be encrypted, as well as the identity of computers and users to be verified and authenticated. Certificate Services establishes a system of trust. The following section will look at the fundamental concepts behind Certificate Services as well as some of the issues to consider when implementing the service in a Windows Server 2003 network infrastructure.

Understanding Certificate Services

Certificate Services is included with Windows Server 2003. It is used to issue and manage certificates for a Public Key Infrastructure (PKI). By installing Certificate Services, you can configure a computer running Windows Server 2003 to receive certificate requests, verify the identity of a requestor, issue and revoke certificates, and publish a certificate revocation list (CRL). In order to successfully implement Certificate Services, it is important that you have an understanding of how it works.

Certificates

Before implementing Certificate Services, you should have a general idea of what a certificate is. A *certificate* is basically a digital statement from a trusted authority that is used to verify the identity of a host. A host's public key is bound to the digital certificate. This certificate basically says that the host holding the key is who it claims to be.

A simple way to really understand the purpose of certificates is to compare them to one's driver's license or passport. A driver's license or passport is issued by a government authority, which is assumed to be trusted, with your photograph and other information to prove your identity. You can use either piece of identification to prove your identity

INSIDE THE EXAM

What Is a Public Key Infrastructure?

You may have come across the term PKI at some point when studying for MCSE exams. A Public Key Infrastructure employs a system that secures communication through the use of digital certificates, public and private keys, and certificate authorities. The various components work together to increase security between two hosts. For example, the purpose of the digital certificates is to verify the identity of an individual, while the public and private keys are used to secure the information exchanged between hosts. And all of this would not be possible without the certificate authorities, which are responsible for generating the key pair used to secure data and issuing the digital certificates.

The purpose of the public and private keys is to secure information being sent between two computers. They also provide a method of verifying that an entity is indeed who it claims to be. So how are the public and private keys used? A key pair is generated by a CA for a requestor. The private key is given only to the host that made the request for the key pair. The corresponding public key is included with the requestor's digital certificate and made available to other hosts. When a message is encrypted using a public key, only the host with the corresponding private key can decrypt the message. Let's take a look at an example: If Ross wants to send Alex a secure message, he can obtain Ross's public key. The public

key is used to encrypt the message, and the message is sent to Ross. Since Ross is the only one with the corresponding private key, he can successfully decrypt the message. In terms of authentication, if Ross wanted to prove his identity to Alex, he could create a digital signature, which is a hash function of the private key. Alex can verify the digital signature using Ross's corresponding public key.

For a host to participate in a PKI infrastructure, that host must have a digital certificate as well as a public and private key. The key pair is usually generated by the Cryptographic service provider (CSP). The CSPs provide the encryption and signature algorithms and determine the algorithms and key lengths used with a certificate. After a key pair has been generated, a request can be sent to a CA for a digital certificate. The request may go to a third-party CA (such as VeriSign), or it may be submitted to a CA on the private network, depending on how the PKI infrastructure is implemented. A request for a certificate will include the public key of the requestor (remember that this is made available to other hosts, along with the digital certificate). The request for a certificate includes the public key of the requestor as well as any other required information, such as name and e-mail address.

(for example, when traveling between countries). Since they are issued from an authority that is trusted, it is believed that you are who you claim to be.

Certificate Authorities

A *certificate authority (CA)* is an entity, such as a computer, that has been delegated the task of issuing digital certificates to users, computers, and organizations that must prove their identity to other entities.

One of the responsibilities of a CA is to receive requests for certificates from entities known as *requestors*. The CA will use the information supplied by the requestor to verify that it is who it claims to be. This must be done before a digital certificate is issued. By having a CA legitimize a requestor, other entities can be assured they are communicating with a trusted and secure source.

When a certificate request is generated, it is sent to a CA for approval. If the request is approved, the CA builds a certificate for the requestor. A request can also be denied or set to pending, at which point the requestor is notified. Once the certificate is completed, the CA stores it in the local database. The requestor also obtains a copy of the certificate and stores it locally.

Another responsibility of a CA is that of certificate revocation. A CA will publish a list of all revoked certificates known as the *certificate revocation list (CRL)*. The purpose of the list is to identify those users, computers, and organizations that no longer have trusted credentials with the CA.

on the

Ö o b

A CA plays an extremely important role in a PKI infrastructure, and therefore it is important that you consider security when planning for CAs. First of all, the physical security of CAs needs to be considered. Certificate authorities should be placed in a secure location where they are accessible only to administrators. Also, since the CA's private key is used in the certification process (to sign all issued certificates), this too must be secured.

Certificate Authority Hierarchies

Certificate authorities can be configured in a hierarchy. At the most basic level, a hierarchy will consist of a single CA. More often, however, a hierarchy will contain multiple CAs consisting of parent-child relationships.

A *root* CA (also referred to as a root authority) is the most trusted CA. Root CAs are often used only to issue certificates to subordinate CAs. A subordinate CA, on the other hand, is one that has been certified by another CA (this can be a root CA or another subordinate CA). Typically, subordinate CAs are used to issue certificates for specific purposes such as secure e-mail and smart cards. These root CAs and subordinate CAs form a certificate hierarchy. Child CAs in a hierarchy are certified by their parent CA. The hierarchy thereby creates a model of trust where each child CA trusts its parent CA leading back to the root authority (see Figure 10-1).

Creating multiple subordinate CAs offers a number of different benefits, including these:

- Subordinate CAs can be configured with distinct issuing policies and be responsible for issuing specific types of certificates.

- Subordinate CAs can be configured for the various organizational or geographical divisions within a company.

- It allows for load balancing so that one CA is not responsible for issuing certificates to a large number of users.

- It creates a level of fault tolerance so that there is always one CA online available to service users requests.

- Multiple CAs also increases security, as users do not need to be in contact with the root CA to obtain certificates. Certificates can be issued by a subordinate CA instead.

- It provides administrators with the ability to take a CA offline.

FIGURE 10-1

Certificate authority hierarchies

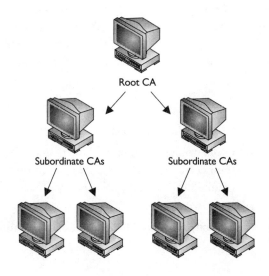

Certificate Authorities Classes

Windows Server 2003 supports two different classes of certificate authorities. The type of certificate authority you create will depend on who you are issuing a certificate to. The CA types include

- Enterprise certificate authorities
- Stand-alone certificate authorities

Enterprise Certificate Authorities   An *enterprise* CA is used to issue certificates to entities within an organization. When you install an enterprise CA, it is automatically registered within Active Directory and thereby trusted by all entities within the domain.

Enterprise CAs have the following features:

- Active Directory and DNS are required.
- You must be a member of the Enterprise Admins group to install an enterprise CA.
- User certificates and the CRL are stored within Active Directory.
- This type of CA is used to issue certificates to entities within the domain.

exam
watch

If you encounter a question where a certificate authority will use domain user account information to verify the identity of a requestor, you will need to install an enterprise CA.

Stand-Alone Certificate Authorities   The second class of certificate authority supported by Windows Server 2003 is a stand-alone certificate authority. This class of CA does not require Active Directory and would be implemented when certificates need to be issued to entities outside of an organization. A stand-alone CA has the following characteristics:

- Active Directory is not required.
- User certificates and the CRL are stored locally.
- Requestors must submit all of the required information needed to complete their certificate. This is unlike an enterprise CA, which can retrieve the required information from Active Directory.
- All certificate requests are set to pending until the identity of the requestor is verified by an administrator. This is unlike enterprise CAs, which can

immediately approve a request using the domain user account information within Active Directory.

on the **Job** *If Active Directory is installed, you have the option of configuring either an enterprise CA or a stand-alone CA. Otherwise, you only have the option of installing a stand-alone CA because it does not require Active Directory.*

Types of Certificate Authorities

Now that you are familiar with the two general classes of CAs supported by Windows Server 2003, let's take a look at the different types of certificate authorities that can be

INSIDE THE EXAM

Qualified Subordination

New features included with the release of an operating system are normally popular exam topics. One of the new features in Windows Server 2003 included with Certificate Services is that of qualified subordination.

Qualified subordination allows you to configure issuance constraints for subordinate CAs as well as configure constraints on the certificates they issue. You can use this feature to define which portion of a namespace a CA can issue certificates for, define acceptable uses for certificates, and also create trust between separate CA hierarchies.

Qualified subordination can be used on an intranet and an extranet. Intranet qualified subordination involves a subordinate CA being issued a certificate from a parent CA. The certificate can contain qualified extensions defining things such as the domain for which it can issue certificates. Extranet qualified subordination is used to establish trusts between CAs in different hierarchies (also referred to as cross-certification).

Name constraints are used to permit or exclude those namespaces for which a qualified subordinate CA and its subordinate CAs can issue certificates. For example, a qualified subordinate CA may have a permitted name constraint of sales.bayside.net and an excluded constraint of bayside.net. This means the CA can issue certificates to users and computers within the sales.bayside.net domain but not the bayside.net domain. Name constraints can be in the form of distinguished names, DNS, e-mail, URL, user principal name, and IP address.

configured. Windows Server 2003 supports four different types of certificate authorities based on the classes that were described previously:

- Enterprise root CAs
- Subordinate CAs
- Stand-alone root CAs
- Stand-alone subordinate CAs

Enterprise Root CA The *enterprise root* CA is at the top of a CA hierarchy. When you install an enterprise CA, it automatically registers itself within Active Directory. Doing so means that all computers and users within Active Directory will trust the CA.

An enterprise root CA can issue certificates to other CAs as well as to users and computers. With multiple CAs within a hierarchy, the enterprise root CA will issue certificates to its subordinate CAs. Depending on how you want to implement CAs, it can also issue certificates to users and computers. However, a common implementation plan is to have the enterprise root CA issue certificates only to subordinate CAs and leave subordinate CAs responsible for issuing certificates to users and computers.

Before configuring an enterprise root CA, keep in mind that it has the following requirements:

- Active Directory must be running.
- DNS must be running
- You must be a member of the Enterprise Admins group to configure an enterprise CA.

on the Job **Multiple root CAs can be configured within a single domain. However, each CA hierarchy can only consist of a single root CA.**

Enterprise Subordinate CAs Within a certificate hierarchy, an *enterprise subordinate* CA exists under an enterprise root CA. Common reasons for implementing enterprise subordinate CAs are for issuing certificates to a particular part of an organization, for specific functions, and for load balancing. Before you can configure an enterprise subordinate CA, an enterprise root CA must already be present. The root CA can be on the local network or a third-party commercial CA.

on the Job **The root CA for your certificate hierarchy can be a commercial CA such as VeriSign. This would be an appropriate solution if certificates will be used outside your organization.**

Stand-Alone Root CAs   A stand-alone CA must be configured if Active Directory is not available. The only requirement for installing this type of CA is that you must have administrative privileges on the local computer. This type of CA should be implemented if you need to issue certificates to entities outside your organization. One of the differences between an enterprise CA and a stand-alone CA is that the stand-alone CA will set all certificate requests to pending until they are approved by an administrator. An enterprise CA, by contrast, can approve certificate requests immediately using account information within Active Directory.

Stand-Alone Subordinate CAs   The stand-alone subordinate CA also does not require Active Directory. However, it does require a root CA. The root CA can be from within your organization or it can be a commercial CA. Also, keep in mind the administrative privileges requirement on the local server. Table 10-1 summarizes the differences between the various CA types.

Installing Certificate Services

There are a number of ways in which you can install Certificate Services. It is not installed by default with Windows Server 2003. However, it can be added after the installation using the Configure Your Server Wizard or using the Add Or Remove Programs applet within the Control Panel. Exercise 10-1 walks you through the process of installing Certificate Services.

TABLE 10-1   Types of Certificate Authorities

CA Type	Description
Enterprise root CA	An enterprise root CA is the top-level CA in a hierarchy. It uses Active Directory to validate the identity of a requestor. It requires Active Directory and DNS.
Enterprise subordinate CA	An enterprise subordinate CA issues certificates to entities within an organization. It is not the most trusted CA in a hierarchy and requires a parent CA. Typically, subordinate CAs are used to issue certificates for specific purposes.
Stand-alone root CA	This CA type does not require Active Directory. It is the top-level CA within a hierarchy. Choose this type of CA when certificates are being issued to entities outside the organization. Typically, a stand-alone root CA is used to issue certificates to subordinate CAs.
Stand-alone subordinate CA	This CA type should be implemented if certificates must be issued to entities outside the organization. A parent CA is required. This can be an external commercial CA.

EXERCISE 10-1

Installing Certificate Services

In this exercise, you will install Certificate Services on a computer running Windows Server 2003.

1. Click Start, point to Control Panel, and Click Add Or Remove Programs.

2. Click Add/Remove Windows Components.

3. From the list of Windows Components, select Certificate Services.

4. Click Yes at the dialog box that appears indicating that the computer name and domain membership cannot be changed once installed.

5. From the list of CA types, select enterprise root CA if it is not already selected. Click Next. Keep in mind that if the server is not a member of a domain, you will have only the option to configure a stand-alone root CA or a stand-alone subordinate CA.

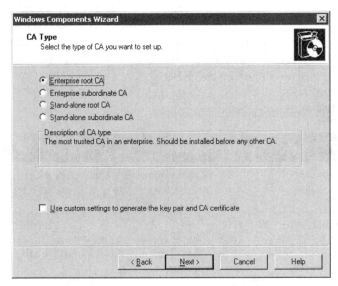

6. Type in a common name for the CA. Click Next.

7. From the Certificate Database Settings dialog box, click Next to accept the default location for the Certificate database and Certificate database log. If Active Directory is not installed, you can specify a shared folder in which to store the configuration information.

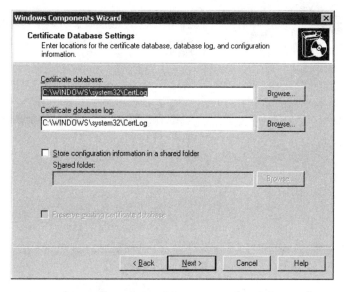

8. A warning message will appear informing you that IIS must be temporarily stopped in order to complete the installation of Certificate Services. Click Yes.
9. Click Finish.

Configuring Certificate Services

Once Certificate Services is installed, you can use the Certificate Authority snap-in to configure and manage the service. To open the service, click Start, point to Administrative Tools, and click Certificate Authority. From the properties dialog box for a CA, you can configure a number of different options (see Figure 10-2).

The General tab provides some basic information about the CA, such as the name assigned to it, the CSP, and the hash algorithm. These settings were initially configured during the installation of Certificate Services.

Policy modules enable an administrator to control the behavior of a certificate authority and determine the action that a CA will take when it receives a certificate request. Policy modules determine whether certificate requests should be issued, denied, or marked as pending when they are received. By selecting the Properties button from the Policy Module tab, you can change the default behavior when a request is received (see Figure 10-3). On a stand-alone CA, the policy module can be changed. The certificate requests will most often be set to pending.

FIGURE 10-2

Certificate
Authority
properties
dialog box

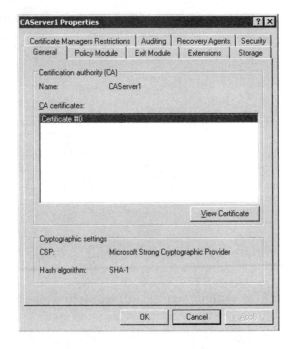

FIGURE 10-3

Configuring the
policy module

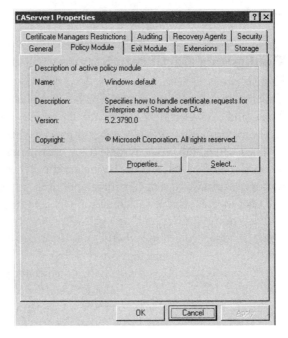

The exit module is used to control any postprocessing of issued certificates, such as publishing them to Active Directory or to a file system. By selecting the Configure button from the Exit Module tab, you can configure a certificate authority to publish issued certificates to Active Directory and/or a file system (see Figure 10-4).

The Extensions tab is used to configure where the CRL is published. You can click Add to configure a CRL distribution point (see Figure 10-5).

The Storage tab provides information about where the configuration data is stored (see Figure 10-6). This data can be stored in Active Directory or on a shared folder; it is configured during the installation of Certificate Services. Remember, with an enterprise CA, the configuration information is stored in Active Directory by default, whereas on a stand-alone CA, the information is stored locally.

The Security tab (see Figure 10-7) allows you to configure CA access privileges. By default, Authenticated Users are assigned the Request Certificates permission. This permission is enabled for all users who are logged onto the domain to request certificates, allowing them to request certificates from the CA. The local Administrators, Domain Admins, and Enterprise Admins groups are assigned the Issue and Manage Certificates permission and the Manage CA permission, which gives them full control

FIGURE 10-4

Configuring the exit module

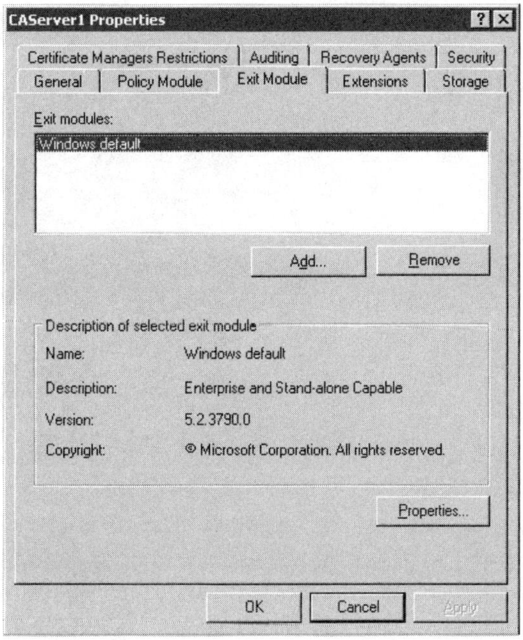

FIGURE 10-5

Configuring the
CRL distribution
point

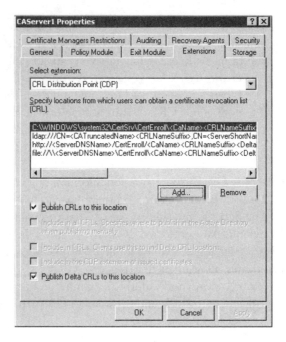

FIGURE 10-6

The configuration
data storage
location

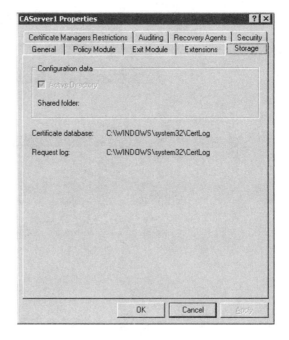

FIGURE 10-7

Configuring
permissions

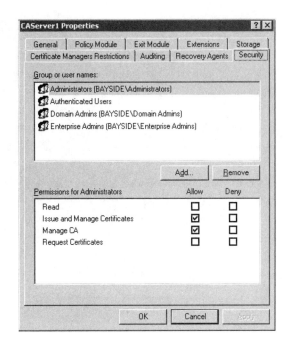

of the CA. If the default permissions do not meet your requirements, you can use the
Security tab to modify them.

The Recovery Agents tab enables you to configure whether private keys are
archived. Windows Server 2003 includes the ability to archive the private key of
specific certificates when they are issued. This allows the private key to be recovered
if it is lost. The process of recovering a private key includes two different phases: key
archival and key recovery.

Normally, an entity's public key is provided when a certificate is requested. In some
cases, an entity can also make its private key available to a CA. The CA will store the
private key within its database in the event it must be recovered. This is known as key
archiving. If a private key is archived, it can be recovered by a key recovery agent.

Certificate Services included with Windows Server 2003 supports security auditing.
Using the Auditing tab shown in Figure 10-8, you can enable auditing of various events.
When an event occurs, it will be written to the Windows Server 2003 Security log.

A user can be designated as a Certificate Manager by being assigned the Issue
and Manage Certificates permission from the Security tab. You can use the Certificate
Managers Restrictions tab to control which certificate managers can manage
certificates for subjects.

FIGURE 10-8

Enabling security
auditing

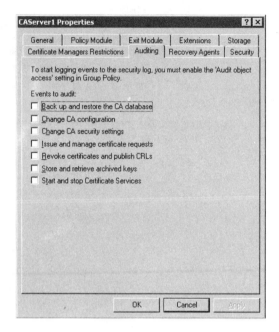

Certificate Enrollment and Revocation

One of the main responsibilities of a certificate authority is to issue and revoke certificates to users, computers, and organizations. In order for an entity to obtain a certificate, a request must first be generated and submitted to a CA. Once a certificate is issued, it can be revoked at any time by an administrator.

Certificate Templates

Certificate templates define a certificate according to its intended use. Each certificate template contains preset configurations depending on what the certificate will be used for. Certificate templates simplify the process of requesting and issuing certificates. Permissions can also be configured for the various templates and they will determine which types of certificates users can request.

watch   *There are two different versions of certificate templates: version1 and version2. Version 1 templates are supported by Windows 2000 clients, while version 2 templates are supported only by Windows XP and Windows Server 2003 clients.*

Windows Server 2003 contains a number of different default templates. The default templates that can be issued by a CA are found within the Policy Settings container. Using the Certificate Authority Manager, you can add additional templates for the CA to issue. For example, if your organization is deploying smart cards for authentication you will have to add the Smart Card Logon template to the Policy Settings container. To do so, right-click the Certificate Templates container, point to New, and click Certificate Template To Issue. From the Enable Certificate Template dialog box, select the template you want to add and click OK.

As already mentioned, you can configure permissions for the various templates. The access control list (ACL) for a template defines which users can enroll for certificates of that type. For example, you can configure permissions on the Smart Card Logon template so it is only available for specific users. Each template is configured with default permissions that can be modified to meet your requirements. Keep in mind that certificate requests are granted only for those users and computers that have been assigned the enroll permission.

To edit the ACL of a certificate template, follow these steps:

1. Click Start, point to Programs | Administrative Tools, and click Active Directory Sites And Services.

2. Click the View menu and select the Show Services Node option.

3. Expand the Services container and expand Public Key Services.

4. Click the Certificate Templates folder.

5. Right-click the appropriate template, click Properties, and select the Security tab.

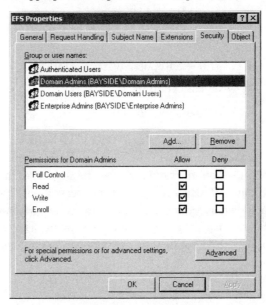

6. Ensure the appropriate users or groups have the Enroll permission to request the certificate type. If you want to give users the ability to autoenroll for a certificate, you must assign the Autoenroll permission.

Certificate Enrollment

The process of generating a request for a certificate is referred to as *certificate enrollment*. The following steps outline the process that occurs when a user generates a certificate request.

1. A key pair must be generated for and assigned to a requestor before a certificate request can be generated.

2. The requestor must gather the information required by the CA to verify its identity and issue a certificate. Before submitting the request, the requestor must gather the information required by the CA in order the verify its identity.

3. The requestor submits the necessary information to the CA along with its public key. All the required information, along with the requestor's public key, is submitted to the CA.

4. The CA verifies the information. It uses the policy rules to determine whether a certificate should be issued.

5. The CA creates a digital statement that contains the requestor's information, which is signed using the CA's private key.

6. The certificate is sent to the requestor and loaded onto the requestor's computer.

There are a number of different ways in which an entity can enroll for a certificate. These include:

- Certificate Request Wizard enrollment
- Web-based enrollment
- Automated enrollment

The Certificate Request Wizard can be used to generate a certificate request to be sent to an enterprise CA. You can launch the wizard from within the Certificates snap-in. Administrators can use the snap-in to manage their user account, computer account, or local services. Other users can use the Certificates snap-in to manage their own account certificates only. When generating a certificate request, you can choose the appropriate certificate template. The templates that a user is able to enroll for will be determined by the permissions configured on the certificate templates.

Users can also enroll for certificates using web-based enrollment by using the Certificate Services Enrollment pages, which are installed on the computer running Certificate Services (although the pages can be added to other systems). You can access the web-based enrollment pages using the following URL: http://server/certsrv/default.asp (see Figure 10-9).

Your third option for certificate enrollment is to use automatic enrollment, which relies on Active Directory. When the settings of a GPO are configured for automatic enrollment, all users and computers within the scope of the GPO will have the certificate issued. Since Active Directory is required for this enrollment method, it is supported only when an enterprise CA is deployed. Using automated enrollment is further discussed in the following section.

on the job

Automated enrollment relies on group policy. Since group policy is available only with Active Directory, this method cannot be used if Active Directory is not available. For example, if you are using a stand-alone CA, certificate enrollment would be done using the web-based certificate enrollment.

Using web-based certificate enrollment

Automated Certificate Enrollment   Using the Public Key Group Policy allows you to automate the enrollment of user and computer certificates. You can use the Group Policy snap-in to configure a Public Key Policy for sites, domains, organizational units, and local computers. Exercise 10-2 walks you through the process of configuring a group policy object for automated certificate enrollment.

EXERCISE 10-2

Configuring Group Policy for Automated Certificate Enrollment

In the following exercise, you will configure automated certificate enrollment using a group policy object.

1. Click Start, point to Administrative Tools, and click Active Directory Users And Computers.

2. Right-click the appropriate organizational unit and click Properties. Select the Group Policy tab.

3. Select an existing group policy object and click Edit. Click New to create a new group policy object.

4. Under the Computer Configuration container, expand Windows Settings, then Security Settings, and click Public Key Policies.

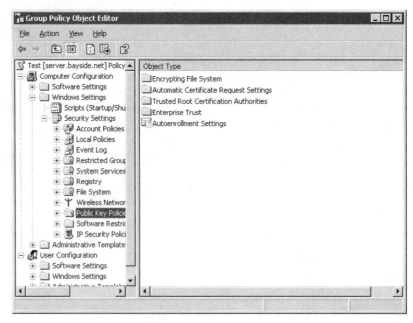

5. Right-click Automatic Certificate Request Settings, point to New, and click Automatic Certificate Request. This launches the Automatic Certificate Request Setup Wizard. Click Next.

6. Select the Certificate template. Click Next. For a certificate template to be issued, the computer must have the Enroll permission for the template.

7. Click Finish.

Certificate Revocation

Revoking certificates falls under the category of certificate management. At some point in time you will more than likely find it necessary to revoke an entity's certificate. For example, if an employee leaves an organization, his or her certificate should be revoked.

Any time a certificate is revoked, it is moved to the certificate revocation list (CRL). The next time the CRL is published, the newly revoked certificate will appear on the list so that other entities can easily identify which users and computers are no longer trusted.

Windows Server 2003 Certificate Services will publish a CRL. This list is used to inform other entities which certificates have been revoked and are therefore no longer valid. The CRL is automatically published once every week, although an administrator can configure the interval for a different time period. For example, if you expect the number of certificate revocations per week to be high, you may want to decrease the publication interval. This can be done through the Certificate Authority snap-in by right-clicking the Revoked Certificate folder and choosing Properties. In the resulting property box, you can make your adjustments to the time cycle for the CRL's publication (see Figure 10-10).

The CRL is automatically published once a week. If, during this period, you revoke a certificate, you can manually publish the CRL. Doing so does not interfere with the regular publication of the CRL. To do so, right-click the Revoked Certificates folder within the Certificate Authority snap-in, choose ALL Tasks, and choose Publish. The CRL is published in the <*systemroot*>\system32\CertSrv\CertEnroll folder. If the CA is an enterprise CA, the CRL is also published in Active Directory.

An Administrator can use the Certificate Authority snap-in to revoke a certificate. Once you revoke a certificate, it cannot be made valid again (unless the Certificate Hold option is selected). If a certificate is revoked, the entity will have to go through the enrollment process again.

FIGURE 10-10

Configuring the
frequency at
which a CRL
is published

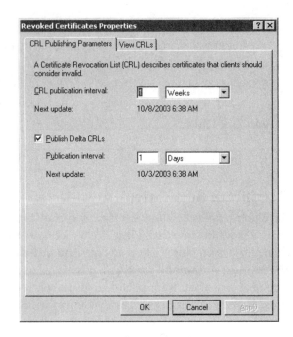

You can use these steps to revoke a certificate:

1. Click Start, point to Programs | Administrative Tools, and click Certificate Authority.

2. Expand the Certificate Authority icon and select the appropriate CA. Select the Issued Certificates container.

3. Right-click the appropriate certificate, point to All Tasks, and click Revoke Certificate.

4. The Certificate Revocation dialog box appears. Select the reason for revoking the certificate and click Yes. If you select the Certificate Hold option, the certificate can be unrevoked at a later time.

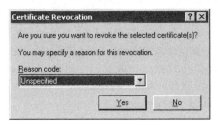

5. The certificate should now appear in the Revoked Certificates container.

Smart Card Authentication

Windows Server 2003 provides built-in support for smart card authentication. Smart cards are similar to credit cards, except that they are used to store a user's private key, instead of storing it on the local computer. The benefit of this is that it makes it more difficult (if not nearly impossible) for a user's private key to become compromised. The following section will look at how to implement smart card authentication in Windows Server 2003.

Planning for Smart Card Authentication

Implementing smart card authentication can increase the overall security of an organization. Before implementing smart card authentication, however, you should consider the points that follow.

One of the things that need to be determined is who will use smart cards for authentication. First of all, not all users within an organization should be using this technology. There are some scenarios in which smart card authentication is not supported. These include

- A user who must join a computer to a domain
- Performing advanced tasks such as installing Active Directory on a server to promote it to a domain controller
- A user who must configure remote access network connections

With this in mind, smart card authentication should not be implemented for those users who perform advanced tasks, such as members of the Administrators and Power Users groups. Smart card authentication should be used for general users, or those users who do not have to perform advanced tasks or administer a network.

Second, you can also use group policy to control how smart cards are used within an organization. A group policy object contains several security settings that apply to smart card technologies. You will need to review these settings and determine which ones you want to implement. Table 10-2 summarizes the various security settings that can be implemented.

TABLE 10-2   Smart Card Security Settings

Security Option	Description
Interactive Logon: Smart Card Required	With this option enabled, users are not able to log on using a password (unless logging on using remote access).
Interactive Logon: On Smart Card Removal behavior	With this option enabled, a computer will automatically lock once a smart card is removed from the reader.

Implementing Smart Card Authentication

Since smart card authentication requires the use of public and private keys, a PKI infrastructure must already be in place. Enabling users to log on using smart cards requires that you configure the appropriate permission for the certificate template and configure a CA to issue the certificates.

on the job

There are two certificate templates available for smart cards: smart card logon and smart card user. You would use the smart card logon template if smart cards are being used only for logons. The smart card user template is required when smart cards are being used for other purposes such as securing e-mail.

The first step in enabling smart card authentication is to configure the necessary permissions for the appropriate template. You can do so using these steps:

1. Click Start, point to Administrative Tools, and click Certificate Authority.

2. Under the appropriate CA, right-click the Certificate Templates folder and select Manage. This will open the Certificate Templates console.

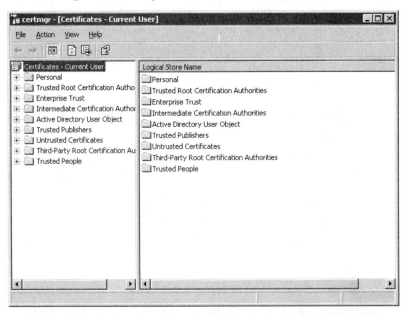

3. Right-click the Smart Card Logon template and click Properties.

4. Select the Security tab and ensure that the appropriate users are assigned the Read and Enroll permissions. You must also ensure that the Enrollment Agent has been assigned the Read and Enroll permissions for the Smart Card Logon template and the Enrollment Agent template.

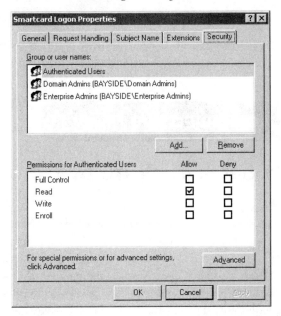

5. Click OK.

Once you have configured the appropriate permissions for the template, the next step is to configure the certificate authority to issue both the Smart Card Logon and Enrollment Agent templates. You can do so using these steps:

1. Click Start, point to Administrative Tools, and click Certificate Authority.

2. Right-click the Certificate Templates folder, point to New, and click Certificate Template To Issue.

3. From the Enable Certificate Templates dialog box, select the Smart Card Logon template and the Enrollment Agent template. Click OK.

The final step in configuring certificate services for smart card authentication is to request an enrollment agent certificate for any users that will be enrolling for smart cards. This can be done within the Certificates snap-in using the following procedure.

1. Click Start, click Run, and type **mmc**. Click OK.

2. Right-click the Certificates folder under Personal, point to All Tasks, and select Request New Certificate. This launches the Certificate Request Wizard. Click Next.

3. From the Certificate type dialog box, select Enrollment Agent. Click Next.

4. Click Finish. Users with the appropriate permissions will now be able to request smart card certificates for authentication.

CERTIFICATION OBJECTIVE 10.02

Planning a Security Framework

When people think of network security, often the first thing that comes to mind is protecting a network from malicious attacks performed by users outside of an organization. However, much of the damage caused to computer systems is the direct result of actions by legitimate users (whether these actions are intentional or not).

Now, you have many ways to increase security within an organization. However, one of the simplest and least expensive ways to protect computers is by implementing clearly defined policies and procedures that are adhered to by all users. The following section will look at how you can use security monitoring as well as change and configuration management procedures to increase and maintain security.

Security Monitoring

Suppose an organization spends numerous hours securing their network, domain controllers, and servers. Then an administrator makes a configuration change to the security settings. Although there may be a change policy in place (which is discussed in the later section "Change and Configuration Management"), changes can be made without notification or approval. When this occurs, an organization may become vulnerable in some way. However, by monitoring security and using the built-in features of Windows Server 2003, you can detect when changes are made to the security configuration and who made them.

Auditing

Being able to monitor security-related events begins with defining an audit policy. An *audit policy* determines what types of security events will be reported to an administrator. For example, an event such as a change being made to security policy settings can be reported back to an administrator. The audit policy will essentially determine what types of security-related activities are monitored.

When planning an audit policy, some of the questions you need to consider include whether you are monitoring domain controller security, the types of events to monitor, and whether to monitor the success or failure of an event. For example, monitoring unsuccessful logon attempts can identify possible password hacks. Table 10-3 outlines the settings within a group policy object that are available within a security policy.

Once you have determined the events to track along with whether to track the successes and failures of events (or both in some cases), you can begin configuring the audit policy. An audit policy can be configured locally or through a group policy object. Exercise 10-3 walks you through the process of configuring an audit policy using settings within a GPO.

TABLE 10-3   Security Policy Settings

Security Policy Setting	Description
Audit account logon events	A request to validate a user account is received by a domain controller.
Audit account management events	A user account or group is created, changed, or deleted.
Audit directory service access	A user gains access to an Active Directory object.
Audit logon events	A user logs on or off.
Audit object access	A user accesses a file, folder, or printer. In order to audit object access, auditing must also be enabled for individual resources.
Audit policy change	A configuration change is made to user security options, user rights, or audit policy.
Audit privilege use	A user exercises a user right.
Audit process tracking	An action is performed by a program or process.
Audit system events	A system event occurs such as the computer being restarted.

EXERCISE 10-3

Configuring an Audit Policy

In this exercise, you will configure an audit policy on a computer running Windows Server 2003.

1. Click Start, point to Administrative Tools, and click Active Directory Users and Computers.

2. Right-click your domain name and select Properties. From the properties dialog box, select the Group Policy tab.

3. Highlight the default domain policy and click Edit.

4. Expand Computer Configuration | Windows Settings | Local Policies | Audit Policy.

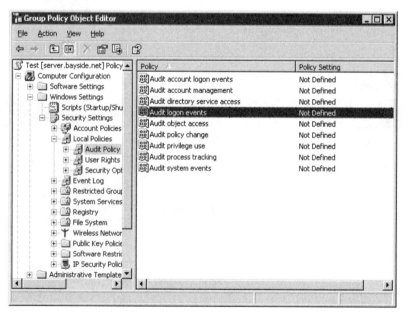

5. Configure the policy settings for the following events:
   - ■ Success/failure logon events
   - ■ Failure of a user to exercise a user right
   - ■ Success/Failure of a change to the security policy
   - ■ Failed attempt of a user to change the properties of a user account or group
   - ■ Failed attempt to access a shared folder

SCENARIO & SOLUTION	
What is the first step in implementing an audit policy?	Your first step in implementing an audit policy should be to determine which events need to be audited. You also need to decide whether to audit the successes and failures of an event.
Should auditing be enabled for all events?	No. You should choose specific events to audit. Auditing consumes system resources, thereby impacting performance. Also, the security log will increase in size and be filled with entries, making it difficult to track events.
How can I determine when an audited event has occurred?	All audited events are written to the Windows Server 2003 Security log, which can be viewed using the Event Viewer. Successful events will appear with a key, while failures appear with a lock.

Change and Configuration Management

Most organizations will employ more than one network administrator. This can pose a serious problem if policies and procedures are not clearly outlined. Let's say, for example, that one network administrator spends countless hours securing the existing infrastructure. One of the other network administrators proceeds to make a change, such as adding a new server to the network, without notifying any of the other administrators. Essentially what this does is create a vulnerability in the security of the existing infrastructure. This is where change and configuration management come into play.

The main idea behind change and configuration management is communication. Any time there is a change to be made, whether it is the addition of another server, or a configuration change on a domain controller, the necessary parties must first be notified. In other words, before any changes are made, the proper channels must first be followed.

Now there are a number of different ways in which an organization can implement change and configuration control. One of the most common ways is to require anyone who has the ability to make changes to the existing infrastructure to first compile a change request form. The information in the change request form may include any of the following items of information:

- Name of the individual requesting the change
- Description of the proposed change
- The system and/or components that the change applies to
- When the change will occur and how long it will take

- Any foreseen problems that may arise from implementing the change
- Rollback plan
- Benefits/reasons for implementing the change

Once an administrator or other user fills out the required information within a change request form, it is submitted to the necessary parties, who will determine whether the change request will be approved. In terms of security, this allows for a review process before a change is implemented to determine any security vulnerabilities that may arise from it.

CERTIFICATION OBJECTIVE 10.03

Planning a Security Update Infrastructure

Microsoft is continually releasing software updates to eliminate various security issues that are reported with an operating system or application. Organizations are faced with two issues. The first issue is ensuring that computers are up to date with security updates, and the second is how to efficiently and securely deploy the updates throughout an organization.

Microsoft offers two tools that can be used to address both of these issues: Microsoft Baseline Security Analyzer and Software Update Services. Both of these tools will be discussed in the following sections.

Microsoft Baseline Security Analyzer

Microsoft Baseline Security Analyzer (MBSA) is a tool that enables you to scan one or more computers to identify any misconfigurations that may leave a computer open to vulnerabilities. You can use the tool to scan a local computer running Windows NT 4.0, Windows 2000, Windows XP, or Windows Server 2003.

MBSA can be executed from any computer running Windows NT 4.0, Windows 2000, Windows XP, and Windows Server 2003 to scan a remote computer. MBSA can scan a system for misconfigurations in the following areas:

- **Windows System**   MBSA will scan for vulnerabilities with the operating system, for example, any unnecessary services that are enabled and any local user accounts that are configured with blank passwords.
- **Internet Information Server**   MBSA will scan IIS versions 4 and 5 for security issues such as whether logging has been enabled or whether IIS has been installed on a domain controller.

- **SQL**   MBSA will scan for vulnerabilities with SQL 7 and SQL 2000, for example, any SQL accounts that are configured with simple passwords and any instances in which access to SQL Server directories is not limited to SQL service accounts and administrators.

- **Security updates**   MBSA will scan the system to make sure it is configured with the latest service packs and security updates.

- **Desktop applications**   MBSA will scan Internet Explorer, Office 2000, and Office XP for misconfigurations.

Installing Microsoft Baseline Security Analyzer

MSBA is a tool offered for free by Microsoft. You can download the tool directly from the Microsoft web site. MSBA will run on Windows 2000, Windows XP, and Windows Server 2003. Before installing the tool, make sure the following three requirements are met:

- Internet Explorer 5.01 or later

- An XML parser (included with IE 5.01 or later)

- IIS common files if remotely scanning computers running IIS

To install the Microsoft Baseline Security Analyzer:

1. Download the Microsoft Baseline Security Analyzer from the Microsoft web site.

2. Double-click the mbsasetup.msi file. This launches the Microsoft Baseline Security Analyzer. Click Next.

3. Accept the licensing agreement and click Next.

4. Enter your full name and organization. Specify whether the application is for the user currently logged on or all users. Click Next.

5. Select a folder to install the application or accept the default location. Click Next.

6. Select the appropriate installation options and click Next.

7. Click Next to install the selected feature, Microsoft Baseline Security Analyzer.

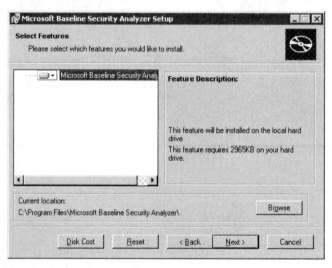

8. Click Next to begin the installation.

9. Click Finish.

Scanning with MBSA

Once MBSA is installed, you can launch the utility by clicking the application shortcut on the desktop (see Figure 10-11). The utility allows you to scan a computer, scan multiple computers, and view an existing security report. In order to scan a computer remotely, the following requirements must be met on the computer you are scanning:

- The remote computer must be running Windows NT 4.0 SP2 or later, Windows 2000, Windows XP, or Windows Server 2003.

- IIS 4.0 or later must be installed if you are scanning for IIS vulnerabilities.

- SQL 7.0 or later must be installed if you are scanning for SQL vulnerabilities.

- Microsoft Office 2000 or later must be installed if you are scanning for Office vulnerabilities.

- The Server service, the Remote Registry service, and File & Printer Sharing must be enabled.

Exercise 10-4 walks you through the process of scanning a computer.

The Microsoft
Baseline Security
Analyzer console

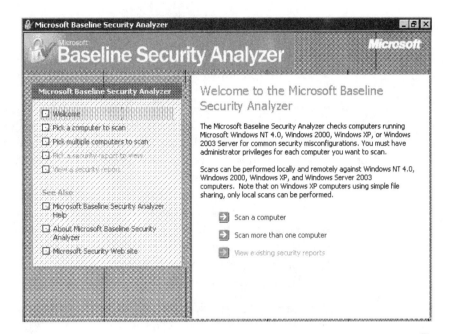

EXERCISE 10-4

Using Microsoft Baseline Security Analyzer

In this exercise, you will use the Microsoft Baseline Security Analyzer to scan a computer running Windows Server 2003.

1. Double-click the MBSA shortcut on the desktop.

2. Click the option to Scan A Computer.

3. Type in the name or IP address of the computer to scan. In this case, make sure the name of the local computer is being used. Make sure all the scanning options are selected.

4. Click the Start Scan link.

5. The Baseline Security Analyzer will begin scanning the local computer for vulnerabilities.

6. Once the scan is complete, the results are displayed.

7. Identify one of the areas in which the computer failed to pass. Briefly outline what you can do to correct the problem.

Microsoft Software Update Services

Critical updates are released by Microsoft to patch security vulnerabilities and other issues for Windows operating systems. One of the tasks network administrators face is deploying critical updates to workstations throughout a network.

Microsoft posts critical updates to the Windows Update web site. Administrators must frequently check the web site for new updates and manually download them. Once the updates are downloaded, an administrator is then faced with the challenge of efficiently distributing the updates throughout the network. This is where Software Update Services comes into play.

Normally, users would download the updates from the Internet and then proceed to install them. However, installing critical updates on a workstation or server does not always have positive results. By implementing SUS, a company can have the updates downloaded onto an internal server and install them within a test environment before installing them in the production environment.

Software Update Services consists of the two components:

- **Software Update Services server** This component is installed on a computer running Windows 2000 or Windows Server 2003. Whenever updates are available on the Windows Update Site, the SUS server can automatically download them (or they can be downloaded manually by an administrator). The updates can then be tested, published for users, and installed on workstations configured to use SUS.

- **Automatic Update Clients** This component is installed on all servers and workstations running Windows Server 2003, Windows 2000, and Windows XP so that they can connect to the server on the internal network running SUS.

Installing Software Update Services

In order to install Software Update Services, the following requirements must be met. A computer configured with the following is capable of handling up to 15,000 automatic update clients:

- Pentium III 700 MHz processor
- 512MB of RAM
- Network adapter
- NTFS partition with 100MB of free space for the SUS installation
- 6GB of free space for storage
- Windows 2000 (with service pack 2 or later) or Windows Server 2003
- Internet Explorer 5.5 or later
- Internet Information Services (IIS)

on the **Job** *Also keep in mind when you are installing Software Update Services that the system partition and the partition on which SUS is installed must be NTFS.*

Once your server has been configured according to these requirements, you are ready to install SUS. You can obtain a copy of the software directly from Microsoft's web site (the software is also free). Once you've downloaded the software, use these steps to install SUS:

1. Locate and double-click Sus10sp1.exe (this is the file downloaded from Microsoft). This launches the setup program for Software Update Services Service Pack 1. Click Next.

2. Accept the licensing agreement and click Next.

3. Select the type of installation. Selecting a Typical installation will install SUS using the default settings. Click Next.

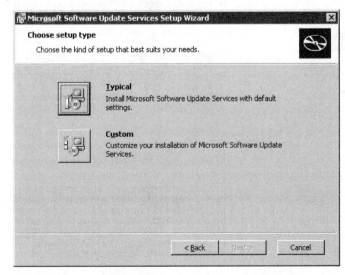

4. The next window displays the URL that clients will use to connect to the SUS server. Click Install.

5. Click Finish. The SUS administration web site opens from which you can configure your SUS server.

Configuring Software Update Services

Once the installation is complete, you will be ready to configure the SUS server. If you followed the steps just outlined when installing SUS and chose a typical installation, the SUS server will be configured with these default settings:

■ The SUS server is configured to retrieve software updates from the Microsoft Windows Update servers.

■ The proxy server configuration is set to automatically select settings.

■ Content that is downloaded is stored locally.

■ All packages are available in all supported languages.

■ Any approved packages that are later updated are not automatically approved.

■ Clients locate the server using its NetBIOS name.

If the default settings are sufficient, you will not need to reconfigure the SUS server. An SUS server can be further configured using the SUS administration tools. You can access the administration site by using the URL http://<*yourservername*>/ SUSAdmin. Alternatively, you can also launch the administration site by clicking Start | Administrative Tools and selecting Microsoft Software Update Services (see Figure 10-12). To begin configuring the SUS server, click the Set Options link.

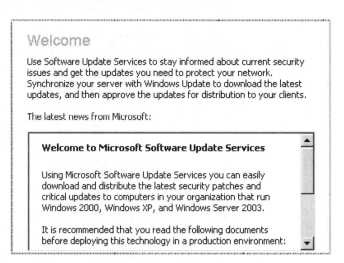

Welcome

Use Software Update Services to stay informed about current security issues and get the updates you need to protect your network. Synchronize your server with Windows Update to download the latest updates, and then approve the updates for distribution to your clients.

The latest news from Microsoft:

Welcome to Microsoft Software Update Services

Using Microsoft Software Update Services you can easily download and distribute the latest security patches and critical updates to computers in your organization that run Windows 2000, Windows XP, and Windows Server 2003.

It is recommended that you read the following documents before deploying this technology in a production environment:

From the Set Options page, you can configure various settings for the server that include

- The proxy server configuration
- The name clients use to connect to the server
- Where the SUS server retrieves updates from
- How new versions of previously approved updates are handled
- Where updates are stored

Under the setting Select A Proxy Server Configuration, you can specify how the SUS server accesses the Internet. Choose one of the following options for how the SUS server connects to the Internet (see Figure 10-13).

- **Do not use a proxy server**   This option should be selected if the server does not connect to the Internet through a proxy server.
- **Use a proxy server to access the Internet**   This option should be selected if the server connects to the Internet through a proxy server.
- **Automatically detect proxy server settings**   Select this option if your network supports automatic discovery of proxy server settings.
- **Use the following proxy server**   If the network does not support automatic configuration of proxy settings, specify the address or port number of the proxy server. If credentials are required to connect through the proxy server, specify the username and password the SUS server will use.

Next you can specify the name that clients on the private network will use to connect to the SUS server. If your network supports NetBIOS, you can specify the

FIGURE 10-13

Configuring the proxy settings for the SUS server

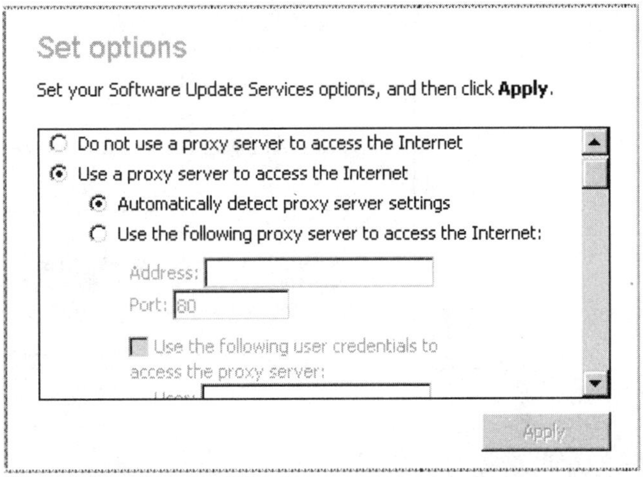

Set options

Set your Software Update Services options, and then click **Apply**.

○ Do not use a proxy server to access the Internet
◉ Use a proxy server to access the Internet
　　◉ Automatically detect proxy server settings
　　○ Use the following proxy server to access the Internet:
　　　　Address:
　　　　Port: 80
　　　　☐ Use the following user credentials to
　　　　access the proxy server:

Apply

NetBIOS name of the server. If DNS is being used, you must specify the DNS name or the IP address of the SUS server (see Figure 10-14).

Next you can configure where the SUS server will retrieve updates from. Here you have two options. The updates can be retrieved directly from the Microsoft web site, or they can be retrieved from another SUS server. For example, you can have one SUS server that pulls updates from the Internet. All other SUS servers on the network can be configured to retrieve the updates from this local server (instead of having all SUS servers on the network retrieve updates from the Internet). Select Synchronize Directly From The Microsoft Windows Update Servers to have the SUS server retrieve updates directly from the Windows Update web site. Select Synchronize From A Local Software Update Services Server to have the SUS server retrieve the updates from another local server. If you select this option, you must also specify the name of the local server (see Figure 10-15).

The next section allows you to configure how new versions of previously approved updates are handled. The two options are these (see Figure 10-16):

■ Automatically approve new versions of previously approved updates.

■ Do not automatically approve new versions of previously approved updates. I will manually approve these later.

If you change the default option so that new versions of previously approved updates are not automatically approved as well, you will have the opportunity to test the new updates before they are available to clients.

Finally, you can also configure where you want the updates to be stored. When an SUS server connects to the Microsoft Windows Update site, it can download two

FIGURE 10-14

Configuring the name clients use to connect to the SUS server

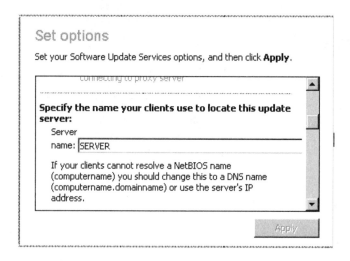

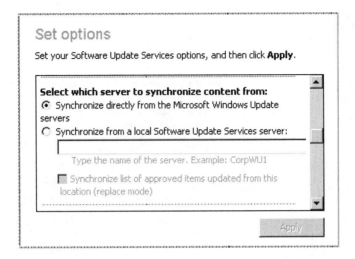

FIGURE 10-15

Configuring
where an SUS
server retrieves
updates from

types of content. First it downloads a file (Aucatalog1.cab) that describes the list of packages. Second, it can download the actual software packages.

You can configure an SUS server to download just the catalog or the software packages as well. If the SUS server downloads only the catalog, clients will retrieve the list of approved software packages from the SUS server and then download them from the Windows Update web site. Alternatively, the software packages can be downloaded and stored on the SUS server. This way, clients do not have to connect to the Windows Update site to retrieve the software. You can also specify the locales that will be downloaded by selecting each language you need to support on the network (see Figure 10-17).

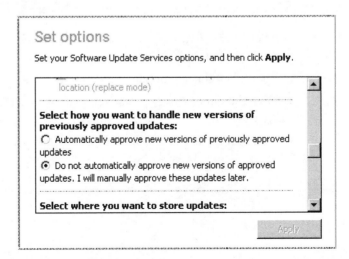

FIGURE 10-16

Configuring how
updated versions
of previously
approved updates
are handled

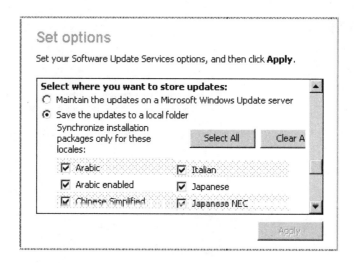

FIGURE 10-17

Configuring
where updates
are stored and in
what languages
they are made
available

Configuring Clients for Automatic Updates

In order to implement a Software Update Services infrastructure, you must also install a special version of Automatic Update on the workstations. The update software allows clients to download the updates from an SUS server instead of using the Windows Update web site. Keep in mind that the updated version of the software is supported only by Windows 2000, Windows XP, and Windows Server 2003 clients.

Updating Client Software   The Automatic Update client (WUAU22.msi) can be downloaded from the Microsoft web site. You can deploy the software locally on each workstation, or it can be deployed from a central location using Active Directory. The following steps outline how the client can be deployed using a group policy object:

1. Click Start, point to Administrative Tools, and click Active Directory Users And Computers.

2. Right-click the appropriate organizational unit and click Properties.

3. From the Group Policy tab, select an existing GPO and click Edit or click New to create a new GPO.

4. Under Computer Configuration, select Software Settings.

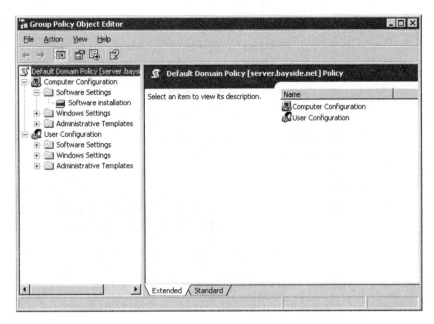

5. Right-click Software Installation, point to New, and click Package.

6. Locate the WUAU22.msi file and click Open.

7. The Deploy Software window appears. Click Assigned and click OK.

Deploying Automatic Client Update Settings   There are a number of different settings that can be configured for the clients. For example, you can specify which server the clients will retrieve updates from. You have two options for deploying the settings: you can do so locally on each workstation, or you can do so through a GPO.

on the **job**

Before you can deploy any settings through a GPO, you must first load the Automatic Update policy settings. This should be done when Software Update Services is installed. If not, open the appropriate GPO (under the Computer Configuration or User Configuration), right-click the Administrative Templates folder, and click Add/Remove Templates. Click Add and locate the Automatic Updates ADM file (wuau.adm), which is located in the Windows\inf directory. Select the adm file and click Open.

You can find the Windows Update settings by navigating to the Administrative Templates/Windows Components/Windows Update folder within a GPO (see Figure 10-18). There are four different settings that you can configure:

- Configure Automatic Updates
- Specify intranet Microsoft update service location
- Reschedule Automatic Updates scheduled installations
- No auto-restart for scheduled Automatic Updates installations

The first setting, Configure Automatic Updates, is used to enable or disable automatic updates (see Figure 10-19). If it is enabled, you can select one of the following settings as to how updates are downloaded and if the administrator is notified:

- Notify for download and notify for install
- Auto-download and notify for install (this is the default)
- Auto-download and schedule the install

Windows Update
settings

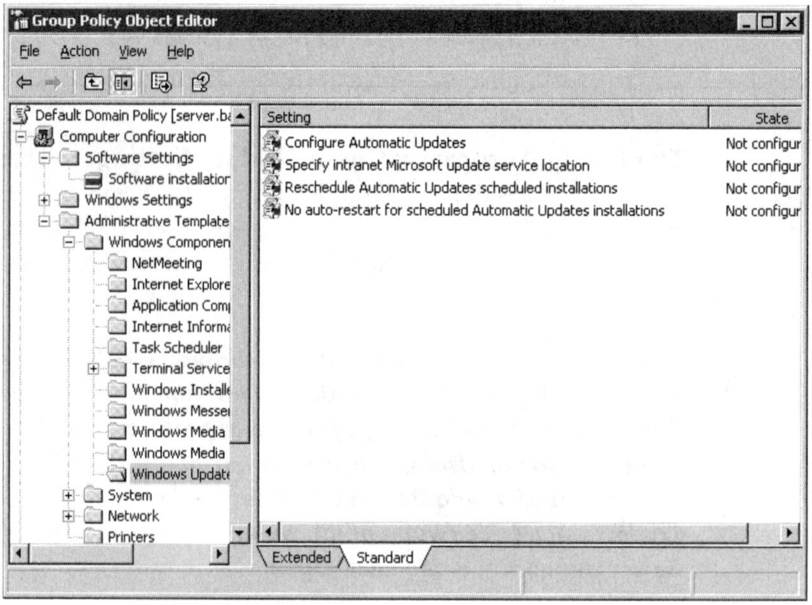

Enabling
or disabling
automatic
updates

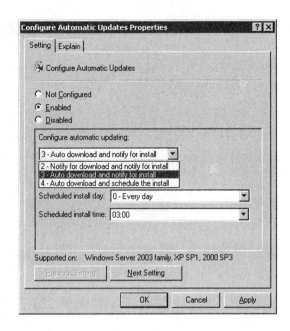

You can also use the schedule options to configure the day and time that installs should take place.

The next setting available, Specify Intranet Microsoft Update Service Location, is used to configure which intranet SUS server clients will retrieve updates from and which server they will send statistics to (see Figure 10-20).

The Reschedule Automatic Updates Scheduled Installations setting is used to define how long to wait after system startup before proceeding with an installation when a scheduled install has been missed. If this option is disabled, the installation will occur at the next scheduled day and time (see Figure 10-21).

The No Auto-Restart For Scheduled Automatic Updates Installations option is used to configure whether or not the computer is automatically restarted after an update is installed. If this option is enabled, the user currently logged in will be notified to restart the computer. The computer will not be automatically restarted (see Figure 10-22).

As already mentioned, automatic updates can also be configured locally. You can do so by creating various Registry entries. Table 10-4 outlines the various entries that should be created.

FIGURE 10-20

Configuring where
clients download
updates from and
send statistics to

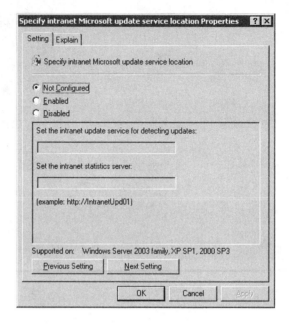

FIGURE 10-21

Configuring
the Reschedule
Automatic
Updates Scheduled
Installations option

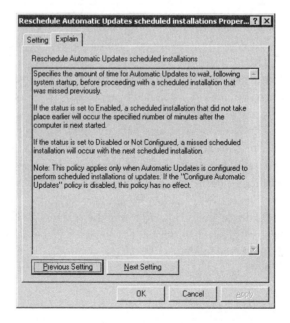

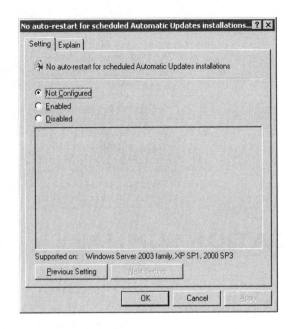

FIGURE 10-22

Configuring the
No Auto-Restart
For Scheduled
Automatic
Updates
Installations option

TABLE 10-4   Windows Update Registry Settings

Registry Entry	Description
UseWUServer	This option is used to specify whether an SUS server is used. Setting the value to 1 indicates the client will download updates from an SUS server.
AUOptions	This option is used to configure how updates are downloaded and whether administrators are notified. The possible values are 2 (notify of download and installation), 3 (automatically download and notify of installation), or 4 (automatic download and scheduled installation).
ScheduledInstallDay	This option specifies the day of the week that updates will be installed. The values range from 0 to 7, where 0 indicates every day and 1–7 indicate specific days of the week, where 1 = Sunday and 7 = Saturday.
ScheduledInstallTime	This option specifies the time of day that installs will take place. The value is specified in 24-hour format.
RescheduleWaitTime	This defines how long to wait after restarting a computer for a missed scheduled install to take place. The value is specified in minutes (1–60).

TABLE 10-4	Windows Update Registry Settings *(continued)*
NoAutoRebootWithLoggedOnUsers	This option specifies whether the computer is automatically restarted after an update is installed. Set this value to 1 to enable the logged-on user to choose whether or not to reboot their computer.
NoAutoUpdate	This option is used to enable or disable automatic updates.
WUServer	This option is used to specify which SUS server the client will retrieve updates from. The SUS server is identified by HHTP name, for example, http://SUSsrv01.
WUStatusServer	This option is used to specify where clients will send status information. The server is identified by HTTP name.

CERTIFICATION SUMMARY

This chapter began by looking at Windows Server 2003 Certificate Services. It is used to issue and manage certificates for a Public Key Infrastructure (PKI). Installing Certificate Services enables a computer running Windows Server 2003 to be configured to receive certificate requests, verify the identity of a requestor, issue and revoke certificates, and publish a certificate revocation list (CRL).

Windows Server 2003 provides built-in support for smart card authentication. Smart cards are similar to credit cards, except that they are used to store a user's private key, instead of storing it on the local computer. The benefit of this is that it makes it more difficult (if not nearly impossible) for a user's private key to become compromised.

Security is often compromised by users within the organization as opposed to external attackers. Other than configuring security settings, one of the simplest things you can do to monitor security is to implement change and configuration management procedures as well as auditing. By implementing an audit policy, you can track security-related events that occur on the network.

Another task faced by network administrators is keeping computers up to date with the latest updates released by Microsoft. Two tools that can be downloaded from the Microsoft web site for free to assist administrators in keeping computers secure are the Microsoft Baseline Security Analyzer and Software Update Services. Microsoft Baseline Security Analyzer (MBSA) is a tool that enables you to scan one or more computers to identify any misconfigurations that may leave a computer open to vulnerabilities. With Software Update Services, a company can have updates downloaded to an internal server, install them within a test environment before installing them in the production environment, and then deploy them to computers throughout the network.

✓ TWO-MINUTE DRILL

Planning for Certificate Services

❑ Certificates are digital statements issued by a trusted authority. Certificates are used to verify an entity's identity.

❑ A CA is an entity that has been delegated the task of issuing digital certificates to users, computers, and organizations.

❑ The certificate revocation list (CRL) is published to identify those entities that are no longer trusted.

❑ A CA hierarchy can consist of multiple CAs that form parent-child relationships. At the top of a hierarchy is the CA root authority. Child CAs (or subordinates) are certified by their parent CA.

❑ Enterprise certificate authorities require Active Directory and DNS.

❑ Stand-alone CAs are configured to issue certificates to entities outside of an organization. Enterprise CAs use information within Active Directory to verify a user's identity.

❑ A user can be designated as a Certificate Manager by assigning them the Issue and Manage Certificates permission.

❑ Version 1 certificate templates are supported by Windows 2000 clients. Version 2 certificate templates are supported by Windows XP and Windows Server 2003 clients.

❑ Certificates requests can be generated using the Certificate Request Wizard, through web-based enrollment, or using automated enrollment.

❑ Smart cards can be used in place of traditional password authentication.

❑ When planning for smart card authentication, you need to determine which users will use smart cards and the policy settings to implement.

❑ Once you enable the Smart Card Required policy setting, any users affected by the policy will not be able to log on with a password.

❑ The Smart Card Logon template is used solely for smart card authentication. The Smart Card User template should be enabled when smart cards are used for other purposes, such as secure e-mail.

Planning a Security Framework

❑ Auditing can be used to track security-related events that occur within an organization.

❑ An audit policy determines the types of events that are monitored. It also determines whether the successes or failures for an event are tracked.

❑ An audit policy can be configured locally or through a group policy object.

❑ Change and configuration management ensures that any changes are approved before they are implemented.

Planning a Security Update Infrastructure

❑ The Microsoft Baseline Security Analyzer is a tool used to scan a computer for security misconfigurations that may leave it vulnerable.

❑ Software Update Services is used to download Windows Updates and deploy them to computers on an intranet.

❑ SUS consists of two components: Software Update Services servers and Automatic Update clients.

❑ The updated version of Automatic Updates must be installed for updates to be retrieved from an SUS server.

❑ Only Windows 2000 and later platforms support the updates version of Automatic Updates.

❑ The SUS web administration tools are used to configure an SUS server.

❑ If NetBIOS is disabled on the network, you must specify the IP address or DNS name of the SUS server that clients will connect to.

❑ Windows Update settings can be deployed through a GPO or configured locally.

SELF TEST

Planning for Certificate Services

1. Your organization is implementing a web server that will be used for customer transactions. The web server will not be configured as a member of the company's domain. Internet customers need to be assured of secure transactions and of the web server's identity. You decide to implement a certificate authority. What type of certificate authority should be configured?

   A. Enterprise root CA

   B. Stand-alone root CA

   C. Enterprise subordinate CA

   D. Stand-alone subordinate CA

2. John is the administrator of a Windows Server 2003 network. He has been asked to configure Certificate Services for his company. Certificates should be approved immediately using domain user account information within Active Directory. The certificate authority will be used only by domain users. Which of the following should you implement?

   A. Enterprise root CA

   B. Enterprise subordinate CA

   C. Stand-alone root CA

   D. Stand-alone subordinate CA

3. You are installing an enterprise root CA for your company network. Which of the following are required to install an enterprise root certificate authority? (Choose all correct answers.)

   A. DHCP

   B. Commercial CA

   C. Active Directory

   D. DNS

   E. IIS

4. A certificate authority has just been installed on your company network. You want to test the configuration and enroll for a certificate using the web-based enrollment page. Which of the following URLs should you use?

   A. http://<servername>/Cert/default.asp

   B. http://<servername>/CertSrv/default.asp

   C. http://<servername>/CertEnroll/default.asp

   D. http://<servername>/Certificates/default.asp

5. The administrators for FKP International want to be able to download updates from the Windows Update web site and install them in a test environment before they are deployed to computers on the company network. Which of the following can be used to facilitate this?

   A. Microsoft Baseline Security Analyzer

   B. Security Configuration and Analysis

   C. Software Update Services

   D. Group Policy

6. John is planning the deployment of software update services for his company. Workstations are currently running a variety of different Windows platforms. Which of the following will support the updated version of Automatic Updates? (Choose all correct answers.)

   A. Windows 95

   B. Windows 98

   C. Windows Me

   D. Windows 2000

   E. Windows XP

   F. Windows Server 2003

7. Mary is configuring a server that will run Software Update Services. She verifies that all the hardware requirements are met. Windows Server 2003, IIS 5.0 and Internet Explorer 6.0 are installed. When she tries to install SUS, the installation fails. What could be causing the problem?

   A. The server is running the wrong version of IIS.

   B. The partition that will store the updates is formatted with NTFS.

   C. Service pack 1 for Windows Server 2003 is not installed.

   D. The system partition must be formatted with NTFS.

8. Mike is planning the deployment of Software Update Services. Multiple SUS servers (SRV01, SRV02, and SRV03) will be added to the network. He is concerned about traffic on the Internet connection generated from all SUS servers retrieving updates from the Windows Update web site. What can he do? (Choose two correct answers.)

   A. Configure the WUServer option to specify which SUS server clients will retrieve updates from using a group policy object.

   B. Using the SUS administration tools, configure the SUS servers to download only the catalog file.

   C. Using the SUS administration tools, configure SRV01 to synchronize with the Windows Update servers.

D. Using the SUS administration tools, configure the SUS servers to synchronize with a local SUS server.

E. Using the SUS administration tools, configure each SUS server to synchronize directly with the Windows Update servers.

Planning a Security Framework

9. Recently a configuration change was made to the security settings within a group policy that left the company network vulnerable to security attacks. This has resulted in the implementation of new security practices. You want to be able to track when a change is made that affects security. What should you do?

A. Implement change control.

B. Configure an audit policy.

C. Run the Microsoft Baseline Security Analyzer.

D. Implement smart card authentication.

10. You have added a new web server to the network and configured it using the company's standard security settings. However, you want to verify that there are no misconfigurations with the server that may leave it vulnerable. What should you do?

A. Run the Security Configuration and Analysis tool.

B. View the current updates available from the Windows Update site.

C. Run the Microsoft Baseline Security Analyzer tool.

D. View the entries within the security log.

11. Mark is concerned about attempted password hacks against his company's domain. The current security configuration limits the number of failed logon attempts before a user is locked out. However, he would like to be notified when a failed logon attempt occurs. What should he do?

A. Implement change control.

B. Enable an audit policy.

C. Implement smart cards.

D. Configure a password policy.

12. Smart card authentication is being implemented throughout your company for all users except administrative staff. When configuring Certificate Services to support smart card authentication, which of the following templates must you configure permissions for?

A. Enrollment Agent

B. Smart Card Logon

C. Smart Card User

D. Smart Card Authentication

13. Ron is putting together a proposal to install Software Update Services. His managers want to know what the requirements are to run the software. Which of the following are considered to be minimum hardware requirements for installing Software Update Services?

   A. Pentium III 500MHz
   B. Pentium III 700MHz
   C. 265MB RAM
   D. 512MB RAM
   E. 4GB storage space
   F. 6GB storage space

Planning a Security Update Infrastructure

14. Felicia is using Software Update Services within a test environment on two computers before implementing the service in the production environment. She installs Software Update Services on a stand-alone server. She has a Windows XP workstation to perform testing with. She wants to configure automatic updates through the Registry so that the local administrator is notified of downloads and installations. How should she proceed?

   A. Configure the AUOptions.
   B. Configure the WUServer option.
   C. Configure the UseWUServer option.
   D. Configure the NoAutoUpdate option.

15. You have enabled Automatic Updates on a Windows XP workstation to use SUS. You now want to specify which SUS server the workstation will download options from. Which Registry value should you configure?

   A. UseWUServer
   B. AUOptions
   C. WUServer
   D. WUStatusServer

LAB QUESTION

The head of security for DKP Int'l is concerned about security breaches. Managers have recently been led to believe that there may be possible attempted password attacks against the network. They have no evidence of this, as there is no security monitoring in place. The head of security has brought these concerns to you and asked you to implement a plan that will address the issue. The managers are concerned that there is currently no way of identifying possible attacks. Since there are also several administrators working alongside of you, they are also concerned about changes that may be made to the existing security configuration and that may leave the organization vulnerable to such attacks. Given this, devise a security monitoring plan that will address the concerns of your managers. Consider the following questions when coming up with a security monitoring solution:

1. How can you reduce the risk of changes being made by one administrator that may have adverse effects on the existing security infrastructure?

2. How can you ensure that security-related events are monitored?

3. Given the concerns in the scenario, which security-related events should be monitored?

4. Outline the steps involved in implementing a Windows Server 2003 audit policy.

5. You have decided to propose the implementation of a change control document that must be used by all administrators. Outline some of the important information that should be included in the document when submitted for approval.

SELF TEST ANSWERS

Planning for Certificate Services

1. ☑ **D.** Since the CA is being used by external clients, a stand-alone CA should be implemented. In order for Internet clients to verify the identity of the CA, it should be configured as a subordinate CA to a commercial CA.
☒ **A** and **C** are incorrect because enterprise CAs are used to issue certificates to entities within a domain. **B** is incorrect because a commercial CA should be used to assure customers of the server's identity.

2. ☑ **A.** Since a CA is required to issue certificates to users using domain user account information, an enterprise CA is required. The CA must be an enterprise root CA because no other CA exists on the network.
☒ **B** is incorrect because in order to configure a stand-alone enterprise CA, a root CA is required. **C** and **D** are incorrect because stand-alone CAs are used to issue certificates to entities outside an organization.

3. ☑ **C** and **D.** An enterprise CA requires DNS and Active Directory.
☒ **A, B,** and **E** are incorrect because these components are not required by an enterprise CA. IIS is required only if web-based enrollment is being used.

4. ☑ **B.** The default URL used to access the web-based enrollment page is http://<servername>/CertSrv/default.asp.
☒ **A, C,** and **D** are incorrect because these answers do not represent the correct URL used to access the web-based enrollment page.

5. ☑ **C.** Software Update Services can be used to download updates from the Windows Update web site. They can be installed in a test environment and approved by an administrator before being deployed to computers.
☒ **A** is incorrect because Microsoft Baseline Security Analyzer is used to analyze a computer and detect security misconfiguration. **B** is incorrect because this tool is used to analyze the security settings configured on a computer against those within a template. **D** is incorrect because group policy is not used to deploy critical Windows updates.

6. ☑ **D, E,** and **F.** In order for computers to retrieve updates from an SUS server, an updated version of Automatic Updates is required. This software is supported only by Windows 2000, Windows XP, and Windows Server 2003 platforms.
☒ **A, B,** and **C** are incorrect because these platforms do not support the updated client software.

7. ☑ **D.** In order to install SUS, the system partition must be formatted with NTFS.
☒ **A** is incorrect because IIS 5.0 and later are supported. The server is currently running IIS 5.0. **B** is incorrect because the partition where the updates are stored must be formatted with NTFS, which is already the case. **C** is incorrect because Internet Explorer 5.01 and later are supported.

8. ☑ **C** and **D**. Traffic on the Internet connection can be controlled by configuring one server to synchronize with the Windows Update servers. The remaining SUS servers can be configured to synchronize with this local SUS server.

   ☒ **A** is incorrect because this option will only determine from which local SUS server a computer will retrieve approved updates. **B** is incorrect because this solution would not limit traffic on the Internet connection.

Planning a Security Framework

9. ☑ **B.** By configuring an audit policy, an administrator can track events that occur on the network. Any audited events that occur are written to the security log.

   ☒ **A** is incorrect because change control is a policy put in place outlining the proper channels a user must take before making configuration changes to the existing infrastructure. **C** is incorrect because Microsoft Baseline Security Analyzer is used to identify various misconfigurations in security on a computer. **D** is incorrect because smart cards are used to replace traditional password authentication.

10. ☑ **C.** One of the features of the Microsoft Baseline Security Analyzer is that it will scan a computer running IIS to identify any security misconfigurations. Therefore, answer C is correct.

    ☒ **A** is incorrect because the Security Configuration and Analysis tool is used to compare the security settings currently configured on a computer with those in a template. **B** is incorrect because this would consume a large amount of an administrator's time. It will also not allow you to identify current misconfigurations on the computer. **D** is incorrect because the security log contains information about audited events only.

11. ☑ **B.** By implementing an audit policy, you can track all failed logon attempts. Each time a user unsuccessfully attempts to log on, an event will be written to the security log.

    ☒ **A** is incorrect because change control is implemented to outline the proper procedures a user must follow before making configuration changes to the existing infrastructure. **C** is incorrect because smart cards are used to store a user's private key instead of storing it on the local computer. **D** is incorrect because a password policy is used to define password requirements such as minimum password length and account lock out settings.

12. ☑ **A** and **B.** In order to implement smart cards for authentication, users must have Read and Enroll permissions for the Smart Card Logon template. The designated enrollment agent must have Read and Enroll permissions for the Enrollment Agent template.

    ☒ **C** is incorrect because the Smart Card User template is used when smart cards are being deployed for purposes other than just authentication, such as secure e-mail. **D** is incorrect because there is no default template included with Windows Server 2003.

13. ☑ **B, D,** and **F.** Microsoft recommends that a computer running SUS be configured with the following minimum hardware requirements: Pentium III 700 MHz, 512MB of RAM, and 6GB of free space to store updates.

☒ **A**, **C**, and **E** are incorrect because these options do not meet the recommended hardware requirements.

14. ☑ **A.** By configuring the AUOptions within the Registry, you can specify how and and when the administrator is notified of updates.

☒ **B** is incorrect because this option is used to specify that the computer retrieve updates from an SUS server. Answer **C** is incorrect because this option is used to enable the computer to retrieve updates from an SUS server. **D** is incorrect because this option is used to enable or disable automatic updates.

Planning a Security Update Infrastructure

15. ☑ **C.** The WUServer option is used to specify which SUS server a computer will retrieve updates from.

☒ **A** is incorrect because this option is used to specify that the computer retrieve updates from an SUS server. **B** is incorrect because this option is used to configure how updates are downloaded and when the administrator is notified of updates. **D** is incorrect because this option is used to specify which SUS server a computer will send status information to.

LAB ANSWERS

1. One of the simplest and least expensive ways of controlling what changes are made to the existing infrastructure is to implement some form of change and configuration management. Many organizations implement change control where any possible changes must first be documented and submitted for approval before they can take place.

2. By enabling an audit policy, you can enable security-related events to be tracked. Each time an audited event occurs, an entry is written to the security log, essentially leaving an audit trail.

3. Audit account logon events (failures), logon events (failures), and policy changes (failures).

4. Once you have determined the events to audit and whether to audit successes and/or failures, you can use the following steps to enable an audit policy:
   A. Click Start, point to Administrative Tools, and click Active Directory Users And Computers.
   B. Right-click your domain name and select Properties. From the properties dialog box, select the Group Policy tab.
   C. Highlight the default domain policy and click Edit.
   D. Expand Computer Configuration | Windows Settings | Local Policies | Audit Policy.

5. A change control document should include information such as who is requesting the change, what the change entails, the impact the change will have, and a rollback plan in the event things do not go as planned.

Appendix

About the CD

The CD-ROM included with this book comes complete with MasterExam, MasterSim, CertCam movie clips, the electronic version of the book, and Session #1 of LearnKey's online training. The software is easy to install on any Windows 98/NT/2000/XP/Server 2003 computer and must be installed to access the MasterExam and MasterSim features. You may, however, browse the electronic book and CertCams directly from the CD without installation. To register for LearnKey's online training and a second bonus MasterExam, simply click the Online Training link on the Main Page and follow the directions to the free online registration.

System Requirements

Software requires Windows 98 or higher and Internet Explorer 5.0 or above and 20 MB of hard disk space for full installation. The Electronic book requires Adobe Acrobat Reader. To access the Online Training from LearnKey, you must have RealPlayer Basic 8 or Real1 Plugin, which will automatically be installed when you launch the Online Training.

LearnKey Online Training

The **LearnKey Online Training** link will allow you to access online training from Osborne.Onlineexpert.com. The first session of this course is provided at no charge. Additional Sessions for this course and other courses may be purchased directly from www.LearnKey.com or by calling (800) 865-0165.

The first time that you run the Training, you will be required to register with the online product. Follow the instructions for a first-time user. Please make sure to use a valid e-mail address.

Prior to running the Online Training you will need to add the Real Plugin and the RealCBT plugin to your system. This will automatically be facilitated to your system when you run the training the first time.

Installing and Running MasterExam and MasterSim

If your computer CD-ROM drive is configured to auto run, the CD-ROM will automatically start up upon inserting the disk. From the opening screen you may install MasterExam or MasterSim by pressing the MasterExam or MasterSim buttons. This will begin the installation process and create a program group named "LearnKey." To run

MasterExam or MasterSim use Start | Programs | LearnKey. If the auto run feature did not launch your CD, browse to the CD and Click on the RunInstall icon.

MasterExam

MasterExam provides you with a simulation of the actual exam. The number of questions, the type of questions, and the time allowed are intended to be an accurate representation of the exam environment. You have the option to take an open-book exam, including hints, references, and answers; a closed-book exam; or the timed MasterExam simulation.

When you launch MasterExam, a digital clock display will appear in the upper-left-hand corner of your screen. The clock will continue to count down to zero unless you choose to end the exam before the time expires.

MasterSim

The MasterSim is a set of interactive labs that will provide you with a wide variety of tasks to allow the user to experience the software environment even if the software is not installed. Once you have installed the MasterSim, you may access it quickly through the CD launch page or through Start | Programs | LearnKey.

Electronic Book

The entire contents of the Study Guide are provided in PDF form. Adobe's Acrobat Reader has been included on the CD.

CertCam

CertCam .AVI clips provide detailed examples of key certification objectives. These clips walk you step-by-step through various system configurations. You can access the clips directly from the CertCam table of contents by pressing the CertCam button on the Main Page.

The CertCam .AVI clips are recorded and produced using TechSmith's Camtasia Producer. Since .AVI clips can be very large, ExamSim uses TechSmith's special AVI Codec to compress the clips. The file named "tsccvid.dll" is copied to your Windows\ System folder during the first auto run. If the .AVI clip runs with audio but no video, you may need to re-install the file from the CD-ROM. Browse to the Programs | CertCams folder, and run TSCC.

Help

A help file is provided through the help button on the main page in the lower-left-hand corner. Individual help features are also available through MasterExam, MasterSim, and LearnKey's Online Training.

Removing Installation(s)

MasterExam and MasterSim are installed to your hard drive. For best results for removal of programs, use the Start | Programs | LearnKey | Uninstall options to remove MasterExam or MasterSim.

If you desire to remove the Real Player, use the Add/Remove Programs Icon from your Control Panel. You may also remove the LearnKey training program from this location.

Technical Support

For questions regarding the technical content of the electronic book, MasterExam, or CertCams, please visit www.osborne.com or e-mail customer.service@mcgraw-hill.com. For customers outside the 50 United States, e-mail international_cs@mcgraw-hill.com.

LearnKey Technical Support

For technical problems with the software (installation, operation, removing installations), and for questions regarding LearnKey Online Training and MasterSim content, please visit www.learnkey.com or e-mail techsupport@learnkey.com.

Glossary

Address Resolution Protocol (ARP)   The Address Resolution Protocol (ARP) is responsible for resolving IP addresses to MAC or hardware addresses.

Automatic Private IP Addressing (APIPA)   APIPA automates IP configuration by enabling computers to assign themselves an IP address from network 169.254.0.0/16.

Basic Firewall   A new feature of Windows Server 2003 is the Basic Firewall. This component, used to protect your private network from unsolicited inbound traffic, can be enabled on a NAT interface. Basic Firewall protects the private network using a combination of dynamic and static packet filtering.

Berkeley Internet Name Daemon (BIND)   One of the most prevalent DNS services is known as the Berkeley Internet Name Daemon (BIND), which is Unix based.

Caching-only DNS Server   DNS servers have a local cache file known as cache.dns. Whenever a DNS server resolves a query, it places the information within the cache. The next time a request for the same hostname is received, the information can be retrieved from the local cache instead of having to resolve the name using other DNS servers. Caching-only DNS servers are not authoritative for any zone information.

Certificate Authority   A Certificate Authority (CA) is an entity, such as a computer that has been delegated the task of issuing digital certificates to users, computers, and organizations that must prove their identity to other entities.

Certificate Revocation List (CRL)   Any time a certificate is revoked, it is moved to the Certificate Revocation List (CRL). Entities can use a CRL to determine which users, computers, or organizations are no longer considered to be trusted.

Certificate Services   Certificate Services is included with Windows Server 2003. It is used to issue and manage certificates for a Public Key Infrastructure (PKI).

Challenge Handshake Authentication Protocol (CHAP)   The Challenge Handshake Authentication Protocol (CHAP) is an industry-standard authentication protocol. Unlike SPAP and PAP, CHAP does not send the credentials across the network. Instead, CHAP uses a challenge-response where the Message Digest 5 (MD5) is used to encrypt the response. CHAP can be used to authenticate non-Windows clients.

Cluster   A cluster is a group of computers working together as if it were a single computer to provide increased availability of services and applications. This allows access and management of the cluster as a single unit.

Default Gateway   This is the IP address of the local router interface where packets that are destined for a remote network are forwarded.

Demand-Dial Routing   Routing and Remote Access allows a computer running Windows Server 2003 to be configured as a demand-dial router. With this configuration, the router can initiate a connection to a remote network to deliver a packet to a remote site.

Department of Defense (DoD) Model   The suite of protocols that make up TCP/IP also map to another conceptual model, referred to as the Department of Defense (DoD) model. This model was developed by the U.S. Department of Defense as a public standard for TCP/IP that would be independent of all software and hardware vendors.

DHCP Relay Agent   A relay agent is responsible for relaying DHCP messages between DHCP clients and DHCP servers that are located on different subnets. If routers are RFC 1542 compliant, they can forward the DHCP-related messages between subnets. If not, a computer running Windows Server 2003 (or Windows NT 4.0 and Windows 2000 as well) can be configured as a relay agent by installing the DHCP Relay Agent component.

Domain Name Service (DNS)   The Domain Name Service (DNS) is used to resolve hostnames to IP addresses. DNS is required within a Windows Server 2003 domain.

Dynamic Host Configuration Protocol (DHCP)   The Dynamic Host Configuration Protocol (DHCP) eliminates most of the administrative overhead associated with configuring IP addresses. It automates the process of assigning IP addresses and other parameters to hosts as well as centralizes administration.

Dynamic Routing   Dynamic routing eliminates the overhead associated with manually updating routing tables. Routers can dynamically build their own routing tables by communicating with other routers on the network.

Dynamic Update Using this feature, resource records no longer need to be manually added to the DNS database. Windows 2000, Windows XP, and Windows Server 2003 clients can dynamically update their own resource records with a DNS server.

Event Viewer The Windows Server 2003 Event Viewer is used to view the contents of various log files. Every computer running Windows Server 2003 has three default log files: Application, System, and Security. Other logs may be available depending on the services installed.

Extensible Authentication Protocol (EAP) The Extensible Authentication Protocol (EAP) is an extension to the Point-to-Point Protocol that provides support for other authentication methods such as smart cards. The authentication mechanism used is negotiated between the remote access client and the remote access server.

Failover Failover is the process of a group being moved from one node to another when a resource fails within the group. Groups can be set to retry the failed resource a certain number of times before the group is moved to the other resource.

Forwarder A *forwarder* is a DNS server that receives DNS queries that cannot be resolved locally and are therefore forwarded to another DNS server.

HOSTS File A HOSTS file is a static text file that contains entries mapping hostnames to IP addresses.

Internet Authentication Service (IAS) IAS is Microsoft's version of a RADIUS server. IAS provides a number of benefits, including centralizing user authentication and administration of remote access policies and centralizing the storage of auditing and accounting information collected from the remote access servers.

Internet Control Message Protocol (ICMP) ICMP is used by TCP/IP for reporting errors and status information when datagrams are sent across the network.

Internet Group Message Protocol (IGMP) The Internet Group Management Protocol (IGMP) is used for multicasting purposes. With multicasting, a group of hosts share a single destination IP address. IP hosts use IGMP to report their multicast group status to routers on the network. Routers are then aware of which multicast groups are on which networks.

Internet Protocol (IP)   The Internet Protocol (IP) performs a number of functions at the Internet layer of the DoD model. Its main purpose is to address and route packets.

Inverse Query   With an inverse query, a DNS client sends a request to a DNS server to return the hostname that is associated with a specific IP address. A DNS server can use the information stored within a reverse lookup zone to return the information to the client.

IP Address   Each host on an IP network is assigned a unique identifier known as an IP address, which is used to route packets between hosts. An IP address consists of two parts: the *network ID* and the *host ID*. The network ID is used to identify a specific network or subnet, whereas the host ID identifies the hosts on a given network or subnet.

ipconfig   This command is used to view the IP configuration parameters on a local computer

IPSec   IPSec is a suite of protocols that work together to protect information transferred between hosts. The data is encrypted on the sending computer and decrypted on the receiving computer.

IP Security Monitor   The IP Security Monitor utility included with Windows Server 2003 can be used to validate that secure communications are indeed taking place where required. The tool can also be used to troubleshoot IPSec-related problems.

Iterative Query   When an iterative query is performed, the DNS server will return an answer to the client. This may be the requested information or a referral to another DNS server.

Lease Process   The steps that a DHCP client goes through to obtain an IP address from a DHCP server are known as the lease process. The DHCP lease process occurs in four distinct phases: DHCPDISCOVER, DHCPOFFER, DHCPREQUEST, and DHCPACK.

LMHOSTS File   An LMHOSTS file is a text file that contains NetBIOS name–to–IP address mappings. Although this is not normally the most efficient means for resolving NetBIOS names, it does offer a solution in a non-WINS environment.

Microsoft Baseline Security Analyzer (MBSA)   Microsoft Baseline Security Analyzer (MBSA) is a tool that enables you to scan one or more computers to identify any misconfigurations that may leave a computer open to vulnerabilities.

Microsoft Challenge Handshake Authentication Protocol (MSCHAP) The Microsoft Challenge Handshake Authentication Protocol (MS-CHAP) version 1 is Microsoft's version of CHAP that is used to authenticate Windows-based clients. It also uses a challenge-response with nonreversible encryption of the password.

Microsoft Point to Point Encryption (MPPE)   MPPE is an encryption method that uses 40-bit, 56-bit, and 128-bit encryption keys to encrypt data. MPPE can be used with PPP or PPTP VPN connections and is used by EAP-TLS and MS-CHAP to encrypt authentication information.

NAT Editor   A NAT editor is an additional software component that can provide translation beyond the TCP and UDP headers so that information can pass through the NAT server.

Network Access Quarantine   Network Access Quarantine, a new feature in Windows Server 2003, protects the private network by placing any remote access connections in a quarantine mode so that network access is limited. Only when it has been determined that the connection meets the organization's requirements or when a connection is brought into accordance with certain criteria, will the remote access connection be removed from quarantine mode.

Network Address Translation (NAT)   Network Address Translation enables multiple computers to share a single Internet connection. NAT translates private IP addresses into a public IP address.

Network Load Balancing   Network Load Balancing is the ability to cluster up to 32 servers running the same services to act as one server. These servers can then be accessed by a large number of clients, with the requests being balanced between the multiple servers.

Network Monitor   Network Monitor is used to capture network traffic for the purpose of managing and optimizing network traffic by identifying unnecessary protocols and misconfigured workstations, as well as detecting problems with network applications and services.

nslookup   The nslookup command-line utility can be used to send forward and reverse queries to a DNS server. Normally, you would use the command to perform a forward query to resolve a hostname to ensure it is able to find a specific client. It can also be used to determine the host associated with a given IP address by performing a reverse query.

Open Shortest Path First (OSPF)   Open Shortest Path First (OSPF) is a routing protocol designed for large internetworks (especially those spanning more than 15 router hops). OSPF uses the Shortest Path First (SPF) algorithm to calculate routes. The shortest path (the route with the lowest cost) is always used first.

Open Systems Interconnection (OSI) Model   The Open Systems Interconnection (OSI) model outlines how a suite of protocols perform together to establish an industry standard for network communication. To ensure communication between hosts, protocols must be designed according to this standard.

Packet Filters   Packet filters are created to control the types of inbound and outbound traffic that are permitted or denied through a computer running Windows Server 2003. Packet filters can be configured to restrict or permit traffic by protocol and IP address.

Password Authentication Protocol (PAP)   The Password Authentication Protocol (PAP) is generally the least secure of all the authentication protocols. When a user authenticates using PAP, the username and password are sent in clear text, meaning they are not encrypted.

pathping   The pathping command generates output as it determines the path from your computer to a remote host. Next, it monitors traffic for a set amount of time, which varies according to the number of hops taken. After the traffic monitoring is complete, pathping presents time and packet loss statistics for each hop so that you can determine where performance losses are occurring.

ping   The command-line utility ping is used to verify connectivity between two hosts or devices using TCP/IP. The ping command sends an ICMP request for response to the remote host

Primary DNS Server   A primary DNS server hosts the main, working copy of a specific zone file locally. Any changes to the zone file must be made on the primary DNS server.

Primary Zone   A primary zone stores the master copy of the zone file locally in a text file. Any updates must be performed on the primary zone.

Quorum Resource   The Quorum Resource is the shared disk for the cluster that holds the database of cluster information. The database information contains data necessary to recover the cluster.

Recursive Query   With a recursive query, when the client sends a name resolution request to a DNS server, it must respond with the information or return an error message that the requested information does not exist. If the DNS server is unable to resolve the request, it cannot refer the client to another DNS server.

Remote Access Policy   A remote access policy allows an administrator to control remote access connections. Each policy consists of conditions, permissions, and profile settings. A remote access policy must exist or all remote access attempts will be denied regardless of a user's permissions.

Resultant Set of Policy (RSoP)   Resultant Set of Policy is an addition to the Group Policy utility that can be used to view the IPSec policy settings on a computer. You can use the tool to troubleshoot policy issues or to test the results of a policy change.

route   route is a command-line utility that can be used to manipulate the routing table.

Routing and Remote Access (RRAS)   The Routing and Remote Access Service (RRAS) allows you to configure a computer as a remote access server, allowing users to dial in or use VPN connections to remotely access the private network.

Routing Information Protocol (RIP)   RIP is a routing protocol that enables routers to dynamically exchange routing information, thereby eliminating the need for administrators to manually update the routing tables when changes to the network topology occur.

Scope   A scope is a range or pool of IP addresses that a DHCP server can lease to DHCP clients. Before a DHCP server is fully functional on a network, it must be configured with at least one scope.

Secondary DNS Server   A secondary DNS server obtains the zone file from another DNS server. It hosts only a read-only copy of the zone file, which is kept up to date through zone transfers.

Secondary Zone   Secondary zones are configured for fault tolerance and load balancing. The zone data is obtained from a master name server, which can be a primary or secondary server.

Service Packs   Service packs are released by vendors to fix known issues with an operating system, keep the product up to date, and introduce new features.

Shiva Password Authentication Protocol (SPAP)   The Shiva Password Authentication Protocol (SPAP) is an authentication protocol used by Shiva remote access servers. It is supported by Windows Server 2003 for Shiva clients. Windows clients also use the protocol to authenticate to a Shiva LAN Rover. SPAP uses a two-way encryption algorithm to encrypt the password, and therefore it is more secure than PAP.

Smart Cards   Smart cards are similar to credit cards only they are used to store a user's private key, instead of storing it on the local computer making it more difficult for a user's private key to be compromised.

Software Update Services (SUS)   Software Updates Services enables Windows updates to be downloaded to an internal server on a private network where they can be installed within a test environment before deploying them in the production environment.

SRV Records   SRV records are used to locate services running on computers, much like the sixteenth character used in a NetBIOS name environment.

Static Mappings   Static mappings can be created for non-WINS clients in the WINS database. Once the static entries are created, WINS clients can resolve the names of non-WINS clients. Any static entries do not need to be updated by the client, nor do they expire. In order to remove these entries, an administrator must manually delete them.

Static Routing   With *static routing*, an administrator must manually configure the routing table by adding entries that tell the router how to reach other networks. Using the route command, an administrator updates the routing table by specifying the network addresses, the subnet masks, and the metrics associated with each route.

Stub Zones   This type of zone is new in Windows Server 2003. A stub zone maintains a list of authoritative name servers only for a particular zone. The purpose of a stub zone is to ensure that a DNS server hosting a parent zone is aware of authoritative DNS servers for its child zones.

Subnet Mask   A *subnet mask* is a 32-bit number that uses 1's and 0's to distinguish the network ID in an IP address from the host ID. The portion of the subnet mask that is set to all 1's identifies the network ID, while the portion set to all 0's identifies the host ID.

System Monitor   System Monitor can be used to monitor the real-time performance of system components, services, and applications on a local or remote computer.

tracert   The tracert tool is used to track the path that traffic is taking between two hosts. By using the output of this command, you can determine this path or the point at which communications fail between the hosts.

Transmission Control Protocol (TCP)   The Transmission Control Protocol (TCP) is a connection-based protocol, meaning that before data can be sent between two hosts, a session must first be established. TCP offers reliable delivery of data through sequencing, error checking, and flow control.

Transmission Control Protocol/Internet Protocol (TCP/IP)   TCP/IP consists of a suite of protocols and utilities that enable network communication between hosts. These hosts can be on the same local area network or span a wide area network.

User Datagram Protocol (UDP)   UDP is a connectionless protocol. This means that UDP does not establish a session before sending data, nor does it provide for reliable delivery. When information is sent, acknowledgments are not returned, so it is just assumed to have been received. UDP is more often used in one-to-many situations where information is sent using a broadcast or for multicasting (TCP is used for one-to-one communication).

Virtual Private Network (VPN)   A virtual private network (VPN) enables you to connect to a remote server using a public network such as the Internet. Once a connection to the Internet is established, the remote access client creates a connection to the remote access VPN server using a tunneling protocol. The tunnel provides secure communications between the remote access client and the private network over the Internet.

Windows Internet Name Service (WINS)   The Windows Internet Name Service (WINS) is Microsoft's implementation of a NetBIOS name server. WINS, which was developed to overcome the problems associated with NetBIOS in a routed environment, provides a centralized method for dynamically registering and resolving NetBIOS names.

WINS Proxy Agent   A WINS proxy agent is a computer on the local subnet that listens for NetBIOS name resolution broadcasts. Once the WINS proxy agent receives a name resolution broadcast, it will forward the request directly to a WINS server on another subnet on behalf of the non-WINS-enabled client and return the results.

Zones   A DNS zone is a section of the DNS database that is administered as a single unit. It maintains the configuration information for the zone as well as the various types of resource records. A zone can consist of records from a single domain or multiple domains.

INDEX

K

L

M

S

Z

INTERNATIONAL CONTACT INFORMATION

AUSTRALIA
McGraw-Hill Book Company
Australia Pty. Ltd.
TEL +61-2-9900-1800
FAX +61-2-9878-8881
http://www.mcgraw-hill.com.au
books-it_sydney@mcgraw-hill.com

CANADA
McGraw-Hill Ryerson Ltd.
TEL +905-430-5000
FAX +905-430-5020
http://www.mcgraw-hill.ca

**GREECE, MIDDLE EAST, & AFRICA
(Excluding South Africa)**
McGraw-Hill Hellas
TEL +30-210-6560-990
TEL +30-210-6560-993
TEL +30-210-6560-994
FAX +30-210-6545-525

MEXICO (Also serving Latin America)
McGraw-Hill Interamericana Editores
S.A. de C.V.
TEL +525-1500-5108
FAX +525-117-1589
http://www.mcgraw-hill.com.mx
carlos_ruiz@mcgraw-hill.com

SINGAPORE (Serving Asia)
McGraw-Hill Book Company
TEL +65-6863-1580
FAX +65-6862-3354
http://www.mcgraw-hill.com.sg
mghasia@mcgraw-hill.com

SOUTH AFRICA
McGraw-Hill South Africa
TEL +27-11-622-7512
FAX +27-11-622-9045
robyn_swanepoel@mcgraw-hill.com

SPAIN
McGraw-Hill/
Interamericana de España, S.A.U.
TEL +34-91-180-3000
FAX +34-91-372-8513
http://www.mcgraw-hill.es
professional@mcgraw-hill.es

**UNITED KINGDOM, NORTHERN,
EASTERN, & CENTRAL EUROPE**
McGraw-Hill Education Europe
TEL +44-1-628-502500
FAX +44-1-628-770224
http://www.mcgraw-hill.co.uk
emea_queries@mcgraw-hill.com

ALL OTHER INQUIRIES Contact:
McGraw-Hill/Osborne
TEL +1-510-420-7700
FAX +1-510-420-7703
http://www.osborne.com
omg_international@mcgraw-hill.com

Sound Off!

Visit us at **www.osborne.com/bookregistration** and let us know what you thought of this book. While you're online you'll have the opportunity to register for newsletters and special offers from McGraw-Hill/Osborne.

We want to hear from you!

Sneak Peek

Visit us today at **www.betabooks.com** and see what's coming from McGraw-Hill/Osborne tomorrow!

Based on the successful software paradigm, Bet@Books™ allows computing professionals to view partial and sometimes complete text versions of selected titles online. Bet@Books™ viewing is free, invites comments and feedback, and allows you to "test drive" books in progress on the subjects that interest you the most.

Prepare

Get the books that show you not only what—but *how*—to study

**MCSE/MCSA
Implementing a Windows
Server 2003 Infrastructure
Study Guide
*(Exam 70-291)***
MCCAW & LIND
0-07-222566-1
$49.99
Available: October 2003

**MCSE Windows Server
2003 Active Directory
Infrastructure Study
Guide *(Exam 70-294)***
SUHANOVS
0-07-222319-7
$49.99
Available: October 2003

**MCSE Planning a
Windows Server 2003
Network Infrastructure
Study Guide
*(Exam 70-293)***
BARTLEY
0-07-222325-1
$49.99
Available: November 2003

**MCSE Designing Security
for a Windows Server 2003
Network Study Guide
*(Exam 70-298)***
GOODWIN
0-07-222747-8
$49.99
Available: December 2003

- **100% complete coverage** of all official objectives for each exam
- **Exam Readiness checklist** at the front of each book
- **Step-by-step exercises** are linked to MasterSims and CertCams on the CD-ROM—so you can watch, listen, and try the exercises live
- **Inside the Exam** sections in every chapter highlight key exam topics covered
- **Simulated exam questions** match the format, tone, topics, and difficulty of the real exam

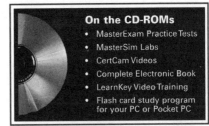

On the CD-ROMs
- MasterExam Practice Tests
- MasterSim Labs
- CertCam Videos
- Complete Electronic Book
- LearnKey Video Training
- Flash card study program for your PC or Pocket PC

Get certified...

in a **flash!**

Card Deck

EXAM PREPARATION **FLASH CARDS**

Available for Windows & Pocket PC!

Study anytime, anywhere
on your laptop or
Pocket PC!

○ Leverage proven flash-card study methods!

○ Dramatically increase memory retention!

○ Create your own custom card sets!

○ Add images & media to reinforce key concepts!

Inside the enclosed CD:

- *Card Deck for Windows*
- *Card Deck CE for Pocket PC*
- *Over 100 sample cards covering all exam topics!*

Pocket PC

Visit us online for more great IT certification card sets based on McGraw-Hill/Osborne publications.

2003 ezflashcards, LLC.

Get Certified In A Flash   **Card**Deck   www.ezflashcards.com